Excel 2024 Essentials

M.L. HUMPHREY

SELECT TITLES BY M.L. HUMPHREY

EXCEL 2024 ESSENTIALS
Excel 2024 for Beginners
Intermediate Excel 2024
Excel 2024 Useful Functions

EXCEL 365 ESSENTIALS
Excel 365 for Beginners
Intermediate Excel 365
102 Useful Excel 365 Functions

EXCEL ESSENTIALS 2019
Excel 2019 Beginner
Excel 2019 Intermediate
Excel 2019 Formulas & Functions

EXCEL ESSENTIALS
Excel for Beginners
Intermediate Excel
50 Useful Excel Functions
50 More Excel Functions

WORD ESSENTIALS
Word for Beginners
Intermediate Word

POWERPOINT ESSENTIALS
PowerPoint for Beginners
Intermediate PowerPoint

ACCESS ESSENTIALS
Access for Beginners
Intermediate Access

See mlhumphrey.com for all titles by M.L. Humphrey

CONTENTS

Excel 2024 for Beginners

EXCEL 2024 ESSENTIALS - BOOK 1

M.L. HUMPHREY

CONTENTS

Introduction

Excel is one of the most powerful software programs for a normal every day user. I would be lost without it at work and I'm not quite sure how I'd keep track of monthly bills without it. (Probably in the margin of a notebook like I used to in the old days.)

But it can be really intimidating for a new user to learn. Especially if you pick up a book that's trying to cover everything you can possibly know in Excel. Because the program can do SO MUCH. This is my fourth time writing a series of books on Excel, and I'd say each time I cover maybe 30% of all the possible things that Excel can do. And yet the collection still ends up being an inch thick in print.

Good news, though, by the time you're done with this first book in the series, I think you'll know about 90-95% of what you need to know to use Excel on a daily basis, and you'll have a good idea of how to learn the rest.

My goal is to give you what you need to know without bogging you down in a lot of stuff you don't need to know. *Intermediate Excel 2024* and *Excel 2024 Useful Functions*, which are the next two books in this series, will keep you going if you want to learn more. But by the time you're done with this book you should feel comfortable opening Excel, entering and moving data around, formatting it, doing some basic analysis, and printing your results.

I want to show you that Excel does not have to be scary, and that anyone can learn it.

Now, that does mean I start with the basics of all basics and cover things like terminology, opening Excel, starting a new file, saving in Excel, etc. For those who already know that, I think there's still value to be had here. We'll cover sorting, filtering, and basic formulas, too. But you can also just jump ahead to the other titles in the series. That's why there are multiple titles. So people can jump in where they need to.

(And if you have some experience and want a little taste of how I teach, check out *Excel Tips and Tricks* which should be free in ebook and provides some simple time-saving tricks I've learned over the years.)

One more thing to note before we get started. This book is written for users of Excel 2024.

At the beginner level, most of what you learn here can be used in any version of Excel. What differentiates this book and the original Excel title I wrote, *Excel for Beginners*, is that I'm not going to hold back on telling you new ways of doing things that are available in Excel 2024 but weren't in earlier versions of Excel.

Again, at the beginner level there's not too much of that. But if you continue with this series then things like pivot charts and the newer functions will be something you can use in Excel 2024 (or Excel 365) but not in earlier versions of Excel. That backwards compatibility issue is probably less of a concern these days than it was back in the day, but I once wasted a week using a function that was available in my version of Excel only to figure out it wasn't available to my consulting client and had to redo everything as a result. Not fun.

Anyway. Your big difference as a beginner in Excel will be the appearance of Excel 2024 versus earlier editions. It seems with each release they like to streamline things more and more so that they are less visually intuitive. Fine for someone like me who has been using variations of Excel for over 30 years, not so great for a new user.

Also, know that my screenshots may look slightly different from what you see on your screen. That's because the section at the top of Excel will display differently depending on the screen size of the computer you're on. Also there are various appearance settings that can impact how Excel looks. Things should always be in the same location, though, so if you get lost look for the little image (the icon) for each option, or for a dropdown menu with that section name.

Finally, I print these books in black and white to make them as affordable for readers as possible, but sometimes it is nice to see color images. The ebook versions of these books are in color and if you go to the About the Author section at the end of this book there is a discount code for buying the ebook off of my Payhip store.

Okay. First up, basic terminology.

Terminology

This chapter includes terms that I'm going to use throughout the rest of the book and also starts some of your basic learning. So even if you think you know Excel, be sure to skim it just in case.

Workbook

A workbook is basically an Excel file.

Workbooks are made up of worksheets. While the default for a workbook in Excel 2024 is to have one worksheet, you can easily add more.

Worksheet

According to Microsoft, a worksheet is "the primary document that you use in Excel to store and work with data." Worksheets consist of "cells that are organized into columns and rows".

That is the official definition, but in more recent versions of Excel I have seen worksheets that did not have columns and rows. They were simply blank pages that could display an image. So the better way to think of a worksheet is as a discrete location in your workbook that contains information. (We will not deal with any situations that involve those blank pages, though, so feel free to forget that for now.)

Note that the Office folks also sometimes refer to a worksheet as a spreadsheet. I don't, because to me that can also mean a workbook.

Cell

Cells are formed by the intersection of a column and a row, and are referred to based upon the column and row where they are located.

So the first cell in a worksheet is Cell A1, where A is the first column and 1 is the first row. When a cell is selected, you can see a border around the edge of the cell, like here where Cell A1 is selected:

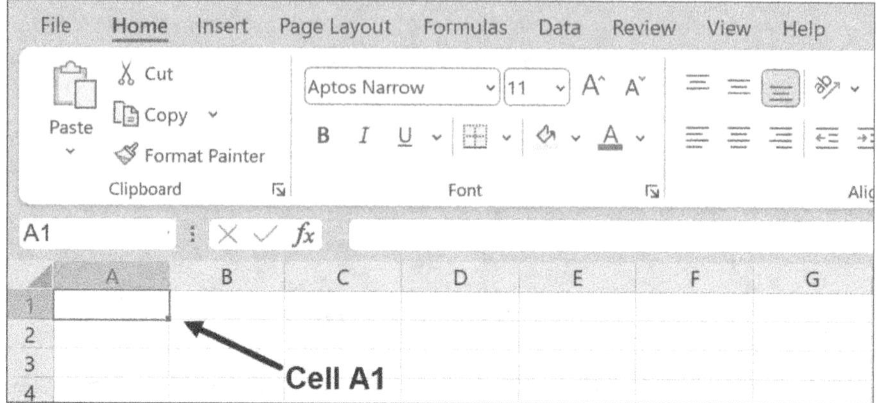

When you enter information into a worksheet, it is almost always entered into a specific cell. You can then refer to that cell to use that information.

Cells generally will contain text, numeric values, or formulas.

Column

A standard worksheet uses columns and rows to create cells which display your information. Columns run across the top of the worksheet and are, by default, indicated with a letter. Here is the top left corner of a worksheet:

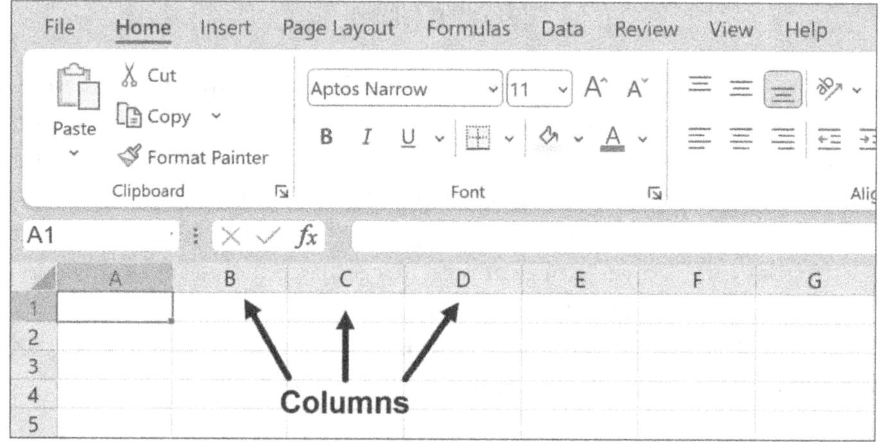

See the letters running across the top there? A, B, C, D, etc.? Each of those letters is at the top of a column.

Every Excel 2024 worksheet has the exact same number of columns. Scroll far enough to the right and the columns will start a double alphabet of AA, AB, AC, etc. This will continue into a triple alphabet AAA, AAB, etc. The very last column in an Excel 2024 worksheet is XFD.

Row

Rows run down the side of a worksheet and are numbered from 1 up to the very last row, which in Excel 2024 is 1,048,576.

Here is that image above but with the rows pointed out instead:

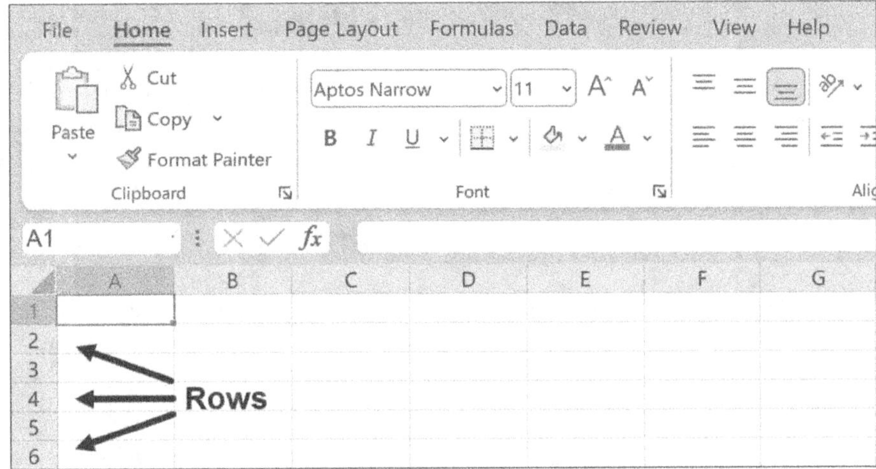

(Note that the number of rows and columns in a worksheet is one area where different versions of Excel can be incompatible. I wrote the first Excel book in Office 2013. In that version, the maximum number of rows was 65,536. You cannot take data that fills all of the rows in a worksheet in Excel 2024 and transfer it to a worksheet in Excel 2013. It wouldn't fit.)

Click

You probably already click on things all the time without thinking about it, but just in case.

If I tell you to click on something, that means to use your mouse (or trackpad) to move the arrow on the screen to a specific location, and then to left-click or right-click (as defined below).

In general, a left-click will select an item whereas a right-click will create a dropdown list of options to choose from. If I don't tell you which one to use, left-click.

Left-Click/Right-Click

If you use a standard mouse, then it's going to be split in the middle with the option to press down on either side. Press on the left side and that's a left-click. Press on the right side and that's a right-click.

With trackpads it can be a little trickier, because they sometimes get creative about where they put things. On my current computer I can left-click on my trackpad by either clicking on a flat button at the *top* of the trackpad or by pressing in the bottom left corner. Right-click also has two options, a visible button at the top right and pressing in the bottom right corner of the trackpad itself.

If you're not sure how to left- or right-click on your computer, experiment a bit. I will mention times to use one or the other throughout this book that you can use as your test cases.

Left-Click and Drag

I may at times tell you to left-click and drag something. What this means is to left-click on that object or in that location, and then hold your left-click as you move your arrow/mouse/cursor to either select a range or to move an object.

Formula Bar

The formula bar is the long white bar at the top of the Excel workspace with the function(x) *fx* symbol next to it.

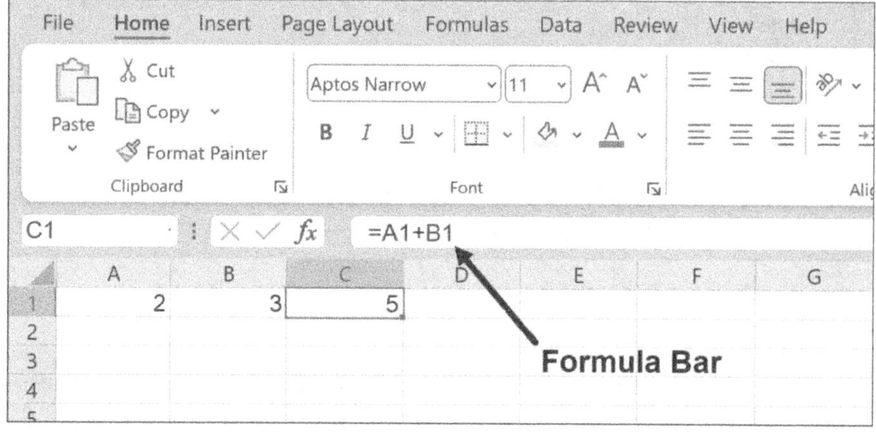

When you click onto a cell, like I have here in Cell C1, the formula bar will show you the contents of that selected cell. If the contents of the cell are just text or numbers you typed in, that's what you'll see. But if a formula was used instead, the formula bar will display the formula that was used.

This is useful because by default the cells in a worksheet only display the results of any formulas that were used.

Above, for example, I used a formula in Cell C1 that adds the value in Cell A1 to the value in Cell B1. You can see the result of the formula, 5, in Cell C1, and the formula used, =A1+B1, in the formula bar.

Tab

I refer to the menu choices at the top of the screen (File, Home, Insert, Page Layout, Formulas, Data, Review, View, Help, etc.) as tabs. Learn this because I am going to use it about a hundred times throughout this book. Maybe more.

I use the term tab because in the past when one of those options was selected, it looked like the top of a file folder. That's no longer the case. In Excel 2024, the selected tab is just underlined, like here with the Home tab:

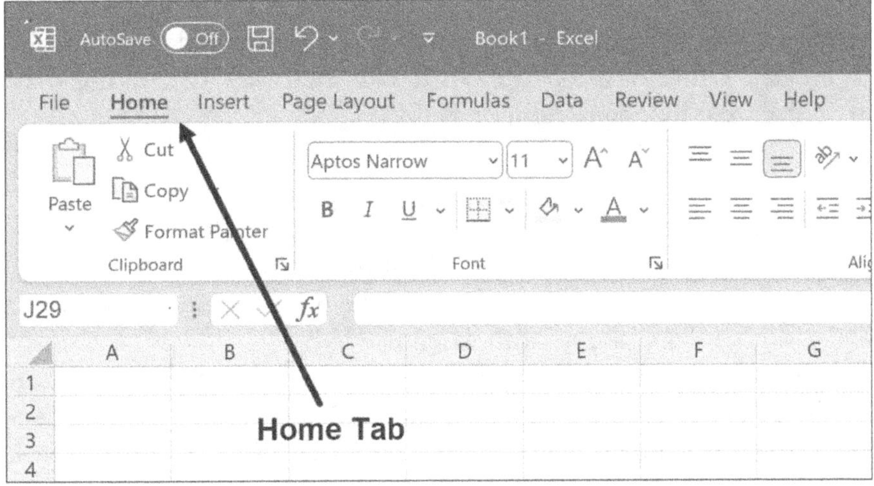

Each tab gives you different tasks you can perform. The Home tab, for example, lets you Paste, Cut, Copy, apply text formatting, and more.

Section

I refer to the different named areas under each tab as a section. The names are at the bottom of the section.

For example, here I have isolated the Font section of the Home tab:

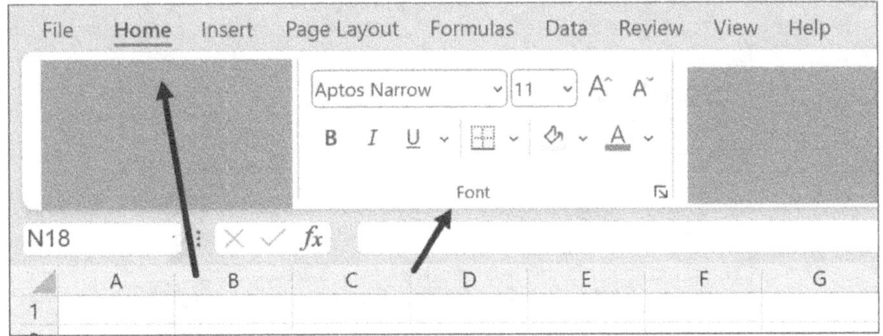

Data

I use the terms data and information interchangeably. Whatever information you have in your worksheet is your data.

Table

I will sometime refer to a table of data or data table. This is just a collection of cells that contain related information and appear to be formatted to belong together.

(In Excel 2024 it looks like Microsoft has introduced a data table concept that is separate and distinct from this. I am not using table or data in that way. We are not that fancy. I just mean a group of data that belong together.)

Scroll Bar

When there is more information than Excel can show you on the screen, it will make scroll bars available so you can "scroll" to see the rest of the information. Scroll bars appear either on the right-hand side or along the bottom when needed.

The primary place you'll see scroll bars is in a worksheet when you have more data in the worksheet than is visible. Here, for example, I have added text into a number of cells in Row 1 and in Column A so that there is data that continues outside of what you can see:

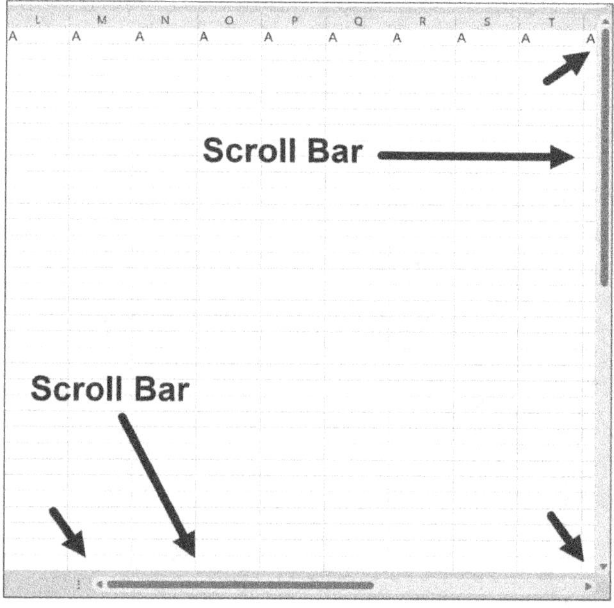

Excel made scroll bars available to navigate all of that data.

Each scroll bar section consists of a light gray scroll area with a darker gray bar that marks where you are in the data. So here, for example, you can see that I am at the very top and far left of the data because the darker gray bars are positioned that way in the scroll bar area.

Scroll bars only let you navigate within the rows and columns where there's data entered. To go past that you can use the arrows at the ends of the scroll bars.

There are a few ways to navigate using scroll bars. One way is to left-click and drag the dark gray bar up and down or side-to-side within the light gray scroll area. As you drag the right-hand bar up or down, or the bottom bar left or right, the visible columns and rows in your worksheet will change.

You can also click into the light gray portion of the scroll bar area to move approximately one screen's worth of columns or rows at a time. It's slower than clicking and dragging the scroll bar itself, but sometimes it's the better option when you want to look through all of the data.

The arrows at the ends will move you one column or row at a time.

Be sure to click into a cell in your current workspace if you use scroll bars to navigate your worksheet. Until you do, if you use Enter or the arrow keys, you'll be moving from whatever cell you were last clicked into, which may be hundreds of rows away. (This happens to me often, especially when using freeze panes, which we'll cover later.)

Select

When I refer to a selected cell it means the cell you're clicked onto, like above with Cell A1 under the definition of cell. As mentioned above, a selected cell will have a different border around it.

It is possible to select a range of cells. To do so with a range of cells that are touching, left-click and drag from a cell at one of the outer corners of the range until all of the cells you want are highlighted.

When you do that, all of the selected cells will be surrounded by a border. Within that border, the first cell you clicked on will be white and the rest will be gray. Like so:

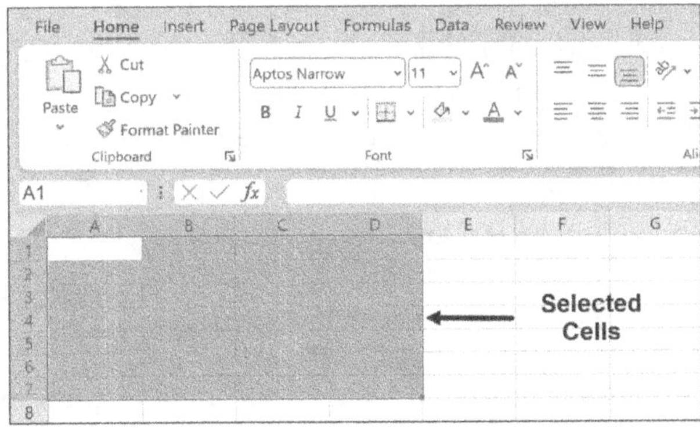

Above I left-clicked on Cell A1 and dragged to Cell D7.

Another way to select cells that are next to each other is to click into the first cell you want, then hold down the Shift key as you use the arrow keys to select other cells.

It is also possible to select cells that aren't touching one another. To do so, select the first cell or range of cells like above, but then hold down the Ctrl key while you select the second cell or range of cells. When selecting ranges of cells, let up on your left-click and drag each time. You can select as many cells or ranges as you want as long as you hold down the Ctrl key each time before you select new cells to add.

(To unselect a cell or cell range, hold down the Ctrl key and click on that cell or cell range again.)

Here I've selected Cells A1 to B2 as well as Cells D3 to E5 and Cells A5 to B5:

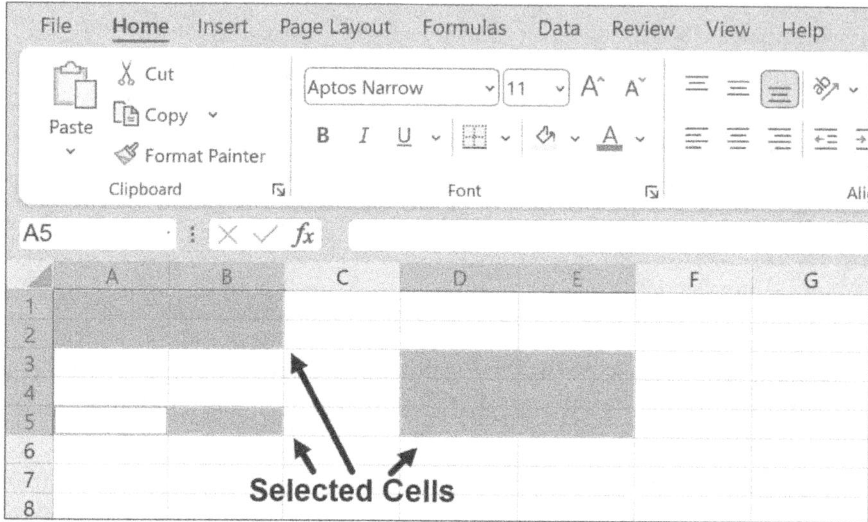

Each selected range of cells is shaded in gray. The cell I first clicked on for the last selected range, Cell A5, is white with a border around it.

When you have more than one cell selected, the one that's white with a border is the one you can type into, but you can format all selected cells at once. (And what I usually use this for, have Excel take that selected cell range and use it in your formula.)

One final comment. To select an entire column or an entire row, just click on the letter for the column or number for the row around the perimeter of the cells in that worksheet.

Dropdown Menu

I will often refer to dropdown menus or dropdowns, which are a list of potential choices that you can select from that aren't immediately visible. In the set of menu options up top, the existence of a dropdown menu is indicated by an arrow next to that option.

In the image below, you can see dropdown arrows next to Paste, Copy, Font Choice, and Font Size.

I've clicked on the arrow for font choice, and you can now see a dropdown menu of other fonts.

(Note also that there is a scrollbar in the font dropdown menu since there are more available fonts than can be displayed at one time.)

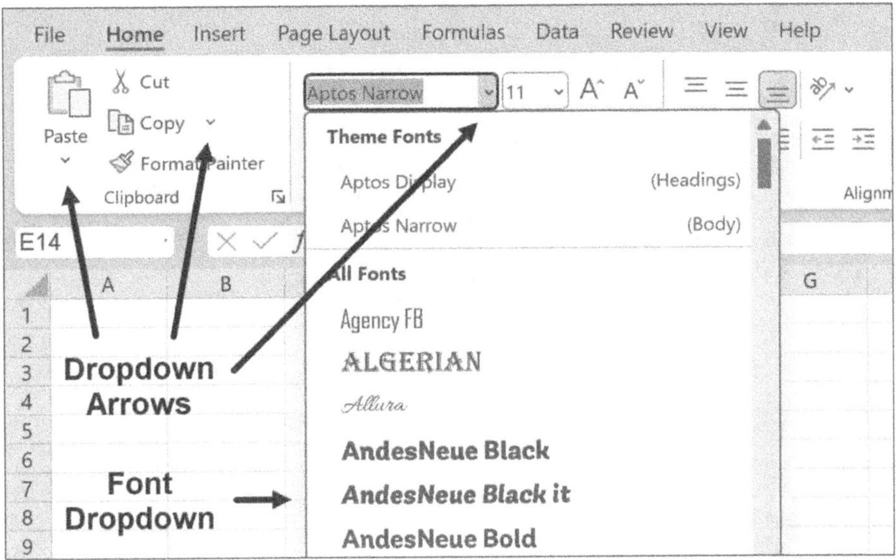

Dialogue Box

Dialogue boxes are pop-up boxes that appear on top of your workspace. They contain a set of available options to choose from. This is the Insert dialogue box, for example:

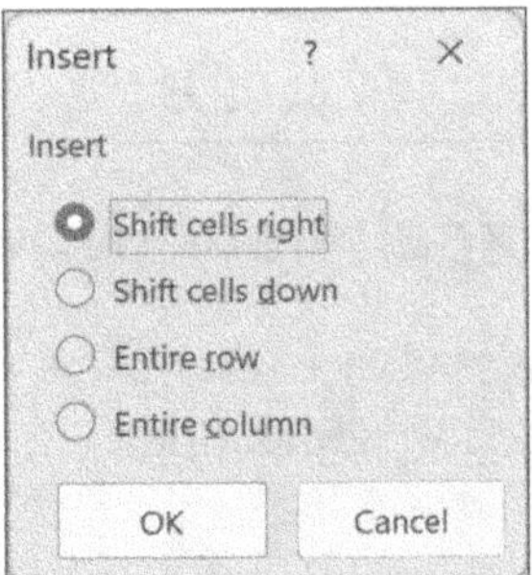

It lets you "insert" cells into a spot on your worksheet. (The number of cells in a worksheet is actually fixed, so what it's really doing is just shifting your existing data to make blank cells available at that particular spot.)

Dialogue boxes are less common now—I think they've largely been replaced by the use of task panes for newer functionality—but they still exist for older functionality, and often contain more options than the menus do.

To close a dialogue box, either make your selection and click OK, click Cancel, or click on the X in the top right corner.

Task Pane

Task panes are separate spaces that can appear to the left, right, or bottom of the worksheet area. They allow you to perform various additional tasks.

The easiest one to see is the Clipboard task pane, which will open if you click on the expansion arrow in the bottom right corner of the Clipboard section of the Home tab:

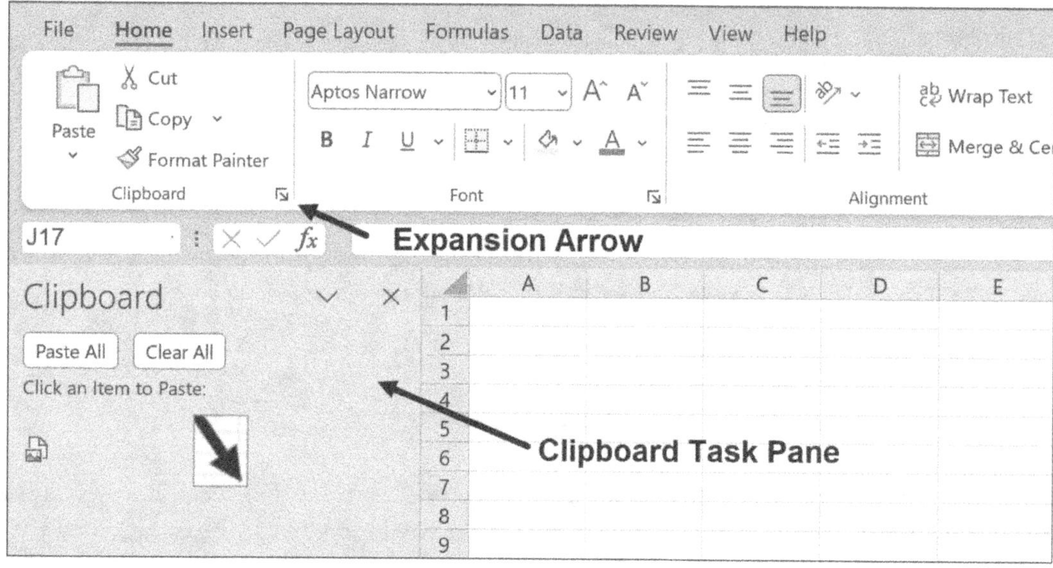

To close a task pane, click on the X in the top right corner of the pane.

Expansion Arrow

Some of the sections in the tabs have what I refer to as expansion arrows. These are arrows in the bottom right corner of that section which open either a dialogue box or a task pane that contains more choices.

For example, the expansion arrow for the Font section of the Home tab will open the Font dialogue box:

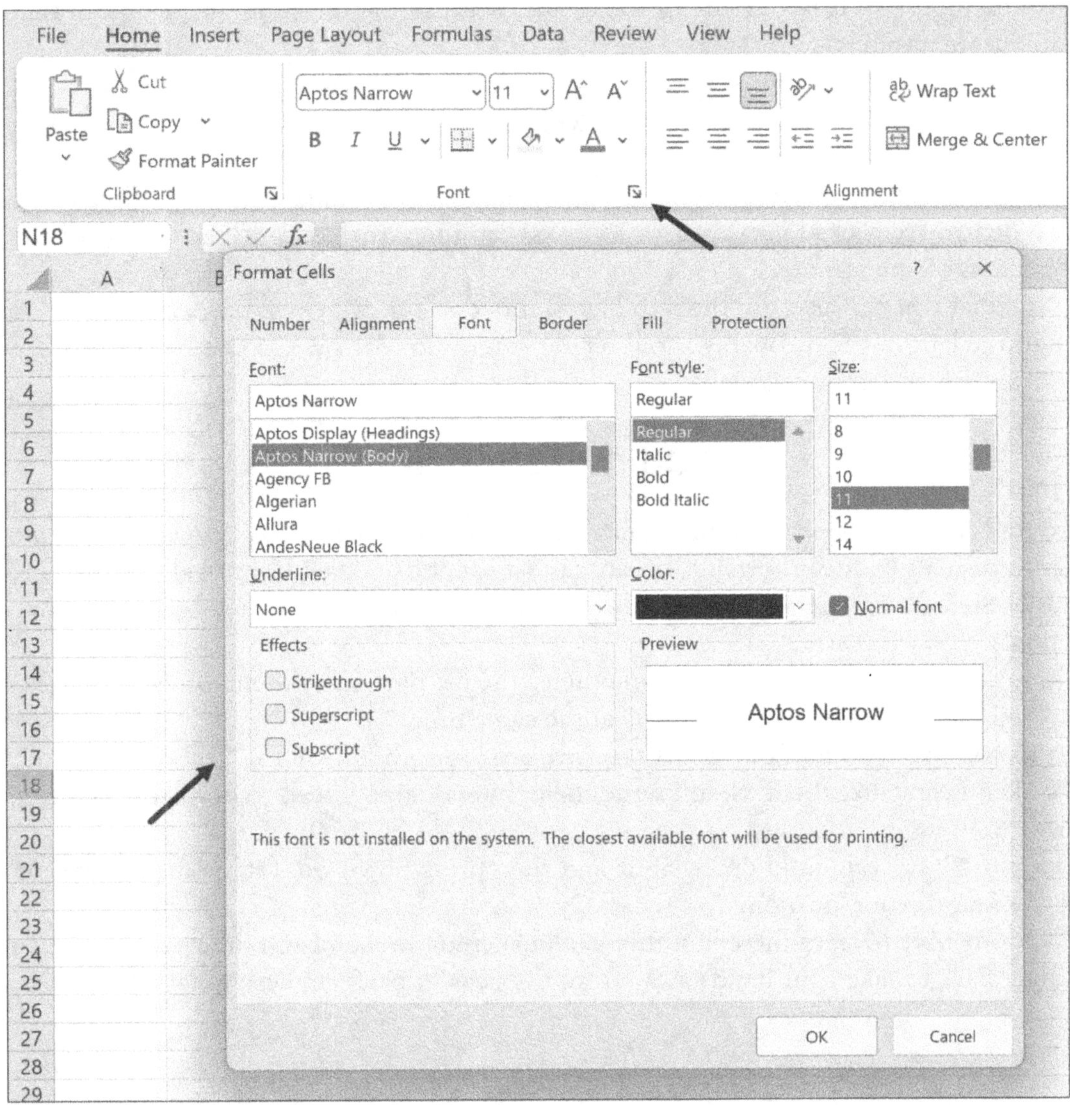

If you are ever looking for something you think you should be able to do and can't find it, it's always worth clicking on one of these to see what else is available.

Cursor

Your cursor is what moves around when you move your mouse. Depending on where you are, it will look like different things. Often in Excel it looks like a variety of arrows, so I may tell you to move the arrow around or the cursor around or even to move the mouse around. All three just mean to get that thing that moves on the screen to a specific spot so you can click.

Pay attention to what your cursor looks like, because the different shapes mean that you can do different things.

Arrow

If I ever tell you to arrow to something, that means to use the arrow keys to navigate to that spot. When you're clicked into a cell in a worksheet, the arrow keys will move you one cell in the direction of the arrow.

(Note that you can also use the Tab key to move to the right one cell, and Shift + Tab to move to the left, but I'll probably avoid telling you to do that since it can be confusing when I refer to the menu options as tabs.)

Control Shortcut

There are various keyboard combinations that you can use in Excel to perform common tasks. I refer to them as control shortcuts, because most use the Ctrl key, but not all of them do. For example, Shift + Tab. A very common one to use is Ctrl + C, which lets you copy your selection.

Note how I write these. I have something, then a plus sign, then something else. That means to hold down both of those keys at the same time.

So to copy, you would hold down the Ctrl key (bottom left of the keyboard for me) and the "c" key. I capitalize them when I write them, but you don't need to do that, just select that letter.

Or, with Shift+Tab, hold down Shift and then press down on Tab as many times as you need to move to your location.

You don't have to learn these, but they can be incredibly useful and time-saving. They mean you don't have to take your hands away from the keys to perform certain tasks, which is very nice.

* * *

Okay, now it's time to dive in on how to actually use Excel.

Absolute Basics

This is the chapter that many may already know and can skip, but it may be worth skimming because you don't know what you don't know. I, for example, never used to use a control shortcut to open a new file until I learned it writing these books. Now I use it regularly.

Open Excel

If you're creating an Excel file from scratch, then your first step needs to be opening Excel, so let's cover that real quick.

If you just installed Microsoft Office, then Excel may be listed in your start menu (generally available by clicking on the Windows icon at the bottom of the screen).

Otherwise, use the search bar at the bottom of your screen or in the start menu to look for Excel. Click on Open when Excel appears on the right-hand side.

I personally like to pin my favorite programs to the bottom of my screen in the taskbar so I can open them easily by just clicking on the icon down there when I need to open Excel.

To do that, you can either right-click on the image of Excel in your search listing and choose Pin to Taskbar (on the left side in the image on the next page).

Or you can expand the menu under Open (on the right side in the image on the next page) and click on it there.

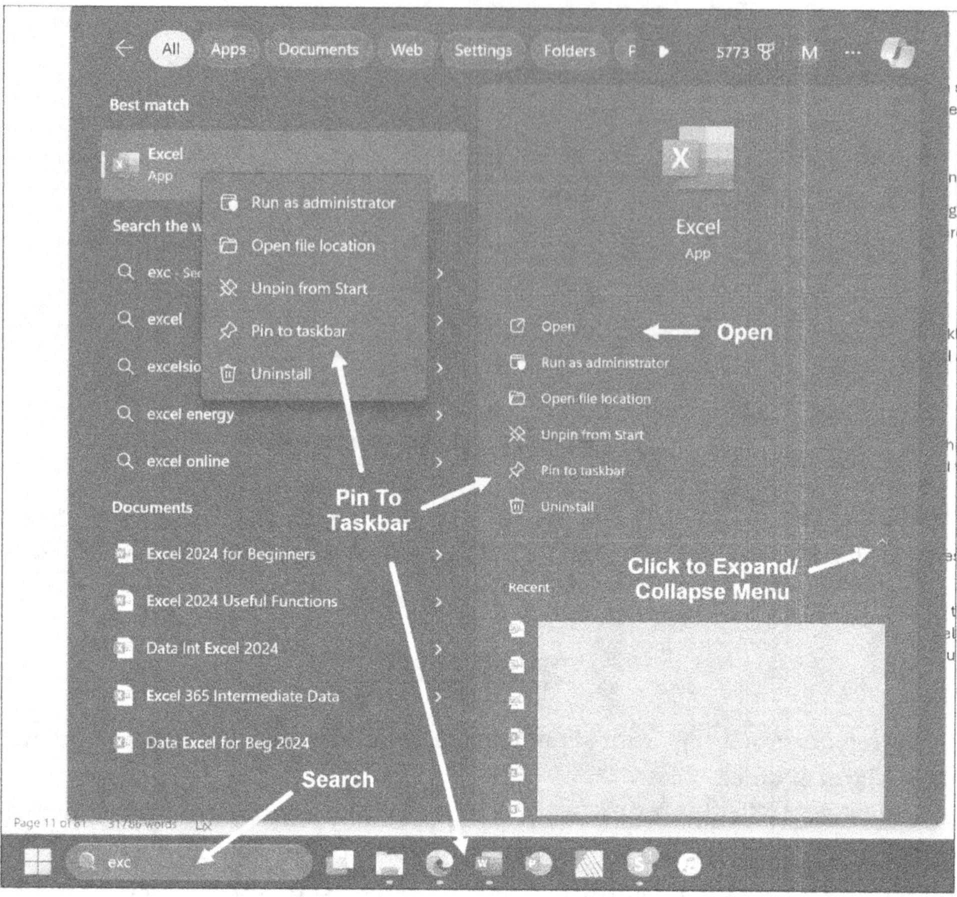

Create a New Excel File

Excel will normally open to the Welcome Screen.

From there the easiest way to start a new Excel file is to click on the Blank Workbook option in the top row.

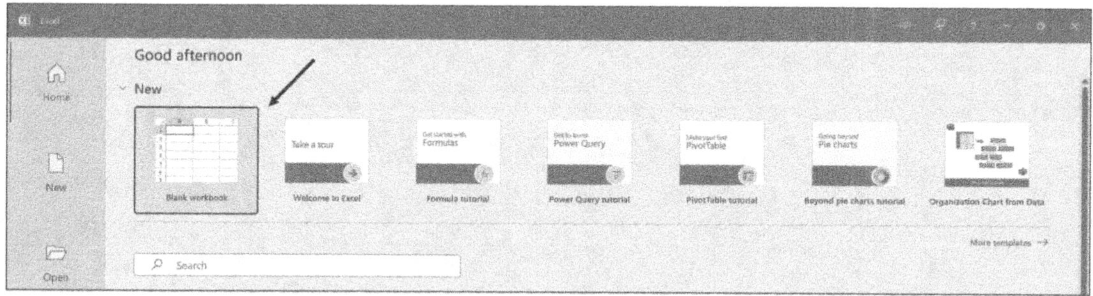

If you're already working in an Excel file and want to open another one, then the easiest choice is to use Ctrl + N.

Or you can click on the File tab to go back to the Welcome Screen where you can then select Blank Workbook.

Open an Existing Excel File

One option for opening an existing Excel file is to go to where you have the file saved and double-click on it. If Excel isn't already open, that will also launch Excel for you.

For files I've worked with before, though, I prefer to open them through Excel. The bottom portion of the Welcome Screen lists the ten Excel files you had open most recently.

Here you can see the top of that section and my three most recent files listed:

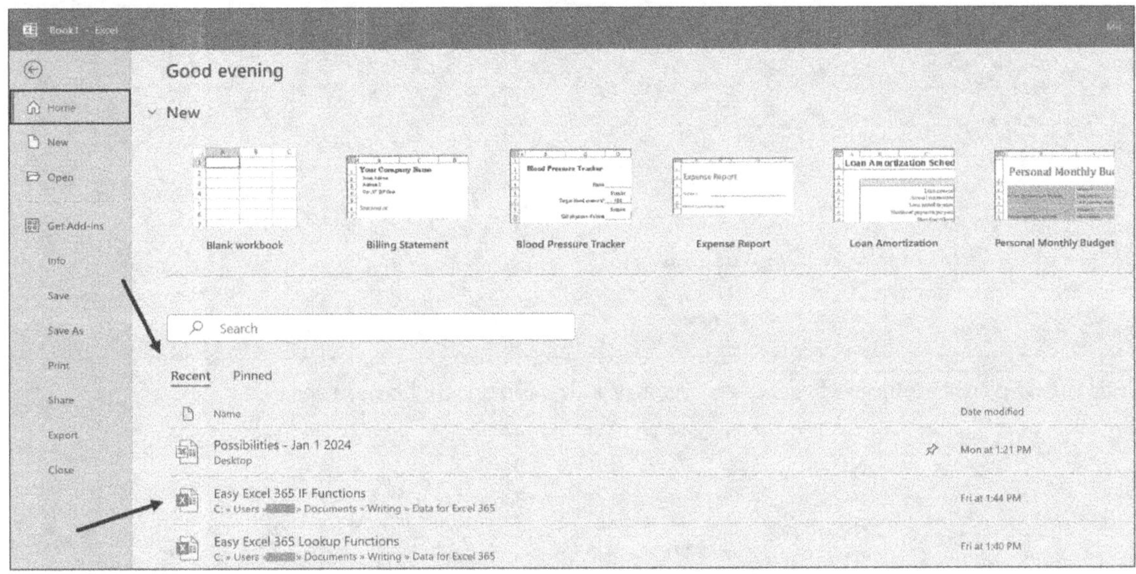

If the file you want is there, just click on the name and it will open.

If it isn't listed but you know you used it sometime recently, click into the white Search field and start typing the file name. When you see the file you want listed as a result, click on the name in the list.

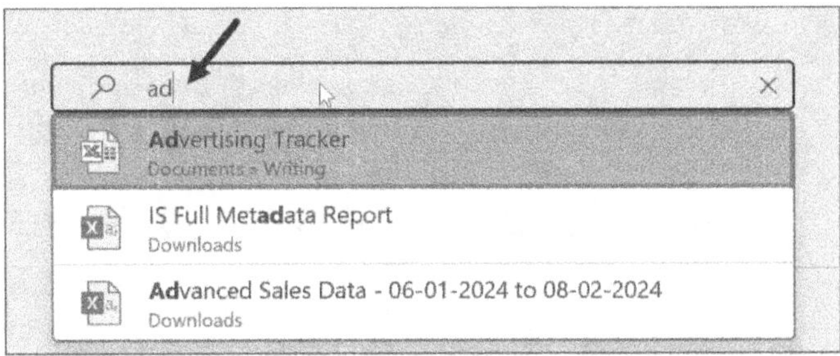

Above, for example, I started to type "ad" because I was looking for my Advertising Tracker file. It gave me three recent files to choose from that have "ad" in the name. I can now click on the first entry in that list, which is the one I was looking for.

A third option you have is to open a file through Excel by navigating to where the file is saved.

To do that, click on the Open option on the left-hand side of the Welcome Screen. That will take you to the Open screen which has Workbooks listed by default but a Folders choice at the top under the Search field. Click on that. It will then show you a list of folders that contain Excel files you recently used:

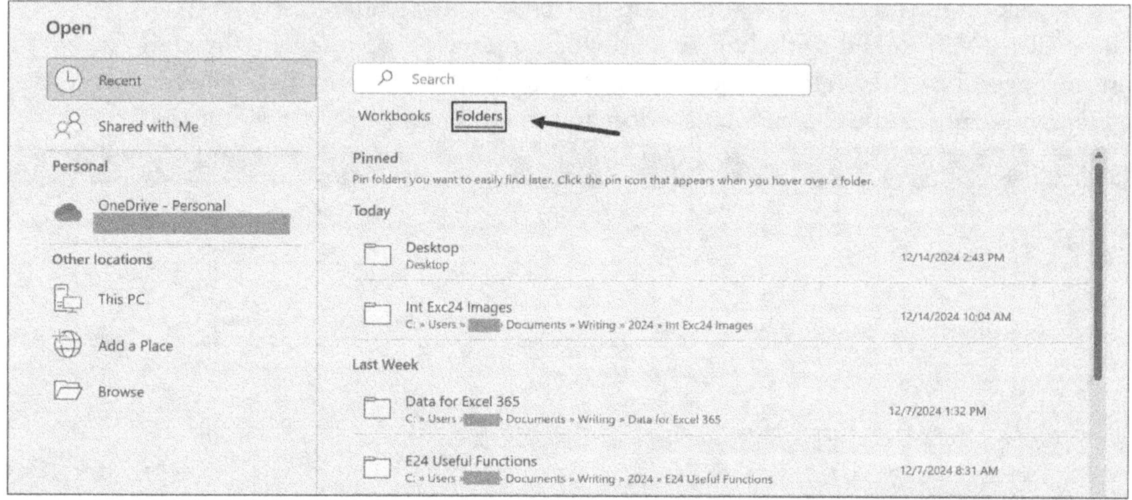

Click on one of the listed folders to see any sub-folders or Excel files.

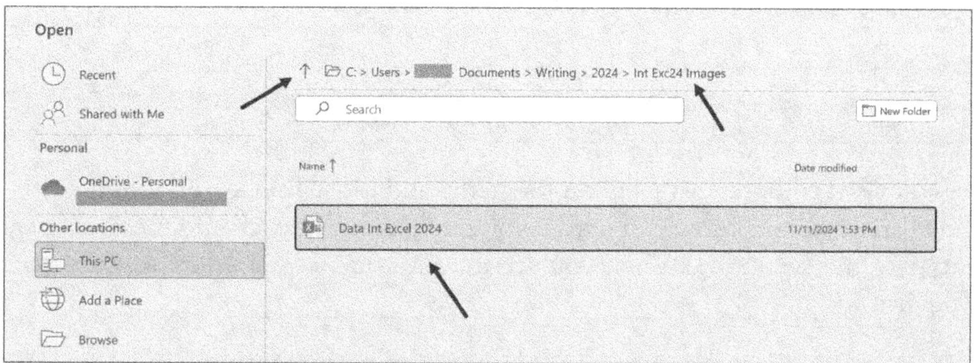

Once you find the file you want, click on it to open it. If you don't find the file you want, you can use the up arrow next to the file path at the top to go back one level and see other folders.

If that still doesn't get you there, then click on Browse, which will bring up the Open dialogue box.

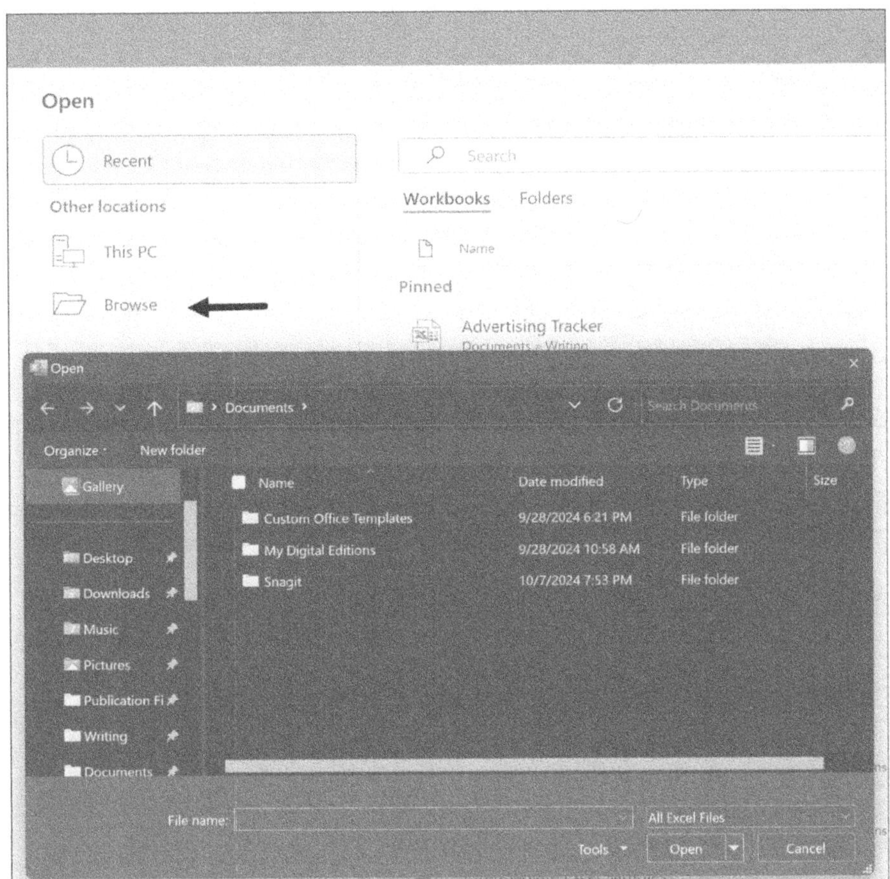

At that point you can just navigate to where the file is saved on your computer like you would have outside of Excel. When you find the file, double-click on it, or click on the name and then click on Open at the bottom corner of the dialogue box.

Pin A File

I have certain files that I go back to over and over. One is that possibilities file you see in the screenshots above, which is actually my budgeting workbook (that is discussed in detail in *Excel for Budgeting*).

I want to be able to find that immediately no matter how many Excel files I've opened in the meantime. The way to make that happen is to pin the file. That makes the file always available in a special list you can access from the Welcome Screen.

To pin a file, hold your mouse to the left of the date modified, like I'm doing here for Easy Excel 365 Lookup Functions:

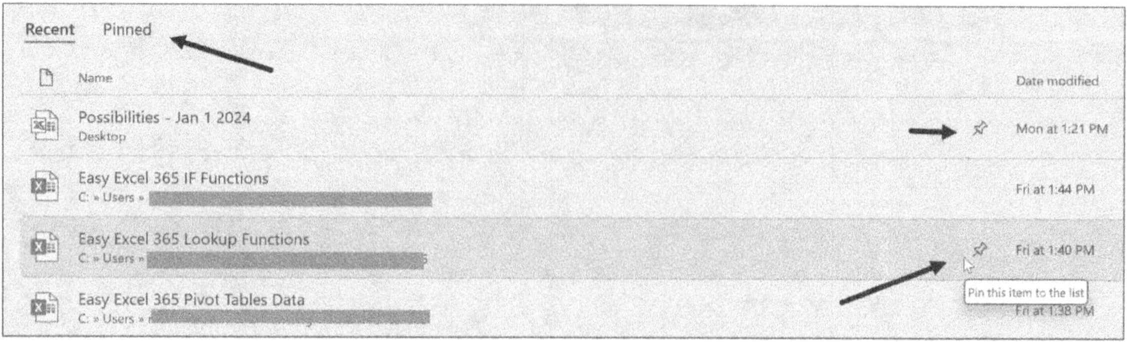

You can see that a text box appeared that says "Pin this item to the list" along with a thumbtack image. Left-click and the file will be pinned. That thumbtack image will remain for that file.

To see your pinned files at any time, click on Pinned at the top of the file listing, and it will switch over to a list that is only your pinned files. Like so:

To unpin a file, just left-click on the pin for that file.

Close a File

The easiest way to close a file is to click on the X in the top right corner when you have the file open:

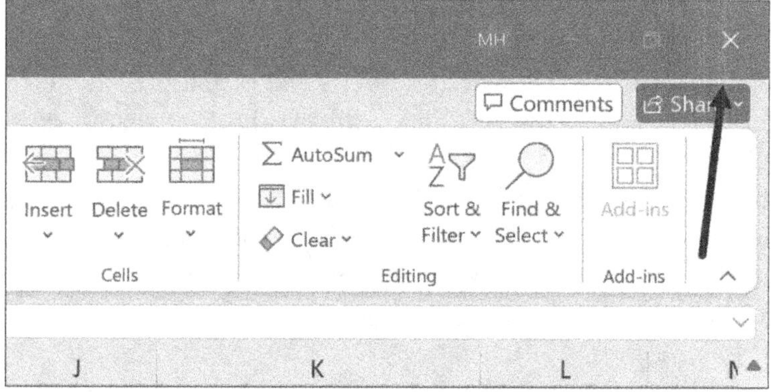

(And, really in Excel, almost anything you can close will have an X in that top right corner, so learn that one well.)

If that was the only Excel file you had open, it will also close Excel.

Another option is to use the control shortcut, Ctrl + W. Or you can go to the File tab and choose Close on the left-hand side menu. Both of those options will keep Excel open.

Save a File

Excel works pretty hard to make sure you don't close a file without saving your changes, so any file that has a change in it that you try to close will pop up with a dialogue box asking if you want to save those changes:

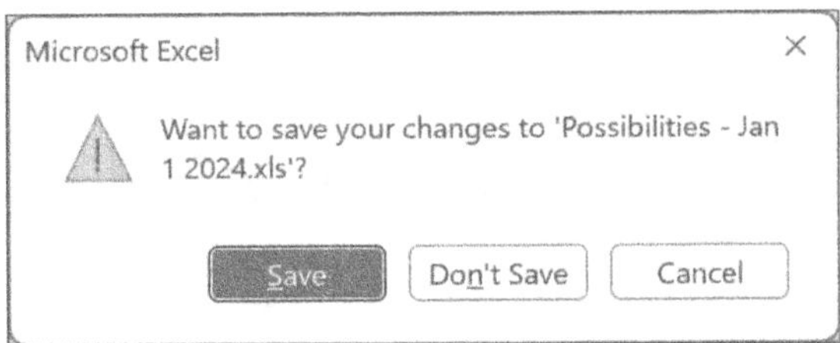

That's probably one of the easiest ways to save changes to a file that you're done with. Just hit Enter when that dialogue box appears and your changes will be saved.

Another option, for a file you're not ready to close, is to use the save icon in the top left corner:

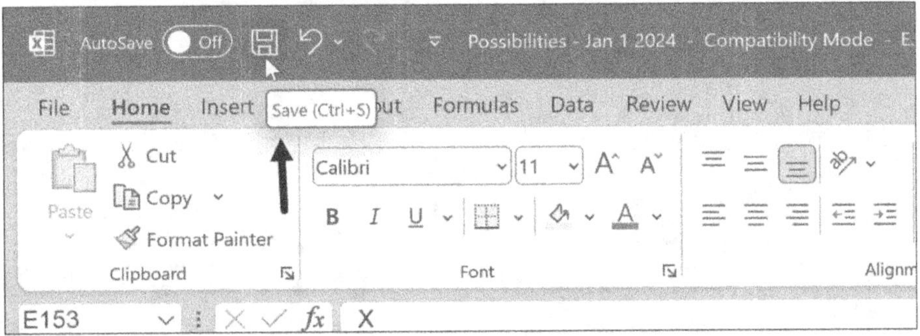

You can also use the control shortcut, Ctrl + S.

All three of the above work great for an existing file where you want to keep the file name, file location, and file type the same, which will be most of the time.

But for a new file there are more steps. When you choose to Save using one of the above methods, Excel will present you with a Save dialogue box where it will ask you for a file name, location, and type. It suggests default values for you:

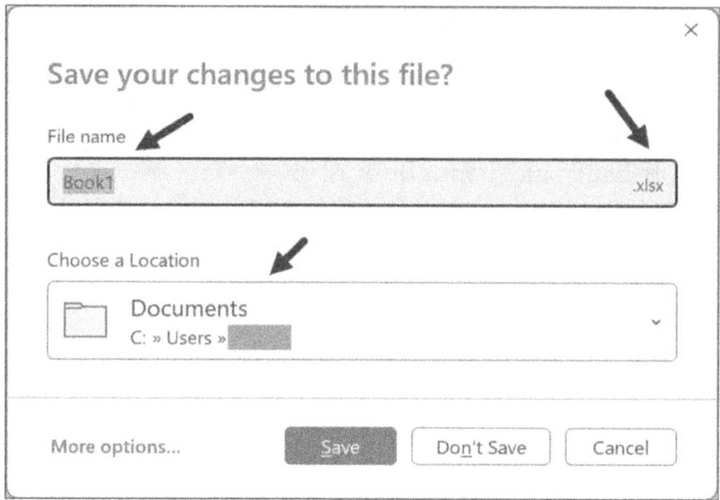

But it is very likely you will want a name other than Book1. That name will already be selected so you just need to type to change the name.

The dropdown for location will show other recent file locations. To choose a location not available in the dropdown, or to change the file type, click on More Options. That will open the Save As dialogue box.

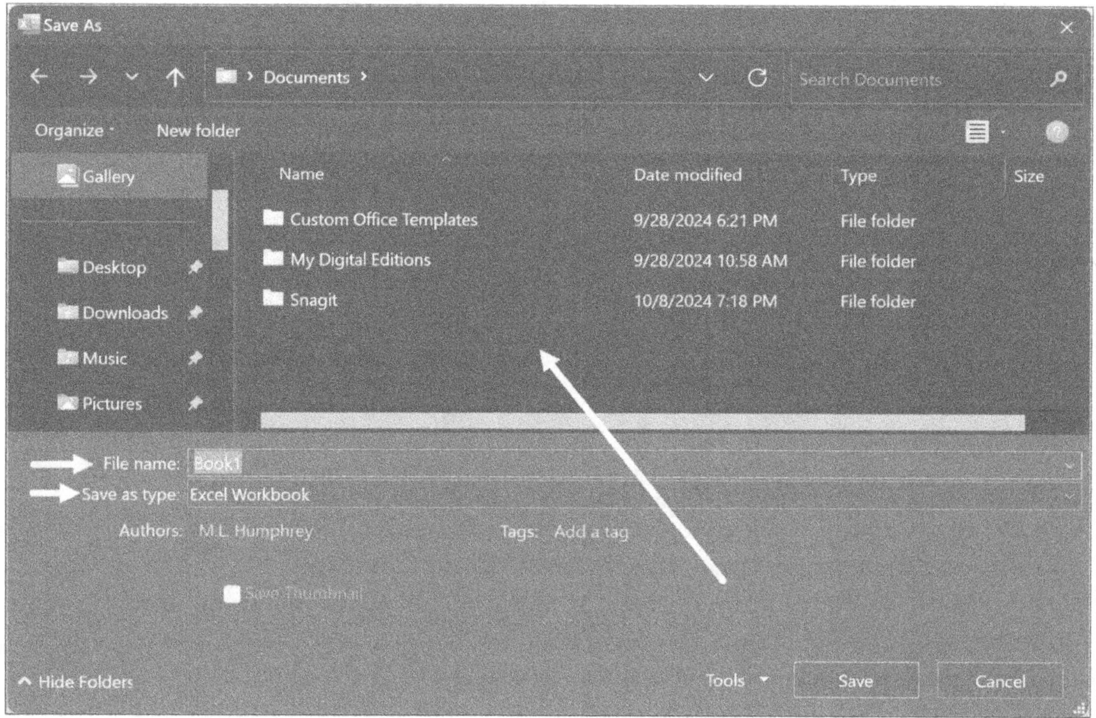

Save As For an Existing File

There are going to be times where you have an existing file but you want to either give it a new name, save it to a new location, or change the file type. When that happens, go to the File tab and choose Save As from the left-hand menu. (See next page.)

Click on one of the listed folder names or click on Browse to bring up the Save As dialogue box.

The File Name field is where you can change the file name.

The Save As Type is a dropdown menu where you can choose a different file type. The standard now is Excel Workbook which is also an .xlsx file. That will usually be fine. But you may run into somebody who needs an older file format. In that case, use Excel 97-2003 Workbook which is also an .xls file. (You may also inherit an older file that's in .xls format and need to upgrade it so you can have the full benefit of Excel 2024.)

The other file type you may run into is a .csv file type. A lot of data output is provided in that format. Excel is going to open it just fine most of the time, but it's a good idea to save it as an .xlsx, Excel Workbook, format if you do any sort of calculations or manipulations with the data.

To choose a new file location, navigate to that location using the side menu and/or folders, just like you would to find a file.

Rename a File

If all you want to do is change a file name and you don't need to keep two versions of the file, then don't use Save As. Instead, go to where the file is saved, click on the file name once to select the file, and then click on it again to highlight the name and make it editable.

Type in the new name you want, click away, and you're done.

Keep in mind that a renamed file cannot then be opened from the recent files list in Excel. Excel will still be looking for that old file name, so won't be able to find the file under its new name. If that's important, your best bet is to rename the file and then immediately open it so the new name is listed in your recent files list.

Move a File

You also should not use Save As if all you really wanted to do was move a file. That also should be done outside of Excel.

Go to where the file is currently saved. Click on it to select it, use Ctrl +X to cut, go to the new location, and use Ctrl + V to paste.

If you're not comfortable using control shortcuts, you can also select the file and then choose the pair of scissors in the top row of the dialogue box or right-click and choose the scissors from the dropdown menu to cut.

You can then go to the folder where you want to place the file and click on the image for paste which looks like a stylized version of a clipboard with a piece of paper on it. You can also right-click and choose the icon from the dropdown menu that appears.

Delete a File

If you ever want to permanently delete a file, that also needs to be done outside of Excel. Go to where the file is located. Click on it and then click on the image of a trashcan in the top of the dialogue box. You can also right-click on the file and choose the trash can from there.

Be careful that you only have the file you want to delete selected and not anything else. (As I have learned from personal experience.)

If you do accidentally delete something you didn't want to, and notice it immediately, use Ctrl + Z to Undo.

Keep in mind that for most computers, a deleted file will be sent to the Recycle Bin and may remain there, capable of being restored, until you proactively go and empty that recycle bin. Excel won't be able to open it though, and you'll get an error message if you try to do so from the files list in Excel.

Navigating Excel

Now it's time to talk about how you move around within Excel. We'll talk about how to actually enter values in the next chapter.

Basic Navigation Within a Worksheet

When you open a new Blank Workbook, Excel you will automatically start in Cell A1 of Sheet 1. For an existing file, you're going to start where you left off. So whatever worksheet and cell where you last were.

The easiest way to move to a different cell in a worksheet is to left-click on it.

The arrow keys will also move you one cell in the direction of the arrow. So use the right arrow to go right, the up arrow to go up, etc.

The Tab key will move you one cell to the right. Shift + Tab will move you one cell to the left.

Enter will move you down. If there's no data in your worksheet, you'll go down to the next row in that same column. If you have data that is organized and you've been consistently completing that data across multiple columns row after row, then Enter might take you to the first empty column in that range in the next row.

Here, for example, I have created a simple data table with three columns of data to enter. When I input the first set of values in Cells A2 through C2 and then hit Enter, it took me to *Cell A3* not cell C3. After I entered information in Cells A3 through C3 and hit Enter it took me to Cell A4.

	A	B	C	D	E
1	Author	Book	Date Read		
2	Grant, Adam	Originals	1/1/2022		
3	Berger, Jonah	Contagio	3/1/2023		
4					
5					
6					
7					

The PgUp and PgDn keys will also work to move you up or down one visible set of rows at a time.

If the cell, row, or column you want isn't visible, then use the scroll bars to get there. Clicking and dragging the dark gray bar is the fastest way to move when there is existing data, but if you don't have data in those rows or columns yet you'll need to use the arrows at the ends of the scroll bars.

Another option is to use the scroll wheel on your mouse.

Just remember with scrolling to click into an actual cell when you get to where you want to go, because otherwise when you type, hit Enter, use the arrow keys, etc. you will still be doing so from that last cell you were clicked into.

Insert a New Worksheet

To add another worksheet to your workbook, the easiest option is to click on the plus sign next to the name of your existing worksheet(s):

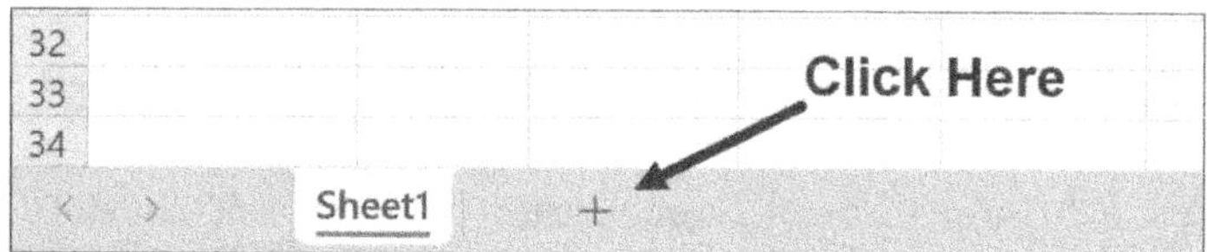

This will insert a worksheet to the right of the one you're currently on.

You can also right-click on an existing worksheet's name , and choose Insert from the dropdown menu. Click on Worksheet (it should be selected by default) and then OK when the Insert dialogue box appears. This will insert a worksheet to the left of the one you right-clicked on.

Another option is to go to the Cells section of the Home tab, click on the dropdown arrow under Insert, and choose Insert Sheet from there.

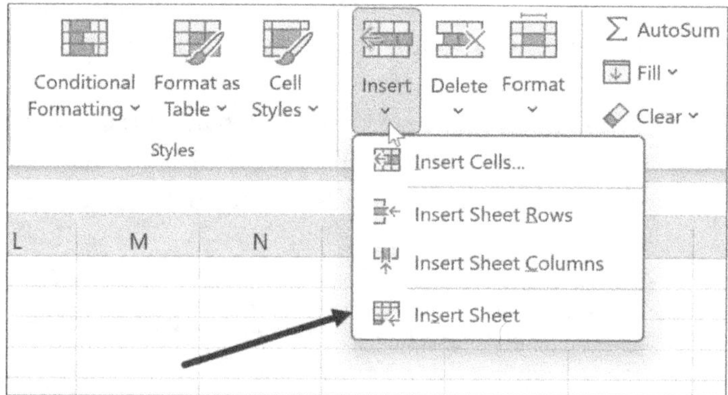

This will also insert a worksheet to the left of the sheet you are currently on.

Select a Worksheet

To select the worksheet you want to see, click on the name tab at the bottom of the workspace:

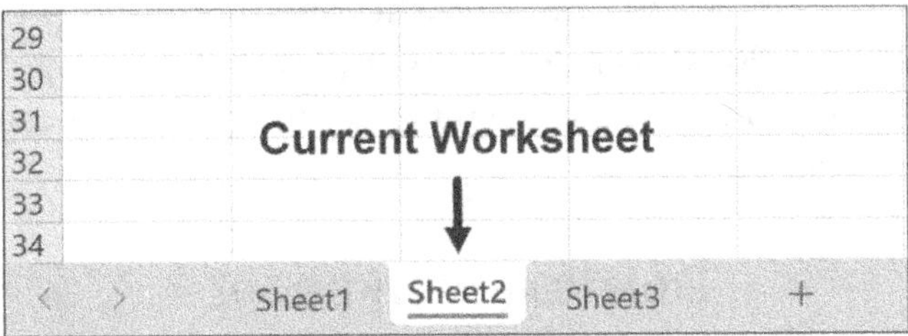

A selected worksheet will be white instead of gray and the name will also be underlined. See here that I have Sheet2 selected and Sheet1 and Sheet3 are more in the background.

(It is possible to select more than one worksheet at a time. I do not recommend it for a beginner. If that ever accidentally happens, click on a different worksheet to unselect all currently selected worksheets. You can also right-click on one of the sheets and choose Ungroup Sheets from the dropdown menu.)

Move a Worksheet

To move a worksheet, simply left-click on the worksheet name and drag to where you want it to go. As you drag along the row of worksheets, you'll see a little arrow that indicates where the sheet will move. Just let up on your left-click and it will drop into that new location.

Rename a Worksheet

Once you have more than one worksheet, chances are you'll want to name them something other than Sheet1, Sheet 2, etc. To rename a worksheet, you can either double-click on the worksheet name, or right-click on it and choose Rename from the dropdown menu:

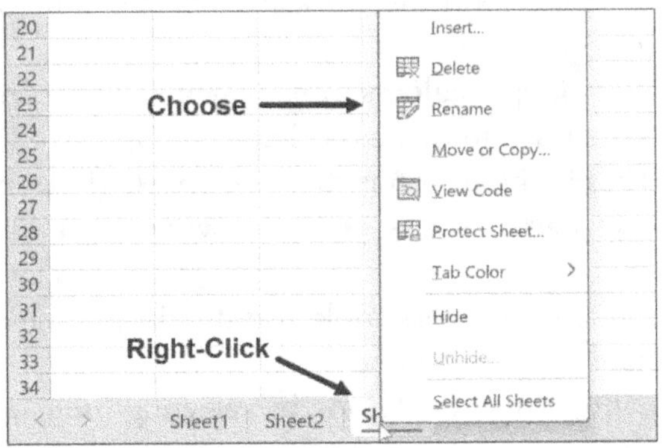

Either option will highlight the name of the worksheet. From there just type in what you want the name to be and hit Enter or click away. You can use Esc to cancel if you decide you don't want to change the name after all.

There are restrictions on how long the worksheet name can be (31 characters) and what characters you can use. Excel 2024 won't let you type past that point, nor will it let you use one of the restricted characters, so if you were typing just fine and now can't type something it's probably safe to assume that's the reason.

Delete a Worksheet

To delete a worksheet, right-click on the worksheet name and choose Delete from the dropdown menu. You can also select the worksheet and then go to the Delete dropdown menu in the Cells section of the Home tab and choose Delete Sheet.

Excel will delete a blank worksheet immediately.

If there is any data in the worksheet, Excel will show a dialogue box asking you to confirm the deletion. Click on Delete to proceed or click on Cancel if you want to double-check what's in there first.

Basic Navigation Between Worksheets

If you have more worksheets than you can see at the bottom of the workspace, use the arrows on the bottom left corner to move the set of visible worksheets left or right by one sheet at time.

Use Ctrl while clicking on the left or right arrows to move all the way to either end of your listed worksheets.

Copy a Worksheet

To keep one version of a worksheet where it already is and create a copy of a worksheet and move it somewhere else, right-click on the worksheet name, and choose the Move or Copy option from the dropdown menu.

This will open the Move or Copy dialogue box, which you can see on the opposie page.

Check the box towards the bottom that says Create a Copy.

You then need to tell Excel where to put the worksheet. If it's in the current workbook, then click on the worksheet name that is one past where you want to place your copied worksheet. Click OK.

If you want to place it in another workbook, use the dropdown menu at the top where it says To Book and select that workbook name.

You can also just move it to a new workbook by selecting (new book) in the dropdown.

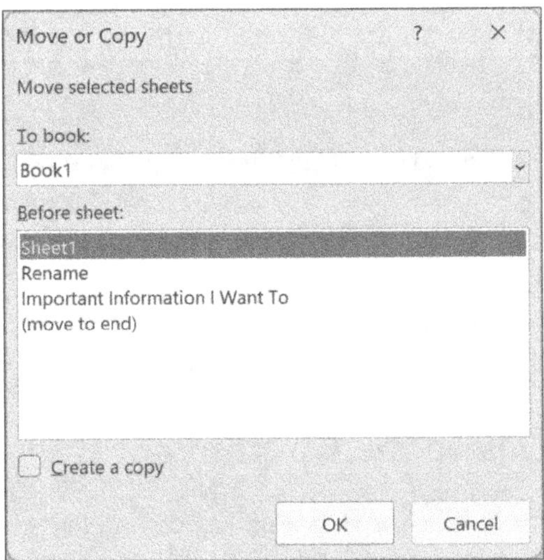

To be listed in that dropdown, a workbook needs to already be open. If it isn't, use Esc or Cancel, go and open that workbook, and then try again.

Move a Worksheet to a Different Workbook

The process to move a worksheet to a different workbook is the exact same as copying it to one, you just don't check the box for Create a Copy.

Select a Column or Row

We already covered this in the terminology section, but I want to cover it again. To select an entire column or row, just click on the letter for that column or the number for that row. Here, for example, I have clicked on the letter "D" to select Column D:

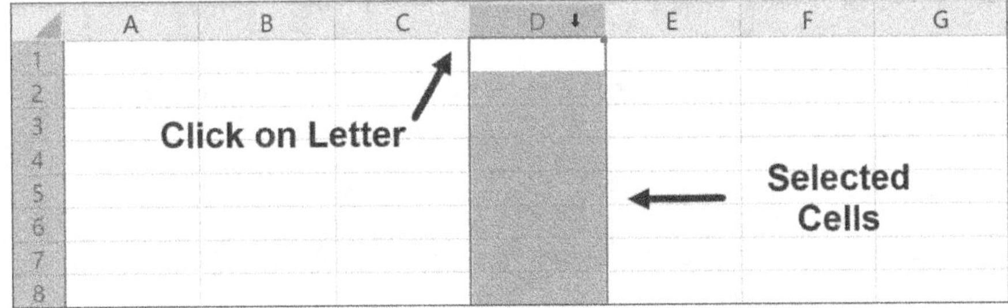

You can see that the cells in that column are all now shaded and also the name of the column is colored differently.

To select more than one column or row at a time, left-click and drag across the letters or numbers for those columns or rows. You can also click on the first column or row in the range, hold down the Shift key, and click on the last one. If they are not all touching, hold down the Ctrl key as you select each one.

Delete a Column or Row

To delete a column, row, or range of columns or rows, select them first and then right-click and choose Delete from the dropdown menu.

You can also select them and then go to the Cells section of the Home tab and use the Delete dropdown. Choose Delete Sheet Rows or Delete Sheet Columns, as appropriate.

Delete the Contents of Cells

Delete will delete the content in all of a range of selected cells.

Backspace will just delete the content in the first cell of the last cell range you clicked on.

Another option is to go to the Editing section of the Home tab and use the Clear dropdown. Clear Contents will clear the text, formulas, etc. but leave the formatting. Clear All will delete the contents as well as any formatting.

Delete a Cell in a Worksheet

Deleting columns or rows is relatively straightforward, because everything else in the worksheet stays properly aligned. Everything that was in Column C may move to Column B, but it's still all in one column.

Deleting cells can be trickier because you're taking part of a row or column and removing it. The other cells in the worksheet have to shift to fill that space. Since you're usually not going to do this if you don't have data in that worksheet, you need to pay attention to the rest of the data in the worksheet.

If you only delete part of a row or column, then data that has to move to fill the deleted space can get out of alignment.

It is relatively easy in Excel to "break" your data. Let's look at that little table I was building before:

	A	B	C	D
1	Author	Book	Date Read	
2	Grant, Adam	Originals	1/1/2022	
3	Berger, Jonah	Contagious	3/1/2023	
4	Godin, Seth	Linchpin	4/1/2021	
5	Clear, James	Atomic Habits	7/6/2022	
6				

This is a pretty basic table of data where I'm listing the author, title, and date read for some books on my shelf. You and I can look at that and know that everything on Row 3 belongs together.

According to this made-up data, I read Contagious by Jonah Berger on 3/1/23, right?

Now, here's where the problem happens. If I delete Cell C3, Excel has to shift things somehow to fill in that gap. I can choose to shift cells left or to shift cells up. If I make the wrong choice and choose to shift up, I get this:

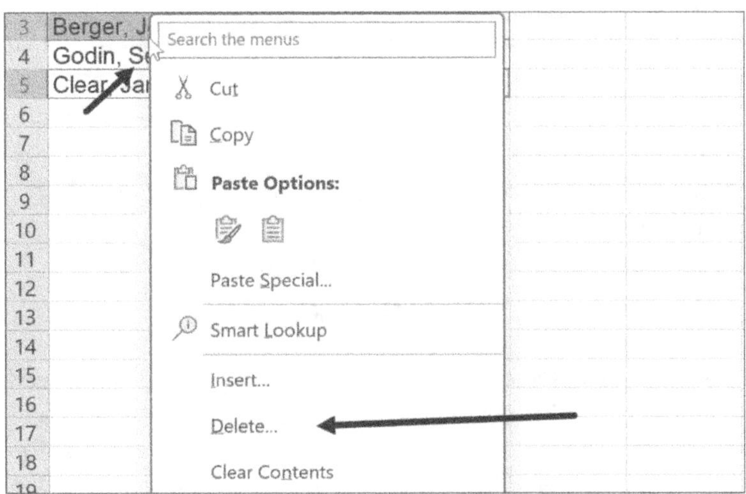

See how the data broke? It now looks like I read that book on 4/1/21 instead, and that I read Linchpin on 7/6/22 instead of 4/1/21. I broke my data. In a normal data table that you create by inputting information in Excel, that can happen very easily.

So when you delete cells in a worksheet, pay attention to what effect that will have on *all* of the data in the worksheet, not just the cells around what you delete.

This is why sometimes it is best to delete an entire row or column to keep things like that from happening. It may also mean deleting more cells to keep everything together. If I'm deleting Cell C3, I really should delete Cells A3 and B3, too. (Or I could just remove the text in Cell C3, but not delete the cell.)

Okay. Lecture over, let's walk through how you actually delete a cell.

Select the cell or cells you want to delete, and then right-click and choose Delete from the dropdown menu.

That will bring up the Delete dialogue box:

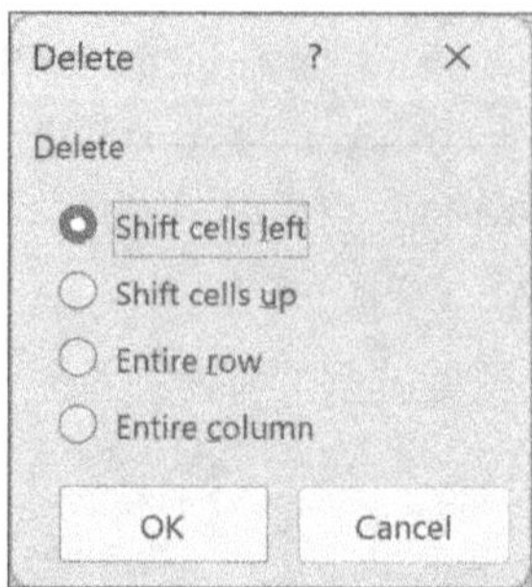

You have two choices there, shift cells up or shift cells left. How do you want to fill in that empty space? When your cell or cells are removed, do you want everything below that to move up, or do you want everything to the right to move over? The appropriate choice is going to depend on your remaining data.

In our example above, I should've chosen to shift cells left. The rest of the table would've remained untouched if I'd done so.

Note that you can also choose to delete an entire row or column using that dialogue box. It's another way to do that without having to select the entire row or column.

Another option is to select your cell(s) you want to delete and then use the Delete dropdown in the Cells section of the Home tab, which will also bring up the Delete dialogue box.

Insert a Column, Row, or Cell

Insert basically works like delete except the Insert dialogue box gives the option of shifting the cells right or down to make room for your inserted cells. Again, this only makes sense to do if you're dealing with cells that already have information in them because the size of an Excel worksheet is fixed.

You can either right-click on selected cells, and choose Insert, or you can use the Insert dropdown in the Cells section of the Home tab.

As with deleting cells, pay attention to your other data to make sure that you aren't breaking your data relationships when you insert cells.

Find Text

I cover advanced find in *Intermediate Excel 2024*, but real quick, if you need to find text in a formula or cell in an Excel worksheet, you can use Ctrl + F to open the Find and Replace dialogue box. Type the text you need to find into the white space next to Find What and then click on Find Next. Excel will take you to the next cell that has that text in it.

Find All will give you a list of all of the locations in your worksheet that have that text in a cell. You can then click on the entries in the list to move to each one.

By default, Find works within one worksheet at a time not the entire workbook. It also is not case-sensitive and looks for the text you tell it to look for in any part of a cell. It does not look at the results of any formulas.

One thing to be aware of in Excel is that it will search in columns or rows that are hidden, too. So sometimes you may think that Excel hasn't moved to the next cell with that value in it, but it really has, it's just not a cell that's visible to you.

Input and Delete Data

At its most basic, inputting data into Excel is very easy. You click into a cell and start typing. When you're done, you hit Enter. Or tab. Or arrow or click to another cell.

But there's a lot more that can go into it, which is what this chapter covers.

Undo

My lifesaver when working in Excel is the ability to undo things. I use Ctrl + Z, which is the control shortcut to undo, all the time. You can use it multiple times in a row if you mess up and don't realize it for a few steps.

It does go back through each thing you did in order, so if you messed up ten steps ago, you'll lose all ten things you've done since then. But better than not being able to, right?

If you know up front that you have a lot of steps to reverse, you can use the Undo dropdown menu available in the top left corner of Excel.

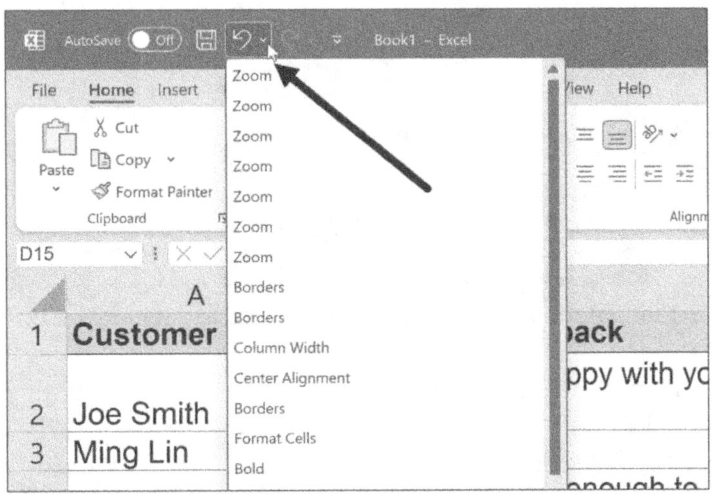

Click on the backwards pointing arrow once to undo your last step, or click on the dropdown arrow next to it and Excel will show you the last 100 things that you did in Excel.

In the image on the previous page, you can see that the last few things I did was zoomed in, added some borders to cells, changed a column width, and more. So if I want to undo that Bold of some text, I'd also lose all of that.

I can do it, though. I just need to click on Bold and that step and everything that came after it will be undone.

Undo is fabulous to use throughout Excel, not just when inputting data. It's one of the easiest ways to undo mistakes when you're learning.

But there are a few places it doesn't work well. For example, if you input the text, "October 4", Excel will treat that like a date and a simple Undo will not change that cell back to text.

99 times out of 100, though, Undo is the way to back out of a mistake in Excel.

Redo

What if you Undo, like I just did, and then realize that was a mistake and want to Redo?

You can either use Ctrl + Y to redo one step at a time, or you can use the Redo arrow up top, which will only be available to select if you already undid something.

It's the arrow that points to the right and it also has a dropdown menu.

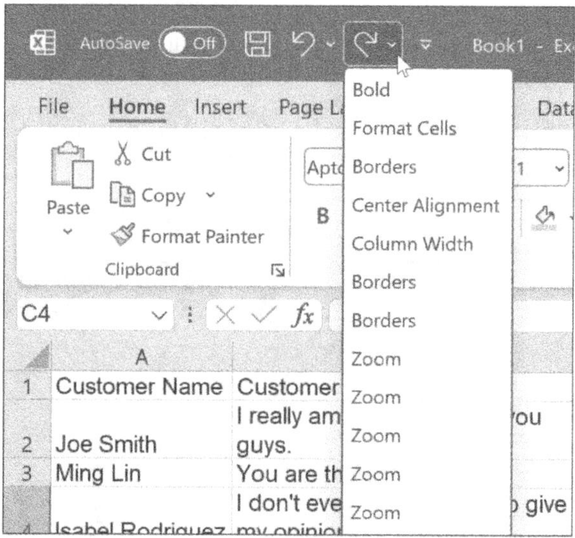

Click on a step in that list and it will redo each step in the list above the one you chose as well as that one.

(Excel will highlight the entries in gray that it's going to redo as you move your cursor over the list to make your selection.)

Same thing with Redo as with Undo, it does them all in order, you can't pick and choose.

Esc

Another little trick I like to use often is Esc. If I start typing a formula in a cell and it becomes a hot mess, I just use the Esc key to get away from whatever I was typing and start over.

It's also a good way to back out of something you've started. Say you copy some data and were going to paste it elsewhere but then change your mind, use Esc to be done with that.

It will also turn off a tool like Format Painter.

Between Undo and Esc that should get you out of 95% of the scrapes you get into. Think of Undo as "Didn't mean to do that, sorry, can we go back?" and Esc as "Wait, let me just stop what I'm doing right now."

Also, if you're ever inputting data and try to Undo and it doesn't work, you may need to use Esc first to back out and then Undo from there.

Okay. On to the inputting text tricks.

Display The Contents of a Cell as Text

If you start the text you enter into a cell with a minus sign (-), plus sign (+), or equals sign (=), Excel will think you're about to enter a formula in that cell. Excel also tries very, very hard to recognize text ("October 2024") as dates and convert them for you, often when you don't want it to.

Fortunately, there is a very simple workaround for these issues. Simply type a single quote mark at the start of the text you're entering into that cell.

So if you want to have an entry that looks like this:

-Item A

what you need to actually type is:

'-Item A

Or if you want:

October 2024

What you need to type is:

'October 2024

Simple as that. The single quote mark is not visible in the worksheet and it won't be visible when you print either. It's just a way to tell Excel "Leave this as is, please".

Include Line Breaks In a Cell

Most people think of using Excel for numbers, but I actually use it for text a lot.

For example, my current day job requires a lot of analysis of bank statements. Sure, bank statements include the dollar value, but just as important in that data is the name of the person who received or sent the money.

Also, I've used Excel in the past for a complex analysis of credit agency regulations across various jurisdictions, because Excel has the ability to filter entries.

Sometimes I want my text to appear on separate lines within one single cell. But you can't just use Enter to make that happen, because Enter will take you to a new cell.

The trick is to use Alt + Enter. If you hold down the Alt key and use the Enter key, Excel will create a line break *within* the cell. Like so:

	A	B	C
1	Rule Number	Text of Rule without Line Breaks	Text of Rule with Line Breaks
2	11-51-501	(1) It is unlawful for any person, in connection with the offer, sale, or purchase of any security, directly or indirectly: (a) To employ any device, scheme, or artifice to defraud; (b) To make any untrue statement of a material fact or to omit to state a material fact necessary in order to make the statements made, in the light of the circumstances under which they are made, not misleading; or (c) To engage in any act, practice, or course of business which operates or would operate as a fraud or deceit upon any person.	(1) It is unlawful for any person, in connection with the offer, sale, or purchase of any security, directly or indirectly: (a) To employ any device, scheme, or artifice to defraud; (b) To make any untrue statement of a material fact or to omit to state a material fact necessary in order to make the statements made, in the light of the circumstances under which they are made, not misleading; or (c) To engage in any act, practice, or course of business which operates or would operate as a fraud or deceit upon any person.

In the image above I used Alt + Enter twice for each break, once to move the text to the next line and once to create that blank line between the sections. See how it makes things much easier to read? Very handy to know.

Auto-Suggested Text

Within a column of data, Excel will by default try to help you by suggesting text that matches what you've entered before. Often when I'm entering data and have control over what I enter, I use this feature to speed things up. It only works with letters or combinations of letters and numbers (it doesn't work with just numbers), so I may sometimes write something as ABC123 rather than 123ABC to save input time if I have that kind of control over my data.

What it does is looks at what you're entering and compares it to your previous entries. If what you have entered so far is a unique match for an entry above, Excel will suggest that entry for you. Let me show you:

On the next page is the table I created earlier for formatting data. I clicked into Cell A5 and typed the letter "j". Excel automatically looked at the other values in Column A and suggested that the entry I want is "Joe Smith" since I only have one entry in that column that starts with a J.

	A	B	C
1	**Customer Name**	**Customer Feedback**	**Customer Score**
2	Joe Smith	I really am not happy with you guys.	1
3	Ming Lin	You are the best.	5
4	Isabel Rodriguez	I don't even care enough to give my opinion.	3
5	joe Smith		
6			

If I agree, I can hit Enter or tab or arrow away from the cell and Excel will populate Cell A5 with "Joe Smith". I only had to type one character instead of nine. Great, right?

If you have a value like 123ABC, though, Excel will not try to suggest anything until you type the "A" even if the only 123 entry is 123ABC.

Also, Excel only does this if there's a unique value it can suggest. So if you have "Joe Smith" in one field and "Joe P. Smith" in another, it won't suggest anything until you get to "Joe P" or "Joe S", because until that point there isn't a unique value to suggest.

Another nice thing about auto-suggested text is it carries over the formatting from the suggested entry. So I can write "Joe Smith" all nicely capitalized, but the next time around I just have to type "j" and not worry about capitalization.

If Excel suggests a value that you don't want to use, then just keep typing.

F2

This is probably a good time to mention F2. If you click on a cell and use F2, it will take you to the end of whatever text you have entered into that cell. This comes in very useful if you just need to make one small change at the end of a cell. So, say I have an entry for "Maria Castilla Ladaron" and I type M and the auto-suggested text gives me that full name, but I want to add "Hernandez" on the end. I can leave that cell and let Excel populate it with the "Maria Castilla Ladaron", and then go back to the cell, use F2 to get right to the end of the text, and type in Hernandez. And done.

I also will use this is if I have entries like Author A, Author B, Author C, and Excel isn't recognizing that as a pattern for Auto Fill. I'll copy Author A to all of my cells and then go back to the ones that should be Author B, Author C, etc. and use F2, to change that A at the end.

Auto Fill

Excel has the ability to recognize patterns and fill those in for you. Some patterns, it only takes one entry. Other patterns, it never figures out.

Here is an example:

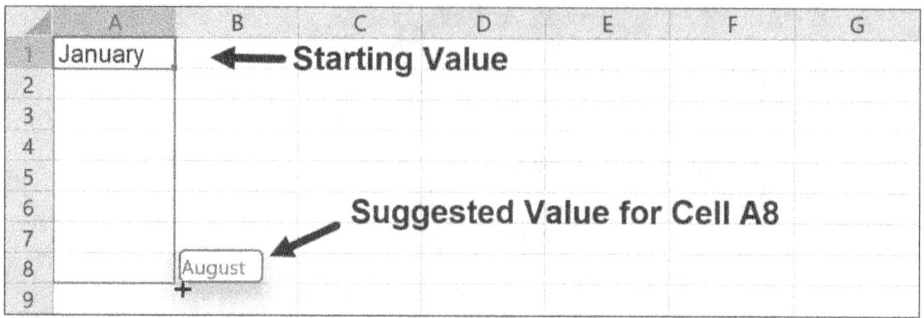

In Cell A1 I entered the value "January". I then left-clicked on the bottom right corner of that cell and dragged downward. As I dragged downward to Cells A2, A3, etc. Excel briefly showed me what value it thought I would want in each of those cells.

Here you can see that I'm at Cell A8 and it's suggesting August after having suggested February, March, April, etc. Perfect.

If I then let up on my left-click, Excel will populate Cells A2 through A8 with the suggested values. Like so:

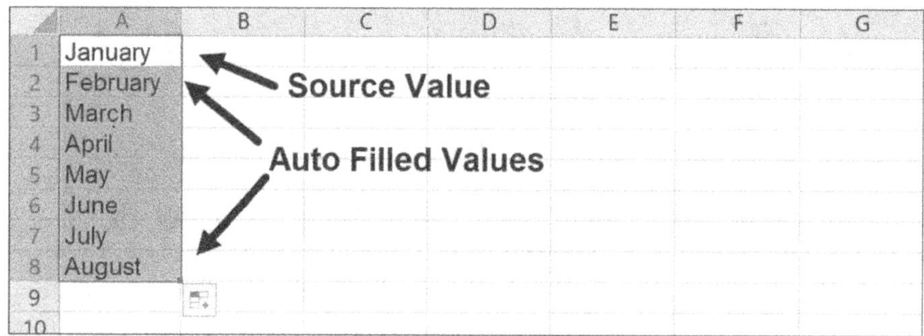

I only had to enter January and then click and drag and Excel did all the rest of the work for me.

I could have clicked and dragged to the right just as easily as I dragged downward. It would have populated values across Row 1 instead of down Column A.

Obviously, not all patterns can be recognized with one value. If you have a custom pattern, you may need a few entries before Excel can identify it. On the next page I have three entries, "Book 1", "Book 2", and "Book 3". I highlighted all three, clicked in the bottom right corner of Cell A3, and dragged, and Excel caught the pattern. You can see it will put "Book 9" in Cell A9.

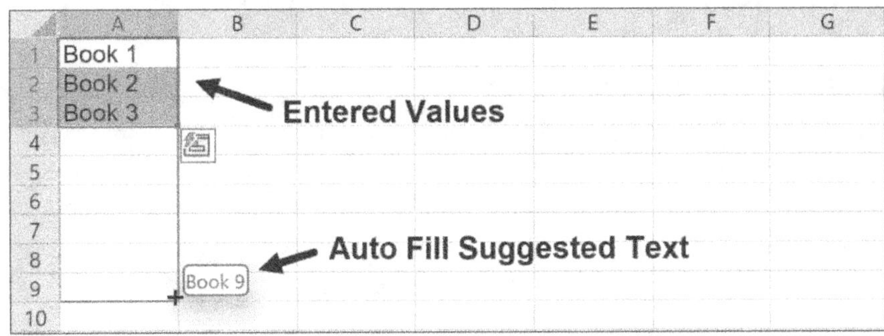

Copy Values Down a Column

If you have a large data table, you can have Excel fill that entire column quickly by double left-clicking in the bottom right corner. As long as there is a column next to the one you're trying to populate that tells Excel how far to go, it will auto-fill all the way down for you.

I actually use this to copy values quickly. Excel will auto fill with a series of values. I then go to the bottom of the portion of the list that is visible on my screen and find what I'm going to call the Auto Fill Options widget:

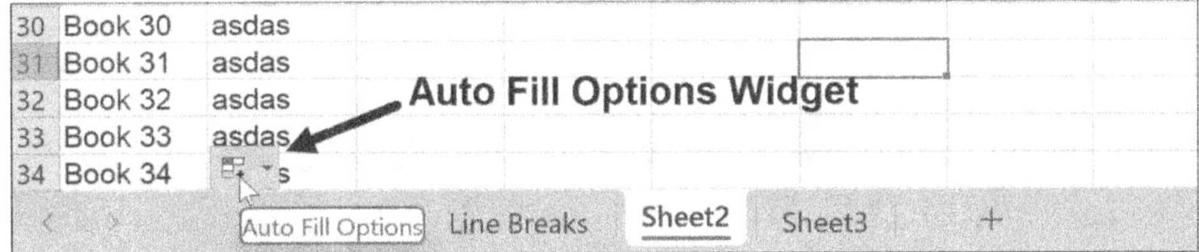

There is a dropdown arrow next to that image. Click on it and you will see a list of options:

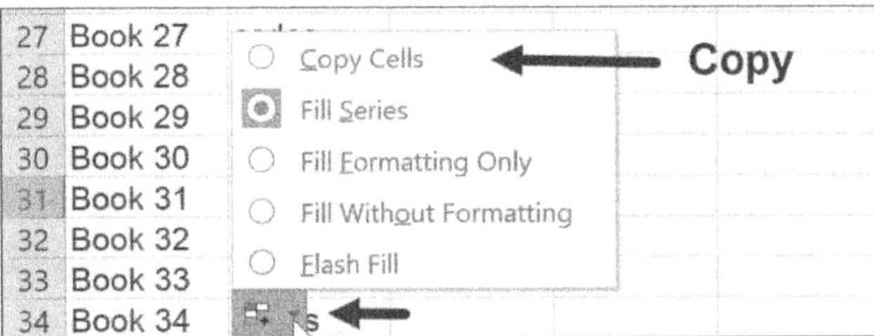

To change the auto fill over to a copy of that starting value, just click on the circle next to Copy Cells. And done.

How to Customize Your Excel Input Options

My current employer uses Office 365, and I have noticed recently that Excel is getting a little too proactive in trying to auto fill values for me. As in, it's doing it on its own without telling me, and not waiting for me to affirmatively tell it to do so. If you run into that issue, you can turn this off.

To do so, go to the File tab, click on Options in the bottom left corner, and when the Excel Options dialogue box appears, go to the Advanced tab:

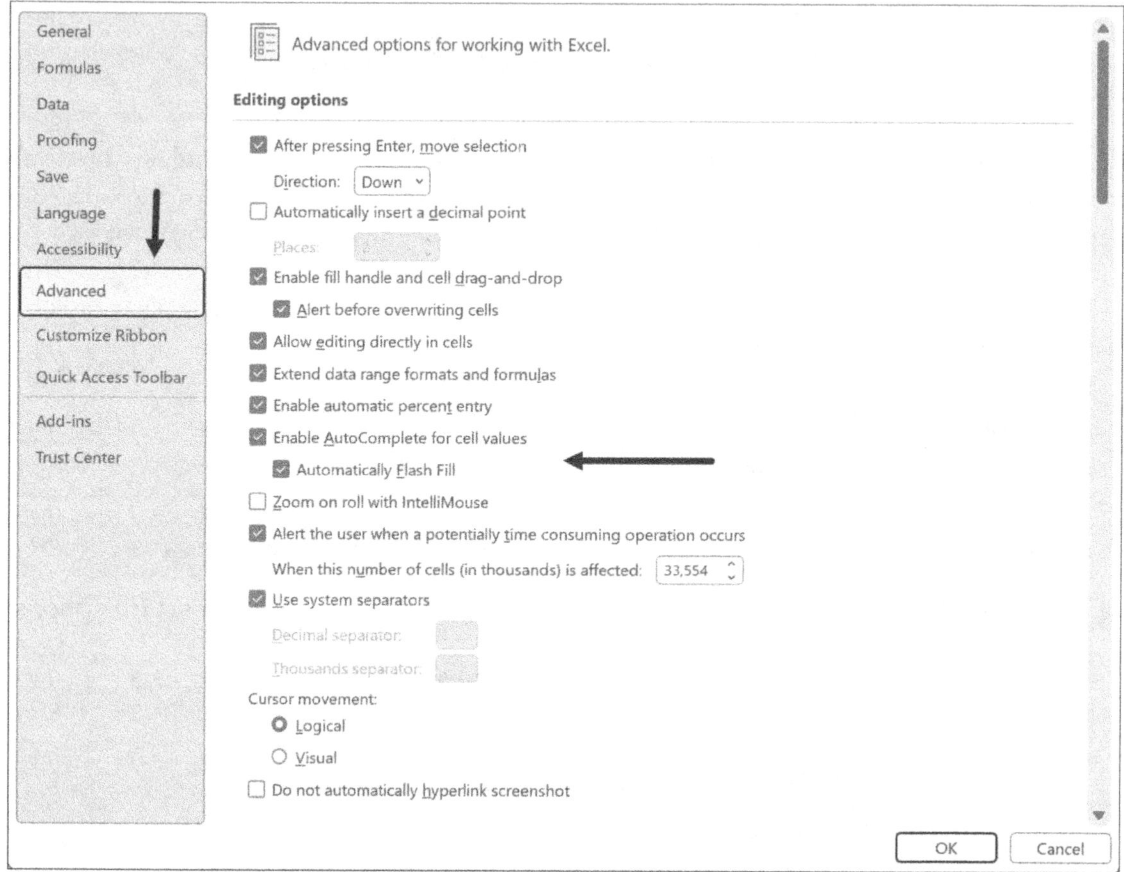

Uncheck the box for "Automatically Flash Fill".

If you like that Excel suggests a word for you like above with our "Jim Smith" then leave the Enable Autocomplete box checked.

While we're here. Go to the Data tab and you'll see a section called Automatic Data Conversion:

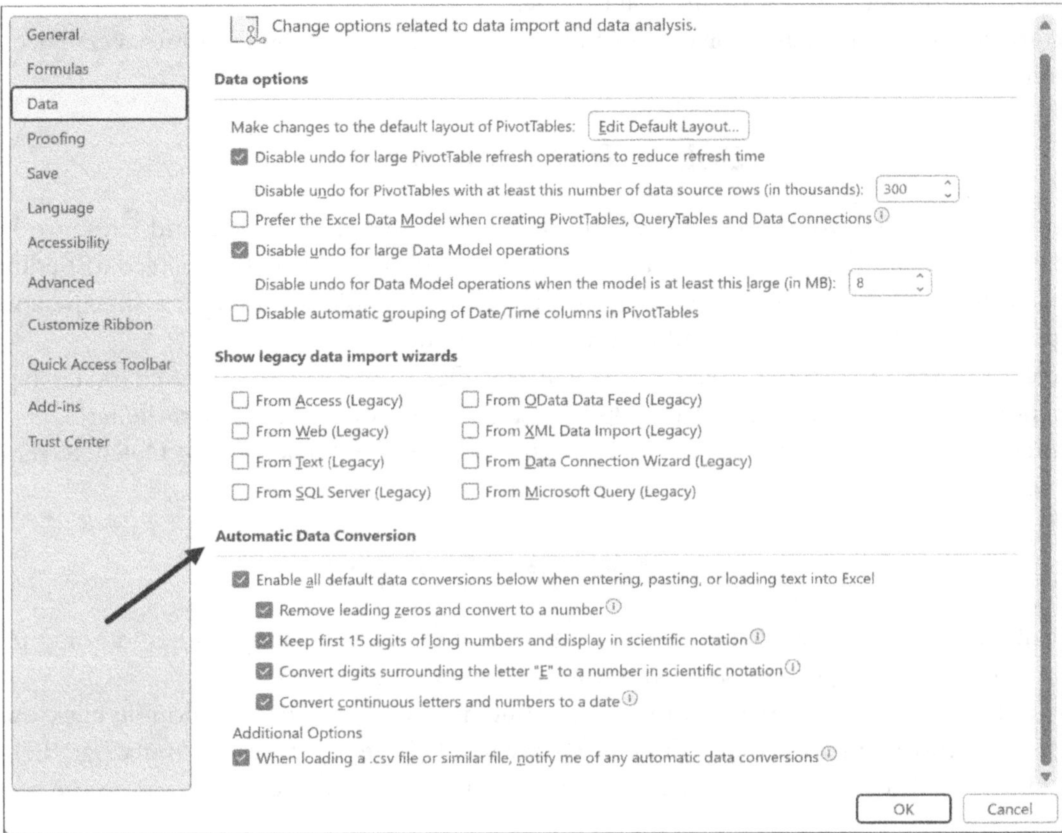

You may want to uncheck one or more of these boxes. For example, I work with zip codes a lot. Some of those have a zero at the start. I can either use the single quote mark (') to tell Excel to leave them alone, format the cell as a zip code, or I can uncheck the box for "remove leading zeros" and Excel will stop turning a zip code that is 01234 into 1234 on me. (Theoretically.)

Note that if you do that, the value stores as text not a number, which for zip codes is fine with me.

I also deal with ISBN numbers which are fifteen digits long and which Excel loves to put into scientific notation. "12345678912345" becomes "1.23457E+13", so I can uncheck that next box, too, although I just did so and it didn't work.

Oddly enough, when I clicked into the cell where I had the value, copied the value, and pasted it into another cell formatted as a text cell, where it still didn't work, somehow the original cell started displaying properly. And then the second one did, too. (Excel is not always perfect. And sometimes they break things while working on other things. It's a very old program with lots of layers of functionality that have been added or refined over the years, and occasionally there will be quirks. Sometimes it really is them not you. Although often enough it will be you. Or me as the case may be.)

So those last two fixes may or may not help, but the Flash Fill one is a lifesaver. Turn that nonsense off.

Delete Text From a Cell

We already discussed how to use Delete to delete the contents of a cell and Clear to delete formatting as well. But if you don't want to delete everything in a cell, but instead just edit part of the contents, then either double-click on that cell to be able to move to a specific spot in that text, or left-click on the cell and then use the formula bar.

From wherever you are in that text in that cell Delete will remove one character (space, letter, number, etc.) to the right and Backspace will remove one character to the left.

You can also select multiple characters in a cell and then use Backspace or Delete to remove your selection.

Add More Text To a Cell

You can add more text to a cell by double-clicking on it or left-clicking on it and going to the formula bar and typing what you need in the spot where it's needed.

By default, the formula bar will only show one line of text. I usually double-click on the cell itself in those situations, but there is an arrow at the end of the formula bar that will expand that to three lines and provide up and down arrows for you to use to see the rest of the text.

Freeze Panes

One final trick for you with respect to inputting data is to know how to use Freeze Panes. Most tables of data you create are going to have a header row that tells you what is in each column. Some may also have a column or two on the left-hand side that tells you what the row of data covers, like a student or customer name.

But as you enter more data in Excel, those rows or columns will disappear. When you get to Row 652 of your data, Row 1 isn't going to be visible anymore. Fortunately, you can use Freeze Panes, which is available in the Window section of the View tab, to tell Excel to keep certain rows or columns always visible.

The dropdown menu for Freeze Panes will give you the choice to Freeze Panes, Freeze Top Row, or Freeze First Column.

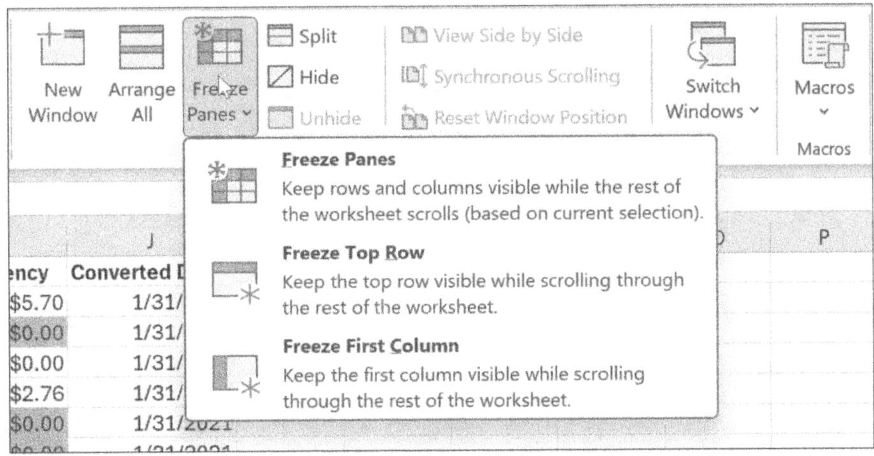

Freeze Top Row will freeze the top row in your visible workspace. So if you want to always be able to see Row 1, be sure it's showing on your workspace before you choose this option.

If you have a data table that starts on Row 10, you can scroll in your workspace until Row 10 is the top row visible, and then choose this option. That will make Rows 1 through 9 permanently hidden until you turn it off, but you will have Row 10 visible at the top of the worksheet even when you're on Row 710.

Same concept works for Freeze First Column. It will keep the first column that was visible in the workspace when you turned it on visible as you scroll to the right. Any columns to the left of that will be hidden until you turn Freeze Panes off.

The final option, Freeze Panes, lets you freeze both columns and rows at the same time as well as more than one row or column at a time. To use this one, arrange your workspace so that the columns and rows you need to be able to see at all times are visible, and then click into the first cell that you *don't* want to have to see (so the one to the right and below the rows and columns you want frozen), and then choose Freeze Panes.

After you turn on freeze panes, you may want to scroll in each direction to make sure that what you're seeing is what you intended to be able to see/not see.

To turn off freeze panes, just go back to that dropdown. You'll see an Unfreeze Panes option. Click on it.

Copy, Cut, and Paste Data

There are going to be times when you need to take information that's in one location in an Excel workbook and move it or use it elsewhere. So copying, moving (known as cutting in Excel), and pasting data is an essential Excel skill to master.

First step, is to select your data. We touched on it before, but let's cover it in more detail now.

Select Cell(s)

To select the information in one cell, just click on the cell.

To select information in cells that are next to each other, left-click on the first or last cell in the cell range and then drag until all of the cells you want are selected.

You can drag in any direction, but that starting cell needs to be in the corner of the range. If you click on one cell, drag right, and then reverse direction and drag left past the first cell, the only cells selected will be from the first cell to the left.

Another way to select a range of cells is to click on the first or last cell in the range, hold down the Shift key, and then click on the cell at the other end of the range.

If you have a data table where the top row and first column of cells are continuously populated with data, then you can click into the top left corner of the table and use Shift + Ctrl + down arrow + right arrow to quickly select all of the cells in the table.

This is very useful when you have large data tables. It's much faster to use Shift + Ctrl to select the data than to try to highlight the rows by clicking and dragging, even though that is doable. (And what I used to do back in the day.)

Just be careful if there are any breaks in your rows or columns because Excel will stop at a blank cell when you use Shift + Ctrl and the arrow keys.

If you need to select cells that aren't touching, then use the Ctrl key to do that. You can combine Ctrl with selecting ranges. So you could select a range of cells, hold down the Ctrl key, and select another range of cells.

To select an entire Column, click on the letter for the column.

To select an entire Row, click on the number for the row.

To select more than one column or row, treat them like cells. Select the first one, and then left-click and drag or use the Ctrl or Shift keys.

Select All

There are going to be times when you want to select all of the data on a worksheet. I will often do this with a worksheet that has formulas so that I can copy the data and replace it with just the results of those formulas. This lets me lock in my results and is often useful when I'm using Excel formulas to transform my data in some way.

To easily select all of the cells on a worksheet, you have two options. One, click anywhere in the worksheet and then use Ctrl + A. Two, you can click in the top left corner of the worksheet where the rows and columns intersect:

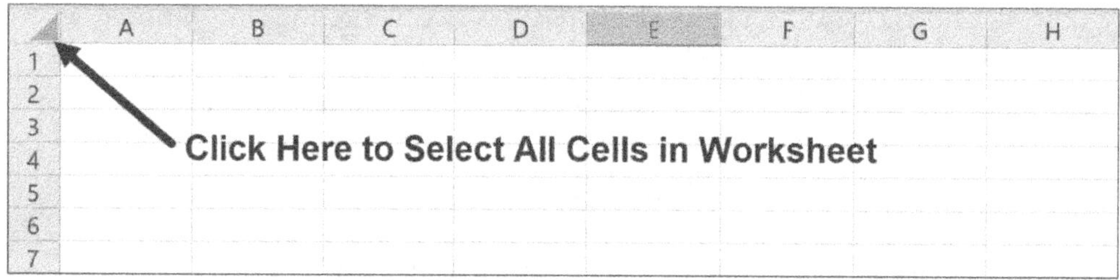

After you Select All, that darker gray triangle will turn green and all of your cells will show that they've been selected.

Terminology

To leave the original data where it is but take an exact duplicate of that data to put elsewhere, you Copy. Easy enough.

To move that data from where it is and put it elsewhere, you Cut.

To place the data in its new location, whether you were copying or cutting, you Paste.

Copy and Paste Data As Is

By default, your data that you copy or cut is going to keep its formatting in its new location. This is the "as is" part. So if it was bolded and bright red, it will stay that way in its new location. If it was highlighted yellow and had a border, same. It all moves.

As defined above, copying data means you leave the original where it is and take an exact duplicate of that data to move elsewhere.

First step, select the cells that contain what you want to copy.

Second step, copy. I generally copy by using Ctrl + C. It's one of the control shortcuts I really recommend you learn because it will save you a ton of time in using Excel.

But if you forget the control shortcut, there are a couple other options. You can go to the Clipboard section of the Home tab and click on the Copy option there:

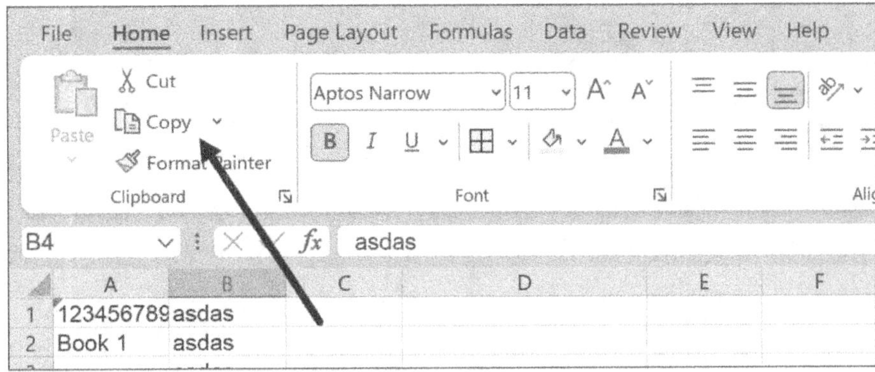

(You don't need the dropdown, just click on the two pieces of paper image.)

Or you can right-click on your selected cells and choose Copy from the dropdown menu:

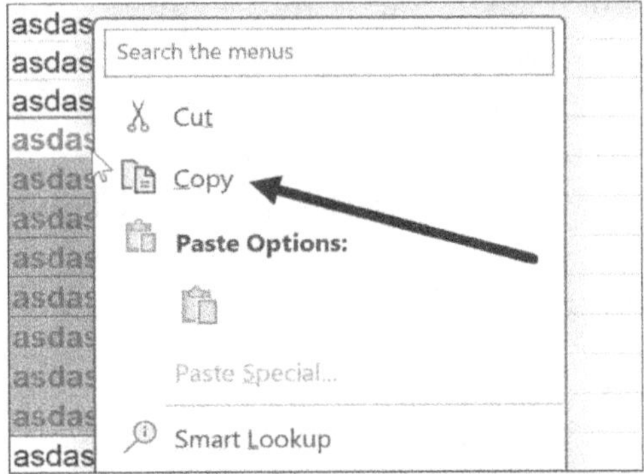

All three get you the same result. Your selected cells will now have a moving dashed border around them, and Excel will be ready for you to paste a copy of those cell contents into a new location.

For the third step, click on the first cell where you want to copy the information to. That can be in the current worksheet, another worksheet, another workbook, or even somewhere like a Word document.

Fourth step, paste. Once again, I tend to use the control shortcut for this, Ctrl + V. But if you only need to paste the data once, you can also just hit Enter.

There are other paste options. For example, you can go to the Clipboard section of the Home tab and click on the Paste option there, or you can right-click and choose the first Paste option from the dropdown menu.

You can see both of those here:

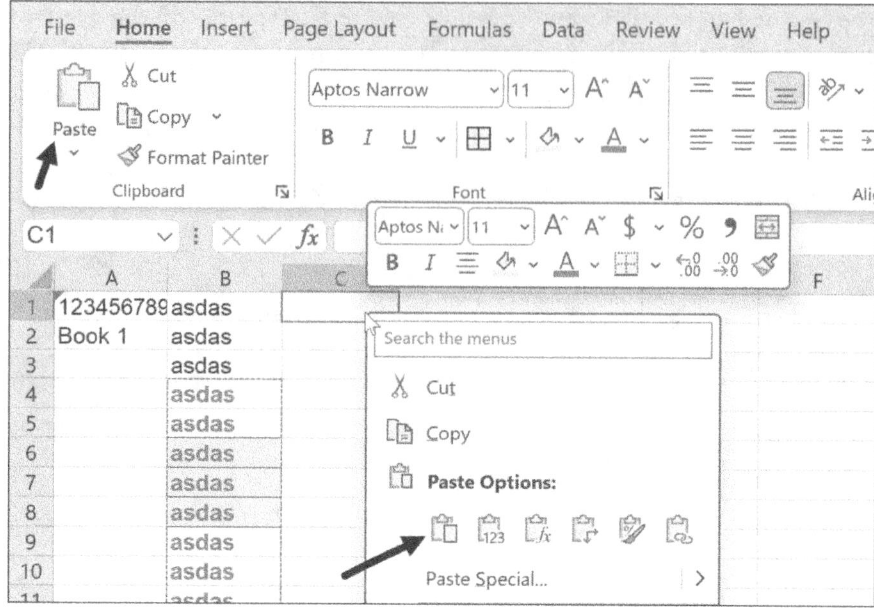

Once you are done pasting your data, if you didn't do it using Enter, then use Esc or click into another cell and start typing to unselect your copied data. (Clicking on one of the tools in the top menu can work to turn it off as well. In general, this isn't going to be an issue that you notice, but in case it does crop up, Esc is your friend.)

A quick note here, since it came up when I pasted this data into a *Word* document to make sure it would work.

This is what that data looked like in Word:

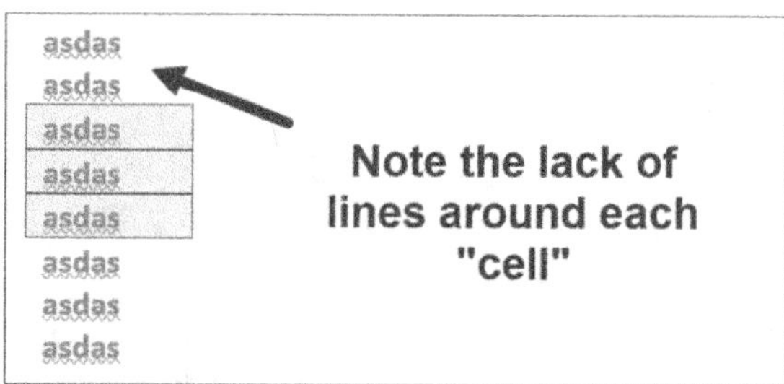

Look carefully at the top two values and the bottom three. See how none of them have a line around them in Word? That's because the default lines that Excel puts around each cell are just there to help you better visualize the separation between the cells. If you actually want your data to copy or print with a border—like the three yellow highlighted cells in the image above—you have to add those borders yourself. (We'll cover how to do that in the formatting chapter.)

I bring this up because in the first Excel for beginners book, I didn't mention that, and then someone sent me a confused email about how tables in Word work (with a built-in border and a set number of cells) versus how tables in Excel work (without borders around cells and no real defined table until you format it to be distinct). So if you're used to working with tables in Word, be a little careful trying to treat data in Excel the same way, because they aren't the same.

Okay. What if you want to move the data altogether, not copy it?

Cut and Paste Data As Is

Cutting data means that you take the contents and formatting that are in a cell or series of cells and you remove it from where it currently is. The cells themselves will remain there, but the contents and formatting of those cells will be gone after you cut those cell contents.

First step, select the cells you want to cut.

Second step, cut. I generally do so using the control shortcut (Ctrl + X), but there is a Cut option in the Clipboard section of the Home tab, as well as a Cut option in the dropdown menu if you right-click.

In Excel, when you cut your selected data, it is still visible in the worksheet. This is different from Word where the text you select and cut will immediately disappear. Which is why in Word you can actually use Cut as another way to delete something, but that doesn't work in Excel.

Third step, go to the top left cell where you want to put the data and paste just the same as you did with copying cells. (Ctrl +V, Enter, or one of the menu options.)

Note that you can only paste data once when you cut it. This is just moving the data from one location to another.

Because you used cut, that will remove the contents and formatting of those cells and place all of it in the new location. Here is a screenshot that's meant to demonstrate the different results between copy and paste:

	A	B	C	D	E	F	G	H
1		asdas		asdas				
2		asdas		asdas				
3		asdas		asdas				
4		asdas		asdas				
5		asdas		asdas		**Copied Cells**		
6		asdas		asdas				
7		asdas		asdas				
8		asdas		asdas				
9								
10								
11				asdas				
12				asdas				
13				asdas				
14				asdas		**Cut Cells**		
15				asdas				
16				asdas				
17				asdas				
18				asdas				
19								

Rows 1 through 8 are what happens when you copy. The original data was in Column B, I copied and pasted into Column D, and I have the option to paste again because you can still see the dotted green line around Cells B1 through B8.

Rows 11 through 18 are what happens when you cut. The original data was in Column B, I cut and pasted into Column D, and that's it. The data moved completely from Column B to Column D. There is no formatting left in Column B and nothing left for me to move.

With both Copy and Cut you are just taking the contents of the cells not the cells themselves so nothing around the copied or cut cells moves.

Cut or Copy Cells With Formulas

One of the biggest strengths of Excel is the use of formulas and functions, that's why each of my Excel Essentials series has at least one full book devoted to them. And one of the key reasons for that is how formulas in Excel copy.

If you CUT a cell that's using a formula, the formula moves to the new location exactly as is. It continues to reference the exact same cells it referenced before.

If you COPY a cell that's using a formula, the formula adjusts based on how far you moved the data. Copy it down one row and it will reference cells that are also down one row from the original formula.

Let's take a very basic example:

	A	B	C	D	E	F
1	Value 1	Value 2			Value 3	Value 4
2	2	3			121	4
3						
4	Formula	Result			Formula	Value
5	=A2+B2	5		Copy C2	=E2+F2	125
6				Cut C2	=A2+B2	5
7						

In Cell A2 I have entered the value 2. In Cell B2 I have entered the value 3.

In Cell A5 I wrote a very basic formula that adds the value in Cell A2 to the value in Cell B2. That formula is:

$$=A2+B2$$

That says to go to Cell A2 and pull in that value, 2, and then add it to the value found in Cell B2, 3.

Your result is 5, which is displayed in Cell B5.

Take a moment to make sure you're good with that. Cell reference + Cell reference means we add what's in those two cells.

Okay. Now back to copy and cut.

In Cell E5 I COPIED the formula that was in Cell A5 and pasted it in. Because Excel adjusts copied formulas and I had moved the formula over by four columns, each of the cell references also changed by four columns. A2 became E2, B2 became F2. I put different values in Cells E2 and F2 so that it could add up to a different result, 125.

In Cell E6 I CUT the formula that was in Cell A5 (and then typed it back in so I could take the screenshot). Because I cut the formula, it did not change at all. It is still adding A2 to B2.

Before you wonder, "Why does Excel do that?", the adjustment to formulas that Excel makes when you copy is one of its key strengths. Because it lets you write a formula once for the first entry in your data table and then copy that formula down the rest of a column or across the rest of a row. Instead of you having to manually adjust a formula 10,000 times, Excel does it for you in the blink of an eye. It is fantastic. But you need to understand that's what happens to avoid making inadvertent errors.

We will revisit this again in the formulas chapter because there are ways to copy formulas and keep Excel from changing a cell reference that I still want to discuss. But first, let's talk about pasting special.

Copy and Paste Just Values

I mentioned before that I sometimes will copy my data and paste over it to get rid of the formulas. Usually I do this because I manipulated my entries in some way.

For example, say I had an ISBN number (which are used to identify books) that was written as 123-43-1234-0123, but my publishing partner wants the number as 1234312340123, with no dashes. Fortunately, I can use Excel functions to do that rather than have to manually change each one. (I could also probably use Replace, but let's pretend I didn't.)

My temptation after I use a formula to do something like that is to delete the original column of values. Problem is, that when I do that, it ruins my results because those results are the outcome of a formula that references the original column.

So if I don't need my formulas to keep running, I like to get rid of them. The way to do this is to use Paste Special – Values.

The initial steps when using Paste Special – Values are exactly the same. You select your cells, *copy* your values, and select where you want that data to go (which can be the same location that you copied from).

But the next step is to either right-click or use the Paste dropdown menu in the Clipboard section of the Home tab, and then click on the paste option with 123 on the clipboard.

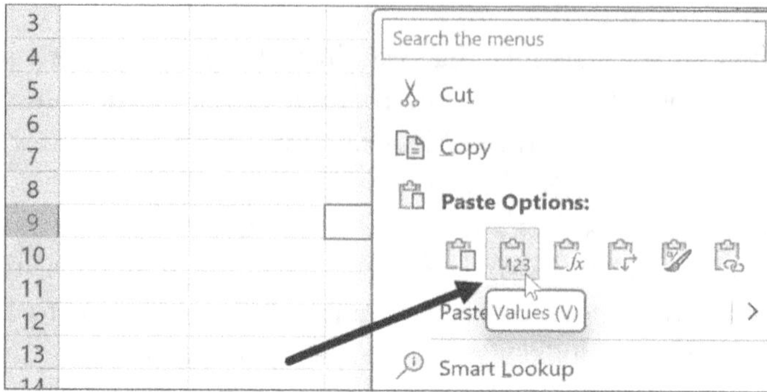

In the image above, I've placed my mouse over it so you can see that it's the "Values" paste option.

In the Paste dropdown it's positioned a little differently:

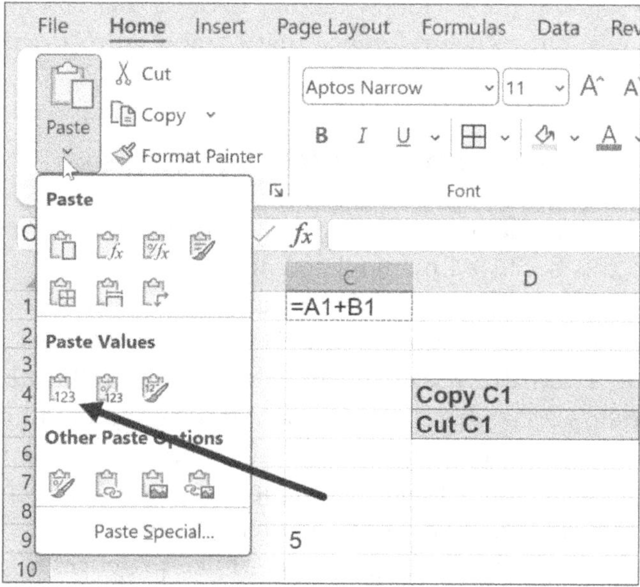

Copy a Column of Data and Paste as a Row or
Copy a Row of Data and Paste as a Column

Another Paste Special option that exists in Excel is to take data that you have in a column and paste it so it's across a row. Or to take data that you have in a row and paste it so that it's down a column.

The Transpose option currently looks like arrows pointing to the right and down in the bottom corner of the clipboard, and as you hold your cursor over that option you should see a preview in the background of what your result will look like:

It is available in the dropdown when you right-click on your selected range, or in the Paste dropdown in the Clipboard section of the Home tab.

You can even do this with a data table, so do both at once. Here's an example:

In Cells A1 through C5 I had a very basic table of data. There were two years of sales results for four vendors.

I selected Cells A1 through C5 and then Pasted Special using the Transpose option into Cell A8. That pasted the values (and formatting) from the table in Cells A1 through C5 into Cells A8 through C12. Note that now the vendor names are across the top and the years are down the left of the table, and the values inside the table also pivoted.

Other Copy-and-Paste-Special Comments

Note that the Paste Special options are only available when you copy. They are not available when you cut your data. So if you want to move the data and change it, it's a two-step process. Change it first, move it second.

As you can see, there are a number of other Paste Special options available in the Paste dropdown menu when you copy cells. I don't think I've ever needed to use any of them, but every tool or function in Excel exists because at some point someone needed it enough for the designers to put in the time to create it. Feel free to experiment and see what they do.

Paste Special – Formatting, for example, might be nice if you have a table of data that is already formatted and need an identical table for new data but don't want to redo all that formatting. You could copy the original table and Paste Special – Formatting to get a blank table with the formatting already in place.

Finally, with each version of Office they like to change the appearance of things. And sometimes it's not quite obvious what something now looks like. So if you ever can't find a paste option you want, click on Paste Special in one of the two dropdown menus. That will bring up the Paste Special dialogue box, which is text-based:

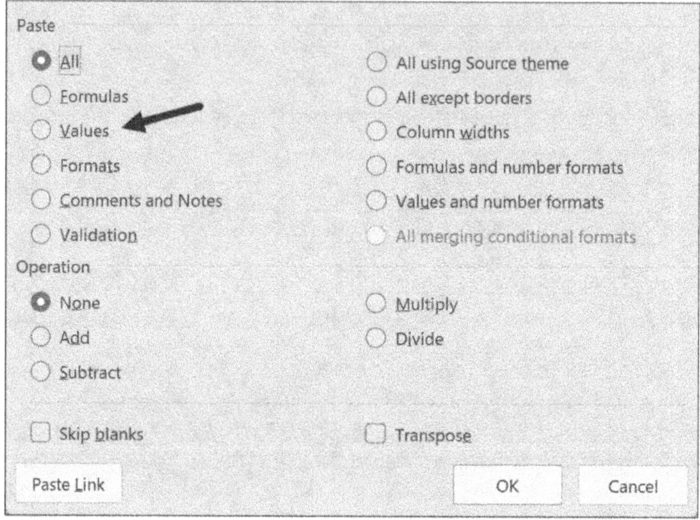

You can then click on the circle next to the option(s) you want and click on OK to apply it.

Copy From Another Program to Excel

One final tip. If you copy text from another program and try to paste into a cell in Excel, Excel will break the text across rows based on where any Enters were. So three paragraphs of text will end up in three cells in an Excel worksheet. If you want all of the text in one cell, double-click on that cell before you paste.

* * *

On to formatting, with one quick detour since the way you plan to use your worksheet will impact how you input and format that data.

A Quick Note on Data Analysis Versus Data Reporting

In the following chapters we are going to cover how to format your data as well as some basic ways to analyze it. Before we do that, I want to take a quick moment and discuss the difference between data that you use for analysis and data that you use for reporting.

If you want to use your data for analysis—meaning you plan to sort, filter, use formulas, create charts, or create pivot tables with it—there are a handful of best practices to follow.

1. Use one row of your worksheet for your data labels, preferably the top row. (This is the row you can freeze and also the one to use for filtering when we reach that discussion.)

2. List all of your data below that label row in continuous rows with one row that contains all of the data for that entry (customer transaction, for example). DO NOT include subtotals or subheadings, those are for reports. If you want to look at your data using specific groupings, then have a column with that information in it for each row.

3. Standardize as many values as possible.

   Customer A should always be Customer A. An entry like State should not be freeform. You want everyone to enter CO for Colorado not CO, Colorado, Colarado, Colo, etc.

4. Format your data in a way that makes it easier to analyze.

   Specific values and random text are not as easy to analyze as category variables. Where it makes sense to do so, such as customer income for financial professionals, it is better to have five buckets that represent income ranges than list the specific income for each customer. The best way to approach this concept is to think about what you'd do if you were doing this manually. Would it matter that one customer earns \$15,234.21 a year and another earns \$17,564.32? If not, then find a way to bucket those values.

5. Store your raw data in one place, correct it in another place, analyze it in a third, and report on it in a fourth.

This can be worksheets in the same workbook, but you want to keep the raw data untouched in case you mess up somewhere along the line. And by keeping the intermediate steps, you can sometimes save having to start over.

Here's an example of what I'm talking about in Items 3 and 4 above:

	A	B	C	D	E
1	**Customer Name**	**Customer Feedback**	**Customer Score**		
2	Joe Smith	I really am not happy with you guys.	1		
3	Ming Lin	You are the best.	5	Standardized Value	
4	Isabel Rodriguez	I don't even care enough to give my opinion.	3		
5					
6		Freeform Text			

This is a data table of feedback from three different customers. One is unhappy, one is pleased, and one really could care less.

You can see that by reading the comments in the freeform text column (Column B). Which is fine to use when you have three customers. But what about 3,000? Or 30,000? Or 300,000? How do you find "good" comments versus "bad" comments?

There are ways that people do that with data analysis, but it's much easier to have values like those in Column C that give that same feedback but in a standardized way. You can see the average rating as easily with 30,000 reviewers as 3.

Do you lose some nuance? Yes, absolutely. And sometimes that's why it's best to capture both.

* * *

What about data for reporting?

In that case, subtotals and subheadings are fine. As are grand totals and special formatting.

A report should be designed in such a way that it's easy for the end user to understand. Expect that data that's prepared for reporting purposes will be printed out. Can it print well? Are there borders? And totals?

Can it be understood just by looking at the printed result? Do the labels and categories make sense to an end-user? Or are the labels still Field1, Field 22, etc.? If you need notes or definitions, are they visible when printed?

This is why data that is formatted for reporting is not good to use for analysis and vice versa. I raise these issues now because if you think about it all ahead of time, you can save yourself a lot of stress and heartache down the road.

Okay, then. Time to learn about formatting.

Formatting

It's all well and good to enter data into Excel. Pretty easy at its core, right, you just click and type. But without formatting your data you can end up with a hideous looking mess that's hard to use. Especially if you want to print anything.

Here, for example, is the print preview for two pages of an imported but unformatted report from one of my vendors:

Title	Author	Units	Publisher I	Currency c	Customer	Customer	Country C	Product T)
A Missing	Aleksa Ba:	3	2.8 USD		3.99 USD		US	EB1
A Dead M:	Aleksa Ba:	1	2.8 USD		3.99 USD		US	EB1
Halloween	Aleksa Ba:	3	0.7 USD		0.99 USD		US	EB1
Excel for E	M.L. Hum	1	385 JPY		550 JPY		JP	EB1
Rider's Re	Alessandr:	1	10.5 USD		14.99 USD		US	EB1
A Buried E	Aleksa Ba:	3	2.8 USD		3.99 USD		US	EB1
A Crazy C:	Aleksa Ba:	2	2.8 USD		3.99 USD		US	EB1
Intermedia	M.L. Hum	1	455 JPY		650 JPY		JP	EB1

Pre-Order	Promo Co	ISBN	Apple Ider	Vendor Id	Vendor Of	Begin Dat	End Date	Publisher
			1.49E+09	1.01E+10		11/1/2019	########	Aleksa Ba:
			1.49E+09	1.01E+10		11/1/2019	########	Aleksa Ba:
			1.49E+09	1.01E+10		11/1/2019	########	Aleksa Ba:
			1.49E+09	1.01E+10		11/1/2019	########	M.L. Hum
			1.49E+09	1.01E+10		11/1/2019	########	Alessandr:
			1.49E+09	1.01E+10		11/1/2019	########	Aleksa Ba:
			1.49E+09	1.01E+10		11/1/2019	########	Aleksa Ba:
			1.49E+09	1.01E+10		11/1/2019	########	M.L. Hum

There are no lines separating the different columns of data. Text is cut off for a number of columns. Whatever is in that End Date column on the second page isn't even visible because the column isn't wide enough to display it. And both Apple ID and Vendor ID are written in scientific notation.

Taking something like that mess and formatting it before you start working with it is essential. Even if you enter your own data, formatting is essential. You do not want to print most data without borders. And I don't think I've ever created a worksheet where I didn't need to adjust column widths. So this chapter matters. A lot.

And because I expect you to come back to this chapter when you need it, I'm going to present the formatting options alphabetically to make them easier to find later. But first, the basics. There are four main ways to format things in Excel 2024:

The first is by using control shortcuts, such as Ctrl + B for bolding text and Ctrl + I for applying italics to text. There aren't a ton of these I use in Excel, but I do use those two all the time.

The second is going to the Font, Alignment, and Number sections of the Home tab and choosing the option you need from there:

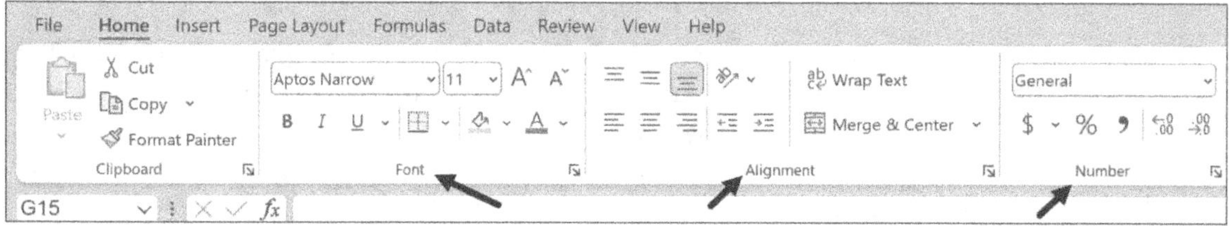

The third, which if you're newer to Excel you may use more than I do, is the mini formatting menu that appears at the top or bottom of the dropdown menu when you right-click after selecting cells in the main workspace:

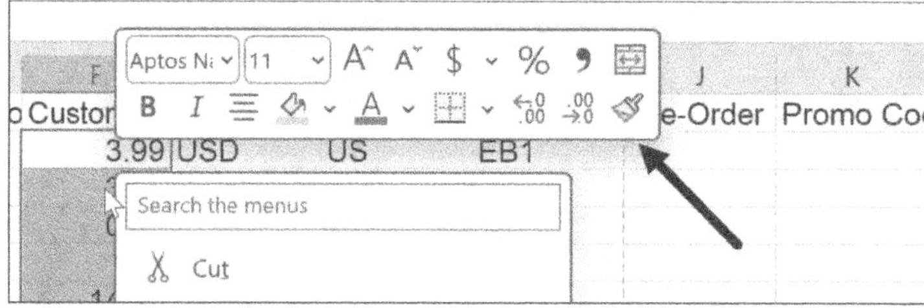

It has a lot of the most common formatting options in it, such as font, font color, font size, fill color, bold, italics, borders, etc.

(You can hold your cursor over each icon to see what it allows you to do if you can't remember.)

The fourth, and least likely to be used, but the one with the most choices, is the Format Cells dialogue box, which you can see on the next page.

To open it, select your cell(s), right-click, and choose Format Cells from the dropdown menu. Or you can click on one of the expansion arrows in the bottom right corner of the Font, Alignment, or Number sections of the Home tab. Note that there are multiple tabs in the Format Cells dialogue box, so you'll need to click over to the one you need.

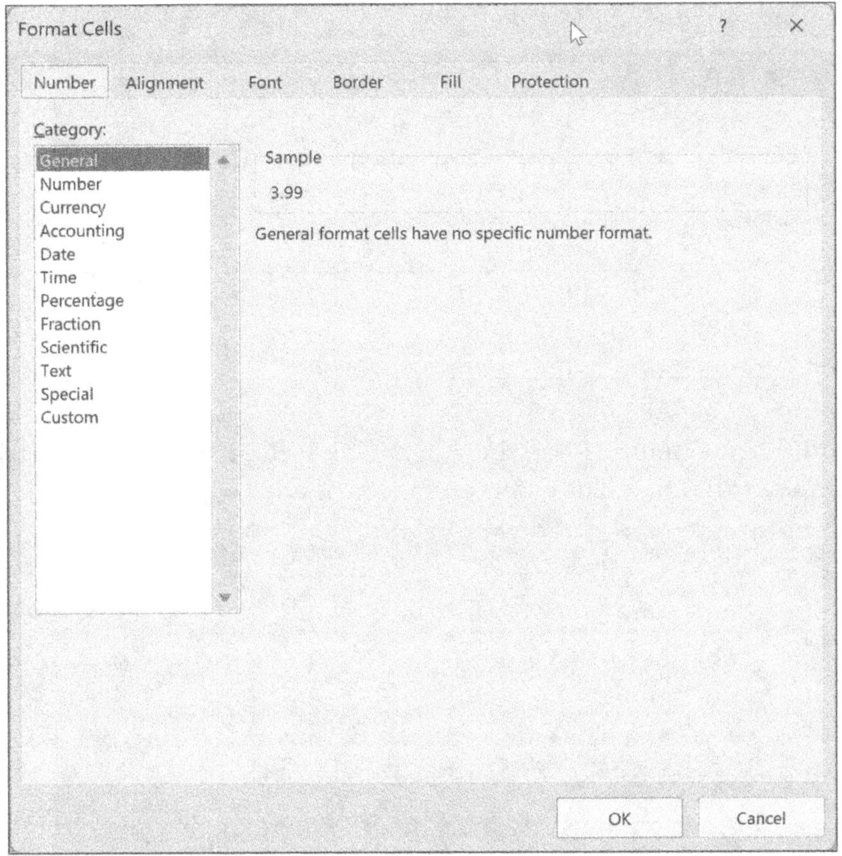

Okay. Let's dive in. Remember, this is listed alphabetically, not from most important to least important.

Align Text Within a Cell

Any text you enter into a cell will by default be aligned to the bottom left side of that cell. Numbers and dates will by default be aligned to the bottom right side of the cell. You can easily see that difference if you increase the height and width of your cells.

You can have your data Top, Middle, or Bottom Aligned, and also Left, Center, or Right Aligned. Which creates nine possible alignments.

Here are examples of each:

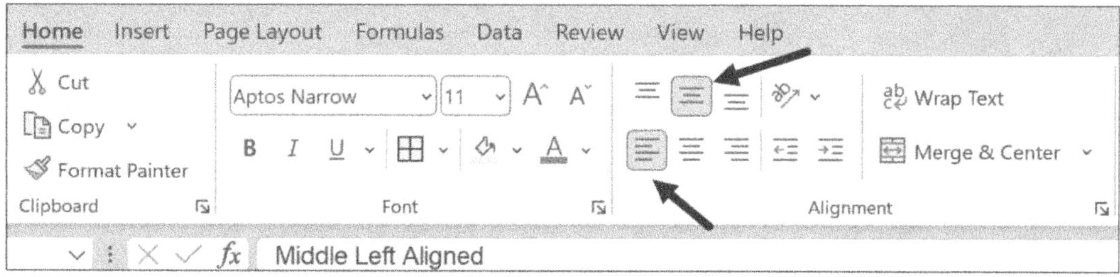

To apply the different options, I use the Alignment section of the Home tab. (The mini formatting menu only has the Center option, so is of limited use for this one.)

The icons/images for each option show the type of formatting that you're applying.

Note above how the Middle option in the top row shows lines that are all centered top to bottom and the Left option in the second row shows lines that all start on the left edge, for example.

Some formatted numbers or dates may not change when you apply alignment, but text should always change.

You can also use the Alignment tab of the Format Cells dialogue box, which you can see on the next page.

There are dropdowns for Horizontal and Vertical that will contain the relevant options and a few more. The Horizontal dropdown menu, for example, includes additional choices such as Left Indent and Right Indent, and the Vertical dropdown menu includes options for Justify and Distributed.

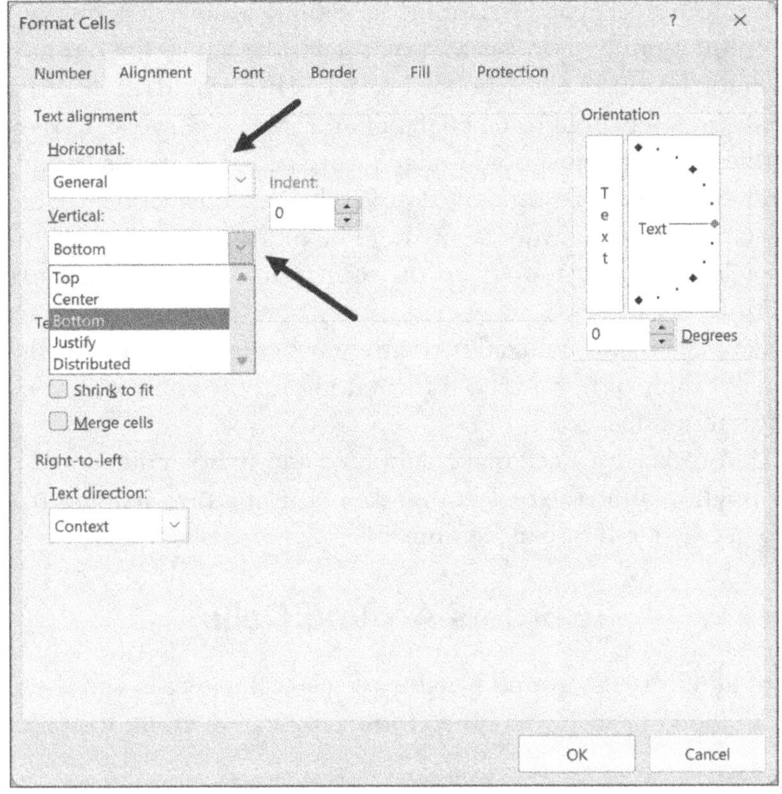

Bold Text

The easiest way to bold the contents of a cell is to click on the cell(s) and use Ctrl + B.

Another option is to select your cell(s) and then click on the bolded B in the Font section of the Home tab or the mini formatting menu.

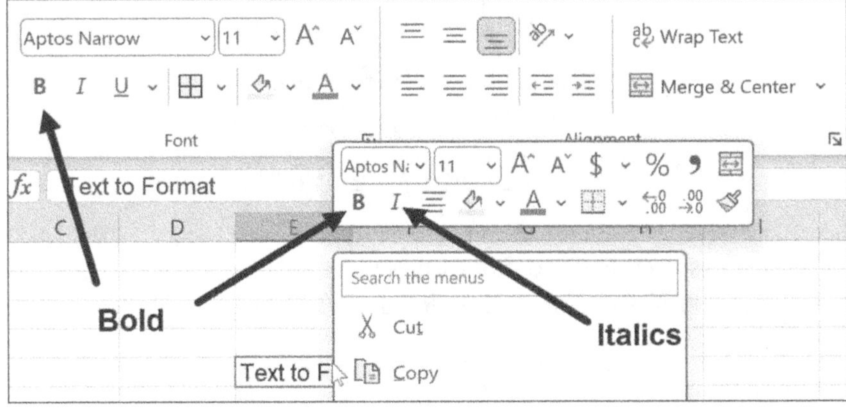

To remove bolding from a cell, you just do the same thing again. Click on the cell and then use Ctrl +B or click on the B in the Font section of the Home tab or the mini formatting menu.

The Font tab in the Format Cells dialogue box has a Font Style set of options that includes Bold and Bold Italic to apply bold to text. Change the style to Regular to remove it.

Sometimes you may want to just bold a single word or set of words within a cell instead of the entire contents of the cell. To do that, double-click on the cell that contains the text you want to bold, select that text, and then apply it. (The mini format menu should automatically appear after you select the text and let up on your mouse, but if it doesn't then the other options are still available.)

If you ever have a cell that has mixed formatting, where part of the text is bolded and part isn't, and you want to apply or remove bold formatting for the entire cell, you may need to use your chosen option more than once.

For example, if you click on a cell that has bolded and unbolded text and use Ctrl + B that is going to apply bold to all of the text in that cell. So to remove bolding from all text in the cell you'd need to use Ctrl + B one more time.

Borders Around Cells

The easiest way to add borders around a cell is to select those cells and then use the borders dropdown menu in the Font section of the Home tab or in the mini formatting menu.

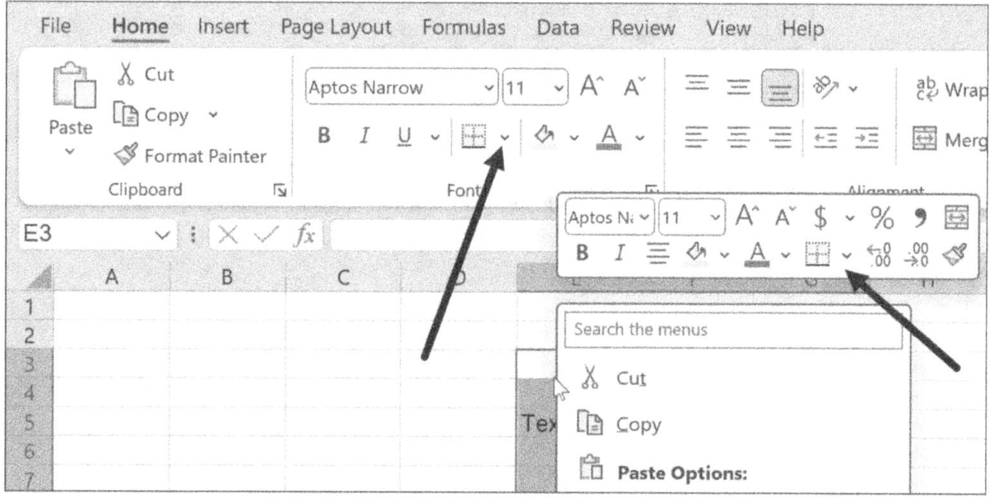

I almost always need to choose from the dropdown menu because I almost never put just a bottom border on a cell, which is the default option.

Click on the arrow next to the current border option to see a full list of choices:

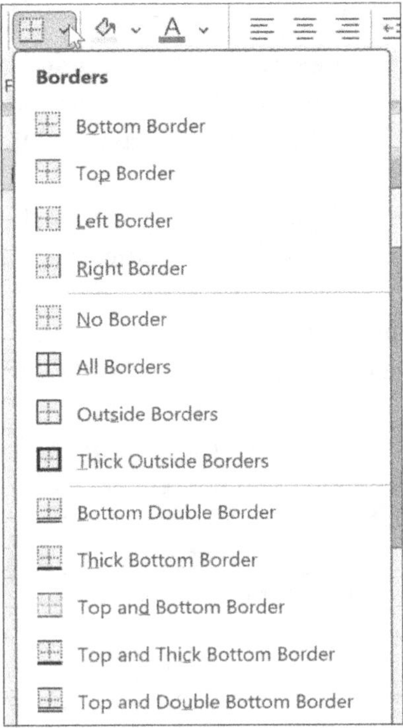

Another option for adding borders is the Draw Border tool in the lower portion of that dropdown menu.

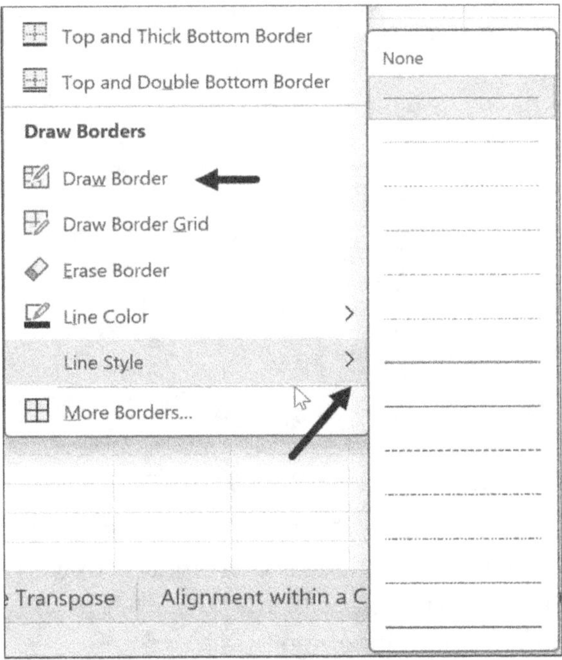

You don't have to select cells first if you use that tool. You can just click on Draw Border and then click and drag in your workspace to put an exterior border around a group of cells.

You can also click on an individual border of an individual cell to put a line on that one border, or click in the middle of a cell and drag a little to put a border around the entire cell. Esc when you're done.

If you don't like the line type or color that Excel uses by default, you can change that in the Draw Borders section of the dropdown menu. In the image above you can see the available Line Style choices, for example.

If you're going to change those attributes, though, you need to change them *before* you apply your lines. Any change you make to line color or line style will only apply to *new* borders not your existing ones.

Finally, you have the option to use the Border tab in the Format Cells dialogue box. That is the only place I know of to get a diagonal line across a cell.

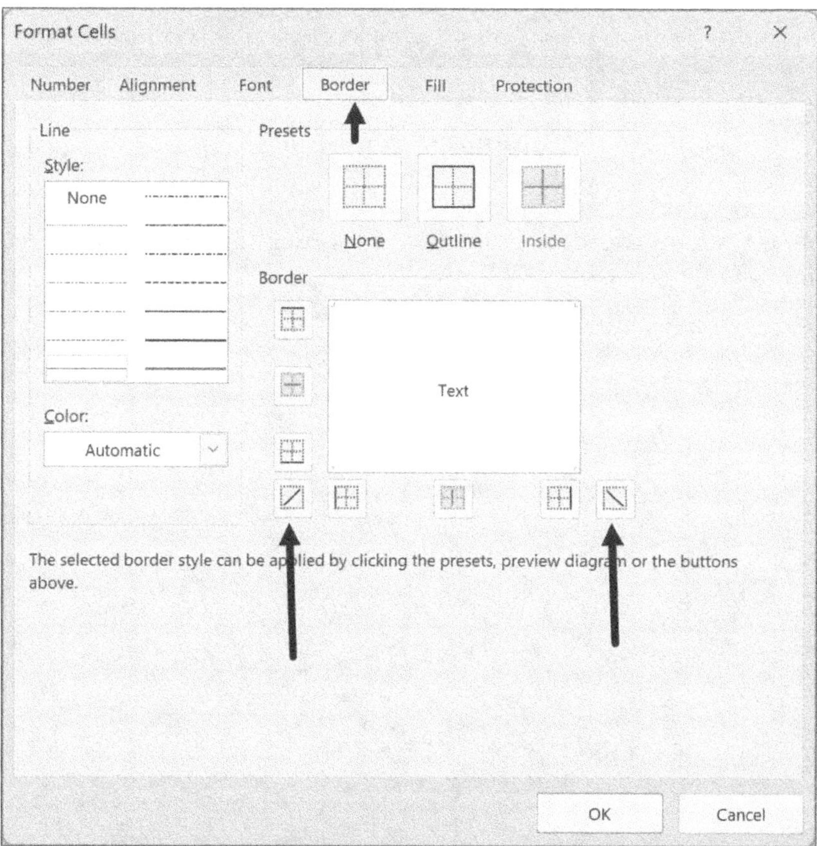

Note that this is a *formatting* line, not a line that corresponds to your text, so if you do this in a cell that has text, you'll get a line that goes from one corner to the opposite corner but your text will still be oriented left to right horizontal by default.

Okay. A few more notes.

When adding a border to cells, I often use a combination of All Borders for all cells in the table and then Thick Outside Borders around the outside edge of the table and the header row.

Now. One tricky thing they've done in recent versions of Excel is make things too subtle. Which means that the border you see on your screen is not the border that will print. See this:

	A	B	C	D	E	F
1		Year 1 Sales	Year 2 Sales			
2	Amazon	$ 1,234.56	$ 1,135.80			
3	Kobo	$ 2,345.67	$ 2,158.02			
4	Nook	$ 3,456.78	$ 3,180.24			
5	Google	$ 4,567.89	$ 4,202.46			
6						
7						
8						
9						

Can you tell in that image that I have two different types of borders applied to those cells? I can't. But when I "print" this to a PDF, this is what I get:

	Year 1 Sales	Year 2 Sales
Amazon	$ 1,234.56	$ 1,135.80
Kobo	$ 2,345.67	$ 2,158.02
Nook	$ 3,456.78	$ 3,180.24
Google	$ 4,567.89	$ 4,202.46

It also looks like this in the print preview in Excel. Note that it changed how my text fits, too. Awful, right? It didn't used to do that.

I don't know which extremely foolish person decided this was a good idea (probably someone who doesn't have to create tables that print from Excel), but it's something to be very aware of when formatting tables in Excel 2024 (or 365). Be sure to look at each table you apply borders to in print preview to make sure the borders look like what you want, and to make sure the text will fit properly, because unfortunately you cannot rely on what's shown in the workspace anymore.

Color a Cell (Fill Color)

You may have noticed that in some of the screenshots I've used a background fill color in a cell like blue or green or orange. I like to do this to distinguish header rows in my tables.

To apply fill color to a cell or cells, select the cell(s), and then go to the Fill Color dropdown in the Font section of the Home tab or in the mini formatting menu:

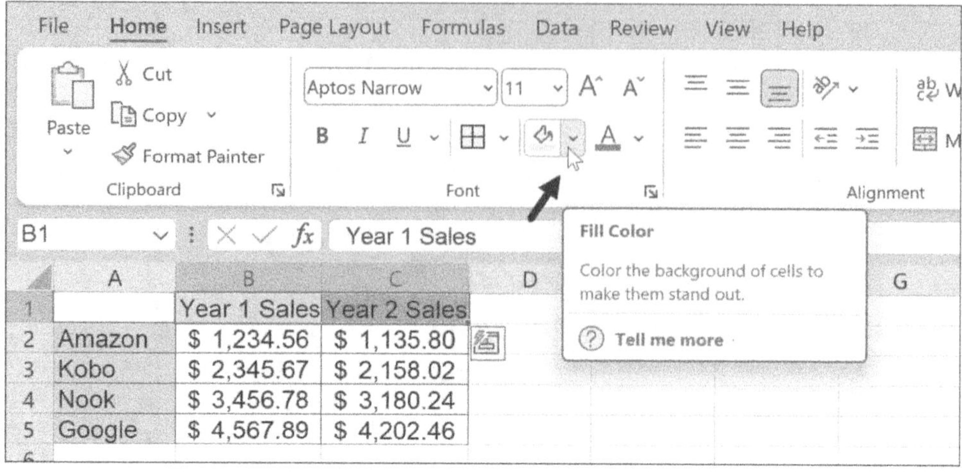

The default is a yellow fill color, which I personally almost never use. Click on the dropdown arrow to see a larger set of color choices:

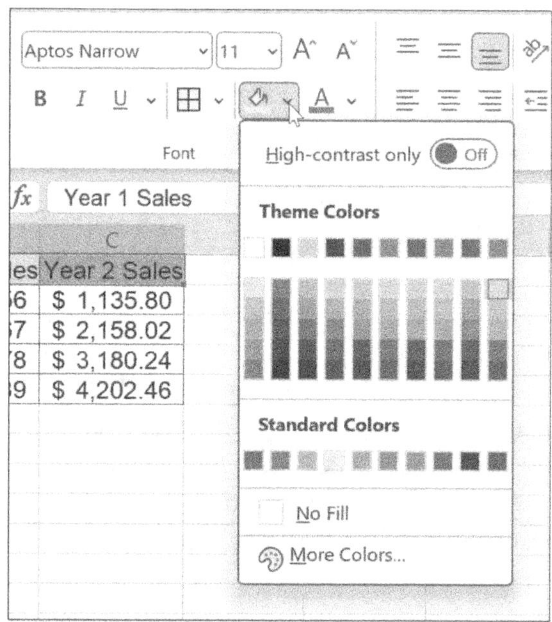

There are seventy different colors to choose from in that dropdown. If one of those works for you, click on it to apply it to your cells.

Note that there is also a No Fill option there in that dropdown that will let you remove any fill that has already been applied.

If you need more color choices, especially for example a specific corporate color, then you can click on the More Colors option. That will bring up the Colors dialogue box which has two tabs, Standard and Custom:

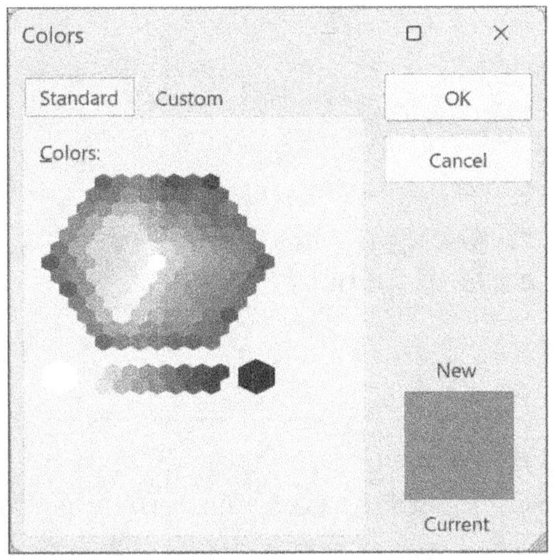 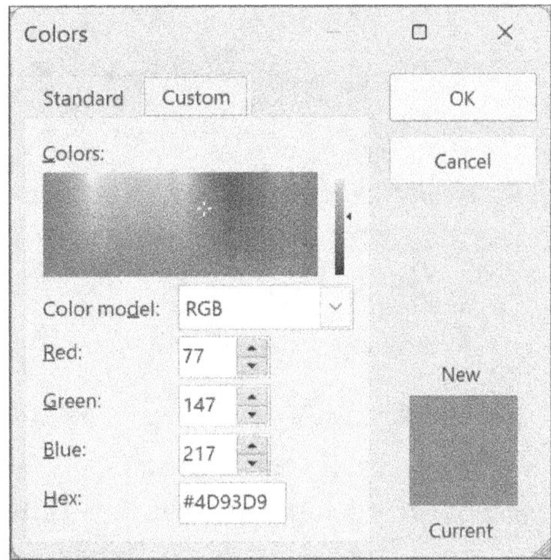

Mine defaulted to the Custom tab when it opened, but let me cover them left to right. The Standard tab has a honeycomb of colors. Click on any spot in the honeycomb to choose that color.

The Custom tab has a rainbow gradient of colors that you can also click on, but where it's more interesting is in the section below that. If you know the exact color you need to use, you can enter the RGB, Hex, or HSL values for that color. (HSL is in the dropdown.) If you have a corporation with a required color palette, they should provide you with those values.

Select your color and then click on OK to apply it.

Note that depending on the color you choose for your background, you may need to then change the font color to keep your text visible. Black on white and white on black are your best contrast choices, but you can also use white or a very light color on a variety of darker backgrounds.

Column Width

As you've seen a couple times already, if your columns aren't wide enough, you may not see all of your text, it will be cut off. For numbers you will see #### in the cell instead of the number. So adjusting column width (and row height) are essential skills to master when working in Excel.

One option is to select all of your columns that have data and then double left click along the border of one of the column names (A, B, C, D, etc.). When that's an available option, the cursor will be a black line with arrows pointing to the left and to the right like in the image on the next page.

	A	B	C	D	E	F
1	**Custo**mer	omer S**core**				
2	Joe Smam	I really	1			
3	Ming Li	You	5			
4	Isabel I	even care	3			
5						

If you do that, Excel will automatically adjust your column widths for all of the selected columns to fit the data in each column. This is what I get with the columns in the image above:

	A	B	C	D
1	Customer Name	Customer Feedback	Customer Score	
2	Joe Smith	I really am not happy with you guys.	1	
3	Ming Lin	You are the best.	5	
4	Isabel Rodriguez	I don't even care enough to give my opinion.	3	
5				
6				

Note that the columns are no longer the same width and that the contents in each cell are now fully visible. If you have numeric values, it will normally resize each column to be wide enough to fully display the largest number in the column. With text it's a little trickier because text can be formatted to wrap to the next line, like in Column B. In that case, it will fit the column to the widest text in a single line instead, like it does for Customer Score in Column C.

If you want all of your columns to be the same width, select all of the columns, and then left-click and drag on the right-hand border of one of the column names to get the width you want. If multiple columns are selected, the width you apply to that one column will be applied to all of the selected columns. Drag left to make the columns skinnier, drag right to make them wider.

If you just want to adjust one column, you don't need to select it first, just left-click and drag from the right-hand side of the column name.

(In each of the instances above, your cursor will be that line with arrows on either side when you can do this.)

Another option is to select the column or columns you want to adjust and then right-click and choose Column Width from the dropdown menu. This will bring up the Column Width dialogue box where you can enter an exact numeric value for your desired column width. That width will be applied to all selected columns.

(I don't use that option often because I am a horrible judge of what a width of 50 is compared to 10 so it's too much trial and error for me to bother with, but it is an option.)

Currency Format

You can easily apply formatting to turn an entry like "25" into a currency format like "$25.00".

There are two main choices available in the Number section of the Home tab, Accounting

No Format		25
Accounting ($)	$	(25.00)
Currency		-$25.00

and Currency. Here are examples of both:

In the first row, you can see how 25 looks when it's just typed into a cell.

The next line shows the accounting format which you can apply by using the $ sign in either

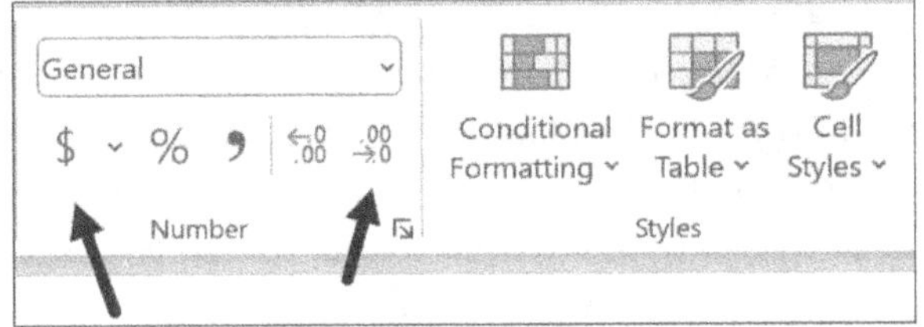

the Number section of the Home tab or the mini formatting menu.

For those of you whose currency symbol is not the dollar sign ($), there is a dropdown next to the $ symbol which includes the British pound, Euro, Chinese Yen, and Swiss Franc symbol.

(This is how it works for me in the U.S. It is possible that versions of Excel sold into different markets will have different defaults or added choices. If the currency you want isn't in either of those lists, click on More Accounting Formats to open the Format Cells dialogue box.)

The final example shows the Currency format. This can be applied by clicking on the

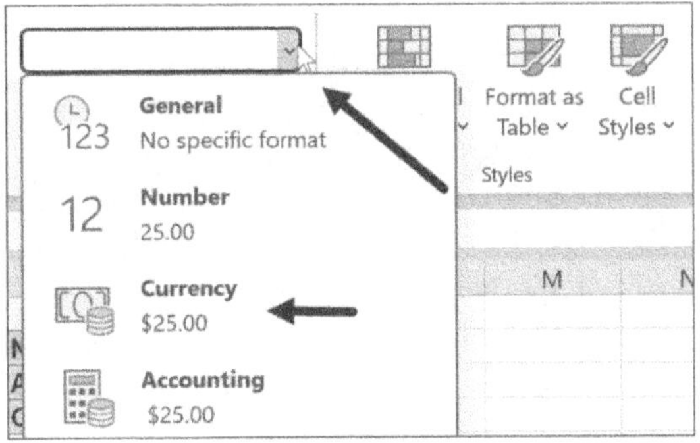

dropdown menu in the Number section of the Home tab:

The format will be listed as General by default.

The main difference between the two is where the $ sign is placed and how they are aligned within the cell. For the Accounting format, the currency symbol will be along the left edge of the cell. For the Currency format, the currency symbol will be directly next to the number.

They also treat negative numbers differently. Accounting uses parens, Currency just uses a

Accounting	Currency
$ 1.00	$1.00
$ 12.00	$12.00
$ 120.00	$120.00
$ 1,200.00	$1,200.00
$ (1,200.00)	-$1,200.00

negative sign.

If you ever want a currency value but without decimal places, you can use the Decrease Decimal option from the Number section of the Home tab or the mini formatting menu. I pointed to it in the second screenshot in this section. Click on it twice to remove both decimal places.

Also, you can use the Format Cells dialogue box to apply currency formatting. On the Number tab, choose either Currency or Accounting from the left-hand menu. If you choose the Currency format, you can also apply a format that colors negative numbers red. If you choose the Accounting format, the Symbol dropdown menu has a much larger list of currency symbols to choose from.

One final note: Just because you format a value as currency or accounting with two decimal places, that doesn't mean that Excel won't retain the original value behind the scenes and use it in any calculations. So if you have a value of 1.2345 and you format it as currency, it will display as $1.23, but Excel will continue to use 1.2345 in any formulas. (There is a function called ROUND that you can use to convert a number to just two decimal places if that's an issue.)

Date Format

Excel loves to turn entries that look remotely like a date into a date, but often it chooses a date format that I don't like, so this is one I change frequently. For example, if you type "January 1, 1990" into a cell, Excel will immediately display that as 1-Jan-90.

If you type "January 1990" it displays that as Jan-90, and behind the scenes turns it into January 1, 1990. (All dates in Excel are stored as numbers so Excel has to assign a month, day of the month, and year to a date even if you don't.)

To apply date formatting or change the formatting of a date, select the cell(s), go to the dropdown menu in the Number section of the Home tab, and choose Short Date or Long

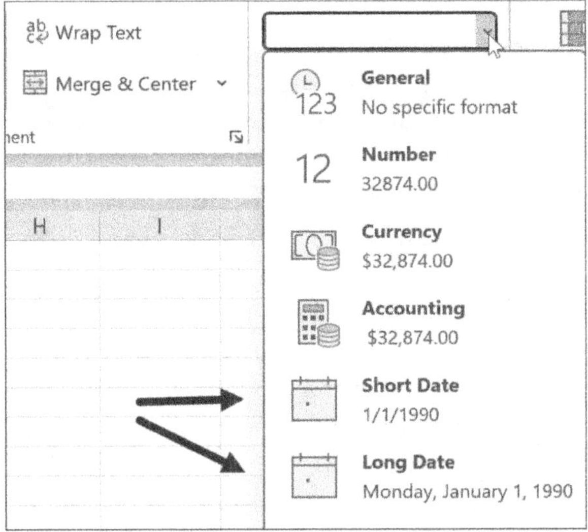

Date:

The nice thing about that dropdown is that it gives you a preview of what this particular cell will look like when you apply that formatting.

Now, I like Short Date and usually use it because it's easy, but there are a lot of other date formats I like that aren't shown in that dropdown. In that case, you need to go to the Format Cells dialogue box. The easiest way to get there is to click on the expansion arrow in the bottom right corner of the Number section of the Home tab. You should already be on the Number tab of the Format Text dialogue box. Next, click on Date or Custom.

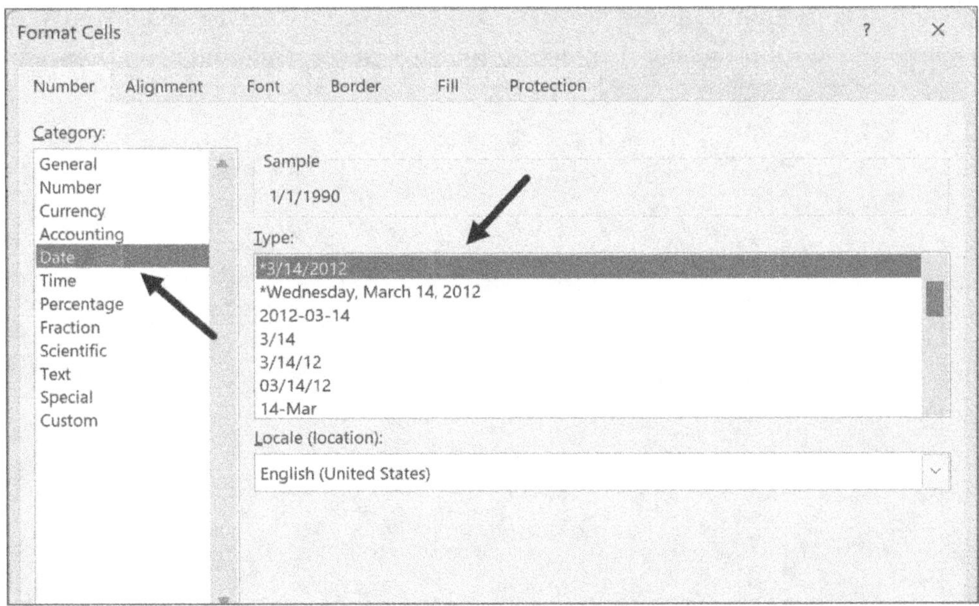

Here is Date:

See all those formats there? Just click on the one you want.

If you think your workbook may be used in different countries, pay attention to which date formats adjust for where the user is, and which don't. Also, different countries write month and day of the month in a different order, so some will write January 4, 2020 as 1/4/20 and others will write it as 4/1/20. If you think your audience may cover both of those uses, then don't choose a format where there can be confusion like that. Choose something like 04-Jan-2020 where it's clear what the date is.

A few more comments on dates:

Excel will sometimes get stuck on date formatting. Once a cell gets formatted by Excel as a date it's very stubborn about it. So sometimes you have to clear all formatting or even delete a cell to get it to work for anything but a date in that specific format.

Also, if you enter a two-digit year for a date, like 1/1/20, Excel has rules it applies to decide which century you meant, 1920 or 2020. It's a good practice, which I fail to follow myself, to use a date format that displays the full four-digit year so you can make sure your date is correct.

Finally, if you just enter a date and month (1/1), Excel will automatically assume you meant the date to be in the current year.

Direction of Text

In addition to the basic alignment of your data within a cell, you can also change the direction that text flows.

By default, as you've seen already, text is left to right along a horizontal line. But especially when building a table that you want to print out, you may want to change that. The text direction options are found in the dropdown that's labeled with an angled ab with an arrow

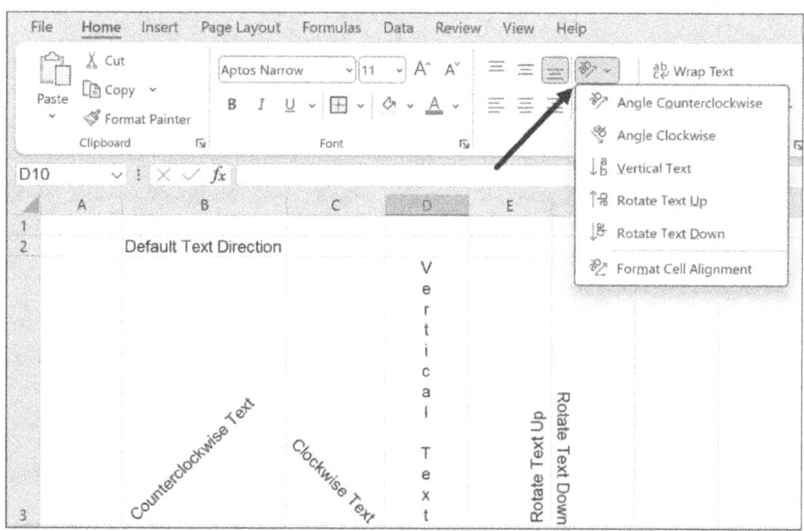

under it in the top row of the Alignment section of the Home tab:

Above you can see how each choice would look in an Excel worksheet. I tend to use that Rotate Text Up option (in Column E) often when building a table with values along the side of a table that need a label. (We'll see an example later.)

Be careful using the clockwise and counterclockwise options, because they change the angle of the cells, too, not just the text in the cell, so if you try to have cells that have clockwise or counterclockwise text in the same row as cells that have "normal" text or are empty, the borders are not going to work.

Here is an example where I applied Counterclockwise Text formatting to six cells in two

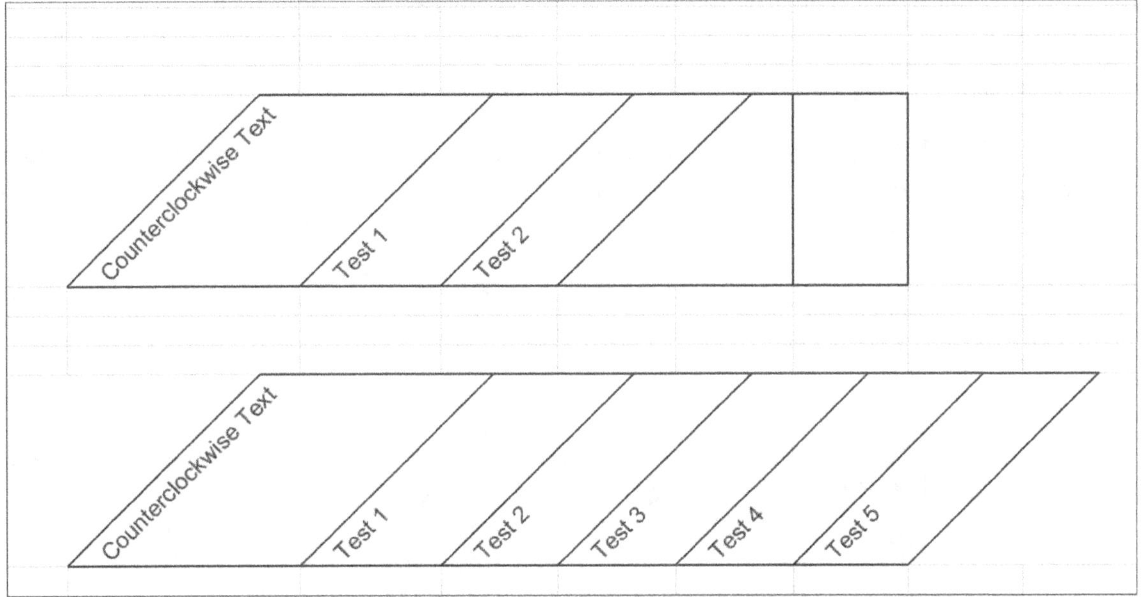

different rows and put borders around the cells in each row.

In the first example, only three of those cells have actual text in them. In the second example, all six have text. Note the issues there with the borders when the cells don't have text? So if you use those two settings, it's an all or none deal for that row.

Also, be careful with entering data in rows below that. You can. It works fine. But that last column extends past the column it labels by two more columns. Printed it will look fine, but pay attention to that when you're creating your data table.

If you want more control over the angle of your text, use the Orientation option in the Alignment tab of the Format Cells dialogue box. That will allow you to type in the exact angle you want:

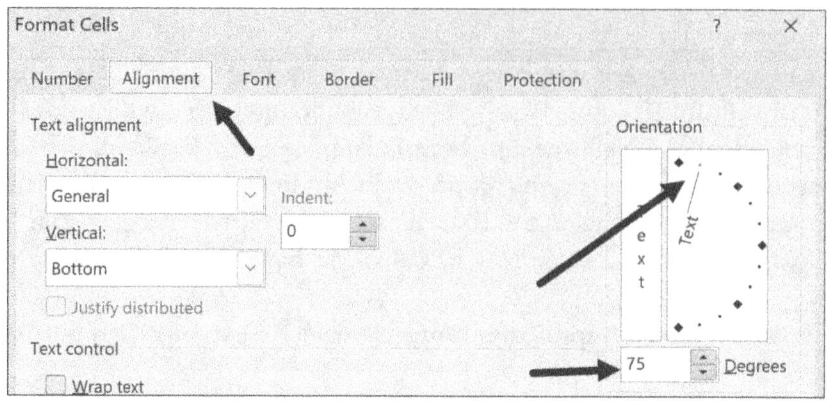

Font

The current default font in Excel is Aptos Narrow. To change that, select your cell(s) or text, and then go to the Font section of the Home tab or the mini formatting menu and use the Font dropdown menu:

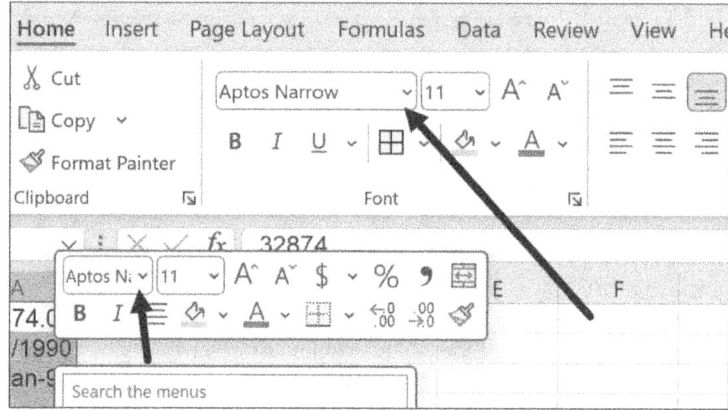

Click on the arrow next to the current font name to see a list of available fonts. Each font listed will be written in that font so you can see what the font looks like when used. On the next page, for example, you can see that Algerian is a very different font from Allura.

Your font list will probably be different from mine. Office offers a large number of fonts for you to use, like Times New Roman, Arial, etc., but I happen to have a lot of other fonts I've purchased. So my list includes all of my available fonts in addition to the ones offered by Office.

To find the font you want, click into that field and start typing and/or use the scroll bars to move through the alphabetical listing.

When you see the font you want, click on it.

If it's displayed in the font box because you started typing the name, hit Enter.

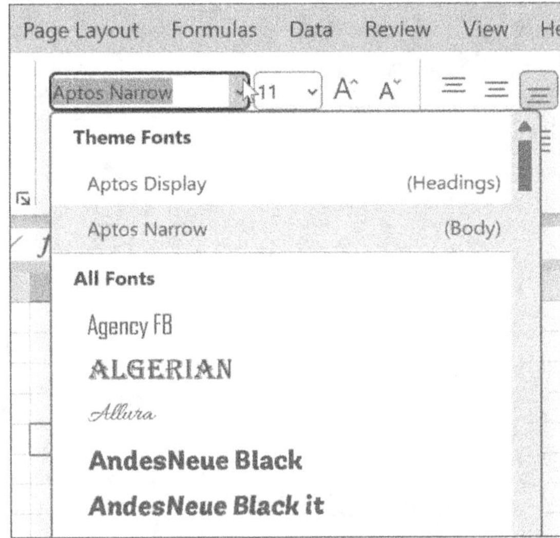

You can also use the Font tab of the Format Cells dialogue box to change the font. There's a listing of all available fonts there as well, but you'll have to use the scroll bars to navigate to the font you want or type out the entire font name to move to that part of the font list.

Font Color

The default color for text in Excel is black, but there will be times when you want to change this. For example, if you use a dark fill color on cells, it's best to then change the text color to white to keep your text legible.

Both the Font section of the Home tab and the mini formatting menu have a dropdown for font color. It will be the letter A above, by default, a red line:

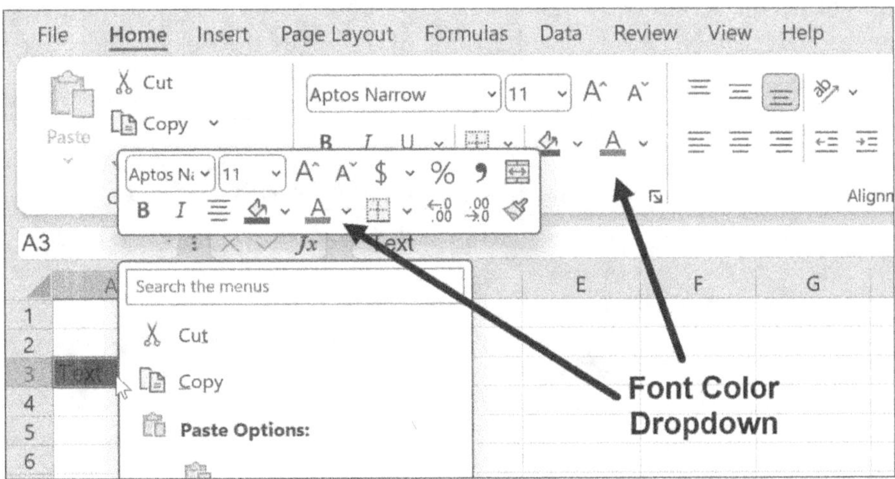

After you've changed your color at least once during an Excel session, that color under the A will be the last color you used. If you want the color under the A, you can just click on the A.

If you want a different color, click on the dropdown arrow next to the A to see more choices:

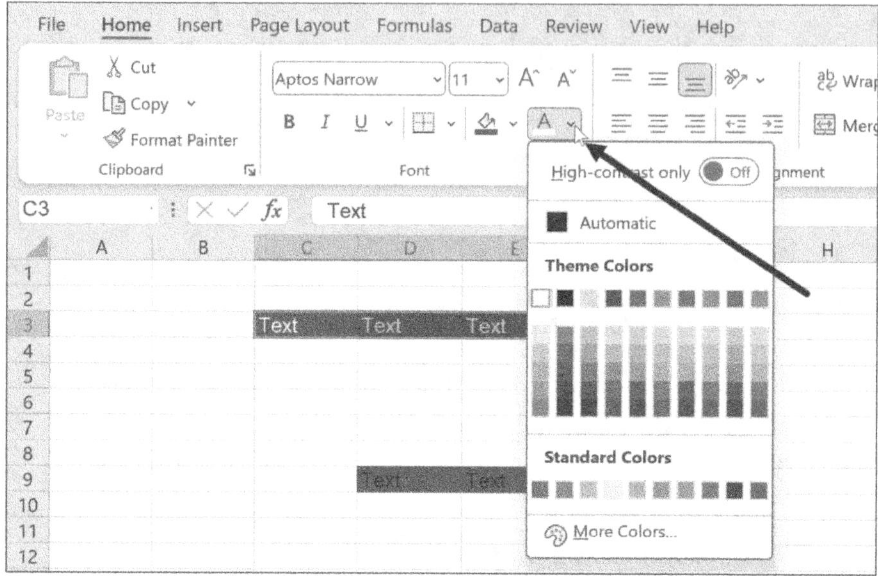

Just like with Fill Color, you'll have 70 choices to choose from in that dropdown, as well as the option to click on More Colors and use a custom color.

In Excel 2024 you have the option in the color dropdown to choose "High-Contrast Only" colors by toggling that option at the top of the dropdown to on. (Click on the word Off to do so.) That will reduce the number of colors you can choose, but it will theoretically ensure that whatever color you do choose will be visible on your current background color.

Here you can see that because I have a dark fill color in the selected cells, Excel is only showing me lighter-colored text options:

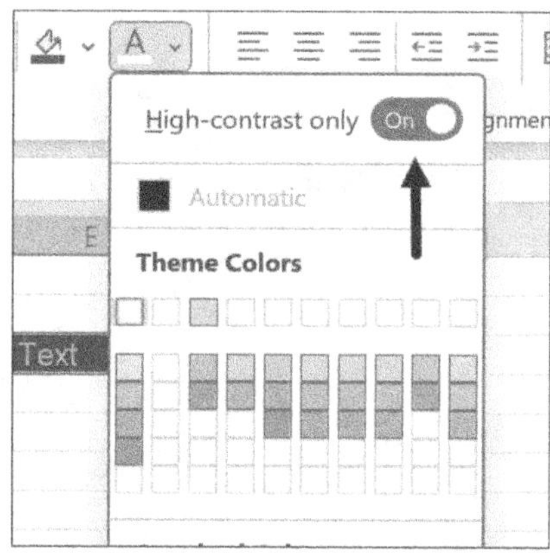

Use your judgment when selecting a color because for me there were still a couple that didn't work well.

To see how a color will look if applied, move your cursor over each option. Click on your choice to apply.

Finally, there is also an option for color on the Font tab of the Format Cells dialogue box.

Font Size

The default font size in Excel is 11 point. If you want bigger or smaller text, you can change that by using the Font Size dropdown menu in the Font section of the Home tab or in the mini formatting menu to pick a new value.

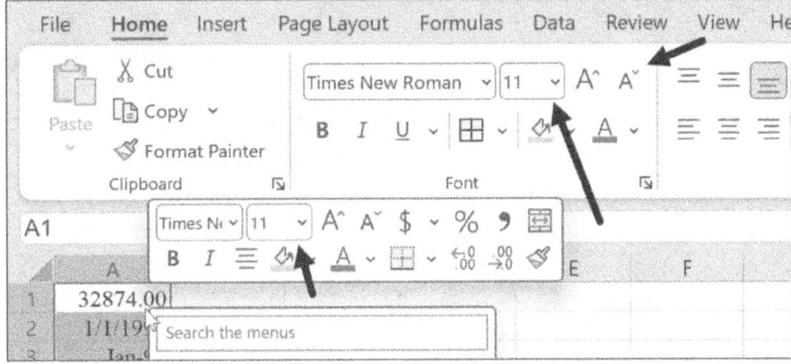

Next to the dropdown menu that lists the current font size are two choices with an A. One has an up arrow; one has a down arrow. Clicking on those will move your font size up or down one spot on the dropdown list of font sizes.

Not every single number is in that list in the dropdown. If you want a different point size, just click into that field and type the value you want. Use Enter ,or click away when you're done.

You can also change the font size in the Format Cells dialogue box.

Italicize Text

You italicize text in the same way you bold text.

Select the cell(s) or text you want to apply your formatting to, and then either use Ctrl + I or click on the slanted I in the Font section of the Home tab or the mini formatting menu.

The Format Cells dialogue box also has an Italic font style option on the Font tab as well as a Bold Italic option.

To remove italics it again works the same as removing bold from text. Select the cell(s) or text, use Ctrl + I or the slanted I symbol. If you select text that is partially formatted as italic and partially not, you may have to do it twice.

Or you can select your text and then use the Format Cells dialogue box to choose the Regular font style.

Merge Cells

There will be times when you want to merge cells together. For example, I will often do this with a header row for a data table. Like in Row 2 of this table:

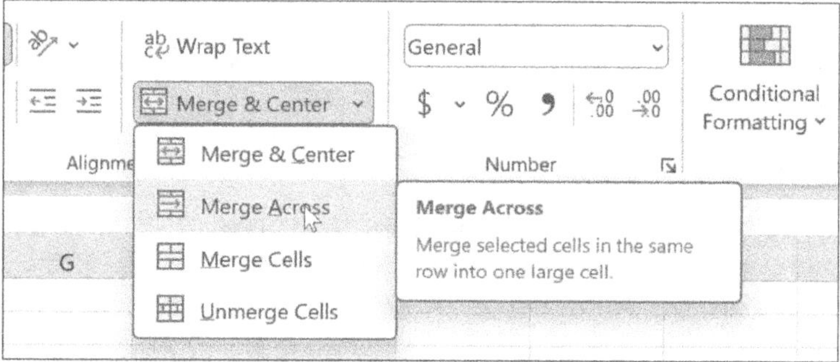

The way to do that is to select the cells you want to merge, go to the Alignment section of the Home tab, and use the Merge & Center dropdown menu:

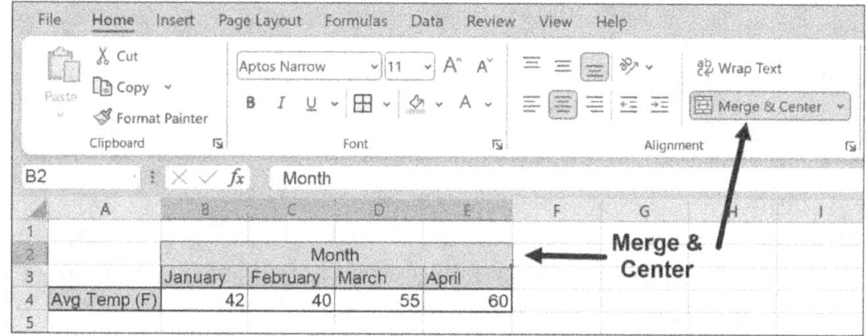

Merge Cells is what I used above. It merged the selected cells but kept the text left-aligned. You can use Merge Cells across any number of rows or columns and it will merge all of the selected cells into one single cell.

Merge & Center may have been the better option to use above, because it not only merges the selected cells but it also will Center align the text across that newly-created cell:

Merge & Center is also an option in the top right corner of the mini formatting menu.

Merge Across is nice when you have multiple rows where you want to merge across columns, but still keep the rows separate. You can select an entire range, say Cells B2 through E4, and Excel will merge B2 to E2, B3 to E3, and B4 to E4 separately. (You'll see some examples of that in these books.)

Use a bit of caution if you already have data in the cells you're trying to merge. Excel will keep whatever is in the top left cell of the selected range and delete the rest. You should see a warning message if that's going to happen.

Unmerging the cells (which is another option in that dropdown) will not bring back the lost contents of those cells. You need to Undo to get the other text back.

Also, If you have cells that were already merged, clicking on one of the merge options will unmerge them.

One final tip: Merged cells should be reserved for when you are creating a report using finalized data, not for a data table that you intend to do data analysis on. Merged cells don't tend to play well with pivot tables, filtering, sorting, or some formulas. If you do use a formula that references merged cells, the cell reference will be the top left corner of the merged cell.

You can see the cell reference to use for a merged cell to the left of the formula bar when you click on the merged cell.

Number Format

If you know going in that you're dealing with a type of number where Excel is difficult (ISBNs, zip codes, etc.), it's best to apply the formatting to those cells before you add your data.

To apply a generic number format to your cells, select the cell(s) that you want to format (including an entire column, if needed), and go to the Number section of the Home tab.

Your first option is to use the comma under the dropdown menu or in the mini formatting menu to apply the Comma Style, which has two decimal places and uses commas to separate the hundreds:

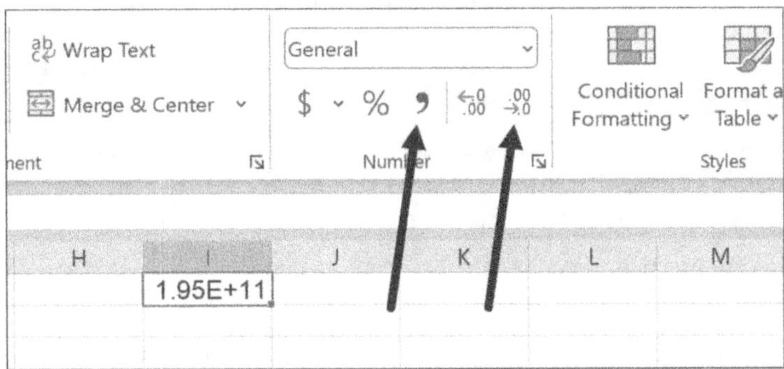

I often don't want decimal places, so will then use the Decrease Decimal option twice to remove them. (You can see the revised result below.)

Another option is to use the dropdown menu in the Number section of the Home tab, which is usually showing as "General" by default, to choose a format:

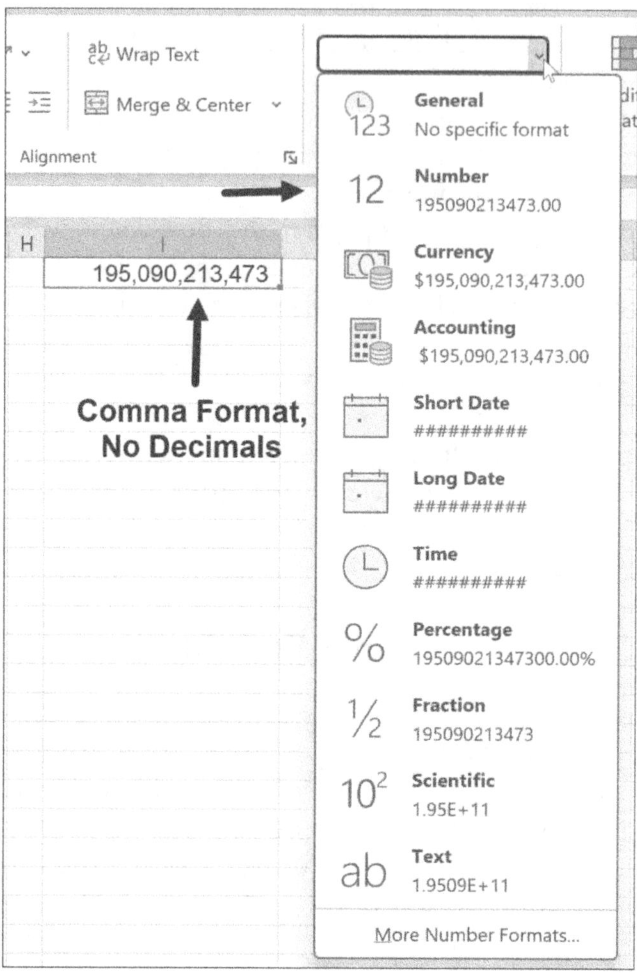

If you have values in the selected cell(s) already, Excel will show you in that dropdown an example of what that value will look like if that format is applied.

A few cautions about numbers in Excel. If you have a large number, like an ISBN number which is fifteen digits, Excel will convert that to scientific notation on you. So if your number looks something like 1.23E+09, that's what's happening

Also, Excel will remove the zero at the start of numbers. This is a problem for zip codes, for example, some of which start with a zero. Since you don't need to do calculations with zip codes, one option is to treat them as text and enter with a single quote mark to make Excel leave those entries as is. The other option is to go to the Number tab of the Format Cells dialogue box, which has a Special format category that includes formats for zip codes.

It also has formats for phone numbers or social security numbers, at least for the United States. Click on each option to see a sample in the dialogue box. Click OK to apply that format to your selected cell(s).

Percent Format

To format numbers as a percentage, select the cell(s) you want to format, and click on the % sign in the Number section of the Home tab or in the mini formatting menu.

Excel is weird but logical with percentages. If the value you're formatting is a decimal (.25) it will convert it to a percentage "normally". In math .25 is the same as 25%.

If the number is a whole number (25), then Excel also adds two zeros at the end and a percentage symbol. So you get 2500%. Perfectly logical when you think about it, but often not expected if you aren't the type of person who thinks mathematically. Which means that if you have values like 25 that are meant to stand for 25%, you need to divide those values by 100 to get them to work with the percentage setting in Excel.

Row Height

Row Height works much like Column Width. Left-click and drag on the line below a row number to adjust the row height manually. You can also double left-click on the line below a row number to resize the row to its contents.

Select multiple rows and use the line below one of the selected rows to adjust multiple rows at once. You can also right-click and choose Row Height from the dropdown menu and then input a specific value.

There is a maximum row height that Excel will adjust to. It is, according to the error message I just got, 409. I have run into this as an issue in the past when I was using Excel for a text-heavy analysis. I had more text than Excel could display in my cell. So if you use Excel for something that involves lots of text in one cell, be aware that it is possible to have your text cut off at the bottom of the cell, and therefore not fully visible. (You can overcome this issue to some extent by widening your columns, but even doing that isn't always enough.)

Underline Text

I underline text far less in Excel than in Word, but it can be needed at times. A basic underline can be applied by selecting the cell(s) or text you want to underline, and then using Ctrl + U or clicking on the U with an underline in the Font section of the Home tab.

If you use the dropdown arrow for the U in the Font section of the Home tab, there is also a double-underline option, which is used in accounting.

In the Font tab of the Format Cells dialogue box there is also an Underline dropdown. It includes Single, Double, Single Accounting, and Double Accounting choices.

To remove an underline, use Ctrl + U again or the U in the Font section of the Home tab. If you applied an underline format other than Single, you will likely have to do that twice because the first time will convert the underline to a single underline. Another option is to change the underline dropdown in the Font tab of the Format Cells dialogue box to None.

Wrap Text

To wrap text, select your cell(s), go to the Alignment section of the Home tab, and click on Wrap Text. (To remove it, just click on the option again.)

Wrap Text is also an option in the Alignment tab of the Format Cells dialogue box.

Why use this? Because by default, text in a cell is going to be on one line. Even if the column of that cell isn't wide enough to display the full text, the text will be visible if that is the only text in that row. But as soon as you put data in a cell to the right, the text will stop at that next cell. Here is an example:

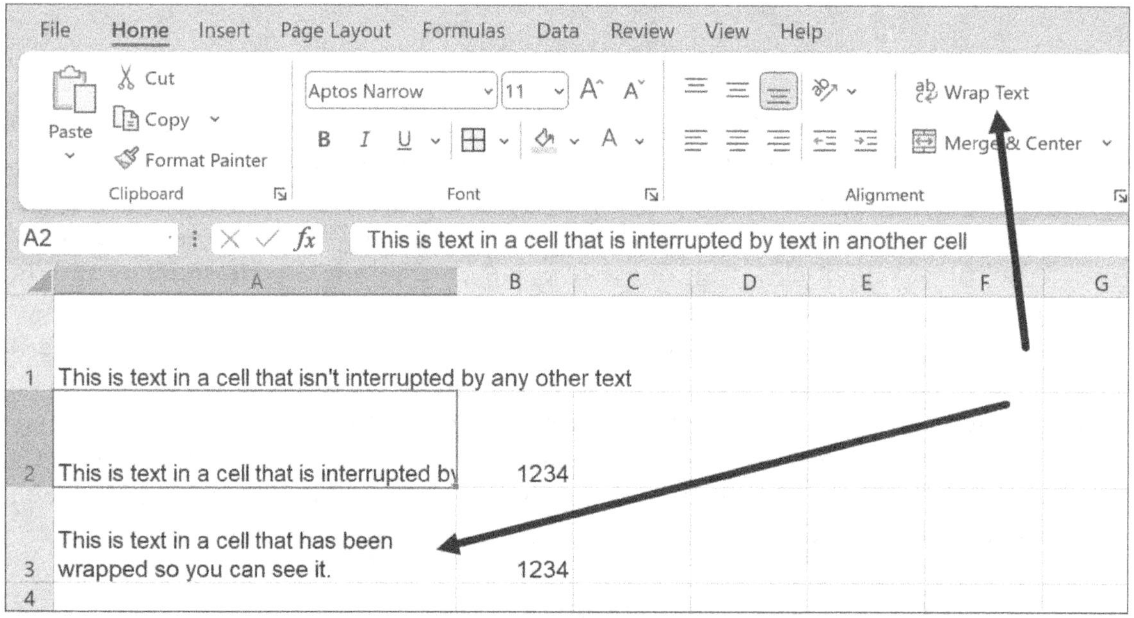

Row 1 has text in Cell A1 but no other text in any cell in the row. You can read the full text even though it stretches to Column C.

Row 2 has text in Cell A2 and a number in Cell B2. The text in Cell A2—which you can still see completely in the formula bar when I click on Cell A2—is cut off at the point where Cell B2 starts.

The way to keep text visible in that situation is to apply Wrap Text. I've done that in Cell A3. Now when the text in Cell A3 reaches Cell B3 it doesn't disappear, it wraps to the next line.

* * *

Before we move on, I want to cover two more formatting tricks.

Copy Formatting

The Format Painter, seen in the Clipboard section of the Home tab or in the mini formatting menu, allows you to take all of the formatting from one cell or range of cells, and apply it to another cell or range of cells.

Say you add a column to a data table and you want the fill, bold, font color, and borders that you were using on all of the other columns in that table to apply to the new column. Easy enough to select an existing column that has your formatting, and then use the format painter to transfer that over to the new column, like I've done above.

The first step in using the tool, is to select the range of cells that have your formatting in them. This can be a cell, a row, a column, or even a series of cells, rows, or columns.

Next, click on the Format Painter in the Clipboard section of the Home tab. (Double-click if you want to use that formatting in more than one location that will require you to select cells more than once..)

Finally, select the cell(s) where you want to apply the formatting.

If you want to apply, for example, the formatting of one column to the three columns next to it, you would select that first column, click on the Format Painter, and then select all three of those columns in the last step. As you can see in the image above, it will apply the formatting of different cells in that range to the selected range, so we have cells highlighted yellow in the exact same spot in each column.

If you do double-click on the Format Painter to use it in more than one location, use Esc when you're done to turn it off.

Be aware that ALL of your formatting will transfer.

Also be careful using this tool, because it will apply the formatting to wherever you move next. So if you select a range of cells and click on the Format Painter and then try to arrow over, the Format Painter will apply the selected formatting to that next cell. Best practice is to always click to select the cells where you want to apply that formatting.

Remember with this one that Undo (Ctrl + Z) is your friend if you apply formatting to the wrong range of cells. Just be sure to use Esc to start over if you do need to undo.

Clear Formatting

To clear formatting from cell(s), go to the Editing section of the Home tab, click on the dropdown for Clear, and choose Clear Formats.

If you use Clear All, that will also delete the contents in the selected cell(s) at the same time.

This can be useful when Excel stubbornly decides to format a cell as a date and won't stop trying to do so.

It's also useful when you have borders or other formatting that extend beyond the boundaries of your data and you want to remove it. For example, I recently had a program that would export data which was in maybe fifty rows, but put borders around all cells in those columns for all 1,048,576 rows of the worksheet.

I was able to select the first row that didn't contain data, use Shift + Ctrl + the down arrow key to select the remaining rows in the worksheet, and then use the Clear Format option to remove those borders.

Analyze Data

This chapter is going to cover three different ways to analyze your data: sorting, filtering, and some basic math. You can do a lot with just those three, which is why I'm covering them in this book. If this doesn't feel like enough, the remainder of the books in this series cover additional analysis tools such as charts, pivot tables (officially written as PivotTables), conditional formatting, and more advanced formulas and functions.

To get started, let me show you the first rows of the data we're going to work with:

	A	B	C	D	E	F	G
1	Royalty Date	Author Name	Marketplace	Transaction Type	Net Units Sold	Royalty	Currency
2	2021-01-31	Author A	Amazon.com	Standard	1	5.70	USD
3	2021-01-31	Author B	Amazon.com.au	Standard	1	5.03	AUD
4	2021-01-31	Author C	Amazon.com	Free - Price Match	65	0.00	USD
5	2021-01-31	Author D	Amazon.com	Standard	1	2.76	USD
6	2021-01-31	Author C	Amazon.fr	Free - Price Match	1	0.00	EUR
7	2021-01-31	Author C	Amazon.ca	Free - Price Match	3	0.00	CAD
8	2021-01-31	Author A	Amazon.com	Standard	1	5.83	USD
9	2021-01-31	Author C	Amazon.de	Free - Price Match	3	0.00	EUR
10	2021-01-31	Author A	Amazon.com	Standard	1	1.75	USD
11	2021-01-31	Author A	Amazon.com	Standard	1	2.74	USD
12	2021-01-31	Author A	Amazon.com	Standard	1	3.12	USD
13	2021-01-31	Author D	Amazon.com	Standard	2	5.52	USD
14	2021-01-31	Author D	Amazon.com	Standard	1	2.76	USD
15	2021-01-31	Author F	Amazon.com	Free - Price Match	1	0.00	USD
16	2021-01-31	Author A	Amazon.co.uk	Standard	1	2.72	GBP
17	2021-01-31	Author A	Amazon.com	Standard	1	2.80	USD
18	2021-01-31	Author C	Amazon.com	Free - Price Match	5	0.00	USD

This is sales data for a variety of authors and book titles that shows date of sale, author, where sold, transaction type, number of units sold, amount earned, and currency it was earned in. There are 631 total entries in this data table.

Not pretty, but it doesn't need to be. It just needs to be formatted in a way that works for sorting, filtering, and formulas as we discussed before.

Look At Your Data

Before you start running any analysis on your data, stop for a moment and look at what you have. Understand what it's telling you.

For example, Column G of this data is Currency, and you can see that there are different values in that column: USD, AUD, EUR, CAD, etc. That tells me that I can't just add the values in Column F to get a total sales value. 1 USD is not equivalent to 1 AUD, is not equivalent to 1 CAD.

Another thing you want to do is look at your various columns, and make sure they are formatted the way they should be. For example, Columns E and F are my number columns. Do they behave that way in Excel?

Looking at Cells E2 through E4 I know they should add up to 67 if Excel treats those values as numbers.

To make sure that Excel does see those values as numbers, I can select those cells, and then look in the bottom right corner of the worksheet.

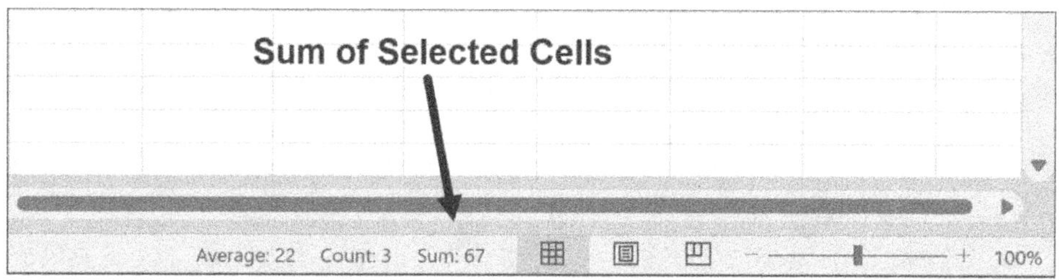

Excel is showing a Sum and an Average for the values in those cells. That means it is treating them as numeric values. If Excel didn't think those were numbers, like in the image below, then it would just give me a count:

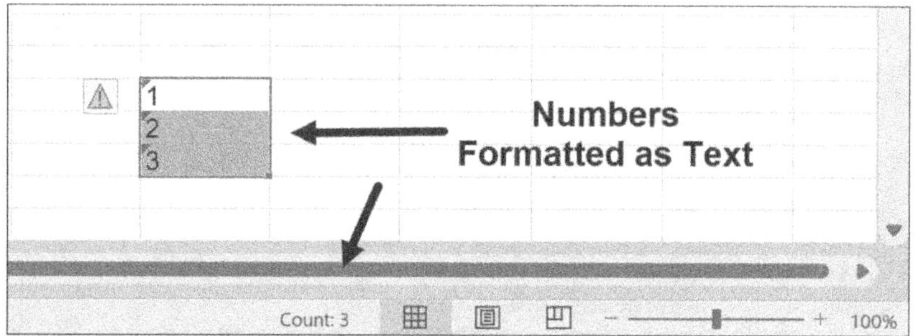

Another way to know you have an issue, is that Excel sometimes flags numbers formatted as text with a green triangle in the top left corner of the cell, as you can see in the image above.

You'll see a caution triangle, like in the image above, when the cells are selected.

Hold your mouse over the caution triangle to see a dropdown arrow. Left-click on the arrow, and you'll see a dropdown menu that shows the reason Excel flagged those cells:

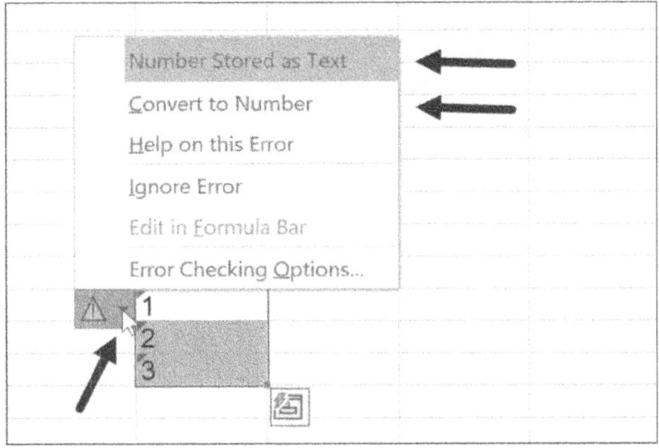

For example, the top line in this example shows "Number Stored as Text". If I want to convert those numbers from text to numbers, I can just click on Convert to Number in that dropdown and all selected cells will convert.

Another thing you want to do with your data before you start, is check for blank lines and blank columns. It is best to remove those if at all possible. At least have the entries in the first row and first column of your data table be continuous. It will make your life easier.

Also, make sure there is just one line per data entry. For example, back in the day Amazon would send sales reports like the one above, but instead of having Marketplace in Column C, they'd put a blank row, and then a row with Marketplace by itself, and then list all transactions for that marketplace below it. Great for a report of sales by marketplace. Awful for a report where you intend to do any sort of analysis.

You do not want breaks for subtotals or subcategories in your data. Convert anything like that into a column that includes those values for each line.

Okay. From here on out, I am going to assume you have good data to work with. First up, filtering.

Filter Data

Filtering lets you take a large data table and narrow down which rows of data are visible, based upon the criteria you choose. So for our sample data, I could use filtering to just look at sales by Author A in the Amazon.de marketplace. Or sales by Authors A, B, and C with a Standard transaction type where the Royalty amount is over 5.00 and the Currency is AUD.

Older versions of Excel were much more limited in terms of how many filter criteria you could apply at once, but Excel 2024 really is not. It's just something to keep in mind if you ever deal with someone with an older version of Excel. (I recommend turning filtering off before you close the file in those situations.)

Okay, first step, how to turn on filtering.

Turn On or Turn Off Filtering

To turn on filtering of your data, click into one of the cells in the top row of your data table, go to the Editing section of the Home tab, click on the Sort & Filter dropdown, and choose Filter.

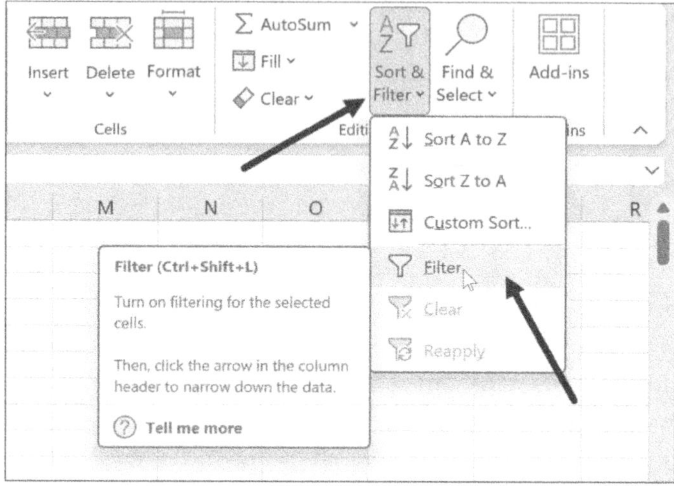

You can see here that Filter also has a control shortcut (Ctrl + Shift + L). That is one I do not have memorized, but I point it out because it could be a useful one to learn, especially since in more recent versions of Excel, I've noticed weird formatting issues with column widths when I have filtering applied to a range of cells. If you ever run into that, turn off filtering, format the cells, and then turn it back on.

To turn filtering off you can just select Filter in the dropdown menu of the Editing section of the Home tab again, or use the Ctrl shortcut.

Another option for turning on filtering, is to right-click on a cell in the data table where you want to filter, go to Filter in the dropdown menu, and then choose your filtering option from there. In that case, it's best to right-click on a cell that meets one of your filter criteria, because it's set up to automatically filter for you based on your selection:

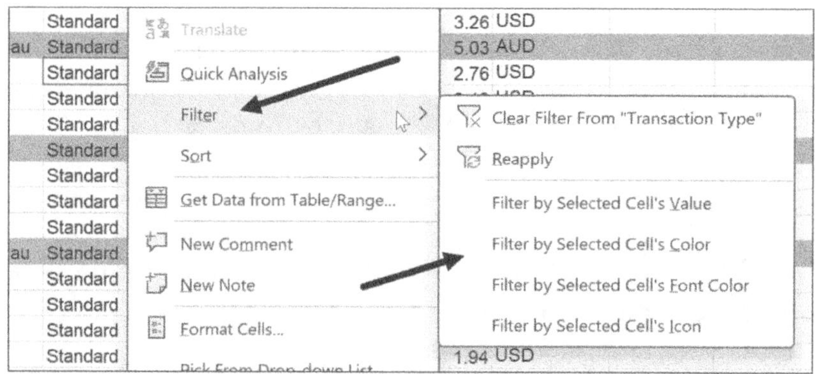

Above you can see that there are options in that dropdown to immediately filter by the selected cell's value, color, font color, or icon.

If you right-click and use the clear filter option that you can see there, that removes the filter for that column, but it leaves filtering in place.

You can also clear filtering from the dropdown menu in the Editing section of the Home tab, by choosing the Clear option, but that will clear filters from all of the columns in the table.

When you turn on filtering, Excel will add little dropdown arrows to every single cell in what it perceives to be the header row of your data table:

	A	B	C	D	E	F	G	H	I
1	Royalty Dat ▼	Author Name ▼	Marketplace ▼	Transaction Ty ▼	Net Units So ▼	Royalty ▼	Currency ▼		Converted Currency
2	2021-01-31	Author A	Amazon.com	Standard	1	5.70	USD		$5.70
3	2021-01-31	Author B	Amazon.com.au	Standard	1	5.03	AUD		$0.00
4	2021-01-31	Author C	Amazon.com	Free - Price Match	65	0.00	USD		$0.00
5	2021-01-31	Author D	Amazon.com	Standard	1	2.76	USD		$2.76
6	2021-01-31	Author C	Amazon.fr	Free - Price Match	1	0.00	EUR		$0.00
7	2021-01-31	Author C	Amazon.ca	Free - Price Match	3	0.00	CAD		$0.00
8	2021-01-31	Author A	Amazon.com	Standard	1	5.83	USD		$5.83
9	2021-01-31	Author C	Amazon.de	Free - Price Match	3	0.00	EUR		$0.00

Note that Column I does not have a dropdown arrow. That's because there was a gap between Columns A through G and Column I, so Excel didn't think Column I was part of the table. (This is why it's best to remove blank columns and rows, so that doesn't happen.)

If I wanted to filter using Column I, I'd need to turn off filtering, and then either click on Column I and turn it on again for just Column I, or delete that blank column and turn it back on for all of my columns.

Another option, if you don't have empty rows at the top of your worksheet, is to Select All or select all of the columns you want to include, before you turn on filtering. Doing it that way would include Columns A through I. (If you try that with data that doesn't start in Row 1, the filters apply in Row 1 not at the top of your data table.)

Another way to apply or remove filtering, is by using the Filter option in the Sort & Filter section of the Data tab.

Filter Dropdown Menu

Click on a filter dropdown arrow to see the options for that column. (An example for Author Name in Column B is on the next page.)

There are three main sections in the dropdown menu. The top section allows for sorting. I never sort data this way, so I'm going to skip it.

The next section allows you to clear a filter from that column, if one is in place, as well as filter by color or by a list of criteria specific to the data type in that column.

The final section lets you choose specific values to include or exclude, and includes a search option.

Your options in each section are going to depend on the type of data Excel thinks is in that column. Text, numbers, and dates are each treated differently.

Author Name is a text field, so the sort below is an A to Z sort, and the values in the bottom section are the unique author names that appear in that column.

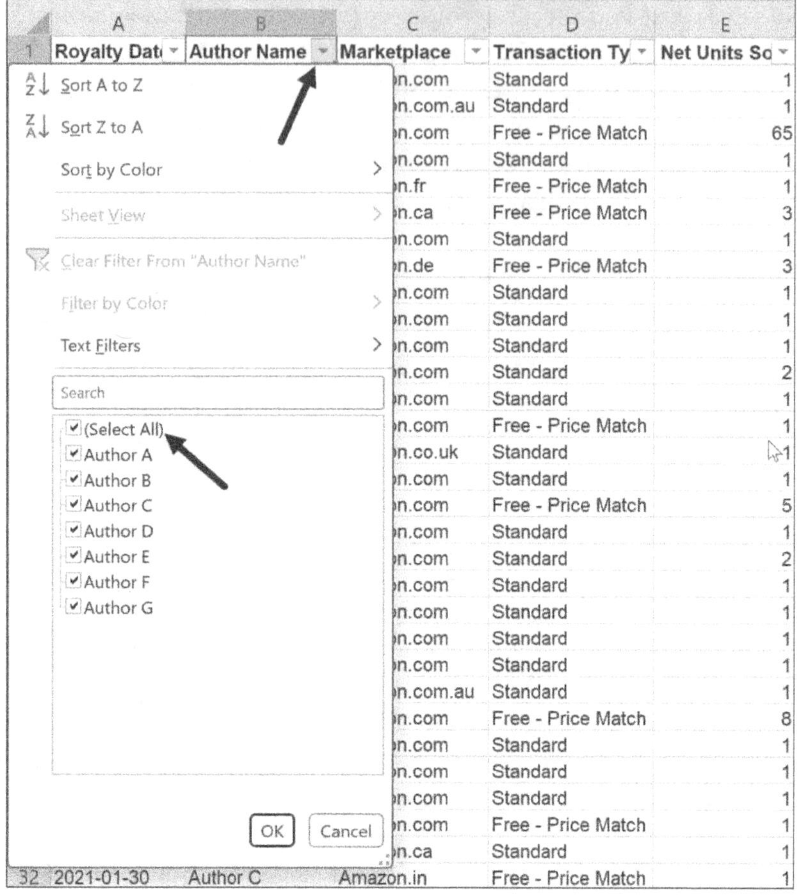

Here are the Text Filter options available in the middle section:

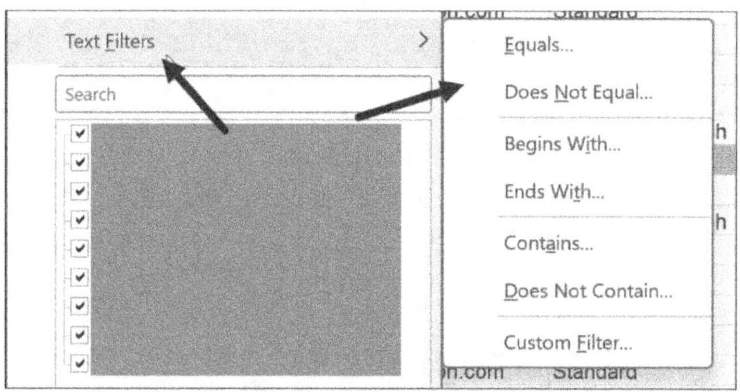

You can choose to look for text that equals, does not equal, begins with, ends with, contains, or does not contain specified text.

For example, one of my vendors used to report sales I had through Overdrive by adding that to the end of the book title. I could filter sales at Overdrive using a "contains" filter, or exclude them with a "does not contain" filter.

For numbers, the bottom section will still list unique values, and you'll have a set of Number Filters options instead:

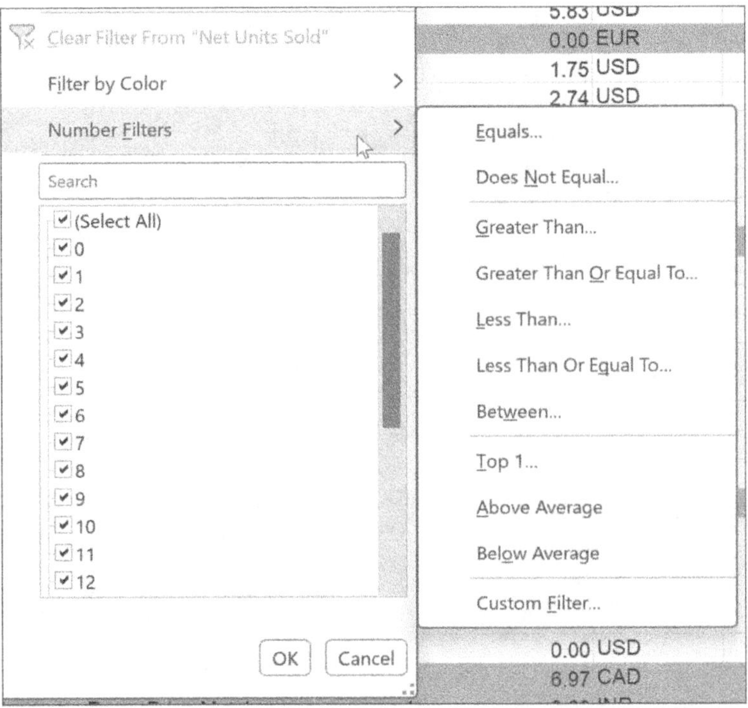

The Numbers Filters choices are equals, does not equal, greater than, greater than or equal to, less than, less than or equal to, between, Top X, Above Average, Below Average, and custom. Custom lets you apply two criteria at once.

Finally, dates, as you can see on the next page, show differently in the bottom section and have their own Date Filters options.

In the bottom section, there are plus signs (+) next to each year and month that you can click to expand the results to see the detail entries.

If a list is expanded, there will be a minus sign (-) that you can click on to collapse the details.

In the image on the next page, I've expanded year (which only has January entries below it), but collapsed month, so you can see both at once.

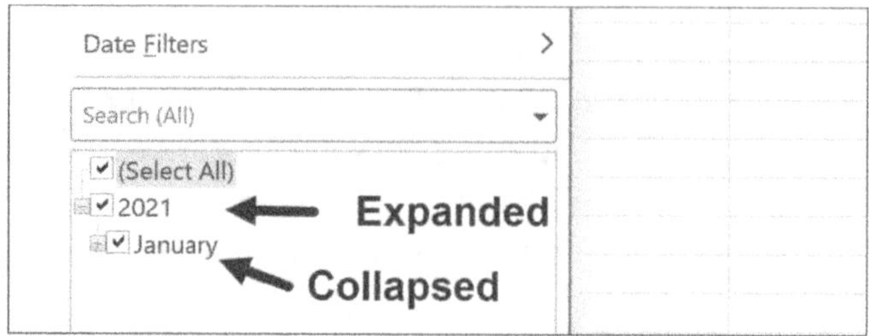

In the secondary dropdown for Date Filters, you can choose Equals, Before, After, Between, and then a large number of options related to the week, month, quarter, or year.

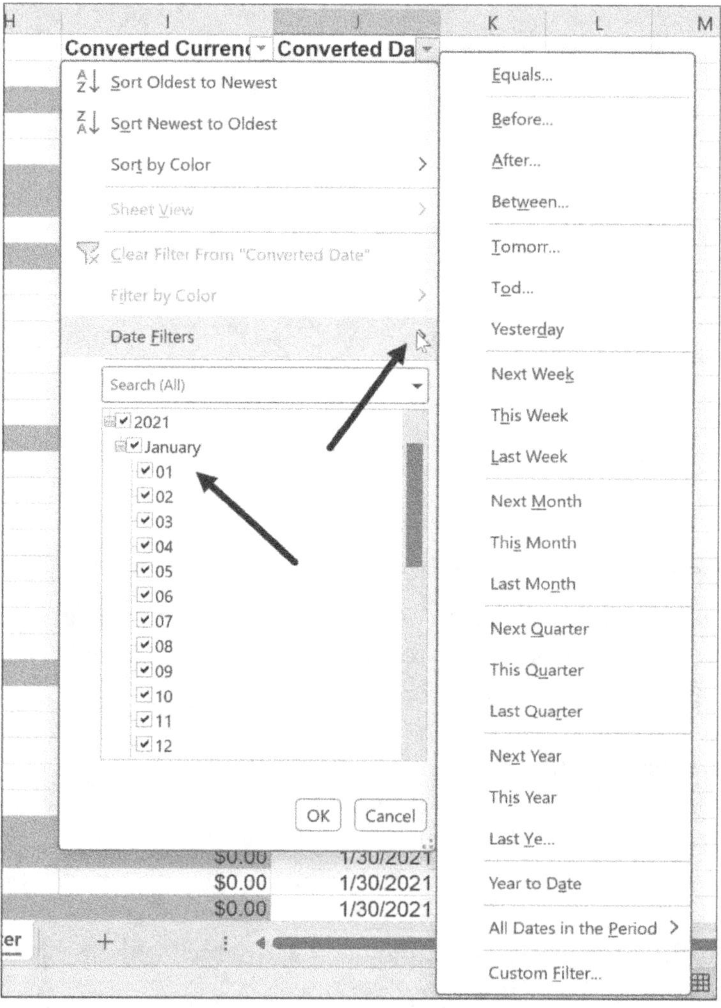

Filtering

There are three primary ways to filter. You can filter by color, by criteria, or by making a specific choice of which values to show.

Let's start with filter by color. I tend to be one of those people who will color the text red if something looks weird, or add fill color to a cell to mark it in some way. If you do that, you can then use the Filter By Color secondary dropdown to see just those colored entries:

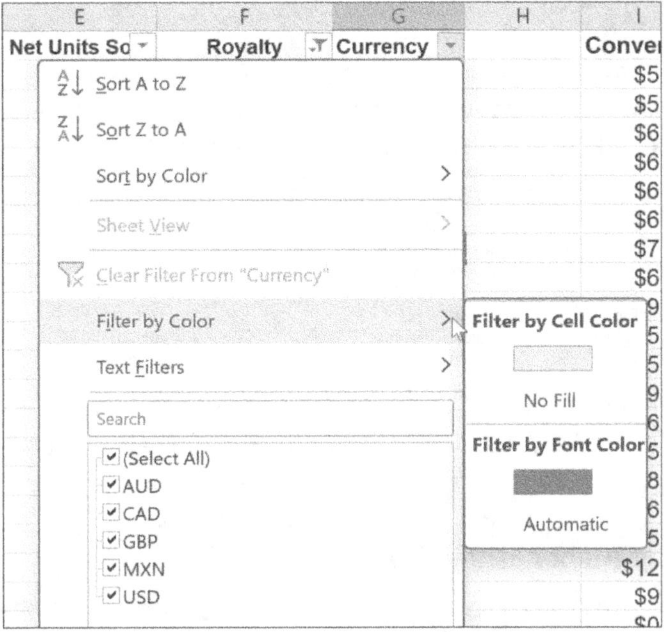

In the image above, you can see that I have entries in that column that are highlighted yellow, as well as entries that have red text. All I have to do is click on the yellow or red in that secondary menu, to narrow my results down to just those values.

Or I can choose No Fill or Automatic color (which just means black for most people) to exclude those entries.

If I were using multiple font or fill colors, all of the colors I was using would show as options in that secondary dropdown menu.

The only drawback on this one, is that you can only filter by one color at a time. So I can filter by one font color or by one fill color, but I can't choose multiple font colors, multiple fill colors, or a combination of a specific font and fill color.

If you're going to take advantage of this, keep that in mind when choosing what to color.

The next filter option is that secondary dropdown list of Text, Number, or Date Filters. I use this one most with numbers.

Here is the dialogue box you'll see if you choose Greater Than or Equal To, for example:

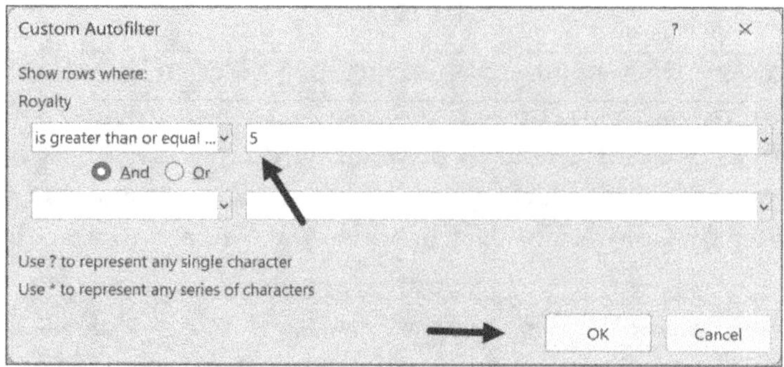

Enter the value you want in the white box, and then click OK. I did so for the Net Units Sold column, and now have all entries where that value is 5 or more:

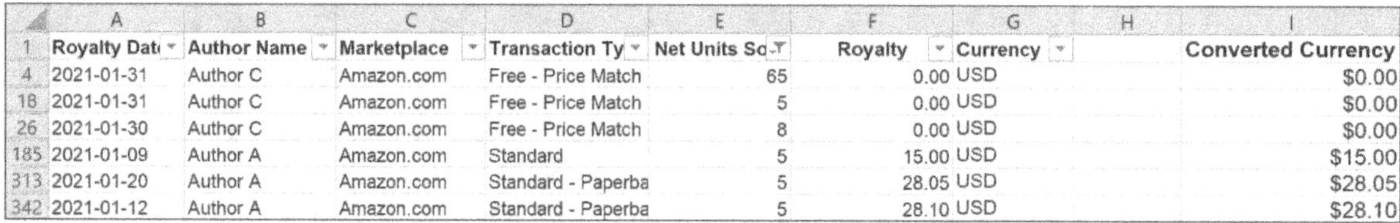

	A	B	C	D	E	F	G	H	I
1	Royalty Date	Author Name	Marketplace	Transaction Ty	Net Units So	Royalty	Currency		Converted Currency
4	2021-01-31	Author C	Amazon.com	Free - Price Match	65	0.00	USD		$0.00
18	2021-01-31	Author C	Amazon.com	Free - Price Match	5	0.00	USD		$0.00
26	2021-01-30	Author C	Amazon.com	Free - Price Match	8	0.00	USD		$0.00
185	2021-01-09	Author A	Amazon.com	Standard	5	15.00	USD		$15.00
313	2021-01-20	Author A	Amazon.com	Standard - Paperba	5	28.05	USD		$28.05
342	2021-01-12	Author A	Amazon.com	Standard - Paperba	5	28.10	USD		$28.10

(Note that even though Converted Currency is not a column I can filter on right now, filters apply to an entire row, so the values in that column still correspond to the values in the data table.)

Finally, we have the checkbox and search options at the bottom.

Let's go back to our Author field listing:

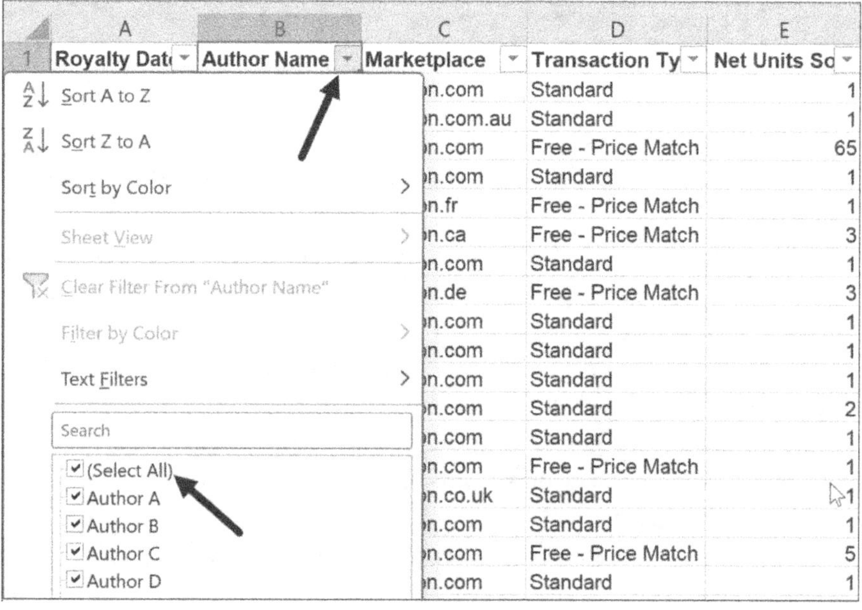

If I want only Author A, the easiest way to get that is to click on the Select All box at the top to unselect all of the entries, and then click on Author A. I can then click on OK to apply. And here we are:

	A	B	C	D	E	F	G
1	Royalty Dat	Author Name	Marketplace	Transaction Ty	Net Units So	Royalty	Currency
2	2021-01-31	Author A	Amazon.com	Standard	1	5.70	USD
8	2021-01-31	Author A	Amazon.com	Standard	1	5.83	USD
10	2021-01-31	Author A	Amazon.com	Standard	1	1.75	USD
11	2021-01-31	Author A	Amazon.com	Standard	1	2.74	USD
12	2021-01-31	Author A	Amazon.com	Standard	1	3.12	USD
16	2021-01-31	Author A	Amazon.co.uk	Standard	1	2.72	GBP
17	2021-01-31	Author A	Amazon.com	Standard	1	2.80	USD
21	2021-01-31	Author A	Amazon.com	Standard	1	1.97	USD

If I wanted Authors A and B, I'd unselect all and check the boxes next to both Author A and Author B.

This works the same for numbers and dates, too. Select All to deselect and then make your choices. For dates, if you want more than one day, month, or year, just expand that section to check the appropriate boxes.

If your list of unique text values is very long, you can use the search box to narrow down the listed results. As you type in your text, the list of values that you can check or uncheck will narrow down to just those that match what you've typed.

Here I've clicked on filter for the Marketplace column and started to type "fr" for France:

	A	B	C	D
1	Royalty Dat	Author Name	Marketplace	Transaction Ty
2	2021-	A↓Z Sort A to Z		Standard
8	2021-			Standard
10	2021-	Z↓A Sort Z to A		Standard
11	2021-			Standard
12	2021-	Sort by Color >		Standard
16	2021-			Standard
17	2021-	Sheet View >		Standard
21	2021-	Clear Filter From "Marketplace"		Standard
22	2021-			Standard
23	2021-	Filter by Color >		Standard
24	2021-	Text Filters >		Standard
28	2021-			Standard
31	2021-	fr ✕		Standard
35	2021-	☑ (Select All Search Results)		Standard
36	2021-	☐ Add current selection to filter		Standard
37	2021-	☑ Amazon.fr		Standard
38	2021-			Standard

You can see it narrowed it down to the one result that contains "fr". I can then click OK and it will apply that filter.

I find that search doesn't work as well with numbers or dates. But the values listed in that section are in numeric and date order, so it's relatively easy to use the scroll bars on the sides to find the values I want. I just have to remember to uncheck Select All first.

Appearance When Data Is Filtered

When your data is filtered, the row numbers will be colored blue. This means there are rows that have been filtered out.

You will also be able to see that the row numbers skip. Your rows will go from Row 2 to Row 8, for example, if the criteria you applied excludes the values in Rows 3 through 7.

Another thing to note is that the dropdown arrow for a column where a filter has been applied will change to a funnel. Since you can filter by more than one column at a time, you may see more than one funnel:

	A	B	C	D	E
1	Royalty Dat	Author Name	Marketplace	Transaction Ty	Net Units So
2	2021-01-31	Author A	Amazon.com	Standard	1
8	2021-01-31	Author A	Amazon.com	Standard	1
10	2021-01-31	Author A	Amazon.com	Standard	1
11	2021-01-31	Author A	Amazon.com	Standard	1
12	2021-01-31	Author A	Amazon.com	Standard	1
16	2021-01-31	Author A	Amazon.co.uk	Standard	1
17	2021-01-31	Author A	Amazon.com	Standard	1

Finally, when you filter your data, you can look in the bottom left corner to see how many entries out of your total lines of data met your filter criteria:

51	2021-01-28	Author A	Amazon.it	Standard	1
53	2021-01-28	Author A	Amazon.com	Standard	1
54	2021-01-27	Author A	Amazon.co.uk	Standard	1
55	2021-01-27	Author A	Amazon.com	Standard	2
56	2021-01-27	Author A	Amazon.com	Standard	2

| < | ... | Currency Format | Dates | Font Color | Merge | Sheet4 | F |

Ready   532 of 631 records found   Accessibility: Investigate

Here it says 532 of 631 records found. That is an easy way to get a count of records that meet your filter criteria.

Also, if you look at that number of total records and it is less than you think it should be, check your data for blank rows, because Excel may have stopped at that point rather than including all of your data.

You can also try to unapply and reapply your filters if you added new data to the bottom of your table and think Excel didn't incorporate it into the filtered data table.

(Ctrl + the down arrow will take you to the last populated field in a data range. That row number minus 1 should be your number of total records if your data starts in Row 1 and there are no blank rows.)

Final Thoughts

I recommend not leaving filtering on. We already discussed that it can be a compatibility issue with older versions of Excel, but also, you don't want to share information that you hadn't planned on sharing. I once had someone provide me a worksheet that was meant to show me our client billing for one specific project but they'd done it using filters. I turned off the filter and was able to see all of our client billing for the entire year.

Also, copy and paste when data is filtered can be tricky. And I honestly think it's gotten worse over the years. Only ever copy and paste one value at a time in your table when your data is filtered.

You can paste one value to multiple cells in a column, no problem, but if you copy three rows of values and try to paste those into another column in your table, they won't paste into the rows you can see, they will paste into the next three rows, even if two of those rows are currently filtered out.

Let's look at an example. Here I have a filtered data table. You can see that it jumps from Row 2 to Row 8 to Row 31 to Row 49.

	A Royalty Dat	B Author Name	C Marketplace	D Transaction Ty	Net
2	2021-01-31	Author A	2021-01-31	Standard	
8	2021-01-31	Author A	Amazon.com	Standard	
31	2021-01-30	Author A	Amazon.ca	Standard	
49	2021-01-28	Author A	Amazon.com	Standard	
55	2021-01-27	Author A	Amazon.com	Standard	
56	2021-01-27	Author A	Amazon.com	Standard	
60	2021-01-27	Author A	Amazon.co.uk	Standard	

I copied the values in Cells A2 through A31, and pasted them in Cell C2. Easy enough to do. Excel lets you do that no problem. This is great if you want to paste into a new worksheet. But note that you can only see one of the dates I copied.

Why is that? Because the values copied to Cells C2 through C5 even though Cells C3 through C5 weren't visible at the time:

	A Royalty Dat	B Author Name	C Marketplace	D Transaction Ty	E Net Units So
1					
2	2021-01-31	Author A	2021-01-31	Standard	1
3	2021-01-31	Author B	2021-01-31	Standard	1
4	2021-01-31	Author C	2021-01-30	Free - Price Match	65
5	2021-01-31	Author D	2021-01-28	Standard	1
6	2021-01-31	Author C	Amazon.fr	Free - Price Match	1
7	2021-01-31	Author C	Amazon.ca	Free - Price Match	3
8	2021-01-31	Author A	Amazon.com	Standard	1

This is an issue I run into all the time using filtering. So be very careful of this. You can copy *one* value and paste it into multiple cells in a filtered table, no problem, but you cannot copy multiple values and paste them successfully into a filtered table.

Sort Data

Now let's talk about sorting. Sorting data lets you put your entries into an order that makes better sense.

For example, in my day job I deal with a lot of financial records. So I might enter data from one bank statement and then another, but at the end of the day I want all of the entries sorted in date order, so I can see what happened in those accounts over time.

Before we start, you need to be careful with sorting, because you can "break your data" very easily. By break your data, what I mean is that your different columns of data are not inherently linked. So when you sort your data, if you fail to include all of the relevant columns, then you can break the relationship between the columns you did sort and the remaining columns.

Let's look at an example. Here I've added fill color to my data for all transactions that are not on Amazon.com:

	A	B	C	D	E	F	G	H	I
1	Royalty Dat	Author Name	Marketplace	Transaction Ty	Net Units So	Royalty	Currency		Converted
2	2021-01-31	Author A	Amazon.com	Standard	1	5.70 USD			$5.70
3	2021-01-31	Author B	Amazon.com.au	Standard	1	5.03 AUD			$0.00
4	2021-01-31	Author C	Amazon.com	Free - Price Match	65	0.00 USD			$0.00
5	2021-01-31	Author D	Amazon.com	Standard	1	2.76 USD			$2.76
6	2021-01-31	Author C	Amazon.fr	Free - Price Match	1	0.00 EUR			$0.00
7	2021-01-31	Author C	Amazon.ca	Free - Price Match	3	0.00 CAD			$0.00
8	2021-01-31	Author A	Amazon.com	Standard	1	5.83 USD			$5.83
9	2021-01-31	Author C	Amazon.de	Free - Price Match	3	0.00 EUR			$0.00

You can see that each row is either all blue or all not blue.

Now what if I want to sort on number of units in Column E, but I only sort on that column? See what happens:

	A	B	C	D	E	F	G
1	Royalty Date	Author Name	Marketplace	Transaction Type	Net Units Sold	Royalty	Currency
2	2021-01-31	Author A	Amazon.com	Standard	0	5.70 USD	
3	2021-01-31	Author B	Amazon.com.au	Standard	0	5.03 AUD	
4	2021-01-31	Author C	Amazon.com	Free - Price Match	1	0.00 USD	
5	2021-01-31	Author D	Amazon.com	Standard	1	2.76 USD	
6	2021-01-31	Author C	Amazon.fr	Free - Price Match	1	0.00 EUR	
7	2021-01-31	Author C	Amazon.ca	Free - Price Match	1	0.00 CAD	
8	2021-01-31	Author A	Amazon.com	Standard	1	5.83 USD	
9	2021-01-31	Author C	Amazon.de	Free - Price Match	1	0.00 EUR	
10	2021-01-31	Author A	Amazon.com	Standard	1	1.75 USD	

Note how the rows are no longer consistently filled or not filled? That's because I "broke" the relationship between Column E and all of the other columns.

To give Excel credit, because I did that with just one column Excel did give a warning, and ask if I wanted to expand my selection. But do that with three or four columns? You're sunk.

This is very, very easy to do, and why you should never work with your raw data. Because you can't fix this later. There's no easy way to reverse a mistake like that once it's made unless you catch it immediately and use Undo (Ctrl + Z) to reverse it.

How To Sort

To sort, first select ALL of the related data for what you need to sort. So all of the rows in your table for a standard sort. This doesn't have to be the full data table, you can just sort a subset, but make sure that you do capture all of the related information to keep from breaking your data.

Next, go to the Sort & Filter dropdown in the Editing section of the Home tab, and choose Custom Sort. (I personally do not use the A to Z and Z to A sort options unless I have just one column of data I'm trying to sort. I want more control over which column is sorted.)

You can also click on the Sort option in the Sort & Filter section of the Data tab, or right-click and go to the secondary dropdown under Sort, and choose Custom Sort from there.

All three will bring up the Sort dialogue box:

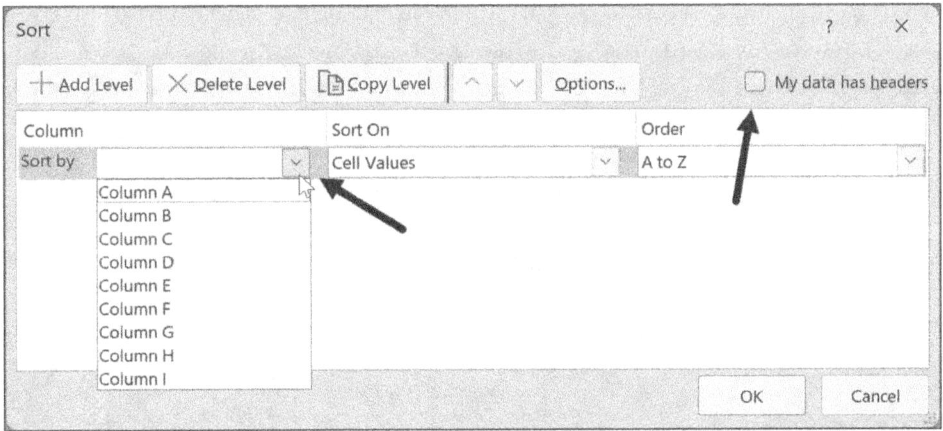

The Sort By dropdown is where you can choose which column to sort on. In this particular instance, Excel didn't recognize that I had a header row in the selected cell range, so it by default just shows me Column A, Column B, Column C, etc.

If you do have a header row, click on the checkbox for My Data Has Headers in the top right corner. That will change the list of columns to sort by to use the names from that first row.

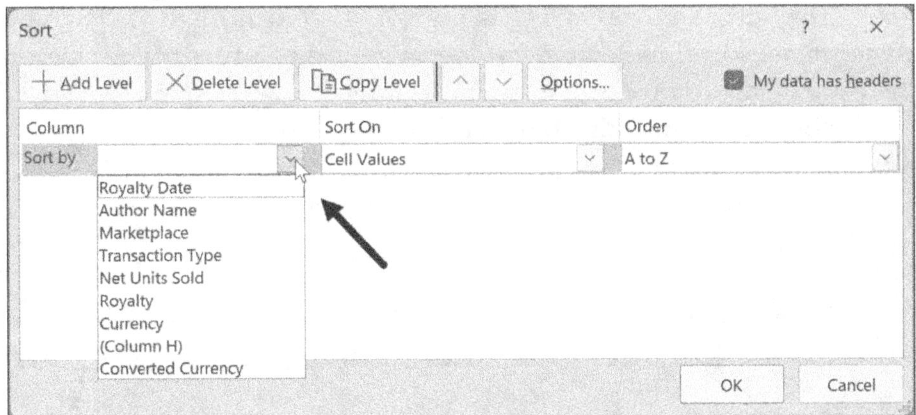

You can also do the reverse, of course, if Excel thinks you have a header row and you don't. Just uncheck the box to see column names instead of values in the first row.

That first level is your primary sort. How would you put these entries together if you were doing so manually. Would you want to look by date, by author, by store, by product type? What's your primary focus?

Choose that in the dropdown.

The next choice is what to sort on. Most of the time it will be the value in the cells. But you can also use this to sort by cell color, font color, or conditional formatting. So if you flag bad entries red and want them all grouped together, you can do that with this dropdown.

Your final choice in that row is how to sort, which will vary based on the type of data and the type of sort, but usually will be ascending or descending.

If you want to then have a secondary sort, click on Add Level and go through those choices for that level. This sort will only happen after the first sort happens. So, for example, if you put date and then author, all of the entries for each date will be grouped together and then within each date the entries will sort by author.

Here I've created a three-level sort:

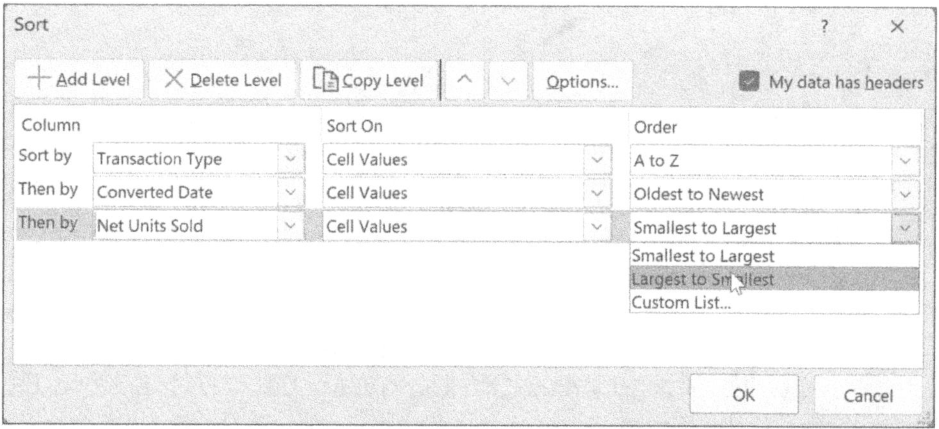

Excel will look at my data and sort it by Transaction Type first, A to Z. Then, within each transaction type, it will sort those entries by date in ascending order from Oldest to Newest. Finally, if there are multiple entries for a specific transaction type on the same day, Excel will sort those entries by number of units sold, in descending order.

Here's what that looks like:

	A	B	C	D	E	F	G	H	I	J
1	Royalty Dat	Author Name	Marketplace	Transaction Ty	Net Units So	Royalty	Currency		Converted Currency	Converted Date
2	2021-01-26	Author F	Amazon.com	Free - Price Match	1	0.00	USD		$0.00	1/26/2021
3	2021-01-30	Author C	Amazon.com	Free - Price Match	8	0.00	USD		$0.00	1/30/2021
4	2021-01-30	Author F	Amazon.com	Free - Price Match	1	0.00	USD		$0.00	1/30/2021
5	2021-01-30	Author C	Amazon.in	Free - Price Match	1	0.00	INR		$0.00	1/30/2021
6	2021-01-30	Author B	Amazon.com	Free - Price Match	1	0.00	USD		$0.00	1/30/2021
7	2021-01-30	Author C	Amazon.co.uk	Free - Price Match	1	0.00	GBP		$0.00	1/30/2021

The top of my data table now contains all of my free entries, because that is the first transaction type alphabetically. The January 26, 2021 entry is listed first followed by entries for January 30, 2021. Since there are multiple sales on January 30, 2021, the entry that had 8 units "sold" is listed above the ones that had 1 unit sold.

Once you sort data, unless it was already arranged in a specific way that can be replicated, you can't go back to the original order. So sorting is one of those steps you take in Excel that will make a permanent change to your data. Which is fine most of the time, so don't let that scare you out of using it. Just something to be aware of.

A few more tips. To remove a sort level, just bring up the Sort dialogue box, select that line, and then choose Delete Level.

To change the order of the levels you want to sort by, open the Sort dialogue box, click on that line, and then use the up and down arrows at the top of the dialogue box to move that level to where you want it.

Basic Math

There is a lot to learn about how to use formulas and functions in Excel. So much it gets its own books. But I want to quickly cover basic math for you.

See the Sum, Average, and Count

You can just select a cell range with numeric values in it to quickly see the average, count, and sum of those values. The result will display in the bottom right corner of your worksheet.

Right-click in that bottom area to change what will calculations will display.

As you can see, your other options are to display calculations of Numerical Count (as opposed to Count which shows the number of cells in the range with something in them), Minimum, or Maximum. Any with a check next to them will display for a selected range of cells. So click on a calculation type to turn it "on" or "off".

Excel will always show Count for selected cells if that option is checked. The other calculations will only show if there are cells in the range that Excel considers numeric, which means dates and/or numbers.

Formulas

To create a formula in Excel, start with an equals sign. Math operators such as the plus sign (+), minus sign (-), division sign (/), and multiplication sign (*) work in Excel. So if you write:

$$=2+3$$

in a cell, that will add 2 to 3 and display a result of 5.

If you write:

$$=2*3$$

in a cell that will multiply 2 times 3 and display a result of 6.

To reference values that are already in cells, just substitute the name of the cells that contain the values. So:

$$=A1+B1$$

will add the values that are in Cells A1 and B1 and display the result.

Those are very basic examples, but Excel can handle extremely complex calculations. If you can write it, Excel will do it. Usually the key is to use your parens to tell Excel which parts of the calculation to do first.

Excel follows standard mathematical rules about calculation order, such as multiplication in a formula before addition. And just like in written math, you can use parens within a formula to control calculation order. A full discussion of the rules Excel follows is under the help topic, Operator Precedence. (See the Learn More chapter to learn about how to use Excel Help.)

Functions

The true power of Excel is in its ability to make calculations that involve many, many cells, which requires using functions.

To use a function, you type the function name, an opening paren, the required information for that function separated by commas, and then a closing paren.

If the formula you're writing only uses that function, then the function comes right after the equal sign that started your formula. Otherwise just include it when it's needed like you would a cell reference or number.

The most basic Excel function is SUM, which adds the values you specify.

Almost every formula you write that uses a function will require cell notation, so let's discuss that now.

Cell Notation

Cell notation is how you tell Excel which cells to include.

To reference a range of cells, use the colon (:) between the first and last cell in the range.

To reference discrete cells or a series of discrete cell ranges, use commas between each cell or cell range.

So if I write:

$$=SUM(A1:C1)$$

That is saying to take the sum of the values in Cells A1 through C1, so Cells A1, B1, and C1. If I write:

$$=SUM(A1, C1)$$

That is saying to take the sum of the values in Cells A1 and C1.

To refer to an entire column you use the letter for that column, a colon, and the letter for that column again (B:B). Same with a row. Number, colon, number. (2:2).

To refer to a range of columns, you use the letter for the first column, a colon, and the letter for the last column. So

$$=SUM(A:E)$$

is saying to sum the values in all rows of Columns A through E.
Same with rows.

$$=SUM(1:5)$$

Is saying to sum the values in all columns of Rows 1 through 5.

When in doubt about how to reference the cells you want to use, start your formula or function, and then select your cells. Excel will write the cell notation for you.

I, for example, never remember how to refer to cells on another worksheet, so I just let Excel do it for me. (The answer is to use the worksheet name with an exclamation point before you list the cell range you want to use from that worksheet. I just go to the worksheet, select the cells, and Excel writes it for me.)

Also, be careful when you write a formula or function that references cells, that you don't accidentally reference the cell you're using to write the formula. That will generate a circular reference error message.

Excel will let you do it, because sometimes people want that, but usually that means you've made a mistake.

Okay. Let's walk through a few more examples.

If you want to subtract all of the values in Column B from the value in Cell A1, you'd write:

$$=A1\text{-}SUM(B:B)$$

This is a cheatsheet way to get around the fact that there is no function for subtraction in Excel. When you subtract a series of numbers, you are essentially adding all but the first one together and then subtracting their total from the first value.

$$=7\text{-}3\text{-}2\text{-}1$$

is the same as

$$=7\text{-}(3+2+1)$$

To add all of the cells in Columns A and B between Rows 1 and 10, you'd write:

$$=SUM(A1:B10)$$

To add the values in Cells A1, B3, and C6 you'd write:

$$=SUM(A1,B3,C6)$$

To add the cells in Columns A and B between Rows 1 and 10 and Columns E and F between Rows 1 and 10, you'd write:

$$=SUM(A1:B10)+SUM(E1:F10)$$

Or, if you want to be fancy:

$$=SUM(A1:B10,E1:F10)$$

When you write a formula in Excel it will highlight the cells that are being used for the formula. Use this to confirm that you have the right cells selected.

You can also go back to any cell that has a formula in it and double-click on that cell, or click on the cell and use F2, to see what cells are being used and in which part of the formula.

Excel color codes the various components in the formula and uses those same colors for borders it places around the cells used in each component.

AutoSum

One more trick you can use in Excel is the AutoSum option.

Click into the cell at the end of a range of values that you want to add, and then use the AutoSum option in the Editing section of the Home tab. Excel will build the SUM formula for you.

Here I did that in Cell E633 and it wrote a formula that adds six-hundred-and-thirty-one rows of data:

C	D	E	F	G
=SUM(E2:E632)				
Amazon.com	Standard - Paperba	1	2.64	USD
Amazon.co.uk	Standard - Paperba	1	4.27	GBP
Amazon.com	Standard - Paperba	1	14.19	USD
Amazon.com	Standard - Paperba	1	4.70	USD
Amazon.com	Standard - Paperba	2	9.16	USD
Amazon.com	Standard - Paperba	1	4.58	USD
Amazon.ca	Standard - Paperba	1	7.95	CAD
Amazon.com	Standard - Paperba	1	14.19	USD
Amazon.com	Standard - Paperba	1	5.40	USD
Amazon.co.uk	Standard - Paperba	1	4.27	GBP
Amazon.com	Standard - Paperba	1	5.75	USD
Amazon.co.uk	Standard - Paperba	1	4.50	GBP
Amazon.com	Standard - Paperba	3	13.74	USD
Amazon.com	Standard - Paperba	1	4.72	USD
Amazon.com	Standard - Paperba	1	5.75	USD
Amazon.com	Standard - Paperba	5	25.80	USD
		=SUM(E2:E632)		
		SUM(**number1**, [number2], ...)		

=SUM(E2:E632)

Pay attention if you use this, though, because it usually stops at any blank cell, so always double-check the formula it writes for you. In the example above it starts with E2, so I know I'm fine, it captured all my entries. But if it were E143, or something like that, I'd know it hadn't captured my full data table, and I'd need to manually adjust the formula.

There are also times when AutoSuml does skip blank cells. I was able to create an example of it here:

tion Type	Net Units Sold	Royalty		Currency	Conver
l - Paperba	1	4.70		USD	
l - Paperba	2	9.16		USD	
l - Paperba	1	4.58		USD	
l - Paperba	1	7.95	5.00	CAD	
l - Paperba	1	14.19		USD	
l - Paperba	1	5.40		USD	
l - Paperba	1	4.27		GBP	
l - Paperba	1		4.00	USD	
l - Paperba	1			GBP	
l - Paperba	3	4.27		USD	
l - Paperba	1			USD	
l - Paperba	1	4.27	6.00	USD	
l - Paperba	5	25.80		USD	
	20		=SUM(G13,G9,G5)		
			SUM(number1, [number2], **[number3]**, [number4], ...)		

The formula it wrote is:

$$=SUM(G13,G9,G5)$$

It's nice if you want that, which there have been times I have. For example, I had a table where I was summing every twelve months of results in a column, and wanted a total of those values, but keep an eye on that, too, and make sure that's what you really want it to do.

Another thing to point out is that even though it's called AutoSum, in Excel 2024 you can use the dropdown for AutoSum to calculate the average, count of numbers, maximum, and minimum values.

Just click on the option you want from the dropdown.

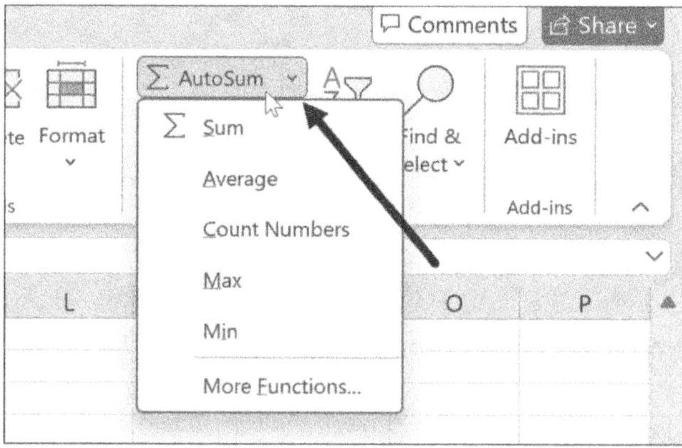

"AutoSum" can also be used to calculate values left to right. So if you want to sum values across a row, just click at the end of the row and then use it.

AutoSum can also be found in the Functions Library section of the Formulas tab.

Other Functions

What we just covered was the down and dirty, very simple version of how to do basic mathematical calculations and use functions in Excel. I've devoted an entire book to this subject, so this was just scratching the surface.

To explore the variety of functions that exist in Excel, click on Insert Function in the Function Library section of the Formulas tab. That will bring up the Insert Function dialogue box where you can click on various function names in the Select a Function section to see a description of what they do.

You can also search in that dialogue box to see if there is a function for the calculation or task you want to perform.

Good functions to explore are SUM, IF or IFS, TEXTJOIN, and XLOOKUP.

Print

Alright, we are almost at the end. The final thing you need to learn as a beginner, is how to print in Excel, which mostly requires learning how to format an Excel worksheet to print well.

To get started, use Ctrl + P or go to the File tab and click on Print from the left-hand menu. Both options will bring up the Print screen:

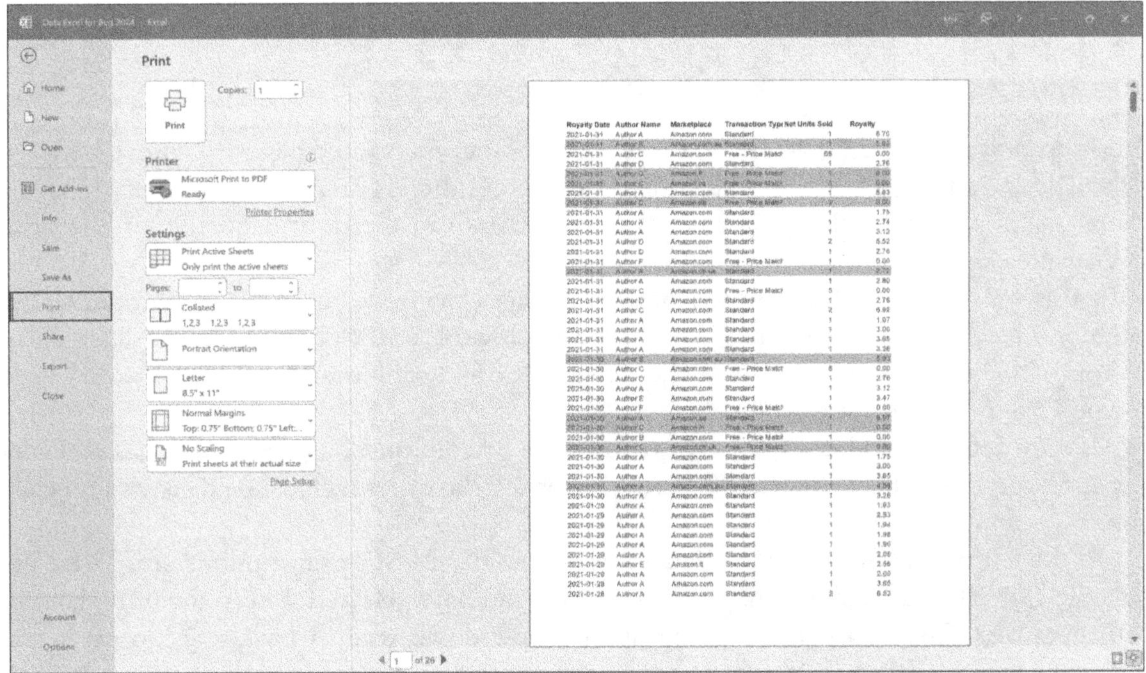

On the right-hand side, you should see a preview of how the first page in the selected worksheet(s) is going to print.

It may not look much like that worksheet.

Note here, for example, that I never put borders around this data, so for print purposes there are no lines on the page to separate columns and rows:

Royalty Date	Author Name	Marketplace	Transaction Type	Net Units Sold	Royalty
2021-01-31	Author A	Amazon.com	Standard	1	5.70
2021-01-31	Author B	Amazon.com.au	Standard	1	5.03
2021-01-31	Author C	Amazon.com	Free - Price Match	65	0.00
2021-01-31	Author D	Amazon.com	Standard	1	2.76
2021-01-31	Author C	Amazon.fr	Free - Price Match	1	0.00
2021-01-31	Author C	Amazon.ca	Free - Price Match	3	0.00
2021-01-31	Author A	Amazon.com	Standard	1	5.83
2021-01-31	Author C	Amazon.de	Free - Price Match	3	0.00
2021-01-31	Author A	Amazon.com	Standard	1	1.75

Also note that there are too many columns to fit on one printed page. I may be able to see all the columns just fine in my worksheet, but that doesn't mean they will print that way. There's also a lot of white space around my actual data.

Below the print preview on the left it will tell you how many pages are going to print:

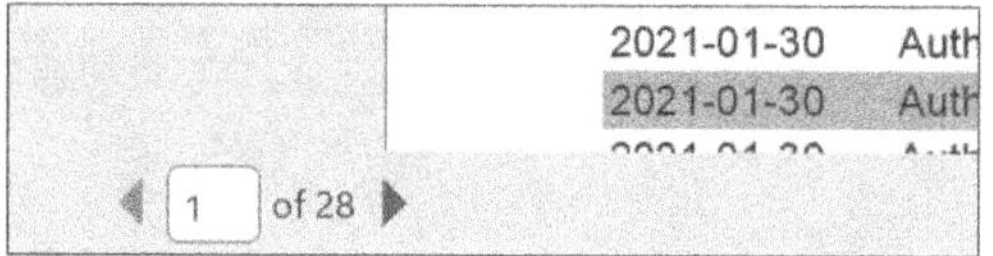

Mine currently says 1 of 28 where 28 is the total number of printed pages. To move between your pages, use the arrows on either side of those numbers, enter a value in the white box where it says your current page, or use the scroll bar(s) on the right-hand side of the print preview area.

In this example, my data spreads onto two pages per row because of the number of columns I have. By default Excel goes all the way down the rows before coming back up to the top of the next section, so to see the remainder of my columns for Row 1 I would need to type 15 into that box at the bottom.

Also, by default Excel does not repeat any rows or columns. So page 1 here has a header row and page 15 will have the rest of it, but the rest of the pages will just be data with no clear labels.

On the left of the print preview section is where all of your print options are. These are dynamic and will change depending on the printer you have selected. I keep my printer set to PDF because Office seems to get hung up and slow down when I have it set to my actual printer, which is usually turned off. So before you work with the options there, change it over to the printer you're going to use so you know what options are actually available to you.

Let's walk through that section from top to bottom. Here is a closer look at that options section now that I've switched over to my printer.

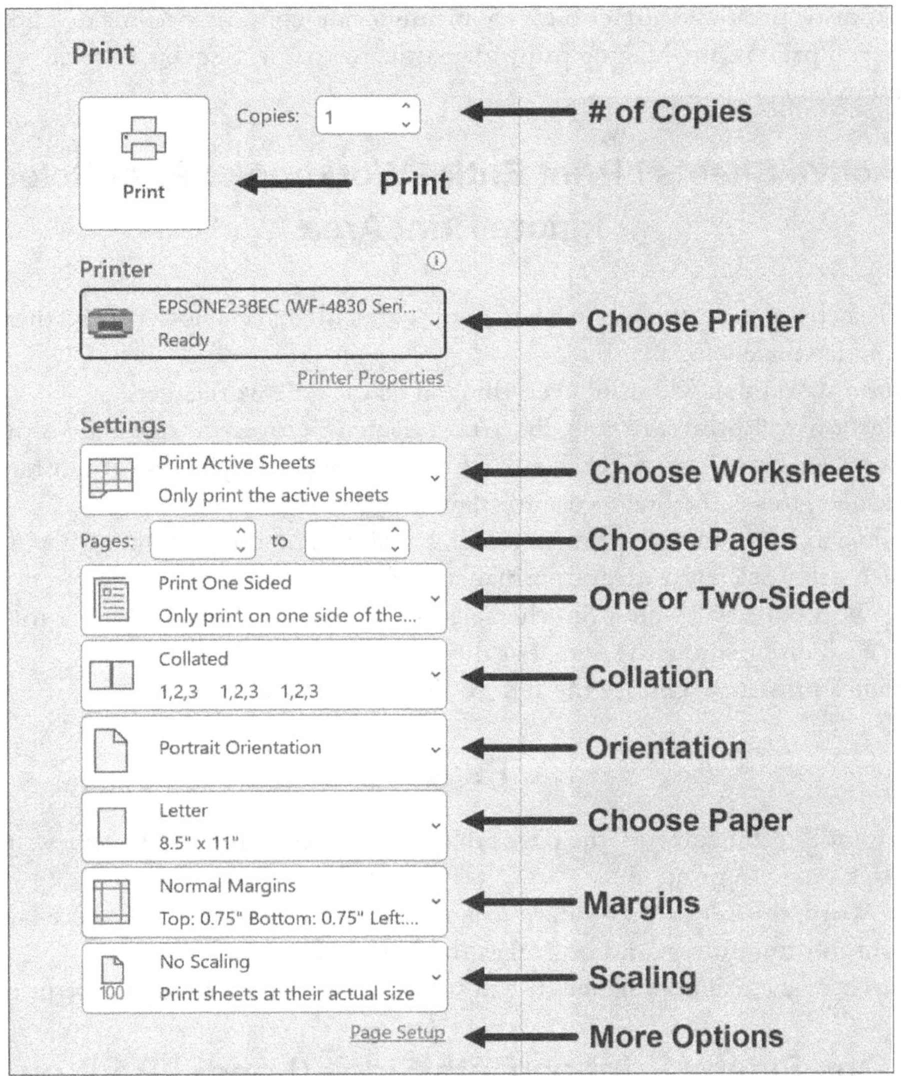

Print

When you're ready to print, click on the print icon there at the top.

Copies

Next to the print icon is an input box for the number of copies to print. The default is 1. You can click on the arrows to move up or down by 1 at a time, or you can just click into the field where it says 1 and type the number you want.

(If you want to print a lot of copies, try printing one copy first to make sure it all looks good before you print more. Making print formatting errors in Excel is just way too common to risk it otherwise.)

Print Active Sheets / Print Entire Workbook / Print Selection / Ignore Print Area

By default, Excel will print the worksheet(s) you currently have selected. The dropdown will show Print Active Sheets for that.

Print Entire Workbook will print everything in all of your worksheets.

Print Selection will print any cells that you selected before you decided to print. If you didn't have any selected, that will be blank. If you just want to print a certain range of cells from a worksheet, this is the one to use for that.

It is possible in Excel to set a print area that will always be the portion of a worksheet that prints. It's like Print Selection except permanent. If you've done that, Print Active Sheets or Print Entire Workbook will only print the cells selected as your print area for that particular worksheet. (We'll discuss how to set that at the end of this chapter.)

To override a print area, choose the Ignore Print Area option.

Pages

If you only want to print some of the pages that you can see in the print preview, it is possible to select a page range to print.

Unlike in Word, this set of pages have to be continuous. The first box there takes the first page you want to print; the second box takes the last.

Your print preview will not change. It will still show all pages that could be printed.

Print One Sided / Print on Both Sides (Long) / Print on Both Sides (Short)

If your printer can do so, you will have the option to print on one side of the page or both sides of the page. The default is one side of the page.

If you choose to print on both sides of the page, you can have it flip on the long side or the short side. In general, I choose long side when printing in portrait orientation and short side when printing in landscape.

Collated / Uncollated

This one only matters if you're printing more than one copy. The choice is between printing all of the first copy, then all of the second copy, then all of the third copy versus printing all copies of page 1, then all copies of page 2, then all copies of page 3.

Collated is when the first copy prints then the second copy, etc. Uncollated is when all of page 1 prints first then all of page 2, etc.

Generally, I choose collated. If I were doing handouts where I handed out each page separately, then I'd do uncollated.

Portrait Orientation / Landscape Orientation

Portrait orientation is when the short edge of the page is across the top and the long edge is down the side. Landscape is when the long edge is across the top and the short edge is down the side.

The default is Portrait Orientation. This is best when you have a limited number of columns and lots of rows. But if you have a large number of columns and want all columns to fit on one page, then Landscape Orientation is the better choice. I often use landscape in Excel.

Letter / Legal / Statement / … / A4 /…

This dropdown is basically asking what paper you're printing on. In the U.S. the default is Letter 8.5" x 11". In other countries it may be A4, which is a standard page size for those countries.

If you need something else, like legal, which will fit more columns in landscape orientation, for example, then choose that paper size from the dropdown. Just be sure that if you're printing to an actual, physical printer that you have that size paper available to print on.

The More Paper Sizes option at the bottom will open the Page Setup dialogue box, but for me the list of choices was the exact same.

Normal Margins / Wide / Narrow / Custom Margins

The next option you have is how much white space you want around the edge of the page. Sometimes if you're very close to fitting all of your information on the page, choosing narrow margins can help, but I tend to leave this one alone.

No Scaling / Fit Sheet on One Page / Fit All Columns on One Page / Fit All Rows on One Page

I use scaling often. It's the easiest way to get all of my information onto one page. So I will use Fit All Columns on One Page if I'm close to getting my data to show on just that one page.

But you have to understand that scaling makes the text smaller to make this happen. And Excel will take you at your word. It will put 50 columns on one page in text so small you can't read it. Or 500 rows on one page.

I often end up using a more advanced scaling option, which we'll discuss under Page Setup.

Page Setup

Clicking on Page Setup launches the Page Setup dialogue box.

It has four tabs: Page, Margins, Header/Footer, and Sheet.

Page Tab

On the Page tab, in the Scaling section, there is an option for Fit To and then two fields that let you specify how many pages wide and how many pages tall you want your printout to be.

Often when I need to scale my data for printing, I will need to do something like 2 pages wide by 3 pages tall, so will use this rather than the scaling dropdown choices available on the Print screen.

Note that 1 wide here would be the same as Fit All Columns on One Page and 1 tall would be the same as Fit All Rows on One Page. This section lets you do both at once, or more than one page for either one or both.

You can also select page orientation and paper source on the Page tab, as well as change the quality of the images you print, but for me at least those options are limited to 300 and 600 dpi.

Margins Tab

The Margins tab I use for Center on Page. I often find when I don't have enough data to fill the printed page, that it looks better if I center my data horizontally.

Header/Footer Tab

The Header/Footer tab has a set of choices for adding a header or footer to each printed page. You can add something as simple as page number or page X of Y. Or you can add something more complex like file name, worksheet name, who prepared the file, date it was printed, etc.

Use the dropdowns that will by default say (none) to choose what you want.

Sheet Tab

The Sheet tab lets you set a print area or set rows or columns to print on every page, but I prefer to do that elsewhere. This tab also lets you choose how pages print so you can have it print across a row and then down columns instead if you want, which is useful if you're printing a range of pages to get the right pages next to each other.

Page Layout Tab

If you go back to your active worksheet and click on the Page Layout tab, you will see in the Page Setup section options for a lot of the print settings we just discussed, such as Margins, Orientation, and Size. They give the same options there as in the print preview screen.

What I use this section for is Print Area and Print Titles.

Print Area

Print Area is where you specify a range of cells on a worksheet that will be all that will print from that worksheet.

This can be useful if you have notes or other data on a worksheet that don't need to print.

To set a print area, select your cells that you want to print, and then click on Set Print Area in the dropdown menu under the Print Area icon.

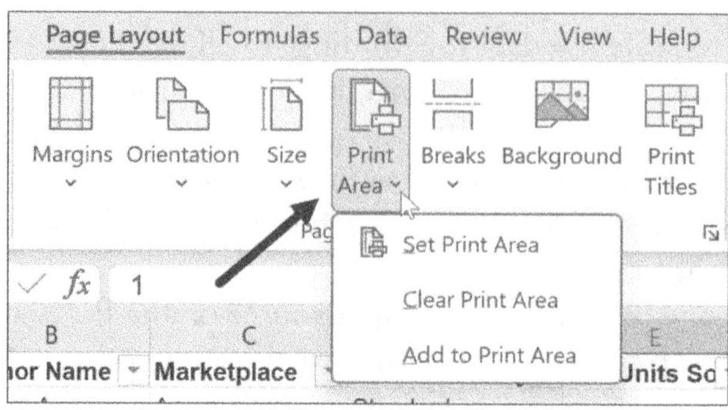

Once you've created a print area, the dropdown will have three choices, Set Print Area, which will override the existing print area you have set, Add to Print Area, which will keep any print area you already set and add the newly selected cells to it, or Clear Print Area, which will remove any selected print area and make it so the whole worksheet prints:

Print Titles

Print Titles lets you tell Excel a series of rows or columns to repeat on every single page that prints.

When you click on Print Titles in the Page Setup section of the Page Layout tab, it will open the Page Setup dialogue box to the Sheet tab.

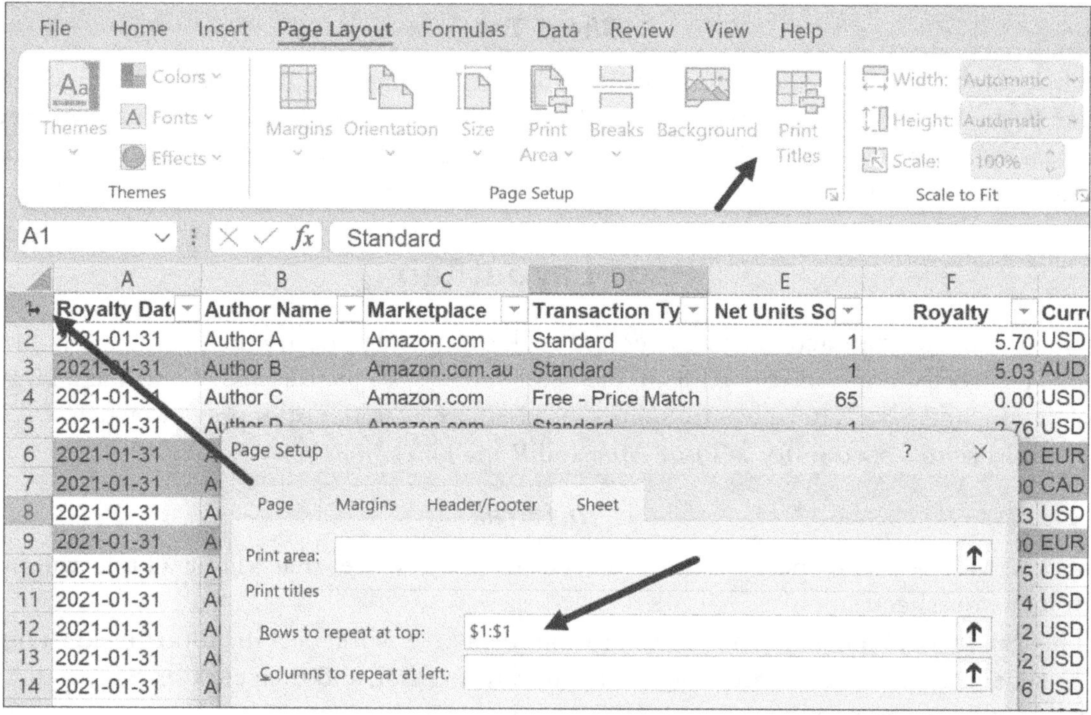

The reason I do this from the actual worksheet instead of the Print screen, is because I can then click into the white cell for Rows to repeat at top, and just click on the 1 for Row 1 to select it. I don't have to remember the cell notation, Excel does it for me.

It is possible to select more than one row or more than one column to repeat on each page. It is also possible to select a row or column that is not the first row or column.

So if you have some introductory text for a report in Rows 1 through 3 but then the header row is in Row 4, you can just select Row 4.

The only thing you can't do, is select multiple columns or multiple rows that aren't touching. Meaning you can't have Row 1 and 4 repeat. It has to be Rows 1 through 4 or Row 1 or Row 4. Keep that in mind when setting up a report or data table.

Learn More

I can assure you that we have not covered everything you will ever want to know in Microsoft Excel. Guaranteed. But hopefully we covered what you need to know on a day-to-day basis.

If you get deeper into data analysis, then you will highly benefit from learning pivot tables, charts, and functions.

If you want to better flag results, then you should learn conditional formatting.

If you have to mess with data a lot, then it's good to learn how to group data, subtotal it, and use functions.

I of course am biased, and think that if you made it through this book and learned from it, then you should keep going with the rest of this series. The next book is *Intermediate Excel 2024*, which covers conditional formatting, pivot tables, charts, grouping data, subtotaling it, and more. Or you can skip ahead to *Excel 2024 Useful Functions*, to learn more about formulas and functions in Excel.

But. If you, like me, tend to learn better by trial and error, then there are plenty of resources that Microsoft provides to help you learn. (The value I bring is structure around how to approach Excel, and what you can safely ignore.)

So. A few tips for learning on your own:

First, you can hold your cursor over many of the options in the toolbar to see more information about that tool or task.

This will usually tell you what that option does, and give a control shortcut if one exists. Many of them end with Tell Me More. Click on that to be taken to the Excel help specific to that tool or task.

Here, for example, is the Format Painter:

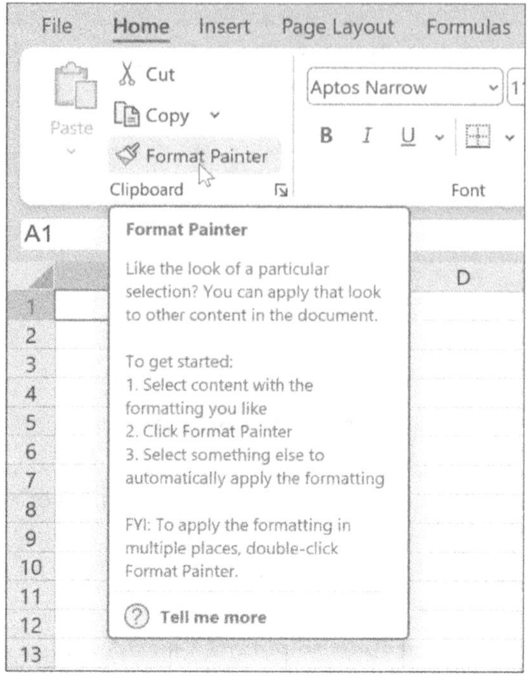

Now, you may be like me, and not like to share every little thing with Microsoft so have turned off all sharing. If that's the case, when you click on Tell Me More, you will get an error message that your administrator has turned this service off.

They haven't. I am my administrator.

What I turned off was "connected experiences". Unfortunately, in Office 2024, rather than let you continue to access Help without being "connected" they force you to choose connected experiences to access it through Excel. (Boo.)

You can turn it back on by going to File and then Options in the bottom left corner. This will bring up the Excel Options dialogue box.

Click on Privacy Settings under General. Scroll down and click the box for "Turn On All Connected Experiences", and then click OK.

You will also need to check the box for Turn On Experiences That Download Online Content. Office will then require you to restart for those changes to take effect. (In my case, I had Skype open, too, and even that is affected. So close anything from Microsoft.)

(Note that if you want to turn these things off, the process is the same, you just uncheck the boxes and restart Office.)

If you don't want that enabled, then use the online search options we'll discuss in a moment.

Okay. So if Help actually works for you, click on that Tell Me More, and Excel will open a task pane on the right-hand side of the screen that lists the help text specific to that task or tool.

Scroll down to read the full text. Click on the X in the top right corner when you're done.

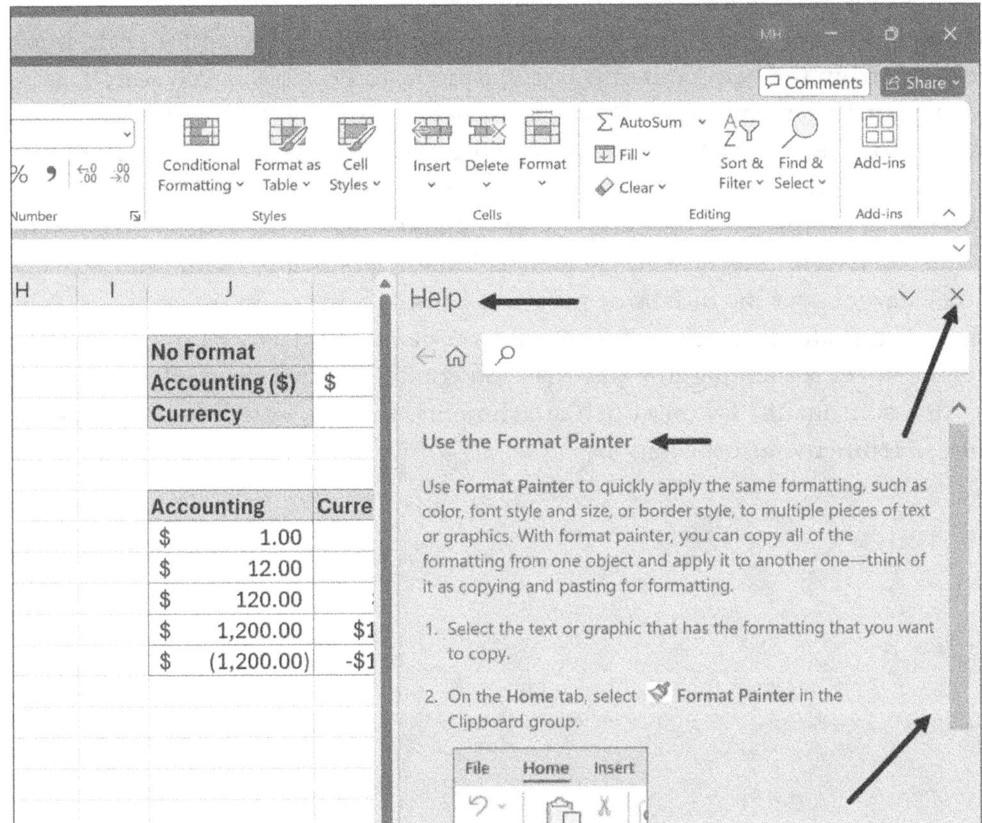

If you want help on something else, you can also use F1, or go to the Help tab and click on Help to open that task pane.

The task pane will open to the main Help page, where you can click on one of the listed topics to learn more, or use the Search box to find the help you need:

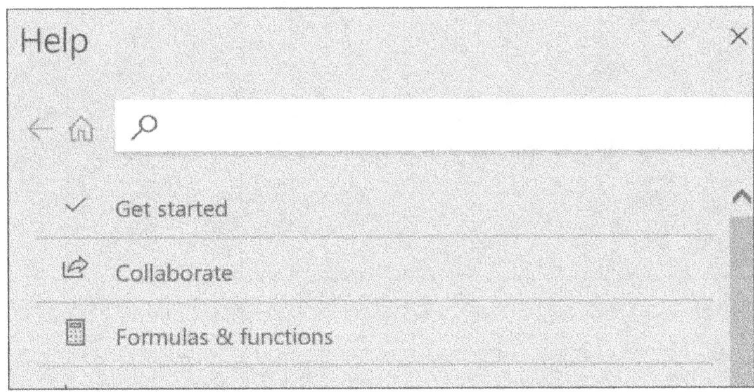

If you go back to the Help tab in the top menu, the Show Training option (which takes a bit to load), has instructional videos you can watch.

The Community and Excel Blog options will take you to websites for each, but honestly once I get away from the help built into Excel, I prefer to do a basic web search.

I type in what I need as well as the version I need it for, so "format painter Excel 2024", and then look for the link to the Microsoft support website (support.microsoft.com).

There are a ton of other free resources out there. YouTube videos are a huge source of information, for example. Just be wary. It's always best to start with the source (Microsoft). I find that they do well at the "how to" guidance, but are less helpful with "can I?".

Also they never cover the pitfalls or pros and cons of various approaches.

Finally, you can always reach out to me if you get stuck. I am happy to help, especially where I didn't cover something in a way that you could follow. (Less so if you try to turn me into your free consultant.) I won't open attachments, though, and I don't always check that email daily, so temper your expectations.

Conclusion

Okay, there you have it. You should be able to work in Excel at this point with some basic data that you can format properly, sort, and filter. You should also be able to do some basic math and navigate around without issues, as well as print your results.

Excel is an incredibly powerful tool. I've been using it for at least 30 years, and I probably only use 20% of its capability. But for most people that's more than they need.

As I mentioned before, this series does continue. If you want to keep going, check out *Intermediate Excel 2024* or *Excel 2024 Useful Functions*.

I also have an older book out there called *Excel for Budgeting* that walks you through how to build an Excel worksheet to use for budgeting purposes, like tracking your spending and income. The companion book for that is *Budgeting for Beginners,* which discusses those concepts. If you don't want to build the actual worksheet, you can just buy a blank template (in .xls format) from my Payhip store. It's linked from my website.

Before we go. You can do this. It may seem daunting, but I have faith in you. Just remember that Ctrl + Z (Undo) or Esc will get you out of almost any misstep you take. You can also just close the file without saving and start over if it's that bad.

And remember to never work directly with your raw data—always keep that set aside for the worst-case scenario.

Take your time.

If you get stuck, remember that Excel is a logical program. Once you learn the structure of it, you should be able to guess how most things are done. Look for the commonalities. (Ctrl + B to bold, Ctrl + I for italics, Ctrl + U to underline, for an example.)

Okay. Good luck with it. Reach out if you get stuck.

Intermediate Excel 2024

EXCEL 2024 ESSENTIALS - BOOK 2

M.L. HUMPHREY

CONTENTS

CONTENTS (CONT.)

Introduction

In *Excel 2024 for Beginners*, we covered the basics you need to know to work in Excel on a daily basis, but Excel is an incredibly powerful tool that can do so much more than that.

So here we're going to continue from that solid foundation and cover some intermediate-level topics.

A lot of this will be more advanced tools for data analysis such as pivot tables (officially PivotTables), which let you take a table of data and quickly build a summary table of that data, charts, which let you visual your data, and conditional formatting, which lets you flag the results that meet your criteria.

If you don't use Excel for data analysis, we'll also cover topics such as converting text to columns, removing duplicate values, grouping and subtotaling data, and how to zoom your view in and out. (I use zoom more than ever these days thanks to video calls.)

I also want to revisit a few topics from the beginner book and dive deeper on them. So we'll discuss more advanced Find options, also cover Replace, circle back to the format painter, and cover how to sort horizontally.

The one big remaining intermediate-level topic we aren't covering here is formulas and functions in Excel. That has its own book, *Excel 2024 Useful Functions*.

Finally, I print these books in black and white to make them as affordable for readers as possible, but sometimes it is nice to see color images. The ebook versions of these books are in color and if you go to the About the Author section at the end of this book there is a discount code for buying the ebook off of my Payhip store.

But for now, let's just dive in and get started, shall we?

Basic Terminology Revisited

This chapter is for those who skipped *Excel 2024 for Beginners* or just want a quick refresh on the terminology I'll be using throughout this book.

Workbook

A workbook is basically an Excel file.

Worksheet

Workbooks are made up of worksheets, which according to Microsoft, are "the primary document that you use in Excel to store and work with data." They consist of "cells that are organized into columns and rows".

Another way to think of a worksheet is as a discrete location in your workbook that contains information.

Column

A standard worksheet uses columns and rows to create cells which display your information. Columns run across the top of the worksheet and are, by default, indicated with a letter.

Row

Rows run down the side of a worksheet and are numbered from 1 up to the very last row.

The number of columns and rows in a worksheet are fixed. When you insert or delete cells, columns, or rows you're actually moving information around, not changing the number of columns or rows in the worksheet.

Cell

Cells are formed by the intersection of a column and a row. They are referred to based upon the column and row where they are located. So the first cell in a worksheet is Cell A1, where A is the first column and 1 is the first row.

Click

If I tell you to click on something, that means to use your mouse (or trackpad) to move the arrow or cursor on the screen to a specific location, and then left-click or right-click as needed.

Left-Click/Right-Click

If you use a standard mouse then it's going to be split in the middle with the option to press down on either side at the front. Press on the left side and that's a left-click. Press on the right side and that's a right-click.

In general, a left-click will select an item, and a right-click will create a dropdown list of options to choose from.

If I don't tell you which one to use, left-click.

Left-Click and Drag

I may at times tell you to left-click and drag something. To do so, left-click on that object or in that location, and then hold your left-click as you move your arrow/mouse/cursor to either select a range or to move an object to its new location.

Formula Bar

The formula bar is the long white bar at the top of the screen with the function(x) (fx) symbol next to it. It shows the true contents of your cell, so, for example, the formula rather than the result of the formula.

Tab

I refer to the menu choices at the top of the screen (File, Home, Insert, Page Layout, Formulas, Data, Review, View, Help, etc.) as tabs. Each one will give you different tasks you can perform.

I may sometimes also refer to these as part of the menu at the top of the screen.

Section

I refer to the different named areas under each tab as a section.

Data

I use the terms data and information interchangeably. Whatever information you have in your worksheet is your data.

Table

I will sometimes refer to a table of data or data table. This is just a collection of cells that contain related information. Excel does now have a defined table functionality, but that is not what I'm referring to.

Scroll Bar

When there is more information than Excel can show you in a dropdown or worksheet, it will make scroll bars available on the right side or bottom of that space so you can "scroll" to see the rest of the information.

Select

When I tell you to select something, that means to click on it, or to choose a range of cells.

Dropdown Menu

A dropdown menu shows a list of potential choices that you can select from that aren't immediately visible. In the set of menu options up top, the existence of a dropdown menu is indicated by an arrow next to the current choice.

You can also right-click on various spots within Excel to see various dropdown menus. Right click on a cell or range of selected cell(s) to see the main dropdown menu in Excel.

Dialogue Box

Dialogue boxes are pop-up boxes that appear on top of your workspace. They contain options you can choose from to perform a task. They are generally there for older functionality, and often contain the largest number of choices.

Expansion Arrow

Some of the sections of the menu tabs have what I refer to as expansion arrows. These are arrows in the bottom right corner of that section which you can click on to open either a dialogue box or a task pane that contains more choices.

Task Pane

Task panes are separate spaces that sometimes appear to the left, right, or bottom of the worksheet area. They allow you to perform various tasks.

The easiest one to see is the Clipboard task pane which will open if you click on the expansion arrow in the Clipboard section of the Home tab.

To close a task pane, click on the X in the top right corner.

Cursor

Your cursor is what moves around when you move your mouse. Depending on where you are, it will look like different things. Often in Excel it looks like a variety of arrows. I may sometimes refer to moving your mouse around. This just means to move the cursor on the screen using the mouse or trackpad.

Arrow

If I ever tell you to arrow to something, that just means to use the arrow keys to navigate to that spot.

Control Shortcut

There are various keyboard combinations that you can use in Excel to perform common tasks. I refer to them as control shortcuts, because most use the Ctrl key, although not all of them do.

For example, Ctrl + C lets you copy your selection.

I write them with capital letters, but you don't need to use a capital of any of the letters, just hold down the keys at the same time.

Some Quick Tips

There were a few items I considered covering in *Excel 2024 for Beginners* but decided to move here instead, so let's cover those quickly.

Move to the End of a Data Range

When you have a table of data in your worksheet, you can use Ctrl + an arrow key to go to the last populated cell in that row or column in the direction of the arrow.

Watch out for gaps in your data, because it will stop just before the next empty cell.

To avoid stopping at each empty cell in a row or column, try starting in the first row or column of your data table. Assuming your table uses header rows or columns, or the first row or column are fully populated, that should work.

If there is no data in the worksheet, then Ctrl + an arrow key moves to the ends of the sheet.

Select an Entire Data Table

If you ever need to select all of your data in a data table, start in one corner of the table, and then use Shift + Ctrl + the arrow keys.

This will also stop at any blank cells, so you may need to use it more than once to capture all of the cells in the table.

Excel Appearance

The biggest impact on how Excel looks for you is likely going to be driven by your screen size. The smaller the screen as perceived by Excel, the less text you'll see for each menu tab. Excel reduces the different tasks down to their icons. You'll need to hold your mouse over each one to see what it does.

For example, I see this in the Data tab when at full-screen:

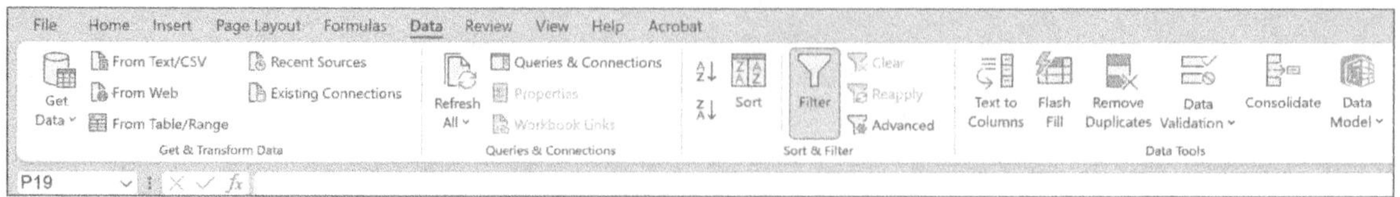

Here is that same section of the Data tab when I've reduced Excel to take up about a third of the screen:

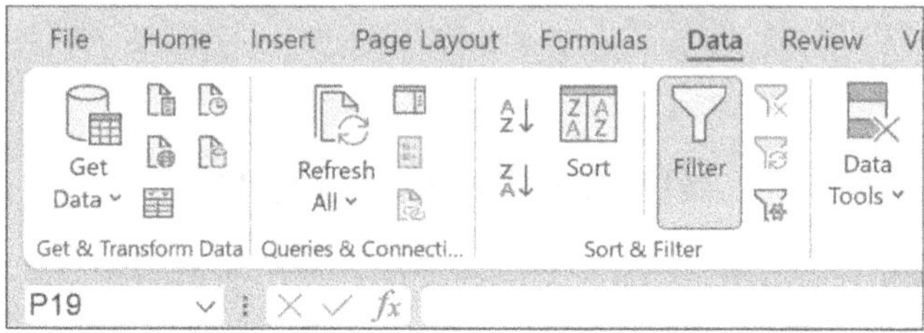

Note how all of the Get & Transform Data options no longer have labels. And the entire Data Tools section is now a dropdown menu.

* * *

Excel and Windows also have different display settings that can drastically impact the default appearance of Excel. The Office Theme settings can be accessed through the choices available in the bottom left corner of the Welcome Screen.

Either click on Account and use the Office Theme dropdown on the Account screen, or click on Options to bring up the Excel Options dialogue box. In the General section of that dialogue box, go to Personalize Your Copy of Microsoft Office, and change the Theme there.

The choices you have in Excel are Dark Gray, Black, White, and Colorful. You can also choose Use System Setting which will use your Windows settings.

I personally use Colorful. White will look much the same.

Sort Horizontal

In *Excel 2024 for Beginners,* we covered how to sort data. Usually you're going to sort results from top to bottom within a column or columns, but occasionally you may want to sort left to right within a row. For example, I once sorted a data table that counted concerns people had raised by most common concern to least common.

To sort horizontally, select your data, and then click on your preferred Sort option to bring up the Sort dialogue box. In the Sort dialogue box, click on Options in the top row.

That will bring up the Sort Options dialogue box:

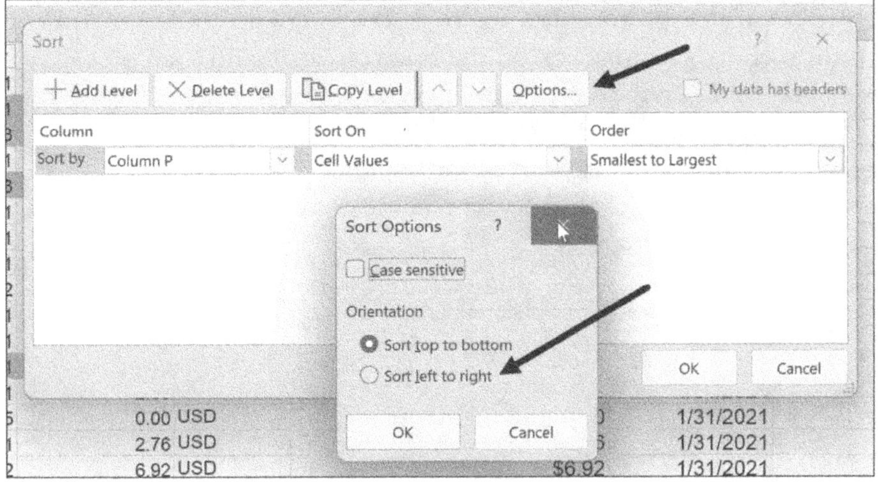

Click on the button for Sort Left to Right, and then click OK to go back to the main Sort dialogue box. Your Sort By option will change to a listing of the rows in your selected data instead of the columns. You can then proceed like a normal sort.

Custom Sort

If you have a text field that shows the day of the week or the month, choose the Custom List option under Order in the Sort dialogue box to find a list to sort that in the correct order:

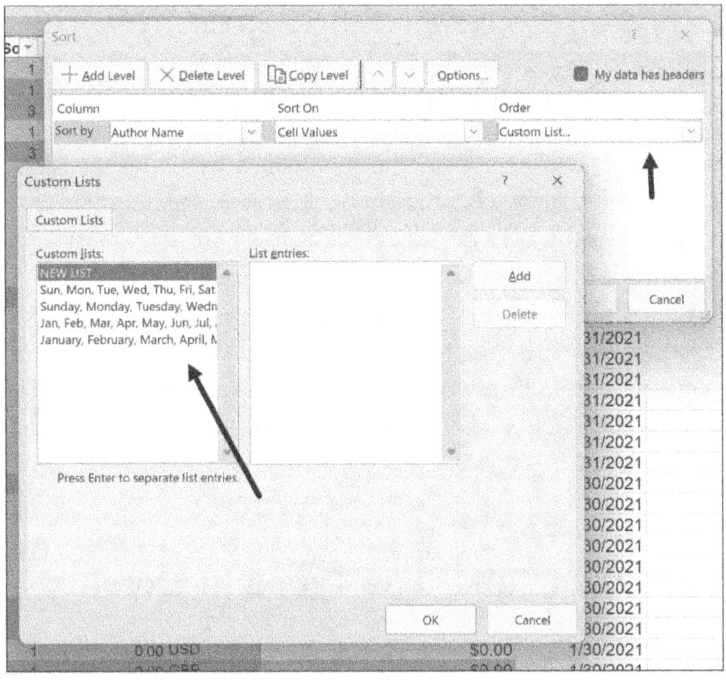

Excel has pre-populated custom lists for both the long and short versions of day of the week and month to choose from. Click on the one you want, and then on OK.

There is also an option there to create your own custom sort list. Choose the NEW LIST option on the left, and click on Add. That will let you enter values in the List Entries field. Type in your list with Enter after each value, and then click on OK.

The Order for that field will then show as your custom list:

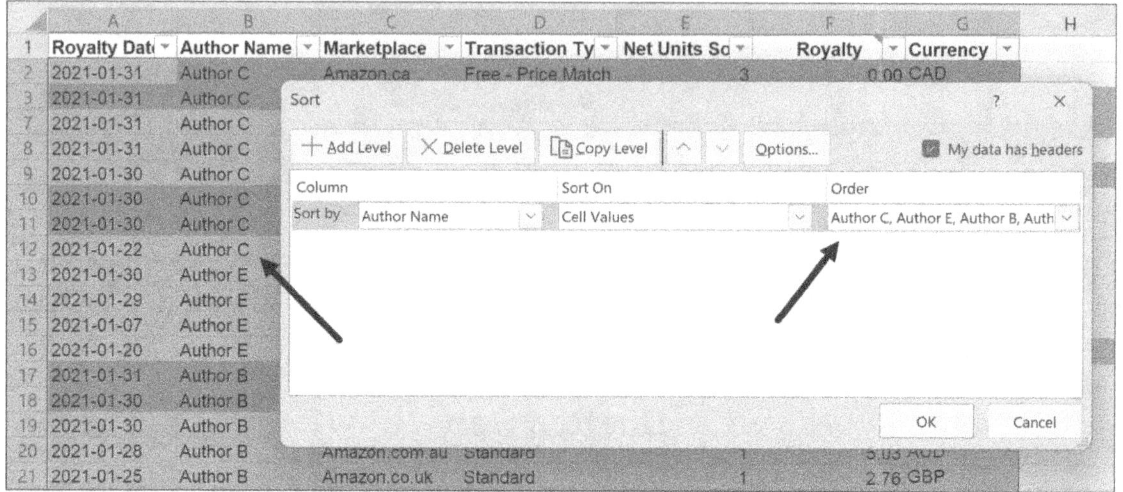

When you click OK the data will then sort in that order. (I sorted the data and then reopened my sort to show you the result and the sort entry at the same time.)

Select Multiple Worksheets

It is possible to have more than one worksheet selected by using Ctrl, and then clicking on multiple worksheet name tabs, or by clicking on your first worksheet name tab, using Shift, and clicking on your last worksheet name tab to select a range of worksheets.

If you do select multiple worksheets, be very, very careful, because if you type something into Cell A3 on your currently-visible worksheet while you have multiple worksheets selected, you will edit Cell A3 on *all* of the selected worksheets. I've used that to my advantage a few times, but more often I've messed up worksheets I didn't realize I was editing.

To unselect multiple worksheets, click onto the name tab for a worksheet you didn't have selected already, or right-click on a name tab for a selected worksheet, and choose Ungroup Sheets.

Open Other File Types In Excel

By default, when you try to open a file from Excel, your choices are going to be All Excel Files.

But there are some files that you can open from Excel that are not considered Excel Files. For example, Apple sends me sales data in .txt files that can be opened by a program like Excel, but aren't considered Excel Files.

To open a file like that, you have to Open the file from within Excel. Click on Open from the Welcome screen, then click on Browse to bring up the Open dialogue box. Change the file type dropdown to All Files, and navigate to where the file is saved.

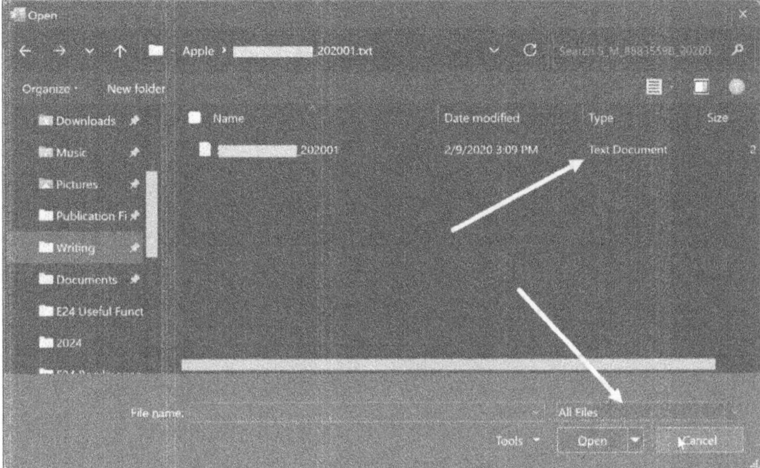

Click on the file name, and choose Open, like you would with any normal Excel file.

For text files, you may need to walk through the Text Import Wizard.

Most of the files like this will be Delimited, so you can just choose Next on the first screen. On the second screen, look in the Data Preview tab to make sure that the right character is selected as your delimiter.

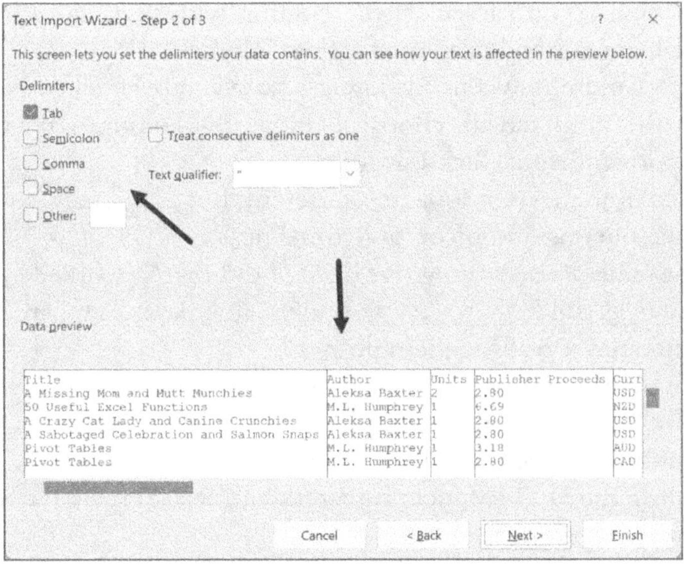

The delimiter is a character that separates columns of data and is deleted during import. Often it's a tab, a solid vertical line, a comma, or comma and space.

If the delimiter is not the correct one, type the correct character into the Other box, or check a different choice in that list.

If you want to work with a file like this that you imported, and keep the changes you make, be sure to Save As and choose a regular Excel file type before you close.

Excel Templates

On the Welcome Screen in Excel, as well as the New screen available under the File tab, you will see that Excel offers templates you can use.

These are pre-formatted Excel files that you can then add data to. I found a useful one that created timelines once by using the search online option. But to effectively use that template, I had to basically deconstruct how it worked. (In that case, the entries in the table had to be sorted in date order or the lines and data on the timeline didn't match.)

So these can be useful, but don't think that they'll necessarily do all the work for you.

To use one, just select it. But be sure to Save As with your file name when you're done.

Reformat a Date Column

It's ironic that while Excel, tries to turn anything close to a date into a date, it also seems to have an issue seeing some date values as dates when it comes to more complex analysis. I run into this with pivot tables and filtering, for example, on a regular basis. Even when a field is formatted as a date, Excel will still treat it as text.

To fix that (sometimes), you can select the column with your dates in it, go to the Data Tools section of the Data tab, and click on Text to Columns.

A Convert Text to Columns Wizard dialogue box will appear. Click Next on the first and second screens. On the third screen, choose Date as the column data format, and choose **DMY** from the dropdown menu. Click Finish.

The date in that column may not look any different, but Excel may now view those values as dates for things like filtering and pivot table timelines.

I say may, because while I was writing this book, I did that, it worked great, and then when I went back to do edits, it suddenly wasn't working. Same data. Same spreadsheet. Nothing I tried fixed it. So sometimes it really is them not you.

Another option if that doesn't work, may be to use the DATEVALUE function to create dates from text entries. They'll come out as the numeric equivalent of a date, so you'll then need to format the entries to a date format, but that's another option.

I also sometimes use the DATE function paired with RIGHT, LEFT, and MID to rebuild a date from a text entry. That one is also hit or miss.

File Naming

If I am going to have a lot of files in a folder that I need to be able to quickly access, like monthly bank statements, I will include at the beginning of the file name the date of the document in YYYYMMDD order. That's year-month-date. The reason to do that is so your files will automatically be in date order, even if one of them is edited at some later point in time.

Please, never, ever name your files using something like 3.30.24. It seems fine, right? But if you have files across multiple years it puts the month files together instead of the year files together. So you have all of March together instead of all of 2024 sorted by month.

Trust me, this matters when you have a lot of records to deal with.

Also, I'm pretty sure that the period in that format interferes with searching your file names. So no periods in a file name either.

You can put the date at the end if you want, but only do that if the rest of the file name is going to be the same. So I could have different versions of this file and name them something like "Excel 2024 for Beginners 20241001" and then "Excel 2024 for Beginners 20241005".

Same goes with using V1, V2, etc. for versioning. Think about how the file names will be listed if you alphabetize them, and name accordingly. Better to use V1 through V23 instead of Final, Final V2, Final Final, etc.

Find and Replace

In *Excel 2024 for Beginners* I briefly touched upon a basic search which can be done by using Ctrl + F to bring up the Find and Replace dialogue box. Now it's time to revisit Find and also discuss Replace.

The control shortcut for Find is Ctrl + F, the control shortcut for Replace is Ctrl + H. They both will open the Find and Replace dialogue box, the only difference is which tab it opens to. In the Editing section of the Home tab you can also use the Find & Select dropdown menu to choose either Find or Replace to also open the Find and Replace dialogue box.

Let's start with Find:

Find

Narrow Results Using Match Case

By default, if I type "sec" into the Find What field, Excel's Find will look for "sec" in any part of any cell. It will return entries for secretive, section, securities, Securities, SEC, etc.

But often I want to narrow the search results down to something more specific, like SEC, which in my day job is the abbreviation for the Securities and Exchange Commission.

To narrow your results based on the capitalization of the word, click on Options in the basic Find dialogue box.

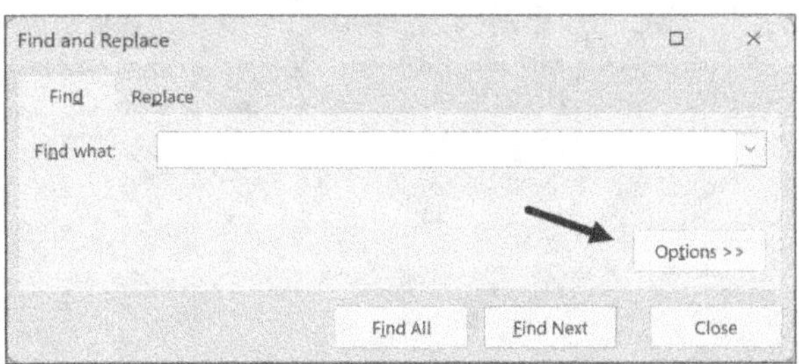

This will expand the dialogue box and show more search options. Check the box for Match Case to limit your search result to only those entries that have the exact same capitalization as your search term:

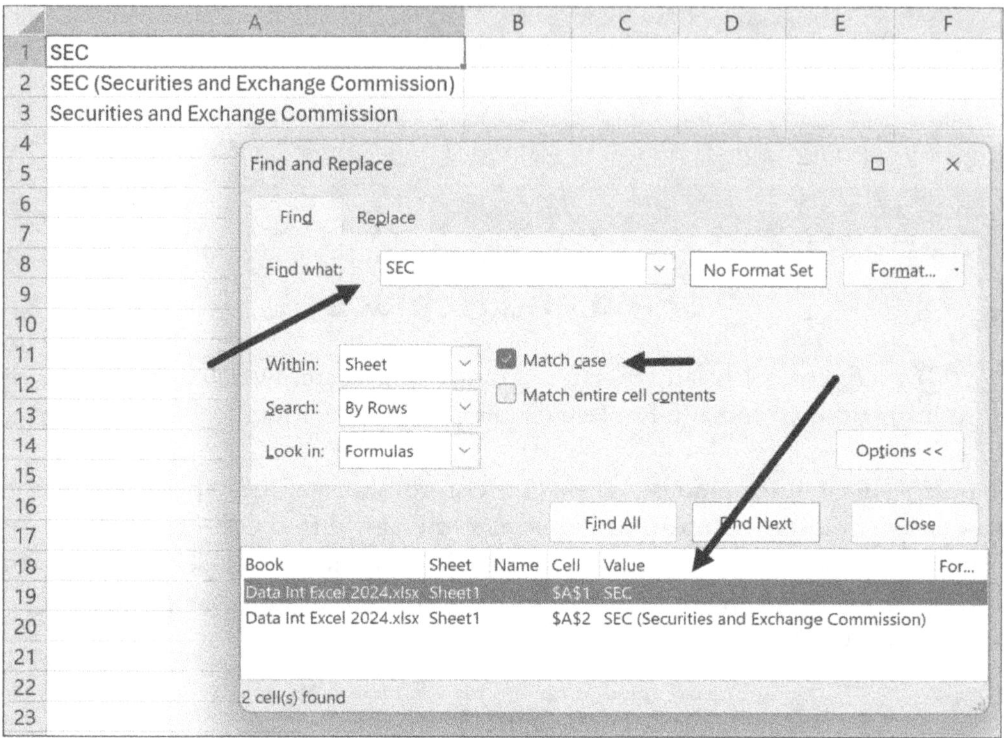

Here you can see that I had three entries that used the letters "sec", but only two that used the capitalized "SEC" that I searched for. By clicking on Match Case, Excel only returned those two results.

Narrow Results to Match Entire Cell Contents

Unfortunately, Excel does not have an option to search for a whole word only like Word does. But it does have the ability to search for only the cells that contain your specified text.

To do that, click on the Match Entire Cell Contents checkbox. Here I've kept Match Case checked and also checked that box to limit my result to just the result that has "SEC" in a cell and nothing else:

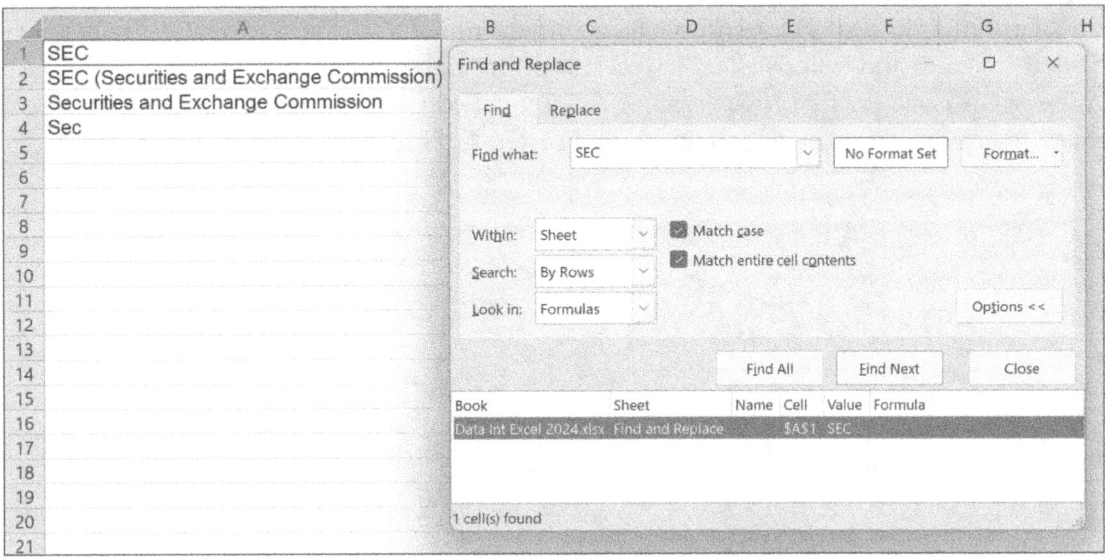

Limit Search By Selecting Cells

Another quick little trick with Find in Excel is to select only some of the cells in a worksheet. That will limit your search to just those cells. I often use this when the data I'm looking for is limited to one column, like customer name.

(This is something to keep in mind in the opposite direction, too. Sometimes you'll tell Excel to search for something you know exists and it won't give you a result. If that happens, check that you don't have some cells selected already that are limiting it to searching in just those selected cells.)

Expand Search Results to Entire Workbook

By default, Excel will only search in your current worksheet. But under the expanded options section you can change the Within dropdown from Sheet to Workbook to look in all of the worksheets in your workbook at once.

Include Formula Results in Search

A normal Excel search looks at the text in your formulas or cells, but not the results of any formulas. Change the Look In dropdown from Formulas to search your visible cell contents.

(That dropdown also allows looking in Notes or Comments if you have those in your workbook.)

Search by Format

If you click on Format on the right-hand side of where you enter the text you want to search for, you can specify an exact format to search for.

In Word I do this a lot to look for italics in my documents. I leave the Find What field blank and set it to italics and it finds all italicized text in my entire document for me.

When you click on that, it will open the Find Format dialogue box. Just choose your formats from each tab like you would in the Format Cells dialogue box.

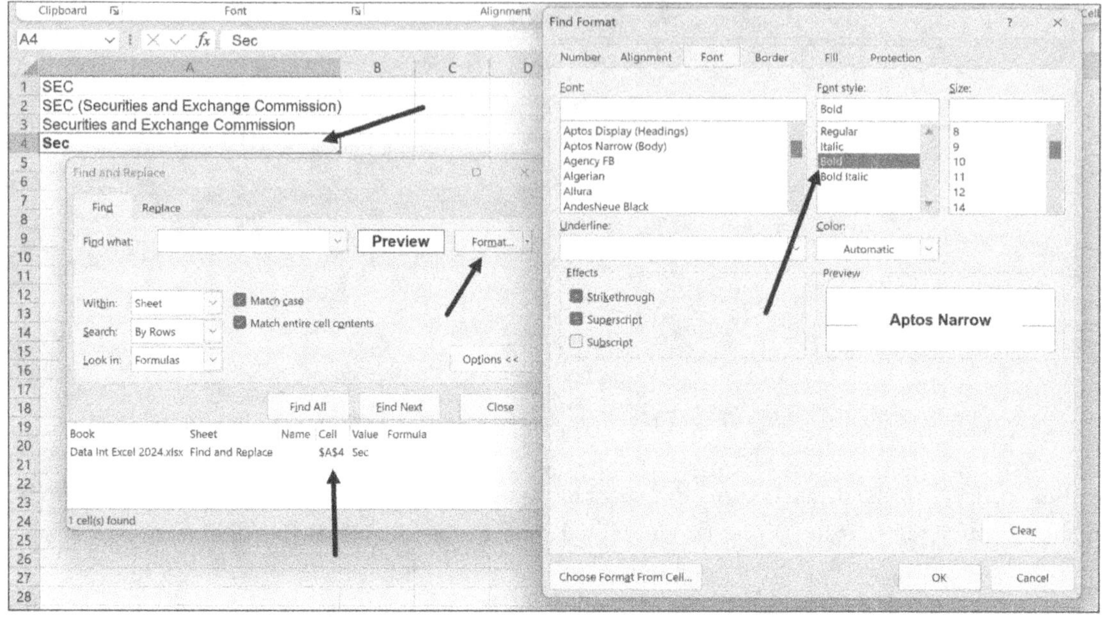

Here you can see that it searched for bolded text for me based on my choice in the Find Format dialogue box. That Preview text in the Find dialogue box shows a sample of the format I told it to search for.

A Caution When Using Find

Be careful once you've used Find after opening Excel, because the Find function in Office tends to default to whatever your last settings were on your last search.

So especially if you use any of the special options to search for something, you need to clear them out if you want to go back to using a basic search. (This happens in Word, too.)

Good news is it resets back to baseline if you close and reopen the program. Not ideal, but if your search just isn't behaving the way you think it should, this is sometimes easier than trying to figure out what setting you need to fix to bring it back to normal.

Replace

Replace lets you find something and also replace it with something else. It's a wonderful, glorious, highly dangerous tool to use.

Here is what the Replace tab of the Find and Replace dialogue box looks like:

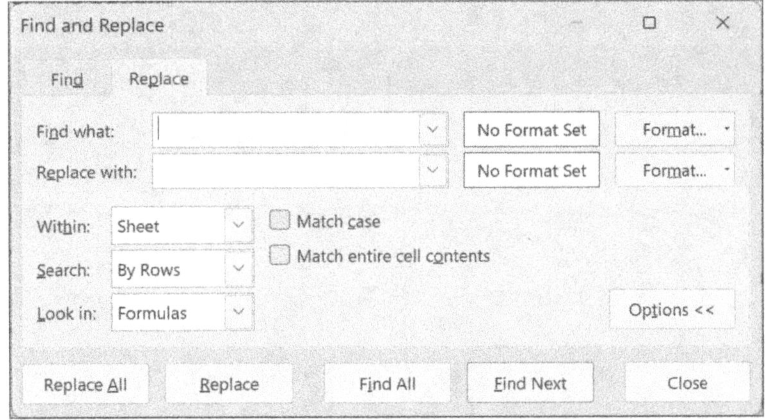

At it's most basic, it's very easy to use. You type what you want to find into the first field, Find What, and then you type what you want to replace it with into the Replace With field.

The problem comes when someone thinks, "Let me replace SEC with Securities and Exchange Commission" and then uses default find parameters. They then end up with "Securities and Exchange Commissionurities and Exchange Commission" where they used to have "Securities and Exchange Commission".

Excel is a tool that only works as well as the user who tells it what to do. And replace is one of those areas where unexpected errors often occur.

To help prevent issues, you can use Find All to see which fields will get changed before you make any replacements.

Or you can use Find Next to go to the next cell where a replacement will be made and only click on Replace if you're sure you want to change that value.

I would also recommend using all of the tricks we discussed above with Find to control your results.

Only use Replace All with extreme caution. And if you do use it, be sure to look through your results before you move on. Replace is one of those areas in Excel where you can irretrievably break your data if you're not careful.

For example, let's say I wasn't careful in our example above, and replaced "SEC" with "Securities and Exchange Commission" in my worksheet without any find constraints. I was then in a hurry to get to lunch and closed and saved without checking the result.

You can't just reverse "Securities and Exchange Commission (Securities and Exchange Commissionurities and Exchange Commission)" by using Replace again. You'd end up with "SEC (SECurities and Exchange Commission)".

Now, that's a pretty obvious error to spot and correct. Where it gets really painful is someone replacing "he" with "she" or something basic like that where maybe some entries already were she and become sshe, or where there were other words that used "he" like "hear" that become "shear". So ALWAYS check the results if you use Replace, and only use it with care.

Remove Duplicates

Remove Duplicates does exactly what it sounds like it does—it looks at your data and removes the duplicates, so that you're left with a list of only the unique values or combination of values.

I use Remove Duplicates all the time. It's an easy way to create a list of unique entries from a column of data. It can also remove duplicate rows of information if those exist in your data table.

Let's look at a couple examples.

Here is a single column of data that spans six hundred rows and has repeating values:

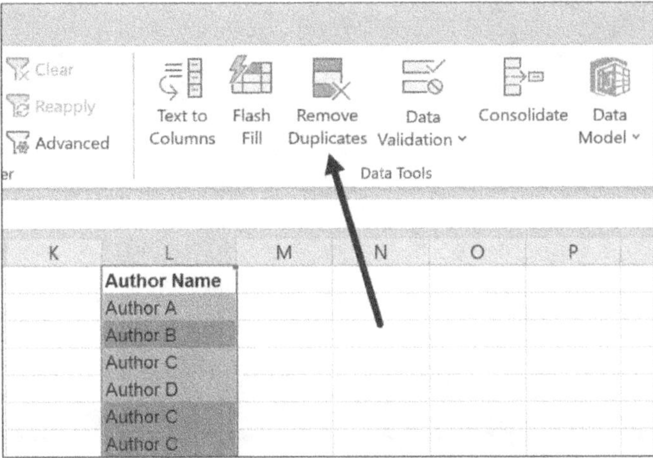

I want to know the unique author names in this column. I could apply the filter option to the column if I was just curious to see approximately how many there are, but if I need to use that list elsewhere, then Remove Duplicates is the way to get it.

To do this, select the column with your data, go to the Data Tools section of the Data tab, and click on the Remove Duplicates option. (It looks like three stacked cells with an X in the bottom right corner.) That will bring up the Remove Duplicates dialogue box:

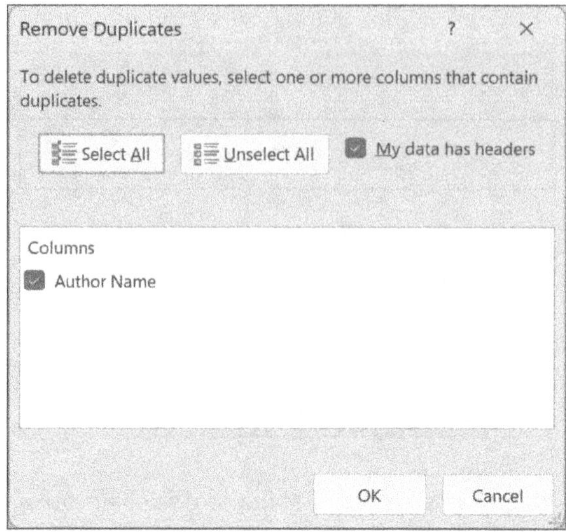

It's very easy when you just have the one column of data. Check or uncheck the My Data Has Headers box at the top so Excel knows whether there's a header row or not, and then click OK.

If you tell Excel there's a header row, it will skip that first row. Otherwise, it will include that value when looking for duplicates.

You'll then see something like this where Excel tells you the number of duplicates removed and number of unique values remaining.

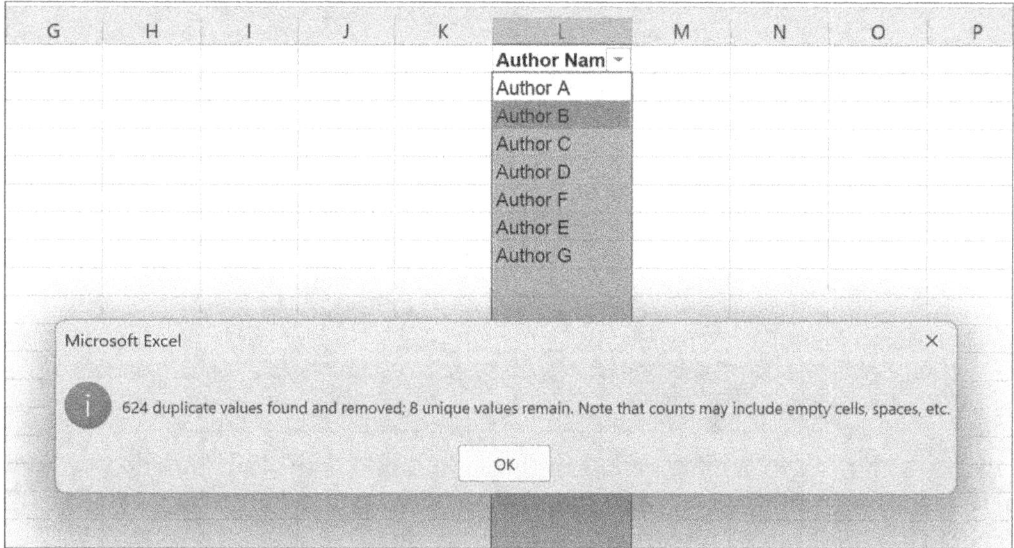

Note that the column I applied it to now has a very small number of unique results left. Ignore the number of unique values it tells you remain, though, since often one of the "unique values" that remains is a blank cell which you really don't want to count.

One thing to be careful of with Remove Duplicates, is that Excel is going to look at the entire contents of your cell to determine whether two cells are identical or not. I recently had a data set where things looked the same on the surface, but weren't. I had "State" in one field and what looked like "State" in another, but the second field had an extra space before the word in one cell and an extra two spaces after it in another. For the purpose of Remove Duplicates, those values were not the same.

So if you are removing duplicates from a very long list, I suggest sorting when you're done, and scanning down the list of values to make sure that you don't have multiples that snuck through because of something like that. (If you know how to use functions, the TRIM function can be applied first to a column of data to remove extra spaces at the start or end of the entries, which will cut down on issues like that.)

While I often use Remove Duplicates for a single column of data, it can also be used for multiple columns. When used that way, it looks for the unique combinations of values across all of the selected columns. That means you may have duplicates of a value in one column, but you won't have duplicates across the entire row.

See, for example, the image below, where you have Author E listed twice in Column E, once for when it occurs with Amazon.com and once for when it occurs with Amazon.it.

If the column(s) of values that you want to apply this to are part of a larger data table, I strongly recommend that you copy and paste the column(s) to a new worksheet first. That's because otherwise you can break your data.

Here is an example:

	A	B	C	D	E	F	G
1	Author Nam	Marketplace	Transaction Type		Author Name	Marketplace	Transaction Type
2	Author E	Amazon.com	Standard		Author E	Amazon.com	Standard
3	Author E	Amazon.it	Standard		Author E	Amazon.it	Standard
4	Author E	Amazon.com	Standard - Paperback		Author F	Amazon.com	Standard - Paperback
5	Author E	Amazon.com	Standard - Paperback		Author G	Amazon.co.uk	Standard - Paperback
6	Author F	Amazon.com	Free - Price Match				Free - Price Match
7	Author F	Amazon.com	Free - Price Match				Free - Price Match
8	Author F	Amazon.com	Free - Price Match				Free - Price Match
9	Author G	Amazon.co.uk	Standard				Standard
10							
11							
12							

In Columns A through C you can see my original data. I copied that data to Columns E through G, selected just Columns E and F, and then removed duplicates.

You can see that after I did that, the values in Columns E and F no longer match to the values in Column G. See how Author F on amazon.com was a Free-Price Match transaction in the original data in Row 6? Now it's in Row 4 and looks like it was a paperback transaction.

This happens because when Excel removes duplicates, it just fills in each new unique combination in the next row available without any consideration for what data is around that.

Excel does sometimes prompt you to make sure you want to do that. Here it did so for a single column within a larger data table:

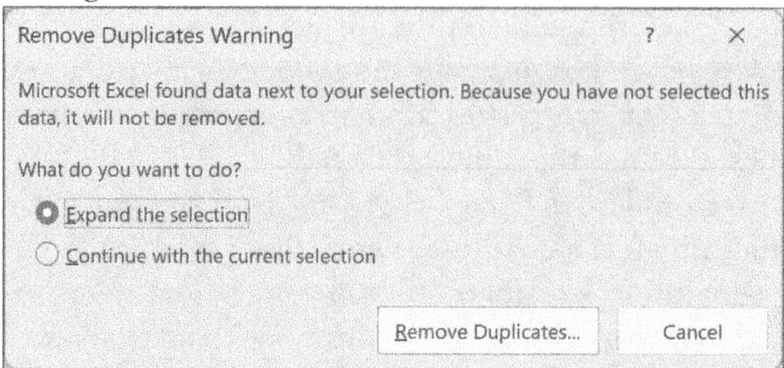

But not always. When I selected two columns from that table, it just went right ahead and removed duplicates without warning me.

This is why I recommend that if you're going to use Remove Duplicates on a data table, that you use it on all columns in that table, or copy the columns you're going to use to a new location first.

Hide or Unhide Columns or Rows

I often hide columns of information that I don't need to see when working with a larger worksheet. Especially if I'm inputting information into a worksheet where I need to enter that information in columns that aren't near each other, say Column B and Column F.

Rather than have to tab or arrow from Column B to Column F for every single row, it's far easier to just hide Columns C through E for a little bit. Another reason to do this is if you build a worksheet that contains columns for calculations that don't need to be visible to all users.

I sometimes will also hide rows of data that I've already verified, for example.

The first step is to select the column(s) or row(s) that you want to hide. Next, right-click and choose Hide from the dropdown menu.

Another option for hide and unhide is to go to the Cells section of the Home tab, and use the Format dropdown. The Visibility section of that dropdown has a secondary dropdown menu called Hide & Unhide that allow you to hide or unhide rows, columns, or sheets.

To unhide column(s) or row(s), though, I select the columns or rows on either side of the ones that were hidden, right-click, and choose Unhide from the dropdown:

If you have multiple sets of hidden columns, or multiple sets of hidden rows, and you want to unhide them all at once, you can click in the top left corner to Select All (or use Ctrl + A), and then right-click on any of the columns or rows in the worksheet, and choose Unhide.

But you can only unhide all columns or all rows at once, you can't do both at the same time.

Another option for hide and unhide is to go to the Cells section of the Home tab and use the Format dropdown. There is a Visibility section that has a secondary dropdown menu called Hide & Unhide.

* * *

One final thing to know about when you hide columns or rows, is that it's not as obvious as filtering. When you filter, the numbering of the rows changes color to let you know.

With Hide, that doesn't happen. Instead you'll just see a very faint double line where the columns or rows are hidden.

And, of course, the column letters or row numbers will also be missing.

Here, for example, I've hidden Columns D through F and Rows 4 through 6:

	A	B	C	G	H	I	J
1	Royalty Da	Author Nam	Marketplace	Currency		Converted Currency	Converted Date
2	2021-01-31	Author A	Amazon.com	USD		$5.70	1/31/2021
3	2021-01-31	Author B	Amazon.com.au	AUD		$0.00	1/31/2021
7	2021-01-31	Author C	Amazon.ca	CAD		$0.00	1/31/2021
8	2021-01-31	Author A	Amazon.com	USD		$5.83	1/31/2021
9	2021-01-31	Author C	Amazon.de	EUR		$0.00	1/31/2021
10	2021-01-31	Author A	Amazon.com	USD		$1.75	1/31/2021
11	2021-01-31	Author A	Amazon.com	USD		$2.74	1/31/2021

Group or Ungroup

There are certain situations where I want to hide column(s) or row(s), but I also want to be able to easily see them, too, as needed. In that case, using group is a better choice than hiding the columns.

For example, the other day I was gathering five years of annual performance data. I had data for each quarter, but I didn't need to see it, I just needed the year-end numbers.

I grouped the columns with the quarterly numbers so I could hide them, while also keeping them easily accessible in case my boss wanted to see the details.

Let's walk through an example. Here's my data:

	A	B	C	D	E	F	G	H
1		Q323	Q423	Q124	Q224	**FY 23-24**	Q324	Q424
2	**Sales**	$1,234.56	$2,354.87	$1,274.96	$4,213.25	**$9,077.64**	$1,237.96	$4,521.87
3	**Costs**	$ 235.79	$ 124.59	$ 546.28	$ 123.69	**$1,030.35**	$ 546.89	$ 364.57
4	**Net**	$ 998.77	$2,230.28	$ 728.68	$4,089.56	**$8,047.29**	$ 691.07	$4,157.30

I want Columns B through E grouped together. To do that, I can select all four columns, go to the Outline section of the Data tab, and click on Group.

Excel places a line above those columns with a minus sign at the end. Clicking on that minus sign hides those columns, and turns the minus sign into a plus sign.

To demonstrate both visible and hidden grouped columns, I went ahead and grouped Columns B through H, too:

	A	F	G	H	I	J
1		FY 23-24	Q324	Q424	Grand Total	
2	**Sales**	**$9,077.64**	$ 1,237.96	$ 4,521.87	**$14,837.47**	
3	**Costs**	**$1,030.35**	$ 546.89	$ 364.57	**$ 1,941.81**	

It's probably a little hard to see in the image above, because the Microsoft folks seem to be going for subtle these days as opposed to easy to see, but there is a line that stretches from where Column B would be to above Column I with a minus sign at the end.

There is also a + sign above Column F.

The minus sign indicates a group of columns that is currently expanded but can be collapsed. The plus sign indicates columns that are currently collapsed/hidden but can be expanded to be visible.

If I click on the minus sign, all of the columns under that line from Column B to Column H will be hidden. If I click on the plus sign over Column F, then the columns that are hidden there (which we know are Columns B through E) will reappear.

Note that there are also numbers on the left-hand side that correspond to each of those lines.

I can click on the 3 to expand all of the groups and make all columns visible, or click on the 1 or 2 to hide the columns in that group.

You may also note a double line between Columns A and F that indicates hidden columns.

To ungroup column(s) or row(s), expand the group, and then select the column(s) or row(s) you want to ungroup, go to the Outline section of the Data tab, and click on Ungroup. If you don't expand the group first, the minus sign along the perimeter will go away, but the column(s) or row(s) will remain hidden, so you'll then need to Unhide them.

If you don't select the grouped column(s) or row(s) first, nothing will be ungrouped when you choose Ungroup.

If you only select a subset of the grouped column(s) or row(s), only they will be ungrouped. Any existing group will be split into two groups on either side of the ungrouped columns or rows.

When columns or rows are grouped, using Tab, arrows keys or Enter will take you to the next visible cell, skipping over those hidden columns or rows.

Subtotals

When you apply Subtotals to a data table, Excel will perform a calculation on your designated fields after every change in the value of a different field. Sum of sales at each change in marketplace, for example.

You have to be careful with this one, though, because the data needs to be sorted properly or your results will be wonky. So, first things first, select the cells in your data table, and sort on the value you want to use. (Marketplace in this case.)

Once your data is sorted properly, go to the Outline section of the Data tab, and click on Subtotal.

This will bring up the Subtotal dialogue box:

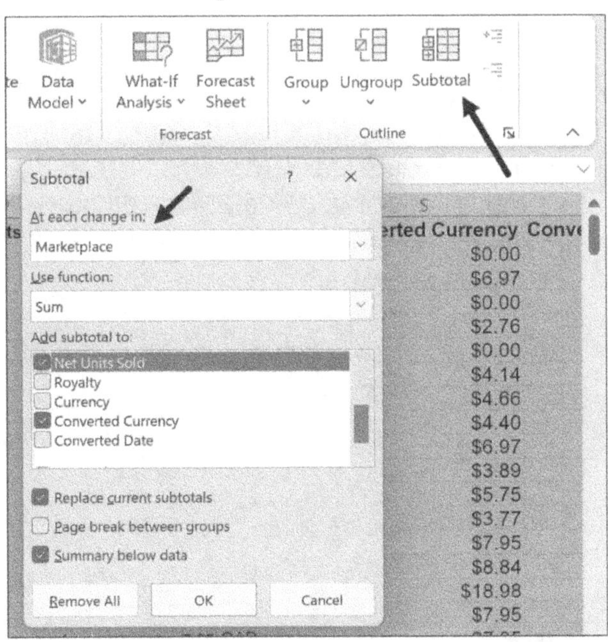

Change the first dropdown to choose the column you sorted on. At each change in the values in that chosen column, Excel will perform the designated calculation.

The next dropdown tells Excel what calculation to perform. The default is Sum, but you can also choose count, average, minimum, maximum, product (multiply all the values), count numbers only, standard deviation, and variance.

Finally, check the boxes next to the columns you want Excel to perform that calculation on. In this case, I want net units sold and converted currency.

Click OK.

Excel will look at the designated column, and each time the value in that column changes it will perform the specified calculation on the values in your chosen column(s).

Here's what I get:

	Royalty Date	Author Name	Marketplace	Transaction Type	Net Units Sold	Royalty	Currency	Converted Currency	Cor
2	2021-01-31	Author C	Amazon.ca	Free - Price Match	3	0.00	CAD	$0.00	
3	2021-01-30	Author A	Amazon.ca	Standard	1	6.97	CAD	$6.97	
4	2021-01-31	Author C	Amazon.ca	Free - Price Match	65	0.00	USD	$0.00	
5	2021-01-31	Author D	Amazon.ca	Standard	1	2.76	USD	$2.76	
6	2021-01-31	Author C	Amazon.ca	Free - Price Match	1	0.00	EUR	$0.00	
7	2021-01-19	Author A	Amazon.ca	Standard	1	4.14	CAD	$4.14	
8	2021-01-19	Author A	Amazon.ca	Standard	1	4.66	CAD	$4.66	
9	2021-01-19	Author A	Amazon.ca	Standard	1	4.40	CAD	$4.40	
10	2021-01-18	Author A	Amazon.ca	Standard	1	6.97	CAD	$6.97	
11	2021-01-15	Author A	Amazon.ca	Standard	1	3.89	CAD	$3.89	
12	2021-01-14	Author A	Amazon.ca	Standard	1	5.75	CAD	$5.75	
13	2021-01-20	Author A	Amazon.ca	Standard - Paperba	1	3.77	CAD	$3.77	
14	2021-01-19	Author A	Amazon.ca	Standard - Paperba	1	7.95	CAD	$7.95	
15	2021-01-27	Author A	Amazon.ca	Standard - Paperba	1	8.84	CAD	$8.84	
16	2021-01-12	Author A	Amazon.ca	Standard - Paperba	1	18.98	CAD	$18.98	
17	2021-01-02	Author A	Amazon.ca	Standard - Paperba	1	7.95	CAD	$7.95	
18	2021-01-12	Author A	Amazon.ca	Standard - Paperba	1	7.95	CAD	$7.95	
19	2021-01-07	Author A	Amazon.ca	Standard - Paperba	1	7.95	CAD	$7.95	
20	2021-01-06	Author A	Amazon.ca	Standard - Paperba	1	7.95	CAD	$7.95	
21			Amazon.ca Total		85			$110.88	
22	2021-01-30	Author C	Amazon.co.uk	Free - Price Match	1	0.00	GBP	$0.00	
23	2021-01-31	Author A	Amazon.co.uk	Standard	1	2.72	GBP	$3.29	

You can see that Row 21 has total values for units sold and converted currency, and that all values for marketplace above that row are Amazon.ca.

By default, all rows of your data as well as the subtotals will be visible.

To collapse your results to just the subtotals, click on the 2 on the left-hand side of the row numbers. You'll then see something like this:

	Royalty Date	Author Name	Marketplace	Transaction Type	Net Units Sold	Royalty	Currency	Converted Currency	Converted Date
21			Amazon.ca Total		85			$110.88	
120			Amazon.co.uk Total		105			$451.74	
620			Amazon.com Total		1,233			$6,176.81	
628			Amazon.com.au Total		7			$49.84	
630			Amazon.com.mx Total		1			$40.25	
632			Amazon.de Total		3			$0.00	
634			Amazon.es Total		1			$2.82	
636			Amazon.fr Total		1			$5.14	
638			Amazon.in Total		1			$0.00	
642			Amazon.it Total		3			$9.34	
643									
644			Grand Total		1440			6846.82	
645									
646									

I recommend always doing that and then scanning the list of bolded entries to make sure they're unique.

This is what that would've looked like if I didn't sort my data first:

	A	B	C	D	E	F
1	Royalty Da	Author Nam	Marketplace	Transaction 1	Net Units S	Royalty
3			Amazon.com Total		1	
5			Amazon.com.au Total		1	
8			Amazon.com Total		66	
10			Amazon.fr Total		1	
12			Amazon.ca Total		3	
14			Amazon.com Total		1	
16			Amazon.de Total		3	
23			Amazon.com Total		7	
25			Amazon.co.uk Total		1	
34			Amazon.com Total		13	
36			Amazon.com.au Total		1	
42			Amazon.com Total		12	

The arrows on the left are pointing at multiple entries for Amazon.com. The arrows on the right are pointing at multiple entries for Amazon.com.au. Something we do not want.

This happens because Excel performs the specified calculation at *each* change in the values in the designated column. If you don't sort your data, Excel can end up creating multiple calculations for the same value.

Remember, Excel is a tool. And it is only as good as the user and the data it is given. Give it bad data, you will get bad results.

Okay, a few more things.

After you collapse your data to just the subtotal rows, you can click on any of the plus signs on the left-hand side to see the detail for that value, or you can click on the 3 to see all of the details again.

Also, the Subtotal dialogue box has a few extra options available at the bottom.

By default the box for Summary Below Data should be checked. That gives you a grand total row for all entries in your data. If you don't want that, uncheck it.

You can also check a box for Replace Current Subtotals to replace any subtotals you have with your new choices.

And if you want each group of results to be on its own page, you can check Page Break Between Groups.

To remove subtotals, I select my data table again, reopen the Subtotal dialogue box, and then click the Remove All option.

Finally, for the extra credit types, you may want to check out the Excel help for subtotals. It will show you how to create subtotals within subtotals. I'm not covering that here because I prefer to work in pivot tables for that sort of thing.

Pivot Tables - Basics

I wrote the first ever Excel Essentials series just so I could teach writers how to use pivot tables, that's how valuable I think they are.

At their most basic, pivot tables (technically spelled PivotTables by the Office folks) are a quick and easy way to take a big table of data and summarize it. You don't have to worry about how things are sorted or which order your columns are in or writing the correct formula, you can just throw it all in a pivot table and Excel will do the hard work for you.

But there is a lot to know to use them effectively.

Now. A few things to keep in mind:

Pre-Prep

You may need to do a little work with your data first to clean it up and standardize it. For example, Excel can't tell that CO and Colorado are the same thing, so will treat them as different values. You'll want to take a copy of your data and fix issues like that before you start using a pivot table to summarize your results.

You should also make sure that your columns are formatted properly so that numbers are seen by Excel as numbers and dates are seen as dates. (See the quick tips chapter for how to fix dates when working with pivot tables.)

Also, remove any subtotals or grand totals, and make sure that each column of your data has a header in the first row of the table. (For me, I prefer that this is also the first row of the worksheet.)

And make sure that each row of data is complete in and of itself. You want to be working with a table of data not data formatted as a report.

Dynamic Nature

Also, be careful where you choose to build a pivot table. Pivot tables are dynamic. The amount of space they take up varies depending on your data and the choices you make about what to include in the table.

If you put a pivot table in a worksheet that has other information, you run a risk that the pivot table will overwrite that other data.

Pivot tables build to the right and down, so if you do put a pivot table in a worksheet that has other information in it, always add that pivot table to the right of and/or below your existing information.

And if you are ever tempted to add notes around an existing pivot table (like I sometimes do), understand that if you update the table you could either accidentally delete your notes, or the data in your pivot table could move so that it no longer matches up with your notes.

(This is one reason why if you use a formula and try to reference values in a pivot table it looks so weird. Excel can't just reference a cell like with normal data entries, it has to instead reference how the value in that cell was built.)

Okay. Now that we've gotten through the preliminaries, let's build one.

Insert

Assuming your header row is in the first row of your worksheet, select the columns that have your data, or use Select All. If your data table doesn't start at the top of the worksheet, then select all of the cells in your table, being sure to include the header row.

Next, go to the Tables section of the Insert tab, and click on the PivotTable image.

If you accidentally click on the dropdown arrow, the option you want is From Table/ Range. (For the level of expertise I expect you to have if you're reading this book, I really do not recommend working with data in another workbook or from another source. It's too easy to break the link between your workbook and that external data source, so we're not going to go there.)

You should now see a PivotTable From Table or Range dialogue box:

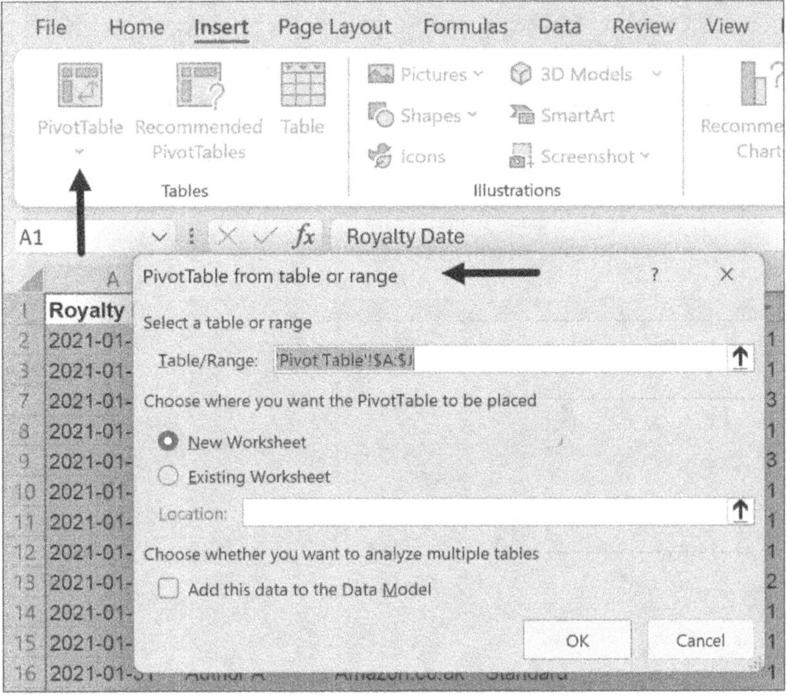

Usually, I just click OK here, because I already selected my data range, I don't work with data models, and I am fine with putting my pivot table in a new worksheet.

However, sometimes I do click on the option for Existing Worksheet instead, and then click somewhere to the right of the data in my current worksheet, to keep the data and the pivot table together in that same worksheet. I usually do that in workbooks where I have a lot of pivot tables I'm going to build to make sure I know the source of the data in each table.

At this point, you may see an error message if any of the cells in the first row of your selected data are blank. That's because Excel needs there to be something to label each column of data with.

If that happens, close out, and either add labels to the blank cells in the first row of your selected cell range, or delete any blank columns in your cell range.

If a blank column header isn't the issue, then you may need to fix your referenced cell range to make sure you captured the header row. Once you've fixed whatever the issue is, go through the above steps again.

By default, Excel will insert your pivot table starting in Cell A3 of a new worksheet:

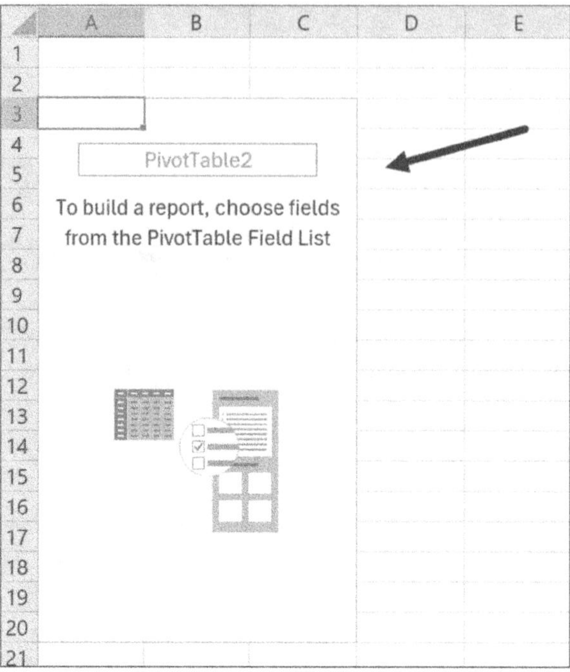

There won't be an actual pivot table there, though, until you tell Excel which fields to use. It just shows you that it's ready to put a pivot table there.

You should also see a PivotTable Fields task pane on the right-hand side of the workspace, as well as two new menu tabs, PivotTable Analyze and Design:

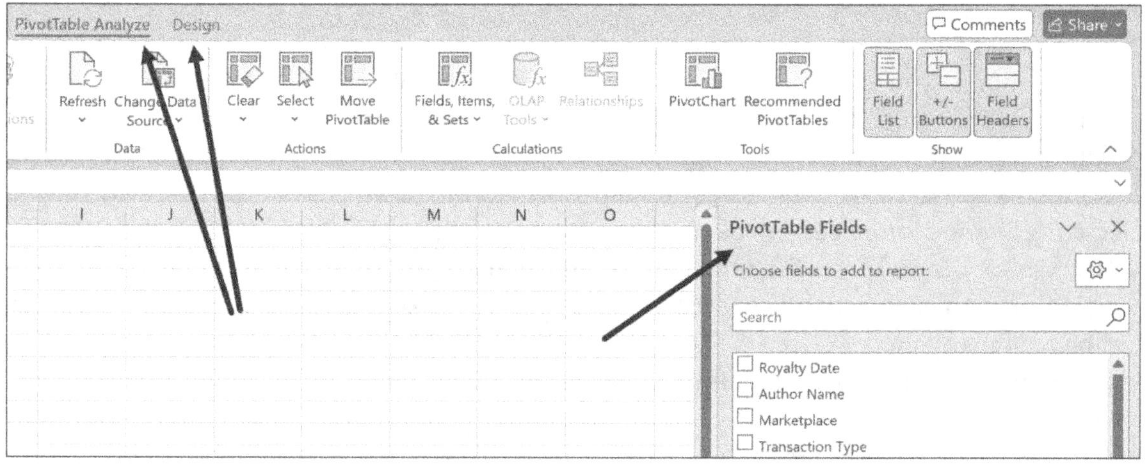

The task pane and tabs will be visible by default any time you're clicked onto a pivot table, but will go away when you click elsewhere in your worksheet or workbook. So to get them back if they ever disappear, just click onto your pivot table.

Build

The way you build a pivot table is by using the PivotTable Fields task pane on the right-hand side of the workspace.

Here is the full task pane:

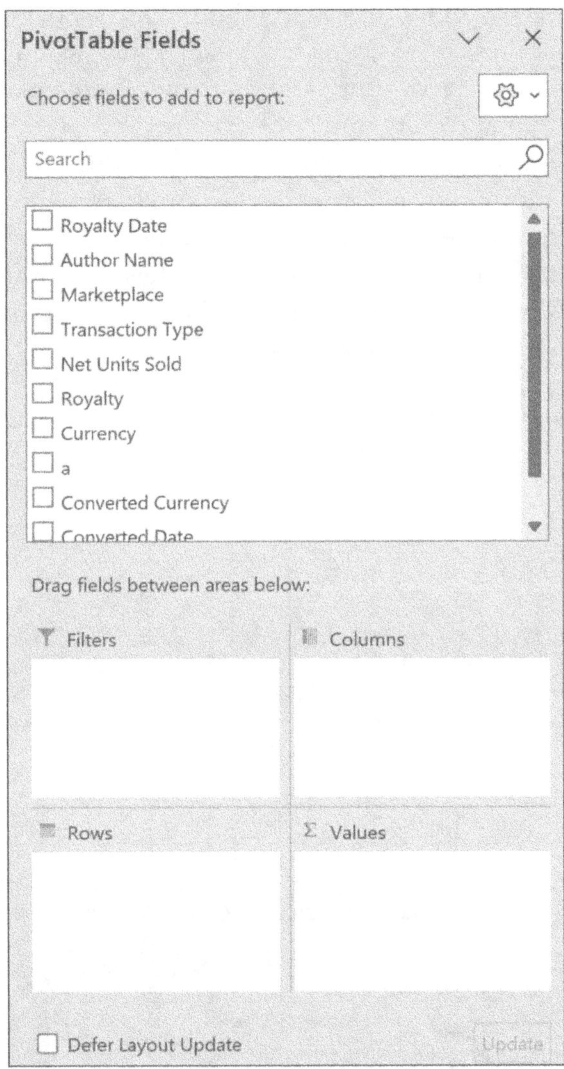

The top section shows all of your available fields. At the start, that will be the names for each column of data you included. (Later it might include extra date-related fields or formulas if you add any.)

The bottom section has four parts: Filters, Columns, Rows, and Values. This is where you put each field to build the table.

The fields you place in Columns and/or Rows will provide the data labels you'll have either across the top (columns) or down the side (rows) of the table. Values is where you put the field(s) you're going to use for calculations.

Filters is for fields you aren't going to use in your columns, rows, or values sections, that you still want to use to narrow down the information displayed in the pivot table.

Let's walk through some examples to see how this works. We're going to use the same data I've been using throughout these books, which contains about six hundred lines of book sales data that includes fields for date of sale, author name, marketplace, type of transaction, number of units sold, currency, royalty, and converted royalty.

First, let's build a table that shows units sold for each author.

My Values field, what I want to use for my calculation, is going to be Units Sold. And then either my Row or Column field needs to be Author Name.

To do this, I simply left-click and drag each of those fields from the top of the PivotTable Fields task pane down to the appropriate section in the bottom of the task pane. I went with the Row section for Author Name because it looked better to me:

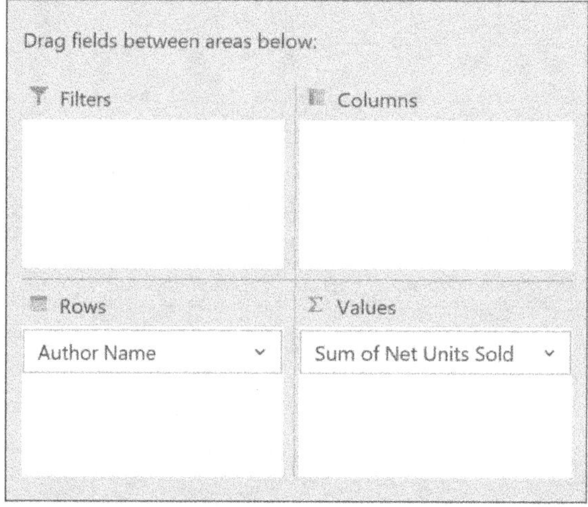

Another option for adding a field to a section, is to right-click on the field name in the top section, and then choose where to place the field from the dropdown menu:

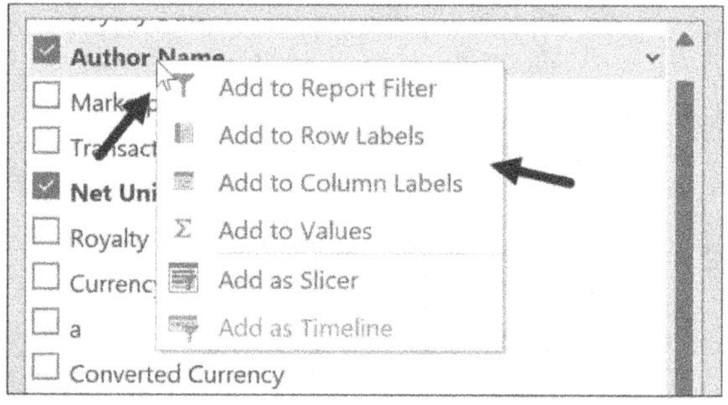

Either way works.

(In older versions of Excel you could also drag the field to the table in the worksheet, but that's no longer available by default. This is why it's always good to know at least two ways to do things in Excel. That way if they change one of the two, you can still use the other method.)

Okay.

Here is the pivot table that created:

	A	B	C
1			
2			
3	**Row Labels** ▾	**Sum of Net Units Sold**	
4	Author C	90	
5	Author E	4	
6	Author B	20	
7	Author A	1242	
8	Author D	80	
9	Author F	3	
10	Author G	1	
11	(blank)		
12	**Grand Total**	**1440**	
13			

Excel automatically built the table as I placed each field.

Now let's make this more complex and add in Marketplace. I want to see how many units each author sold in each marketplace.

I also want to be able to see total sales by marketplace and total sales by author, which means one has to be in the Rows section and one has to be in the Columns section, they can't be together.

Because it was easy, I added Marketplace into the Columns section:

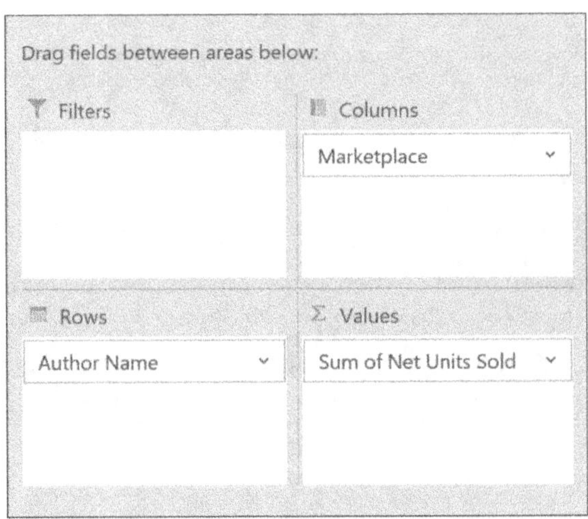

This is what that pivot table looks like:

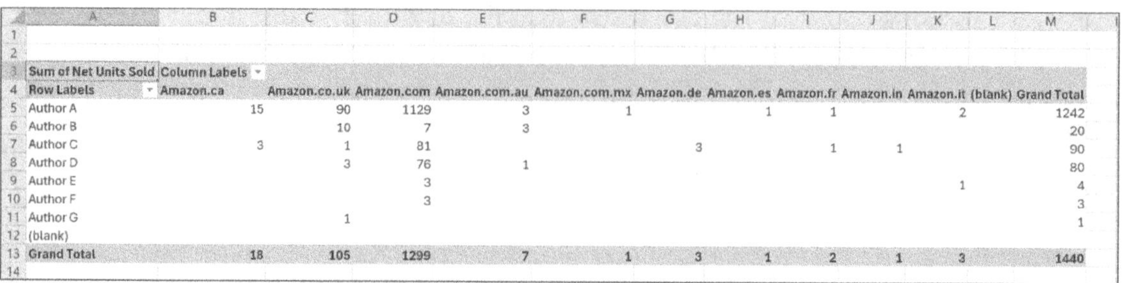

| Sum of Net Units Sold | Column Labels | | | | | | | | | | | |
Row Labels	Amazon.ca	Amazon.co.uk	Amazon.com	Amazon.com.au	Amazon.com.mx	Amazon.de	Amazon.es	Amazon.fr	Amazon.in	Amazon.it	(blank)	Grand Total
Author A	15	90	1129	3	1		1	1		2		1242
Author B		10	7	3								20
Author C	3	1	81			3		1	1			90
Author D		3	76	1								80
Author E			3							1		4
Author F			3									3
Author G		1										1
(blank)												
Grand Total	18	105	1299	7	1	3	1	2	1	3		1440

I can easily see how many units each author sold in each marketplace, as well as totals for each author and totals for each marketplace.

Not bad for clicking and dragging three field names into place, huh?

Filter Pivot Table Data

Now let's apply a filter. To do that, add the field you want to use as your filter to the Filters area of the PivotTable Fields task pane.

For this example, I used Transaction Type:

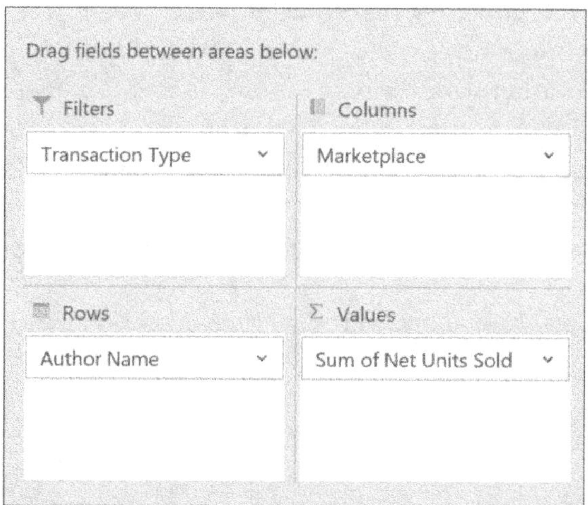

Doing that adds a dropdown menu above the pivot table that you can then use to change what information is displayed in the pivot table itself.

Here, for example, I limited the results to Free-Price Match. Now the pivot table only shows results for transactions that were free price match transactions:

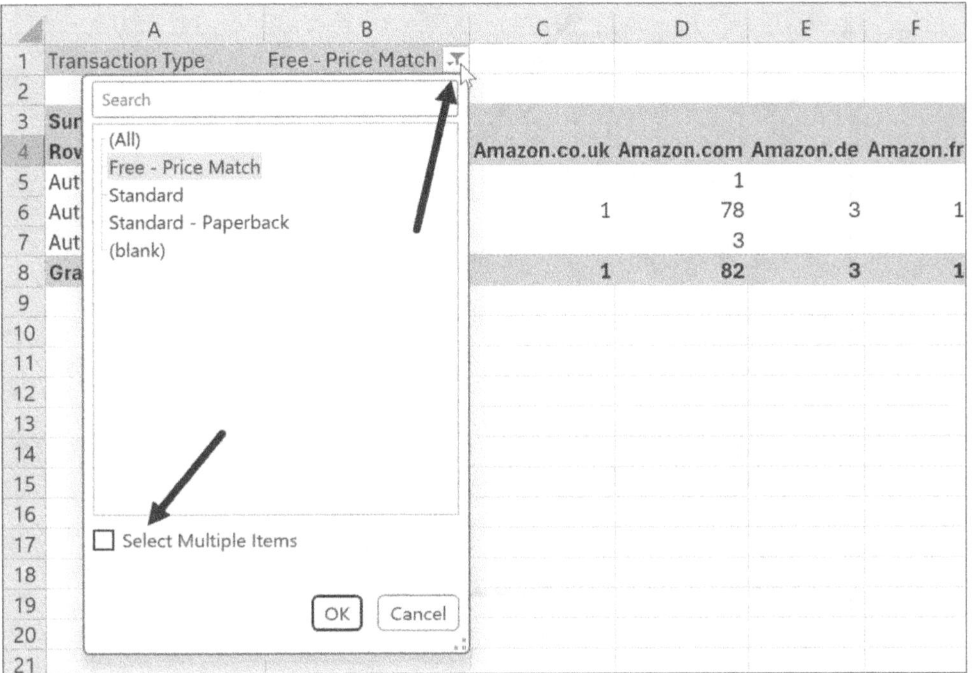

The filter dropdown works just like when you filter columns in a normal worksheet.

Click on the dropdown arrow or funnel on the right-hand edge of the cell (see below) that displays the current filter to see the dropdown.

Check the box for Select Multiple Items at the bottom of the dropdown so you can then check and uncheck the boxes to select the values you want to filter by. The default is All, so if you only want one or two values, uncheck that box for All to unselect all values first, and then check the ones you want.

You can also use the search field to narrow your results.

When you select a single value to filter by, like I did above, Excel will show that value, as you can see in Cell B1 of the pivot table we just built.

If you use multiple criteria, though, it will just say Multiple Items instead. In a situation like that, it may be better to use a Slicer, which is discussed in the next chapter.

Filter Values in Rows or Columns

There will be times when you want to use a field for your rows or columns sections, but you also want to limit which of those values display in the pivot table. You can't put that field in the Filters section, because you're using it in the Rows or Columns section already, and Excel won't let you do both.

Fortunately, you can still filter those values. Just click on the arrow next to Row Labels or Column Labels in your pivot table to bring up a filter dropdown menu for that field:

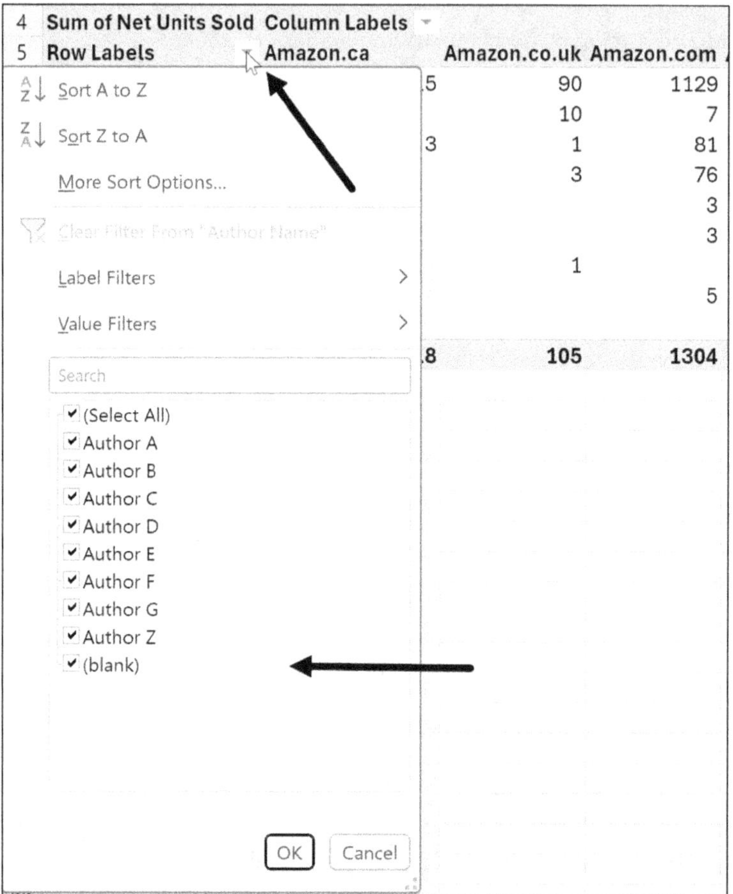

At that point it's just working with filters again.

If you have multiple fields in your rows or columns sections and want to filter on one of them, click on one of the values in the table for that field first, and *then* click on the arrow next to Row Labels or Column Labels.

Multiple Fields in a Section

You can use multiple fields in the Columns, Rows, Filters, and/or Values sections. To have multiple levels, just drag more than one field to that section.

For Columns and Rows, order matters. It's like with sorting. Put the field you want to be primary on top, and list secondary, tertiary, etc. fields below that in order of priority. Values for the primary field will only show up once. Values for the other fields can repeat.

Here, for example, I have a pivot table with Transaction Type in the first position and Author Name listed second:

		Amazon.in
6	**Free - Price Match**	
7	Author C	1
8	Author F	
9	Author B	
10	**Standard**	
11	Author A	
12	Author D	
13	Author B	
14	Author C	
15	Author E	
16	Author G	
17	**Standard - Paperback**	
18	Author A	
19	Author D	
20	Author E	
21	Author B	
22	**Grand Total**	1

Note how you only see each transaction type listed once, but Author B is listed three times, once per transaction type.

For Values, the order just dictates which one will be displayed first in the table. Here I have Net Units Sold in the first position and Converted Currency in the second position:

	A	B	C
1			
2	Transaction Type (Multiple Items)		
3			
4	**Row Labels**	**Sum of Net Units Sold**	**Sum of Converted Currency**
5	Author A	1242	$6,415.27
6	Author B	19	$59.52
7	Author C	3	$8.98
8	Author D	80	$305.28
9	Author E	4	$17.55
10	Author G	1	$0.42
11	(blank)	1440	
12	**Grand Total**	**2789**	**$6,807.02**
13			

For Filters the order doesn't matter.

One final note here. Be very careful if you have multiple fields in more than one section of your pivot table. It can be done, but it can also get really messy really fast. Always ask yourself if what you've done is the best way to present this information. Maybe two tables is a better choice.

Expand/Collapse Fields

When you have more than one field in a column or row in a pivot table, you can expand and collapse the levels to show or hide the detail below. This can be done one entry at a time, or across all entries at once.

It's easy enough to hide or show the detail for one particular entry, you just click on the plus or minus sign to the left of the label. Plus expands, minus collapses (hides).

Here I've put Author Name on top and Marketplace underneath in the Rows section, and then clicked on the negative sign next to Author A to collapse that detail.

	Sum of Net Units Sold	Column Labels								
		<12/10/2020	<12/10/2020 Total	2020	2020 Total	2021				2021 Total
	Row Labels	<12/10/2020		Qtr4		Qtr1	Qtr2	Qtr3	Qtr4	
6	Author A			1	1	880	114	122	120	1236
7	Author B					17	3			20
8	Amazon.co.uk					10				10
9	Amazon.com					4	3			7
10	Amazon.com.au					3				3
11	Author C					90				90
12	Amazon.ca					3				3
13	Amazon.co.uk					1				1
14	Amazon.com					81				81
15	Amazon.de					3				3
16	Amazon.fr					1				1
17	Amazon.in					1				1
18	Author D			1	1	50	16	8	5	79
19	Amazon.co.uk					3				3
20	Amazon.com			1	1	46	16	8	5	75
21	Amazon.com.au					1				1

Author A now has a plus sign I can click if I want to expand that part of the table again. Authors B, C, and D still have a minus sign and show all of their related marketplace details.

To collapse or expand all entries for a specific level at once, right-click on one of the values (Author A, Author B, etc.), go to the Expand/Collapse option in the dropdown menu, and then use the secondary dropdown menu to make your choice.

For each level you have in a pivot table, the bottom of that dropdown will show an option to expand or collapse to that level:

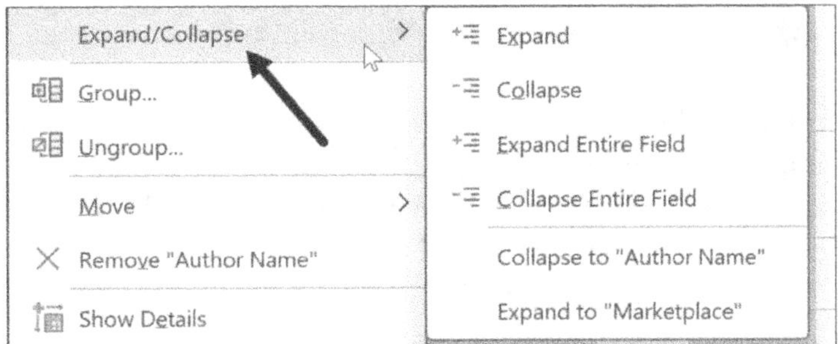

Expand Entire Field shows all of the detail for all values at that level in the table; Collapse Entire Field hides all the details for all values at that level.

Collapse and Expand just collapse or expand for that item at that level in the pivot table.

(I usually just end up playing around with the different choices when I need this rather than memorizing it.)

Remove a Field

The easiest way to remove a field that you were using to build your pivot table is to just uncheck the box next to its name in the PivotTable Fields task pane.

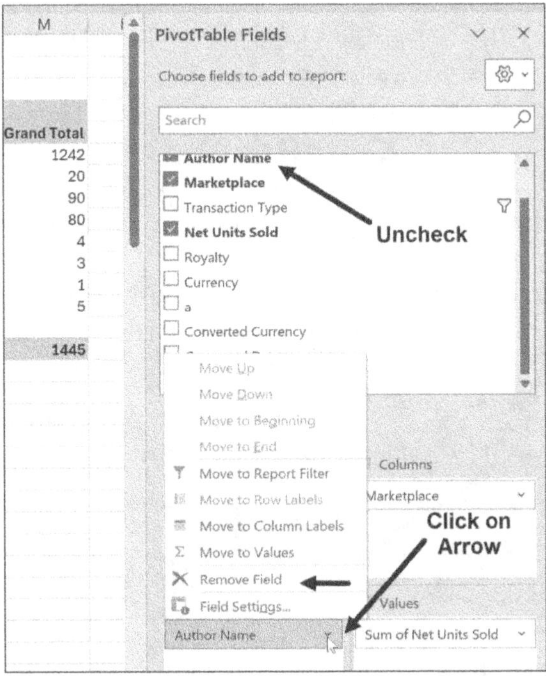

You can also left-click on the arrow next to the name of the field in the bottom section, and choose Remove from the dropdown menu.

This is the best approach if you were using that field more than once in the table (which we'll discuss later).

Another option is to right-click on a value in the pivot table itself, and then choose "Remove [Field Name]" from there.

If you were using that field as a filter, it is best to unfilter first before you remove the field, or the data in your table may remain filtered.

Move a Field

To move a field to a different section of your pivot table (Rows to Columns, Columns to Rows, Filters to Rows, etc.), you can left-click on the field name in the bottom section of the task pane and drag it to the section where you want it.

You can also left-click on the arrow for that field in the bottom section of the task pane to choose a new location from that dropdown menu.

Or you can right-click on the field name in the top of the task pane, and choose a location from that dropdown menu.

If you already had the field in a section, Excel will remove it from that prior section to place it in the new one.

(Also, note that Undo is a little tricky here. If you move a field, realize that was a mistake, and want to move it back, you will probably need to click into your worksheet first before Undo will work.)

Sort Results

You can sort the data in your pivot table. For example, I often want my largest values in my grand total column at the top.

To sort, right-click on a value in the column you want to sort by, go to the Sort option, and in the secondary dropdown menu choose the type of sort you want:

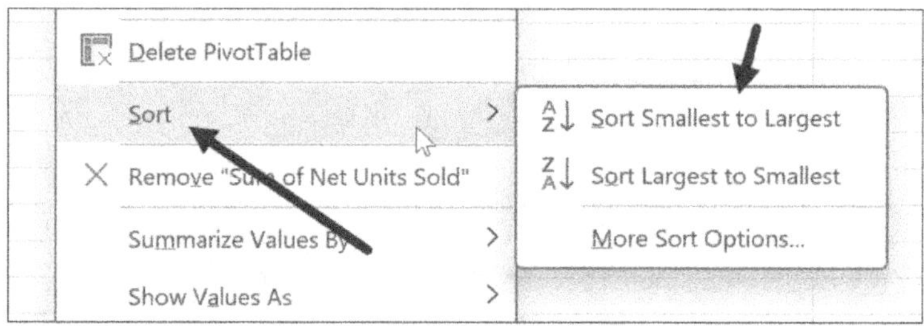

The nice thing about sorting in a pivot table is that all of your values stay together. You don't have to worry about breaking your data if you don't select the whole table first.

If you sort your column values, the sort will automatically be a left to right sort, but if you want a left to right sort for the calculated values in your table, you need to use More Sort Options in the Sort secondary dropdown. That will bring up the Sort by Value dialogue box, where you can then tell Excel you want a left to right sort:

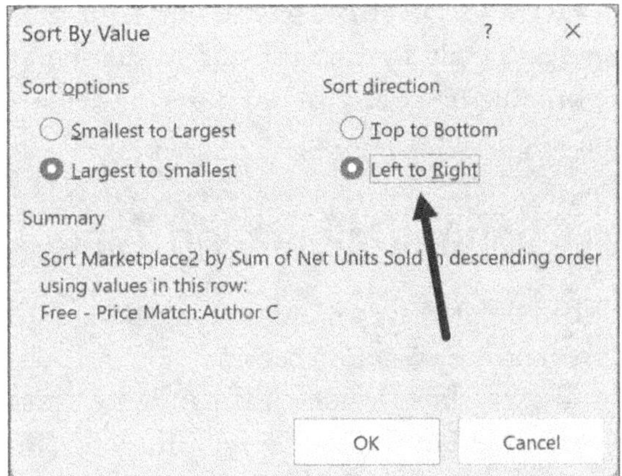

Move Column or Row Entries In the Pivot Table

You can also manually rearrange the column or row entries in your pivot table.

To do so, right-click on a value that you want to move, go down to the Move option, and then use the secondary dropdown menu to choose whether to move the value to the Beginning, the End, up one space, or down one space:

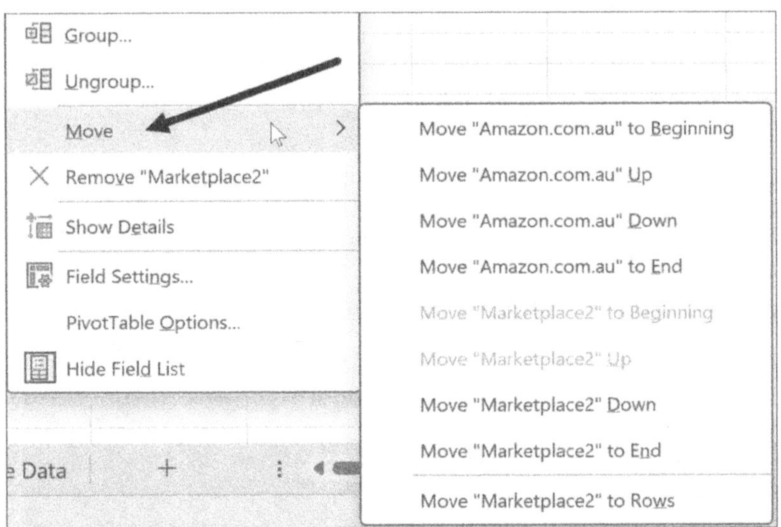

When working with values in the Columns section, think of Up as meaning "to the left" and Down as meaning "to the right".

It can help to think through the ultimate order you want your values in before you start doing this. For example, it's easier to move a field to the beginning and then down one, rather than move it up five times.

And sometimes you can save a lot of effort by moving your fields to the beginning or end in the order that puts the one you truly want at the end in that end position last.

We'll discuss a few more organizing your table options in the next chapter, but for now let's cover some more basics that you need to know.

Change Calculation Type

One of the issues I run into often with pivot tables and my data, is that Excel defaults to count when I drag my number fields into the Values section.

Fortunately, Excel will still sum those values if I ask it to, and it also does indicate what calculation it is performing on a field in the Value section of the PivotTable Fields task pane. (If you look above, you'll see that it was summing net units sold, for example.)

If you ever need to change the type of calculation, one option is to click on the dropdown arrow for that field in the Values section, and then choose Value Field Settings from the dropdown menu:

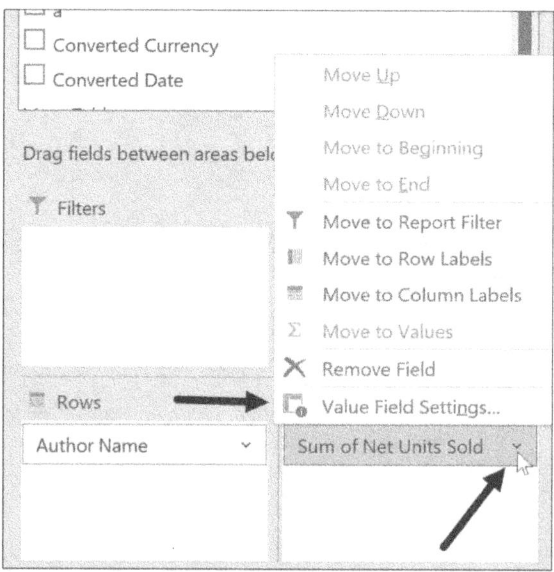

That will open the Value Field Settings dialogue box:

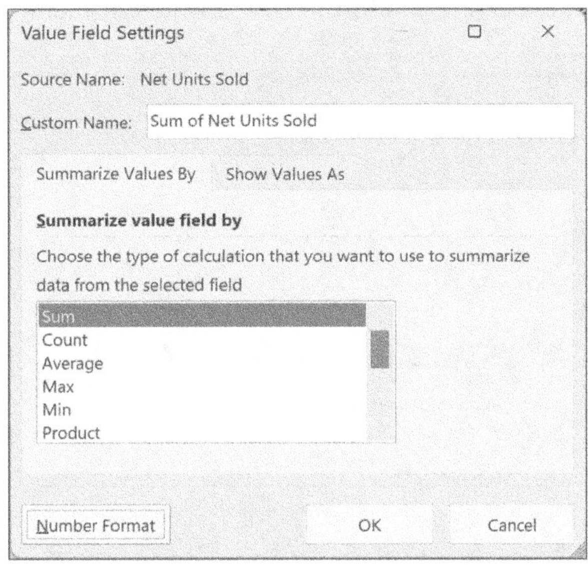

In the Summarize Value Field By section of the dialogue box, you will then see a list of the possible calculations that Excel can perform. It's the standard list of Sum, Count, Average, Max (maximum), Min (minimum), Product, Count Numbers, standard deviation, and variance that you will see throughout Excel. Just click on the option you want and then click OK. (I usually also format my cells at this point in time. We'll talk about that in a moment.)

When you change the calculation type, the Custom Name field will update accordingly.

Another way to choose the calculation type is to right-click on a calculated value in the pivot table itself, and then use the secondary dropdown menu for Summarize Values By:

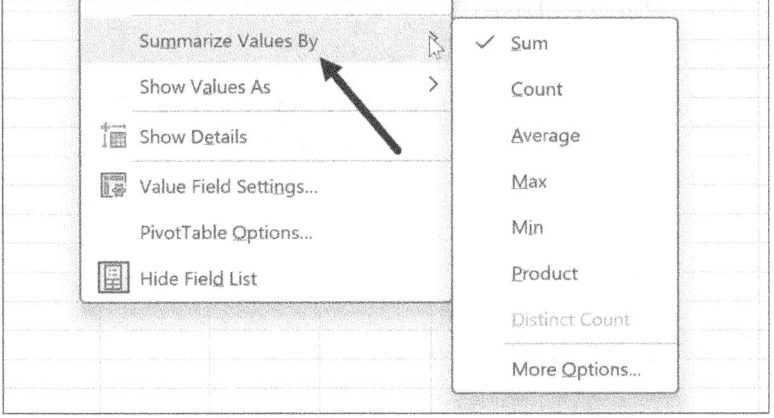

That approach doesn't require opening the dialogue box, so is pretty handy to use. It is a more limited list, but usually I just want Count or Sum, so it would work for me, I'm just used to the other way.

Excel also has a Show Values As option in that dropdown menu or as a tab in the Value Field Settings dialogue box:

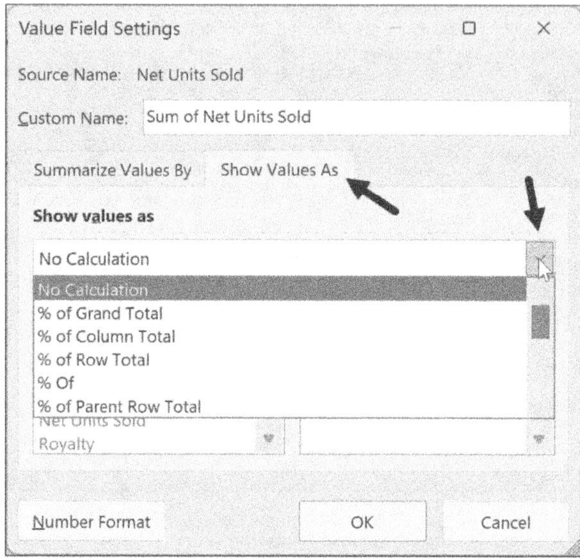

By default, that is going to show as No Calculation, which basically means it will display the result of the calculation you chose for Summarize Values By. (Sum, Count, etc.) But if you click on the dropdown arrow in the dialogue box, or use the secondary menu from the pivot table, you can choose to have Excel show your result as a percentage calculation, a difference from some value, a running total, a rank, or an index:

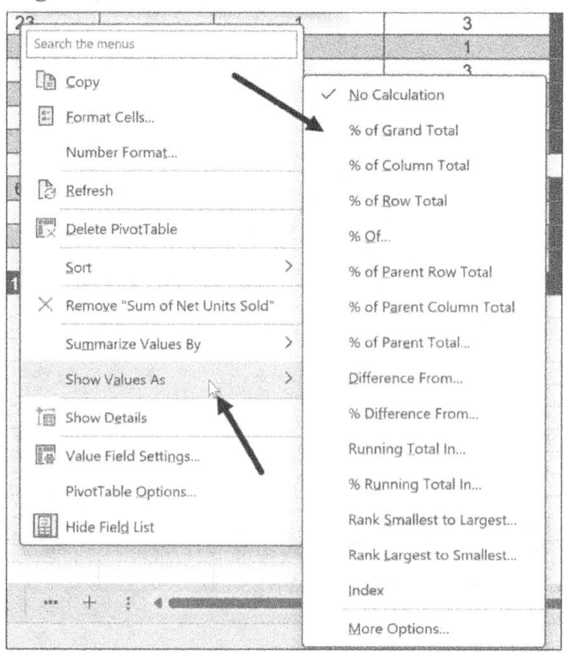

For example, I am sometimes not as interested in the number of units sold by an author in a marketplace as I am in what *percent* of sales that author represents in each marketplace. I have some marketplaces (the U.S.) with much larger absolute sales numbers, so sales in other markets (like France) look small in comparison no matter what. But it's valuable to know if Author A is 60% of sales in both of those markets or only one of them. That can help me make advertising decisions for each market.

The first step if you're going to do this, is to choose the correct calculation for Summarize Values By. (Sum or Count, usually.) After you do that, go to Show Values As, and pick the type of calculation you want displayed.

Here is that same data from our author and marketplace pivot table above, but now set to show the percentage of the column total instead of units:

	A	B	C	D	E	F	G	H
1								
2								
3								
4	Sum of Net Units Sold	Column Labels						
5	Row Labels	Amazon.ca	Amazon.co.uk	Amazon.com	Amazon.com.au	Amazon.com.mx	Amazon.de	Amazon.es
6	Author A	83.33%	85.71%	86.91%	42.86%	100.00%	0.00%	100.00%
7	Author B	0.00%	9.52%	0.54%	42.86%	0.00%	0.00%	0.00%
8	Author C	16.67%	0.95%	6.24%	0.00%	0.00%	100.00%	0.00%
9	Author D	0.00%	2.86%	5.85%	14.29%	0.00%	0.00%	0.00%
10	Author E	0.00%	0.00%	0.23%	0.00%	0.00%	0.00%	0.00%
11	Author F	0.00%	0.00%	0.23%	0.00%	0.00%	0.00%	0.00%
12	Author G	0.00%	0.95%	0.00%	0.00%	0.00%	0.00%	0.00%
13	(blank)	0.00%	0.00%	0.00%	0.00%	0.00%	0.00%	0.00%
14	Grand Total	100.00%	100.00%	100.00%	100.00%	100.00%	100.00%	100.00%

It's a little hard to read because of all of the 0.00% entries, but if you can wade through that, you can see that Author A tends to be the majority of sales in each marketplace, but is not in Australia (AU) and Germany (DE). That would be worth exploring more. (And we can fix that formatting to make this easier to read.)

Note that it is possible in the Values section to add the same field more than once. So you can, for example, show the sum or count value AND a % value.

Here, for example, I have actual number of units sold by author as well as the percent of the total:

	A	B	C
1			
2			
3	Row Labels	Units Sold	Percent of Units Sold
4	Author C	90	6.25%
5	Author E	4	0.28%
6	Author B	20	1.39%
7	Author A	1242	86.25%
8	Author D	80	5.56%
9	Author F	3	0.21%
10	Author G	1	0.07%
11	(blank)		0.00%
12	Grand Total	1440	100.00%
13			

(I took out marketplace because it would have been way too busy and also renamed the columns to something friendlier and formatted them to center the values.)

A Caution

If you ever build a pivot table that has more than one different field in the Values section, be careful about using different calculations for each column. If you put a column that has a count of values next to another that has a sum of values next to another that has an average, it is possible someone will mistake the type of calculation being performed in one of those columns. You can do it, no one will stop you, just step back and ask yourself how someone who didn't build the table and is maybe in a hurry is going to interpret it. This is when changing your column labels will really be useful.

Rename a Field

Speaking of. You can rename a field that you're using in your pivot table by clicking on the cell that has the field name in it and then changing the name in the formula bar. If you try to use the original field name, though, you will get an error message that the name already exists. So if I want to rename "Sum of Net Units Sold" which was built using the "Net Units Sold" field, I can use "Units Sold", no problem, but I can't use "Net Units Sold" again.

You can also change the name by going to the Active Field section of the PivotTable Analyze tab, but that takes more effort.

Format Values

Another issue I almost always encounter with pivot tables is that the numbers won't be formatted the way I want them to be. For example, my currency values never seem to be formatted as currency by default.

You can technically just select the visible cells in the table, go to the Home tab, and use the formatting options there like you would with any other cell in Excel, but I do not recommend that. Because the formatting you apply to those cells will not carry through if the table updates.

The better way to format your values is to use the Value Field Settings dialogue box. (Right click on the field name in the Values section and choose Value Field Settings from the dropdown to open it.)

From the dialogue box, click on the bottom left corner where it says Number Format. That will bring up the Format Cells dialogue box, where you can then choose the number format you want applied to that field. Click OK to close the Format Cells dialogue box, and then OK to close the Value Field Settings dialogue box when you're done.

Here, for example, I've changed the formatting of the percentage values to not have two decimal places, which makes it a little easier to read:

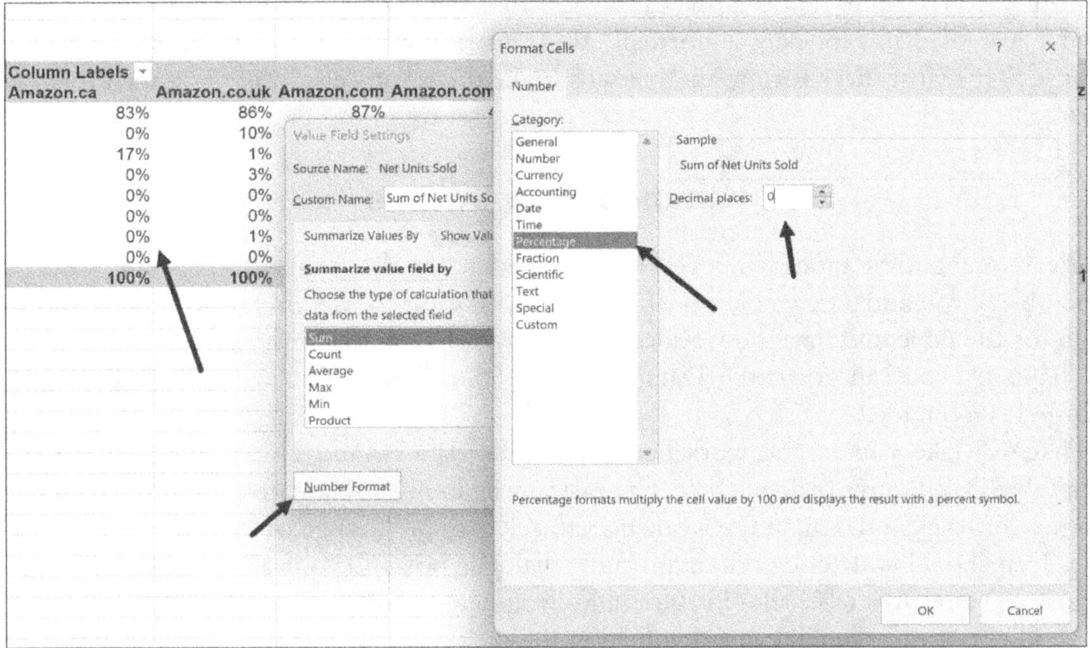

(I made the change and then reopened both dialogue boxes so you could see what each one looks like.)

Refresh Pivot Table

Your pivot table will not automatically recalculate everything when you add new data to the original data source. To update your table, go to the Data section of the PivotTable Analyze tab, and you'll see Refresh:

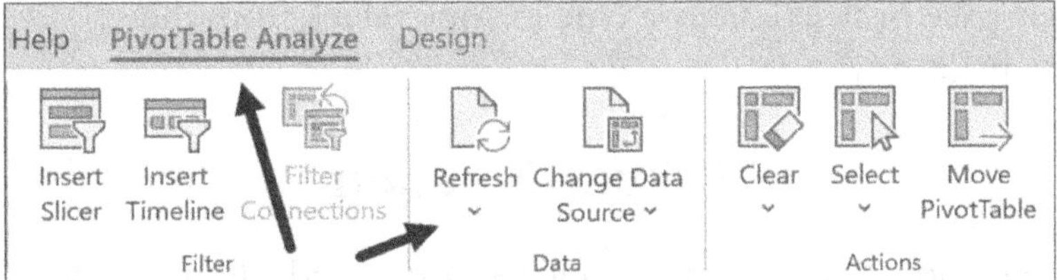

Click on the image there and your table should update to show your changes.

You can also choose Refresh All from the dropdown there, and that will update all pivot tables in the workbook.

There are control shortcuts for this, too, but I never use them. They are Alt + F5 and Ctrl + Alt + F5, respectively.

(One thing to be careful of with Refresh is that it can undo some of your custom formatting, so try to finalize your data before you get fancy with the formatting. Microsoft support seems to think that the PivotTable Options choices can fix this, but it didn't for me when I just tried it. Honestly, I normally don't need pretty formatting of my pivot tables because they're just there for my analysis and I take the results elsewhere if I need them for a report.)

Change Data Source

There are going to be times when you need to change the data that Excel is using for a pivot table. Maybe you add a new column of data that you want to use, or you were selecting a cell range for the table and have now added more rows of data that you need to capture. When that happens, you can go to the Data section of the PivotTable Analyze tab, and click on Change Data Source.

That will take you to the worksheet where the data is, and also bring up the Change PivotTable Data Source dialogue box. The easiest way, in my opinion, to change the data source is to just left-click and drag in the worksheet to select the full range of cells to use in the pivot table. That should update the cell range in the dialogue box and you can then just click on OK to close it. Your pivot table should automatically update based on your new cell range.

Another option is to click into the field in the dialogue box and manually adjust the range of cells being referenced. I do this when I add another column of data because I can just click at the end, backspace out the last listed column letter, and type in the new letter.

Just be careful with this approach, because using arrows to move within the text in that input field does not work well. (It will start populating a cell range for you in the midst of the one you already had.) If you go with this approach and are making significant changes, I think it's best to delete out what's there first, and then you can hold down Shift as you arrow around to select the new cell range.

If you don't want to do that, then click exactly where you need to make your edit in that field, and use backspace or delete before type in your values from there.

Just do not use the arrow keys.

A Quick Caution

One final note here about refresh, change data sources, and filtering. I've noticed lately that Excel is a little less stable when using these than it used to be. It sometimes doesn't update the values. So be sure to "gut check" that your table results look right. Maybe make sure the grand total is what you expect, or that all the values you should be seeing are there.

Do humething to independently confirm your results if you're using refresh, change data sources, or filters.

There have been a couple times in Excel 365, where I have had to do a brand new pivot table to get it to work properly. Also, when I was playing around here with two fields in the Filter section and then removed them, one of the filters continued to apply to my table even though I'd supposedly taken it away. That's why I suggested unfiltering your table first.

Pivot tables are great and invaluable, so don't let that scare you away from using them. Just understand that for anything you do in Excel, you should always make sure the result makes sense.

Clear Your Pivot Table

If you ever build a pivot table and want to just start over from scratch, you can go to the Actions section of the PivotTable Analyze tab and choose Clear.

If you have filters in place on your table, you can use Clear Filters from the dropdown menu to reset those.

Pivot Tables – More Advanced Topics

The last chapter covered the basics of building a pivot table and editing it a bit. I'd say I can get away with only the information in that chapter for probably 90%-95% of what I do with pivot tables. (There are a few more items in the formatting chapter that I use regularly.) But there are a lot of bells and whistles with pivot tables, and they're adding more functionality all the time, so let's walk through some of those more advanced topics now.

Working with Dates

In more recent version of Excel, pivot tables have gotten really useful for working with dates. But only if Excel recognizes the field as a date field. Given Excel's tendency to turn anything remotely close to a date into a date, it is kind of ironic how difficult it can be sometimes to get Excel to treat an actual date as a date for pivot table purposes. (I put some tips at the start of this book, but sometimes even those don't work.)

Okay. So what can Excel do with dates?

When you add a date field to the Rows or Columns section of a pivot table, Excel will create up to four separate date fields for you in that section. You'll have the actual date field, but Excel will also create fields for year, quarter, and month based on your date values. (Assuming your dates span multiple months, quarters, and/or years.)

Here I dragged Royalty Date to the Columns section and you can see the new fields Excel created for me.

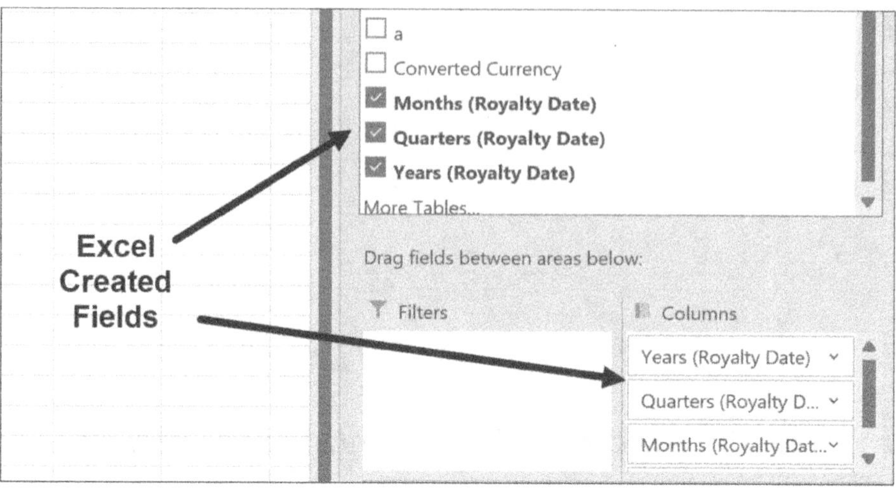

This is either going to be very useful to you or very annoying, depending on what you were trying to do.

I find it very useful, because usually I am not concerned that X event happened on a specific date; I am more interested that it happened in 2022 or in January of 2022. Which means I really like that Excel breaks my date data down for me automatically. Then I can just uncheck the fields it created that I don't want to use.

Once Excel creates those options for you, they'll still be listed as available fields that you can add to your table at any time.

Now, I mentioned in the quick tips section that when I wrote the first draft of this book I was able to get Excel to work with my date column no problem with that convert text to columns trick, but then it stopped working and nothing I did could get Excel to treat that column of values as a date for a pivot table.

I could see that the number for that cell was a date value. I could use it in math. But Excel treated each date as a unique value for my pivot table. (I eventually did a full repair on my version of Office, something I've never had to do before.)

Good news is that dealing with that led me to discover another option for displaying your dates by month, quarter, and year that I hadn't known before. (I do not in fact know everything. I am very lazy. I learn what I need and do it that way until I get stuck and need to learn a new way. Anyway.)

If Excel doesn't automatically create month, quarter, and year versions of your date values for you, but the entries are formatted as dates, right-click on one of the values in your table, and choose Group. That will bring up a Grouping dialogue box:

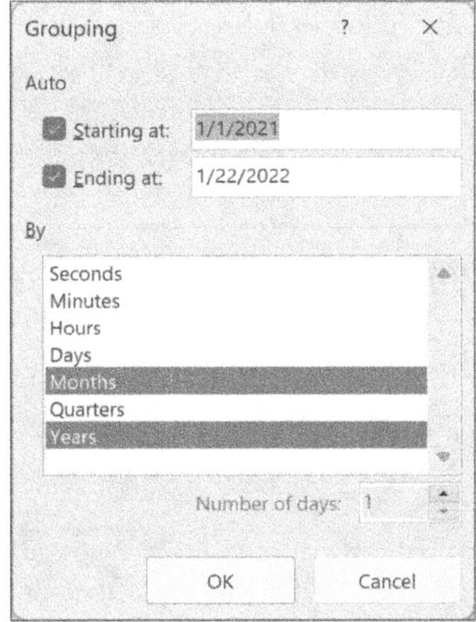

You can choose from there months, quarters, or years. (Days, hours, minutes, or seconds, too.) Click on the one you need, and then OK, and it will break your data down by those categories.

Now, be careful with this. Because I had dates as text and it let me do it but then showed the date values as 1905 dates. So you still need to go through all the steps to turn your date into a date entry in the data table first. But it seems to work even when Excel is being weird.

Insert Timeline

Insert Timeline creates a dialogue box that you can use to filter your pivot table in real-time based on a date field. It is also more visible than filtering. You can always see exactly which date criteria are being applied to a table.

To create a timeline, go to the Filter section of the PivotTable Analyze tab, and click on Insert Timeline. That will bring up the Insert Timelines dialogue box:

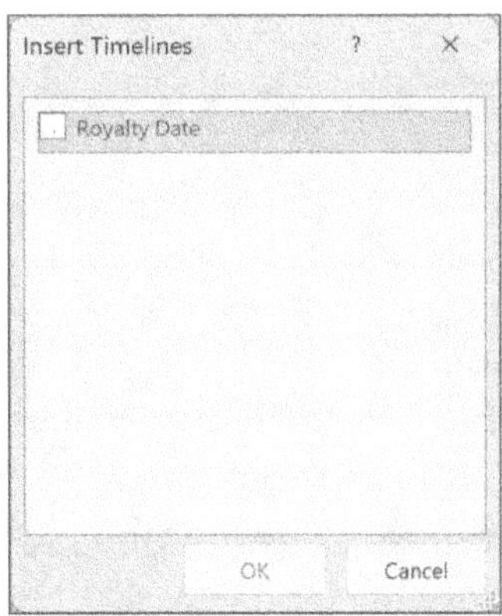

Timelines are only available for fields that Excel thinks are dates for pivot table purposes. So when you click on that option, the only fields that will show are those fields.

Click the checkbox for the one that you want, and then click OK.

Excel will then create a timeline dialogue box for that specific field that you can use to filter your pivot table:

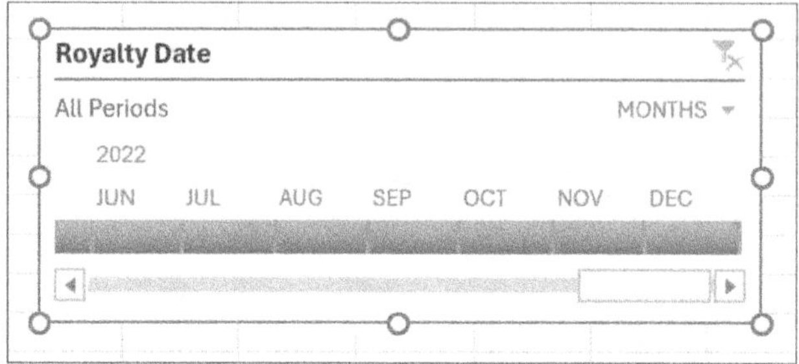

The range of values in the dialogue box will cover the entire date range of values for that field, even if some days, months, quarters, or years in the midst of the range have no data related with them. If you select days, months, quarters, or years that have no results, the pivot table will be blank.

There is a dropdown in the top right corner of the timeline that you can change to different time periods. If your dates cover it, you should be able to choose years, quarters, months, or days. After you do that, just click on the timeline to choose a specific value or range of values.

So I can do MONTHS, and then click on Jul for a specific year, and have only results for July of that year show in my pivot table.

If you want to select a range of months, days, years, etc., click on the starting value you want and hold down the Shift key while you click on the last value in you want.

Here, for example, I've selected January to March 2021:

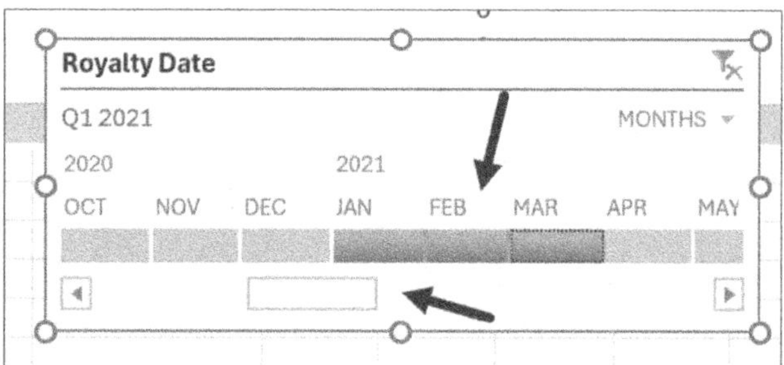

It is not possible to select non-contiguous dates. So you can't select June and October 2021, you have to select June *through* October.

There is a white outlined scroll bar below the date values that you can use to move through the entire range of available dates on the timeline.

To remove your timeline filter from your pivot table, just click on the funnel with an X in the top right corner of the dialogue box.

Right-click on the dialogue box and choose Remove Timeline to get rid of it. Your data may remain filtered if you were also using that field to build the table.

Insert Slicer

Insert Slicer lets you have a visible filter for all of your non-date fields. It can also be found in the Filter section of the PivotTable Analyze tab. Click on Insert Slicer, and then check the box for the field(s) you want to have a slicer for. Click OK when you're done.

Excel will insert slicers for each selected field. The slicers show all possible values for that field. Here, for example, are filters for net units sold and transaction type:

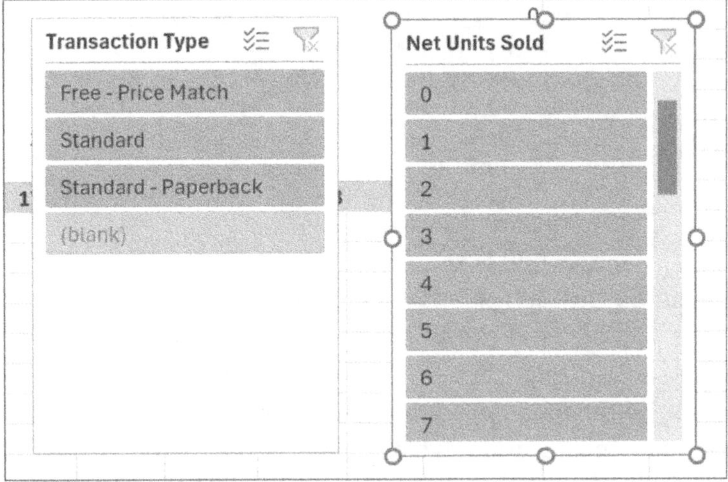

Click on a value to filter the pivot table by that value. Hold down the Ctrl key to select more than one value at once or the Shift key to select a range of values.

The multiselect option, at the top, next to the funnel, will let you choose more than one value without having to hold down the Ctrl key.

Turn off the filter by clicking on the funnel with an X in the top right corner.

Close the slicer by right-clicking and choosing the Remove option.

Grouping Row or Column Values

You can also manually group values in the rows or columns sections.

For example, in this data set I have three transaction categories: Free – Price Match, Standard, and Standard – Paperback. If I want to combine Standard and Standard-Paperback into one entry, I can do that.

To group values together, click on the first value you want in your group, and then hold down Ctrl and click on the other values you want to include.

Right-click when you have them all selected, and choose Group from the dropdown menu. (Or you can choose Group Selection from the Group section of the PivotTable Analyze tab.)

By default, Excel will give that new grouping the name Group1.

It will also assign all remaining values for that field to their own group with a group name that is identical to the value. For example, you can see here that I have a Group 1 that contains my two standard transaction types, as well as a group named (blank) that contains (blank) and one named Free – Price Match that contains Free – Price Match:

	A	B
1		
2	Author Name	(All)
3		
4	**Row Labels**	**Sum of Net Unit**
5	**Free - Price Match**	
6	Free - Price Match	
7	**(blank)**	
8	(blank)	
9	**Group1**	
10	Standard	
11	Standard - Paperback	
12	**Grand Total**	

If you create more than one group for values in a field, Excel will just keep naming the groups with the next available number, so Group 2, Group 3, etc.

To change the name of a group, click on the name in the pivot table, go to the formula bar, and change the text in the formula bar to the name you want.

Here I'm clicked onto Cell A9 and have changed the name to Standard Transactions:

A9		fx	Standard Transactions	
	A			
1				
2	Author Name	(All)		
3				
4	**Row Labels**		**Sum of Net Units Sold**	**Sum o**
5	**Free - Price Match**			
6	Free - Price Match		91	
7	**(blank)**			
8	(blank)		1440	
9	**Standard Transactions**			
10	Standard		306	
11	Standard - Paperback		1043	

To add to an existing group, you need to select the fields that are already members of that group and then select the new values you want to include. So in the example above, I'd need to select Standard and Standard – Paperback, and then click on the field that was missing at that same level, and choose Group again..

To ungroup values, right-click on the group name, and choose Ungroup from the dropdown menu. Or click on the group name and then choose Ungroup from the Group section of the PivotTable Analyze tab.

See Underlying Data

If you ever need to see the specific entries from your original data table that led to a value in your pivot table, either double-click on that value, or right-click and choose Show Details.

Excel will create a new worksheet that has a data table showing all of the specific rows of data that led to that value:

	A	B	C	D	E	F	G	H	I
1	Royalty Date	Author Name	Marketplace	Transaction Type	Net Units Sold	Royalty	Currency	a	Converted Currency
2	2/1/2021	Author A	Amazon.co.uk	Standard	1	1.64	GBP		1.98
3	2/1/2021	Author A	Amazon.co.uk	Standard	1	1.64	GBP		1.98
4	2/1/2021	Author A	Amazon.co.uk	Standard	1	1.62	GBP		1.96
5	2/1/2021	Author A	Amazon.co.uk	Standard	1	1.67	GBP		2.02
6	2/1/2021	Author A	Amazon.co.uk	Standard	1	1.72	GBP		2.08
7	3/1/2021	Author A	Amazon.co.uk	Standard	0	0	GBP		0
8	6/1/2021	Author A	Amazon.co.uk	Standard	1	3.61	GBP		4.37
9	6/1/2021	Author A	Amazon.co.uk	Standard	1	2.13	GBP		2.58
10	7/1/2021	Author A	Amazon.co.uk	Standard	1	2.04	GBP		2.47

Be careful with this one, though, because when I was just playing with it, it did not adjust when I changed my entries in the original data table and tried to Refresh. There was no connection between the two anymore. This could be due to my security settings, or whatever was impacting Excel's ability to recognize my dates, but it's something to watch out for.

I think for my purposes, I would generate the detail, review it as needed, and then delete that worksheet immediately. If I need it again, it's just one click to create it.

Recommended Pivot Tables

In the Tools section of the PivotTable Analyze tab, there is an option for Recommended PivotTables. It takes your data and suggests some possible pivot tables to build with it. If you see something you like, just click on the one you want and then OK.

Personally, I don't use it because it doesn't save me time, but if you ever forget how to build a pivot table or aren't sure how to approach your data, it could be a good starting point.

Calculations

If you want to create a calculation within a pivot table, it is possible. To do so, go to the Calculations section of the PivotTable Analyze tab, and click on the dropdown arrow for Fields, Items & Sets, and choose Calculated Field.

You can then build a formula in the dialogue box that opens using the field names as your inputs

I rarely if ever use this and am going to assign it to an advanced use of Excel rather than walk you through it here. I just wanted you to know it exists if you ever think you need it. For me, personally, if I want to do more with my pivot table data, I copy and paste special-values and then go from there. The only reason I'd do calculations in a pivot table was if I expected to use that pivot table with data that was going to update periodically and that's just not something I've ever needed in 30 years of doing some pretty intensive data analysis in Excel.

Pivot Tables – Formatting

I do format my pivot tables in Excel, especially if I'm going to copy and paste that data for further use elsewhere. The two biggest changes I make are to remove subtotals and grand totals and to change my report layout to make the pivot table a data table.

Subtotals and Grand Totals

The default when you have multiple fields in rows or columns is for Excel to insert subtotals for you. Which is great if you're treating your pivot table as some sort of report. But I am often trying to get data I can then work with elsewhere, so I don't want those subtotals. It clutters things up, gets in the way, and I'd just want to delete them later,.

To remove any subtotals or grand totals used in your pivot table, go to the Layout section of the Design tab. You will see two dropdowns, Subtotals and Grand Totals. Here is the dropdown for Subtotals:

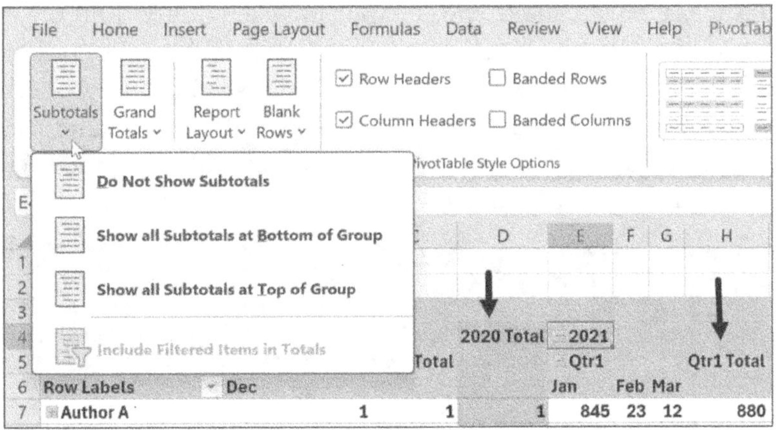

Click on the dropdown arrow for each one and select the option you want.

As you can see, for subtotals there are options for where your subtotals appear, "top" or "bottom". That means before the detail or after it. The default is top but sometimes I prefer it to be on the bottom.

Report Layout

To change how your data displays in your pivot table, go to the Layout section of the Design tab, and click on the Report Layout dropdown menu:

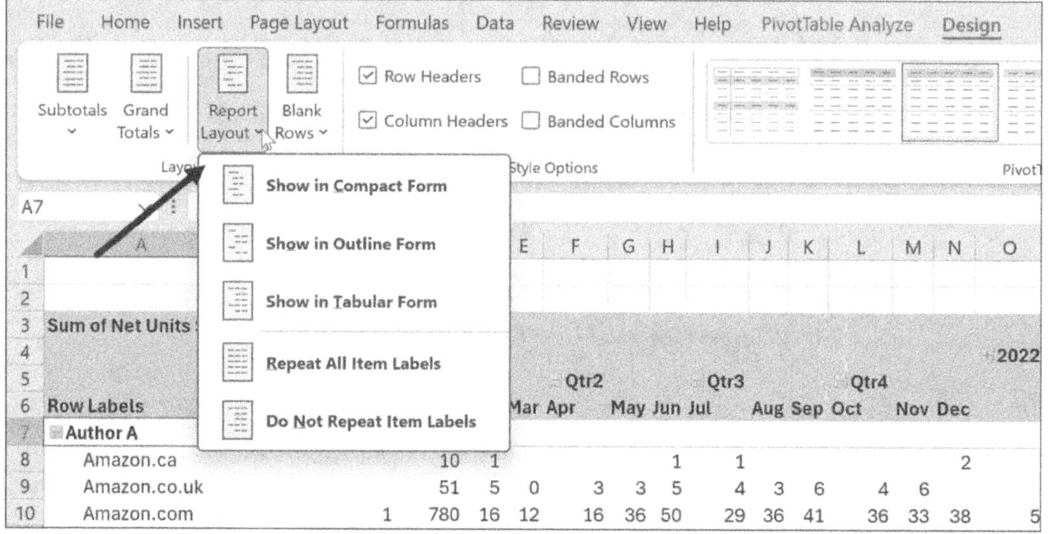

There are two sections there.

The top lets you decide if you want your pivot table rows to be Compact, which is the default, Outline format, or Tabular format. You can sort of see what the layout will look like in those little thumbnails, but I usually end up applying each one to find the one I want.

The second section lets you decide about repeating values for your columns.

By default, Excel does not repeat item labels. You can see below that 2021 shows once in Row 4, but not above each quarter and month that is part of 2021. Same with Qtr1 of 2021. Qtr1 shows once in Row 5 above Jan, but not above Feb and March. Fine for a report, but not for a data table that requires more analysis.

	Sum of Net Units Sold	Column Labels																
3																		
4			2020		2021													2022
5			Qtr4		Qtr1			Qtr2			Qtr3			Qtr4				
6	Row Labels		Dec		Jan	Feb	Mar	Apr	May	Jun	Jul	Aug	Sep	Oct	Nov	Dec		
7	Author A		1		845	23	12	19	39	56	35	40	47	40	40	40		5
8	Author B				17			2	1									
9	Author C				90													
10	Author D		1		47		3	4	2	10	1	5	2	2	3			

To reformat a pivot table for data analysis I change the settings to Tabular form, Repeat Item Labels, no subtotals, and no grand totals. That gives me this:

	A	B	C	D	E
1					
2					
3	Sum of Net Units Sold		Years (Royalty Date)	Quarters (Royalty Date)	Months (Royalty Date)
4			2020	2021	2021
5			Qtr4	Qtr1	Qtr1
6	Author Name	Marketplace	Dec	Jan	Feb
7	Author A	Amazon.ca		10	1
8	Author A	Amazon.co.uk		51	5
9	Author A	Amazon.com	1	780	16
10	Author A	Amazon.com.au		2	
11	Author A	Amazon.com.mx			1
12	Author A	Amazon.es			
13	Author A	Amazon.fr			

Much better. I can now copy this worksheet and paste special – values into another worksheet, and have all of my rows and columns fully complete so I can do more analysis.

Other Formatting

Most of your pivot table formatting options will be in the Design tab. We already talked about the options on the left-hand side that cover subtotals, grand totals, and report layout. Now let's cover the rest:

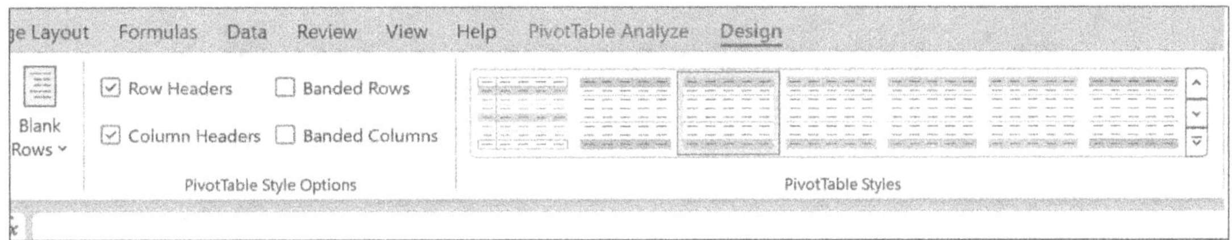

I want to start on the right-hand side with the PivotTable Styles section. If you look really close, you may be able to see that there is a box around the third option displayed there. That's because that is the current style that is by default being applied to my pivot table.

It has a color across the top row and the grand totals row at the bottom. When there are two fields used for rows, it also puts a light blue line between different values for the top-level field. (Not a row, a line.)

All but the first option in that first row are just different colored versions of that format. The first option uses a colored row to separate the different values when there are two levels in the row section.

If you look at the right-hand side there, you should see an up and a down arrow as well as a down arrow with a line behind it. Click on that arrow with the line behind it to see more formatting choices:

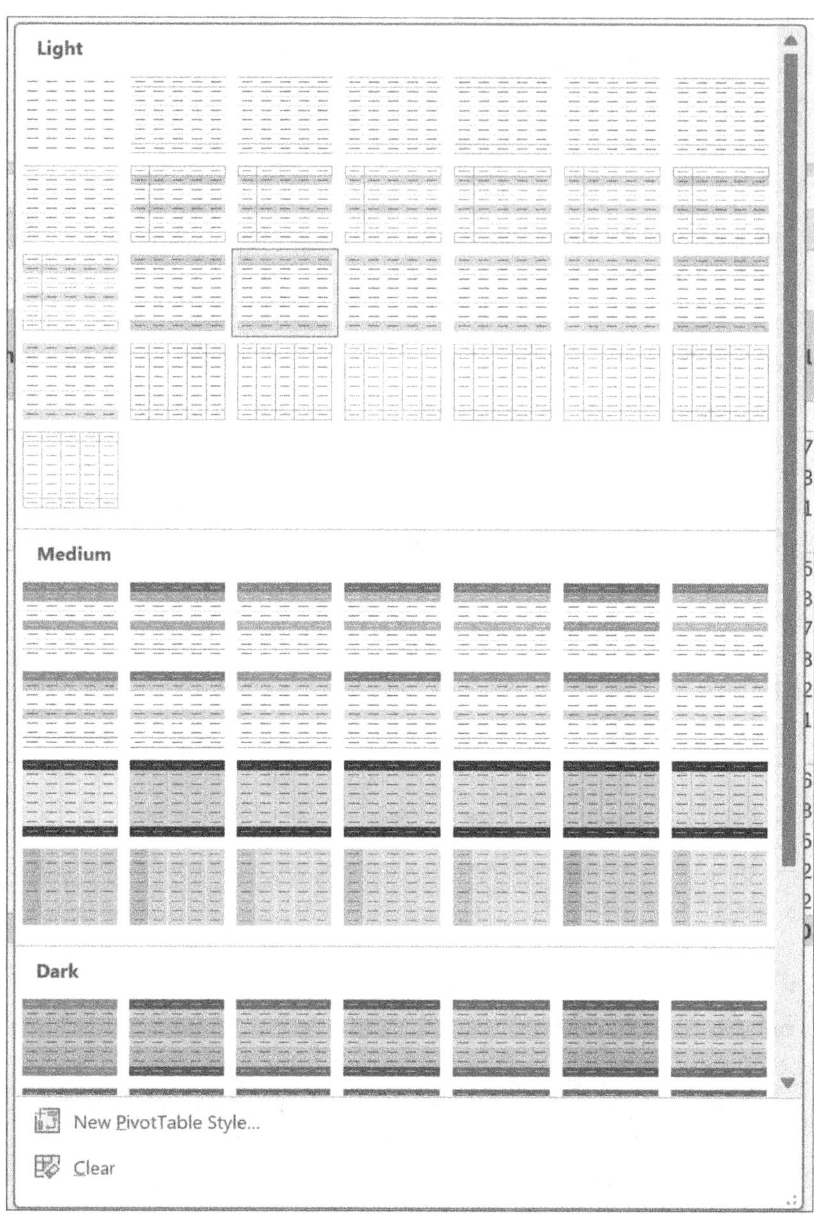

Hold your mouse over each one to see how it will look with your data (like I have on the next page).

If you like an option, click on it to apply.

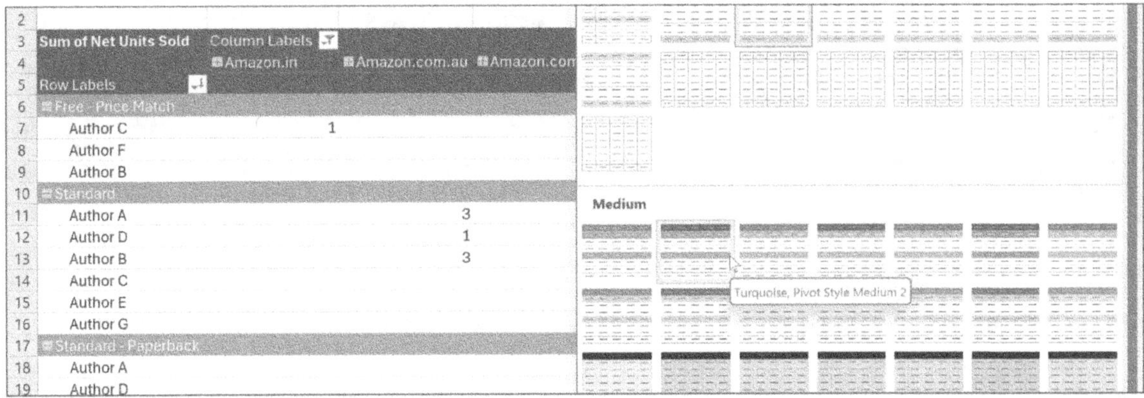

You should choose a style based upon the nature of the pivot table you created.

For example, some of the styles have a different format for the bottom row. Great if you have grand totals in your final row, but weird if you don't.

Same with the final column of the table. Some styles have a different format, which is great if you have a grand total column, but you shouldn't use it if you don't.

As you can see here, while I like this style and its color choices, the formatting isn't working with my data, because I do have a grand total column but this format doesn't treat that last column differently:

Sum of Net Units Sold	Amazon.in	Amazon.com.au	Amazon.com.mx	Amazon.com	Amazon.co.uk	Amazon.ca	Amazon Europe	Grand Total
Free - Price Match								
Author C	1			78	1	3	4	87
Author F				3				3
Author B				1				1
Standard								
Author A		3	1	218	23	7	3	255
Author D		1		26	1			28
Author B		3		5	9			17
Author C				3				3
Author E				1			1	2
Author G					1			1
Standard - Paperback								
Author A				905	63	7	1	976
Author D				46	2			48
Author Z				5				5
Author B				1	1			2
Author E				2				2
Grand Total	1	7	1	1294	101	17	9	1430

I could try to find another style that works better. (You basically go down the column to find the varying styles and then across to find different color schemes.)

Or, I could start with this, and then customize it using the Font section of the Home tab.

In the table on the next page I bolded the last column, added fill color to the bottom row, changed my font color, and added a line to separate my left-most column and my right-most column. I also centered all of the numbers, and hid Rows 3 and 5:

	Amazon.in	Amazon.com.au	Amazon.com.mx	Amazon.com	Amazon.co.uk	Amazon.ca	Amazon Europe	Grand Total
Free - Price Match								
Author C	1			78	1	3	4	87
Author F				3				3
Author B				1				1
Standard								
Author A		3	1	218	23	7	3	255
Author D		1		26	1			28
Author B		3		5	9			17
Author C				3				3
Author E				1			1	2
Author G					1			1
Standard - Paperback								
Author A				911	67	8	1	987
Author D				50	2			52
Author E				2				2
Author B				1	1			2
Grand Total	1	7	1	1299	105	18	9	1440

Not bad. But you have to be careful when you depart from an existing pivot table style, because if you then change your data or refresh the table, you can lose some of that formatting. Not all, weirdly enough, but some.

So preferably save your formatting for last.

Custom Style

It is possible to create a customized pivot table style by going to the very bottom of the PivotTable Styles dropdown and clicking on New PivotTable Style.

That will bring up a dialogue box where you can fully customize the table appearance and save that customized look for use with the current table or any others in the workbook. If you're going to routinely update your data that feeds the pivot table and you don't like any of the default styles, you should either go with a default style or create a custom one.

If you choose to customize, in the dialogue box click on the name of each table element in the list, and then click on Format to bring up a Format Cells dialogue box, which will allow you to control any font attributes, borders, and fill colors. Make your choices, click OK, and then move on to the next element.

The Preview in the main dialogue box should show you what your table will look like with all of the elements formatted according to your choices.

If there is a style that already is partially what you want, right-click on it and choose Duplicate from the dropdown menu. That will start you with a style that already has all of that formatting applied, and you can then make additional changes from there.

When you're done, if you want all new pivot tables to automatically use the style you created, click on the Set As Default box at the bottom before you click OK.

* * *

Three more formatting options to discuss form the Design tab:

Blank Rows

The Blank Rows option in the Layout section of the Design tab lets you add blank rows between each grouped item in your rows. For a table like the one above it really doesn't do much, but if I take that same table and add a subtotal for each top-level category, then it does help a bit with visual separation:

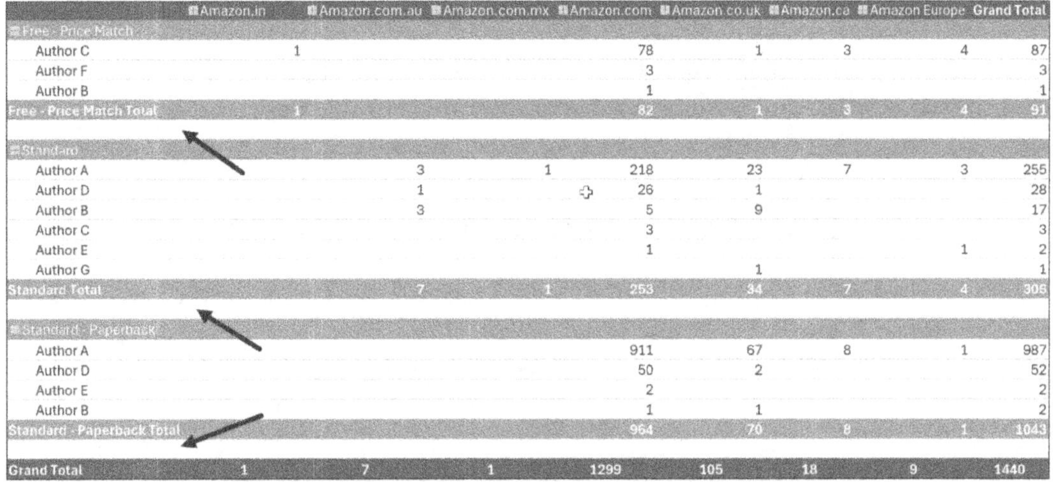

	Amazon.in	Amazon.com.au	Amazon.com.mx	Amazon.com	Amazon.co.uk	Amazon.ca	Amazon Europe	Grand Total
Free - Price Match								
Author C	1			78	1	3	4	87
Author F				3				3
Author B				1				1
Free - Price Match Total	1			82	1	3	4	91
Standard								
Author A		3	1	218	23	7	3	255
Author D		1		26	1			28
Author B		3		5	9			17
Author C				3				3
Author E				1			1	2
Author G					1			1
Standard Total		7	1	253	34	7	4	306
Standard - Paperback								
Author A				911	67	8	1	987
Author D				50	2			52
Author E				2				2
Author B				1	1			2
Standard - Paperback Total				964	70	8	1	1043
Grand Total	1	7	1	1299	105	18	9	1440

Banded Rows and Banded Columns

You can add banded rows or banded columns to any pivot table from the PivotTable Style Options section of the Design tab. Banded just means that every other column or row will be a different color. For example, here is banded columns:

4		Amazon.in	Amazon.com.au	Amazon.com.mx
6	**Free - Price Match**			
7	Author C	1		
8	Author F			
9	Author B			

See how every other column is a different color?

Here is banded rows:

4		Amazon.in	Amazon.com.au	Amazon.com.mx
6	**Free - Price Match**			
7	Author C	1		
8	Author F			
9	Author B			

The appearance of banded rows or columns is going to vary depending on the PivotTable Style you're using. For this style, for example, clicking both banded rows and columns just added a nice little line around each cell:

4		Amazon.in	Amazon.com.au	Amazon.com.mx	Amazon.com
6	Free - Price Match				
7	Author C	1			78
8	Author F				3
9	Author B				1

But for other styles it has a much bigger impact and I wouldn't recommend using both at the same time.

When choosing which one to use, if you think your data will primarily be read left to right, then banded rows can create good visual separation that makes that easier to do. If you think your data will primarily be read top to bottom, then banded columns will help.

Row and Column Header Formatting

There are also checkboxes in the PivotTable Style Options section of the Design tab for row headers or column headers. What unchecking those boxes does will depend on the style you chose. I recommend just clicking on them to see what you get.

* * *

We'll circle back to pivot tables later to cover pivot charts, but for now let's move on to conditional formatting, with a quick stop to learn how to create a two-variable analysis grid first.

Two-Variable Analysis Grid

Before we move on to our next tool in Excel, conditional formatting, I want to real quickly show you how to build what I call a two-variable analysis grid.

This is a table of values that represent the outcome of combining two different variables. For example, hours worked and pay. The higher your pay, the less you need to work to make the same amount, right? Or you can make up for earning less per hour by working more hours.

A two-variable analysis grid puts that information into a very practical lookup table which is simple to build, and which I'm going to use in the next chapter.

Okay. First thing you need to do is build the table with the values you want to use:

	A	B	C	D	E	F	G	H	I
1			Hours Worked						
2			20	25	30	35	40	45	50
3		$15							
4		$20							
5		$25							
6	Pay Rate	$30							
7		$35							
8		$40							
9		$45							
10		$50							

Building this involved a lot of the basic formatting we already covered in *Excel 2024 for Beginners*. I merged and centered the header sections across the cells, added fill color, changed the font color, centered the values I wanted to use, changed the text orientation along the left-hand side, and added borders:

Now we need to figure out the formula. In this case it's pretty basic, because we want to multiply hours times pay. In Cell C3 that would be:

$$=B3*C2$$

so I typed that in there.

Now, here's the fun part. We don't have to rewrite that formula for every cell in the table. Instead, we can change the formula so that it continues to reference Row 2 and Column B, but adjusts otherwise. Then we can just copy it.

You do that by putting a dollar sign in front of the part of each cell reference that you want to keep the same. Like so:

$$=\$B3*C\$2$$

I put a dollar sign in front of the B in B3 and in front of the 2 in C2. Now when I copy that formula to all of the other cells in the table, the formula in each cell will continue to reference Column B and Row 2 but will otherwise adjust. Like this:

	A	B	C	D	E	F	G	H	I
1			Hours Worked						
2			20	=C2+5	=D2+5	=E2+5	=F2+5	=G2+5	=H2+5
3	Pay Rate	15	=$B3*C$2	=$B3*D$2	=$B3*E$2	=$B3*F$2	=$B3*G$2	=$B3*H$2	=$B3*I$2
4		=B3+5	=$B4*C$2	=$B4*D$2	=$B4*E$2	=$B4*F$2	=$B4*G$2	=$B4*H$2	=$B4*I$2
5		=B4+5	=$B5*C$2	=$B5*D$2	=$B5*E$2	=$B5*F$2	=$B5*G$2	=$B5*H$2	=$B5*I$2
6		=B5+5	=$B6*C$2	=$B6*D$2	=$B6*E$2	=$B6*F$2	=$B6*G$2	=$B6*H$2	=$B6*I$2
7		=B6+5	=$B7*C$2	=$B7*D$2	=$B7*E$2	=$B7*F$2	=$B7*G$2	=$B7*H$2	=$B7*I$2
8		=B7+5	=$B8*C$2	=$B8*D$2	=$B8*E$2	=$B8*F$2	=$B8*G$2	=$B8*H$2	=$B8*I$2
9		=B8+5	=$B9*C$2	=$B9*D$2	=$B9*E$2	=$B9*F$2	=$B9*G$2	=$B9*H$2	=$B9*I$2
10		=B9+5	=$B10*C$2	=$B10*D$2	=$B10*E$2	=$B10*F$2	=$B10*G$2	=$B10*H$2	=$B10*I$2

The formula in Cell I10 is

$$=\$B10*I\$2$$

Pretty cool, huh?

(You can see all the formulas in a worksheet by going to the Formulas tab and clicking on Show Formulas under Formula Auditing. That's why you can also see that I built the values used in the table with formulas. I told you, I'm lazy.)

Here are the actual results of the calculations:

C3			f_x	=$B3*C$2			

	A	B	C	D	E	F	G	H	I
1			Hours Worked						
2			20	25	30	35	40	45	50
3	Pay Rate	$15	$300	$375	$450	$525	$600	$675	$750
4		$20	$400	$500	$600	$700	$800	$900	$1,000
5		$25	$500	$625	$750	$875	$1,000	$1,125	$1,250
6		$30	$600	$750	$900	$1,050	$1,200	$1,350	$1,500
7		$35	$700	$875	$1,050	$1,225	$1,400	$1,575	$1,750
8		$40	$800	$1,000	$1,200	$1,400	$1,600	$1,800	$2,000
9		$45	$900	$1,125	$1,350	$1,575	$1,800	$2,025	$2,250
10		$50	$1,000	$1,250	$1,500	$1,750	$2,000	$2,250	$2,500

Do the math yourself, and you'll see that it worked for each of the cells.

Okay, now let's go use this table to demonstrate conditional formatting.

Conditional Formatting

Conditional formatting is a great way to visualize differences in your data. You can think of it as having Excel go through your results and highlight or otherwise call out results that meet various criteria. Just this week I used it to identify some duplicates in a list of values I had, but more often I use it to identify the "best" or "worst" in a range or to show how a range of values compare to one another.

Let's dive in and look at some examples because this one is very visual.

Looking at the analysis grid we built in the last chapter, let's say we know that you need to earn at least $1,200 a week. We can use conditional formatting to analyze the results in that table and color code them so that all values over $1199 are shaded in green.

Here that is:

	A	B	C	D	E	F	G	H	I
1			Hours Worked						
2			20	25	30	35	40	45	50
3	Pay Rate	$15	$300	$375	$450	$525	$600	$675	$750
4		$20	$400	$500	$600	$700	$800	$900	$1,000
5		$25	$500	$625	$750	$875	$1,000	$1,125	$1,250
6		$30	$600	$750	$900	$1,050	$1,200	$1,350	$1,500
7		$35	$700	$875	$1,050	$1,225	$1,400	$1,575	$1,750
8		$40	$800	$1,000	$1,200	$1,400	$1,600	$1,800	$2,000
9		$45	$900	$1,125	$1,350	$1,575	$1,800	$2,025	$2,250
10		$50	$1,000	$1,250	$1,500	$1,750	$2,000	$2,250	$2,500

This makes it much easier to see what combinations of hours and pay reach your goal. Basically, for this range of hours worked, you need a minimum of $25 an hour, and that only gets you to your goal if you work at least 50 hours. On the higher end, $50 an hour is great as long as you get at least 20 hours.

Very useful. So let's walk through all the many, many choices you have for conditional formatting of your data.

Apply

There are five categories of conditional formatting: Highlight Cells Rules, Top/Bottom Rules, Data Bars, Color Scales, and Icon Sets

To apply conditional formatting, select the range of cells you want to apply it to, click on the arrow next to Conditional Formatting in the Styles section of the Home tab, hold your mouse over the category you want to use, and then click on the subcategory you want from the secondary dropdown menu:

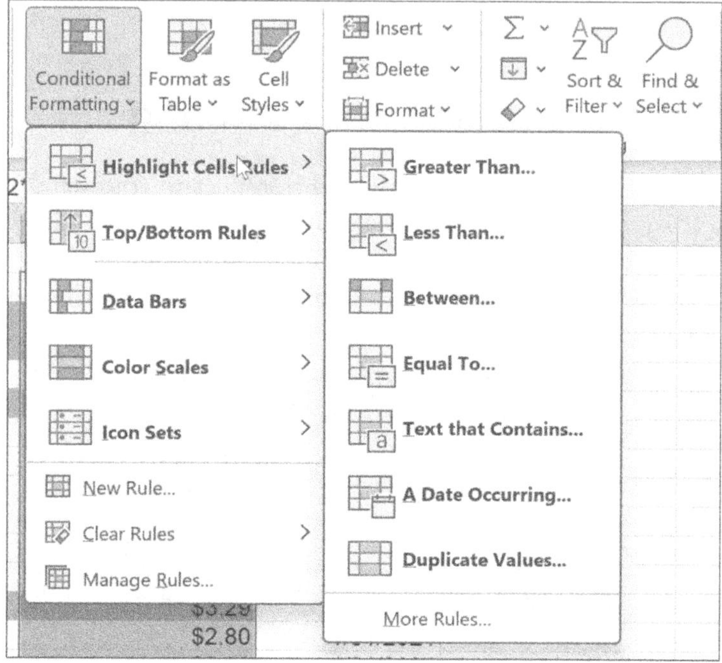

Most options will bring up a dialogue box where you can enter specific criteria and choose a format. Enter the criteria you want to use, choose the format you want, and then click OK. (We'll walk through this in much more detail in a moment.)

Usually I will apply one of the defaults and then go in and edit from there if I want something different in terms of criteria. For example, you may have wondered above why I did over $1199 instead of equal to or greater than $1200. It's because, as you can see in the secondary dropdown menu above, greater than is one of the listed choices, whereas greater than or equal to requires a little more effort to apply.

(In the main dropdown menu, the New Rule option will bring up the New Formatting Rule dialogue box which gives you more choices but also takes more effort.)

Okay, so let's walk through each of the five categories now.

Highlight Cells Rules

You can see the secondary menu for highlight cell rules on the prior page.

Greater Than, Less Than, Between, and Equal To

The first four options there are Greater Than, Less Than, Between, and Equal To. They work pretty much the same. Select the one you want and you'll see a dialogue box. This is the one for Between:

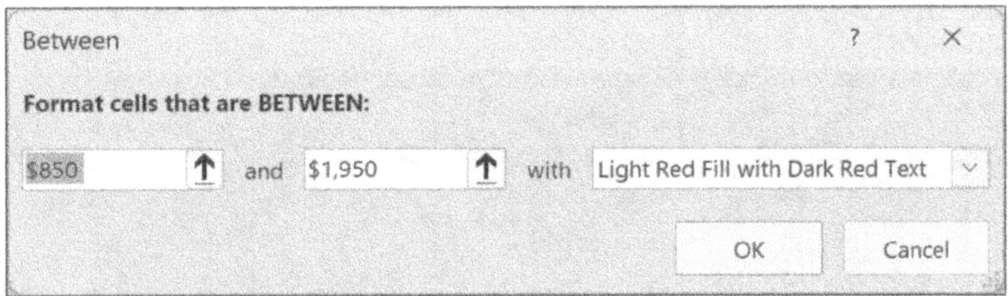

Excel guesses the values you might want to use, but you can just click into each box and type the value you want.

The dropdown on the right-hand side tells you how cells that meet that criteria will be formatted. The default is Light Red Fill with Dark Red Text. The other pre-formatted choices are Yellow Fill with Dark Yellow Text (which I have never used in my life), Green Fill with Dark Green Text, Light Red Fill, Red Text, and Red Border.

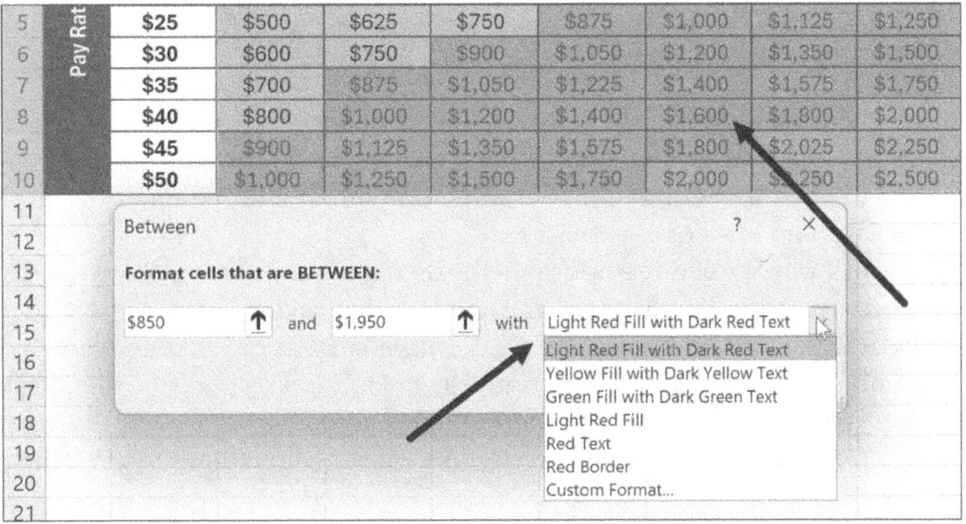

As you can see, whoever put the defaults together assumed you'd mostly want to flag "bad" things since red tends to mean bad in the U.S., especially when used with yellow and green. I personally want to flag things green often, so I almost always have to use that dropdown menu.

If you choose the last item in that dropdown, Custom Format, that will bring up a Format Cells dialogue box where you can apply pretty much any formatting you want to the cells that meet your criteria. If you want purple bolded text with a green striped background, go for it.

(Stripes are under the Pattern Style dropdown on the Fill tab. But just because you can do something does not mean it's actually a good idea to do it. Just sayin'.)

Text That Contains

The highlight cells rules secondary dropdown also has an option for text that contains something. Click on that to get the dialogue box and then type in the text you want. Like so:

Royalty Da	Author Nai	Marketplace	Transactic	t Units So	Royalty	Currency
2021-01-31	Author A	Amazon.com	Standard	1	5.70	USD
2021-01-31	Author B	Amazon.com.au	Standard	1	5.03	AUD
2021-01-31	Author C	Amazon.com	Free - Price	65	0.00	USD
2021-01-31	Author D	Amazon.com	Standard	1	2.76	USD
2021-01-31	Author C	Amazon.fr	Free - Price	1	0.00	EUR
2021-01-31	Author C	Amazon.ca	Free - Price	3	0.00	CAD
2021-01-31	Author A	Amazon.com	Standard	1	5.83	USD
2021-01-31	Author C	Amazon.de	Free - Price	3	0.00	EUR
2021-01-31	Author A	Amazon.com	Standard	1	1.75	USD
2021-01-31	Author A	Amazon.com	Standard	1	2.74	USD
2021-01-31	Author A	Amazo				

Text That Contains

Format cells that contain the text:

USD ⬆ with Light Red Fill with Dark Red Text ⌄

OK   Cancel

Note that Excel is applying the conditional formatting in the background even though I haven't yet clicked on OK. Pay attention to this to make sure you're getting the result you want.

I just tested this, and it is not case sensitive.

It will also work with a cell reference, so if the text you want is in a cell in your worksheet, you can click on that cell rather than type the text into the dialogue box.

And it works with wildcard characters. So if I have entries for USD and .com.usd, and I want that second one only, I can type ?usd into the field. Excel will only highlight cells where there is some text in front of usd.

I could also use usd? as my input to only return entries where there is something beyond usd in a cell.

A Date Occurring

Another option in the highlight cells rules secondary dropdown is for a date occurring, but I find this one of limited use because of the choices it gives you:

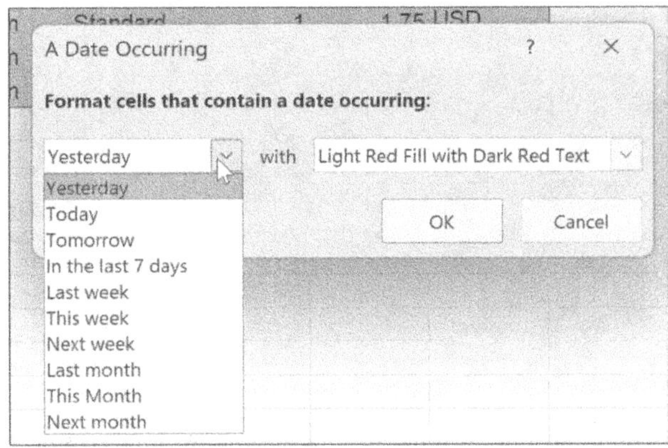

The choices there are yesterday, today, tomorrow, in the last 7 days, last week, this week, next week, last month, this month, and next month. Those are great choices for someone trying to use conditional formatting for something like receivables or payables. You are owed money and you want to see who is past due. Or you need to pay some bills and you want to see which ones are due in the next week so you can pay them.

But I often work with older data sets than that, and as far as I know there's no customizing this one beyond these choices.

Duplicate Values

The final option in that secondary dropdown is for Duplicate Values. I recently used this for a data analysis because I had multiple entries for some case numbers, and I wanted to quickly look at those duplicates to see if they were legitimate, or if someone had double-entered information. This worked well for that because my data was sorted by case number and so the duplicates were right next to each other.

Where it doesn't work as well is when the data is more spread out. Because if you have 10, 10, 20, 20, 30, and 30 at different points in your data, Excel will highlight all six cells the same color even though you technically have three distinct sets of duplicate values.

It also doesn't work as well where there are lots of duplicates.

But for something like subtotals where you want to make sure you didn't have any repeats, it can be pretty useful:

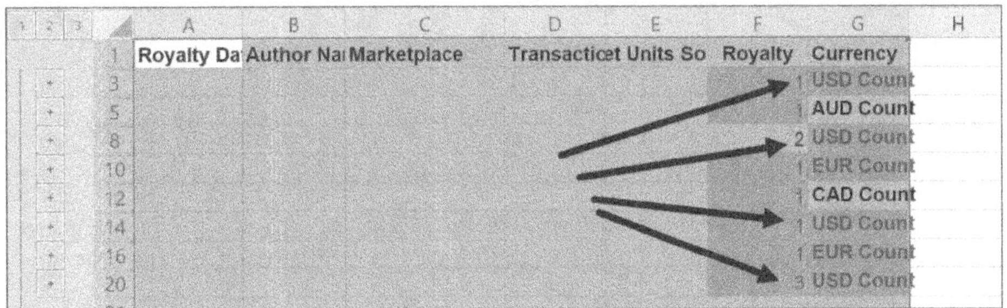

Top/Bottom Rules

Our next category of rules are the top/bottom rules:

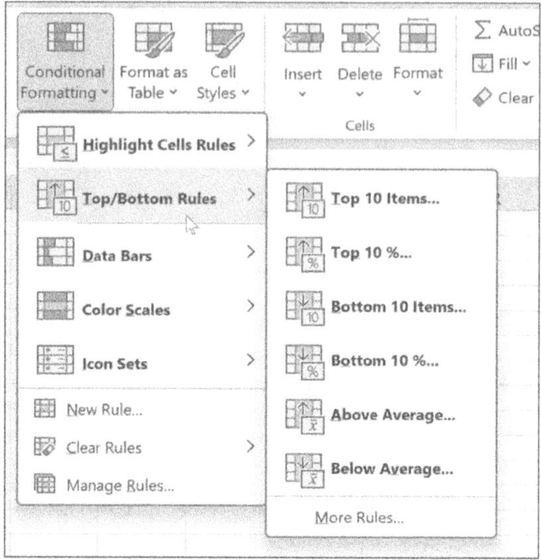

Note that each of the options there in the secondary dropdown uses 10. So top 10, bottom 10, top 10%, bottom 10%. The reality is that when the dialogue box comes up, you can choose whatever number you want to use. Here I changed the value to 3 instead, for example:

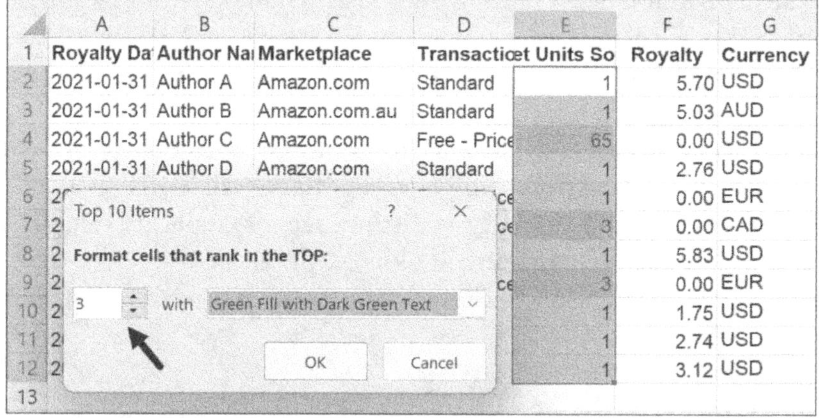

(I also changed the color.)

This dropdown also includes a choice for flagging above average and below average results. The average value it will work off is the average you can see in the bottom right corner of your worksheet when your cells are selected.

In this example that is 8, so most of my cells are highlighted as below average because I had a couple of big numbers in the mix:

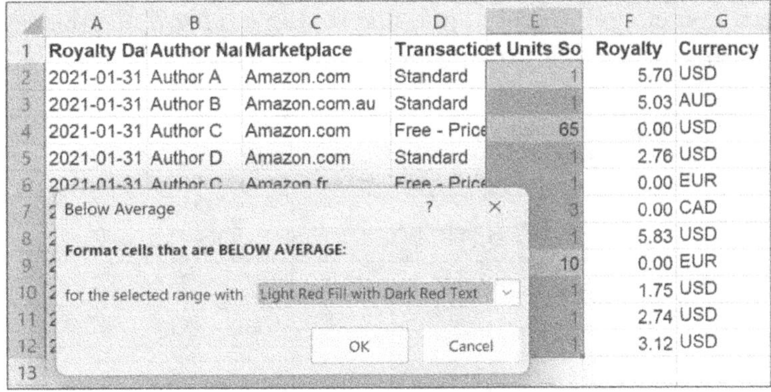

Data Bars

The next category of conditional formats is Data Bars. The secondary dropdown for this one just gives you a choice between solid bars and gradient bars in a variety of colors. By default, he longer the bar the higher the value compared to the other selected cells.

Initially, Excel will determine the range of values to use based on the values in your selected range. Click on More Rules at the bottom of the secondary dropdown menu to set those values yourself via the New Formatting Rule dialogue box:

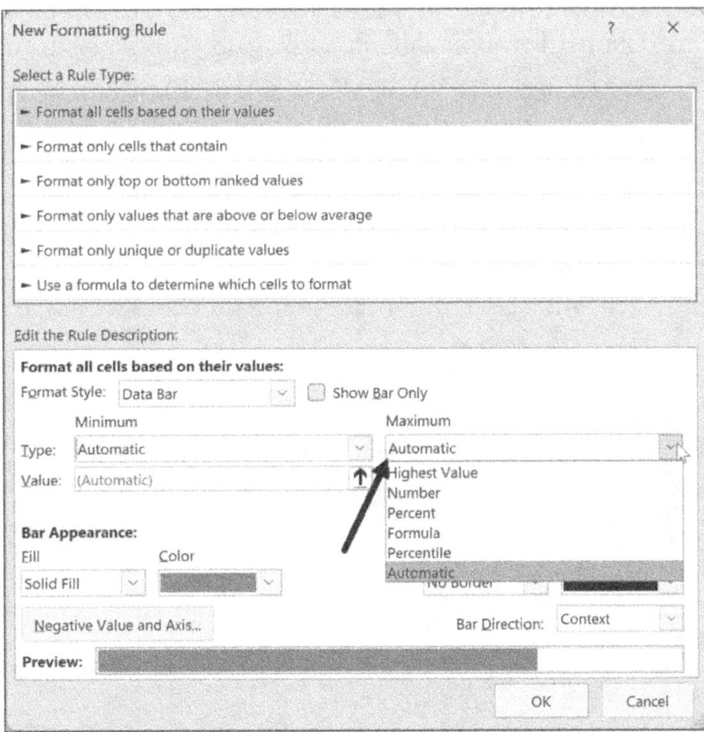

This is also where you can tell Excel to just display the bars and not the associated numbers.

Here are three examples of the green gradient data bar option applied to ten values, but with different settings:

Default	Bars Only	Range of -20 to 20
1		-5
2		-12
3		3
4		4
5		5
6		6
7		7
8		8
9		9
10		10

The first two have values from 1 to 10. The first column is the default data bar setting where the bar gets larger as the number increases, until it fills the cell when the number is the largest in the range. The second is the exact same, except I chose to hide the actual numbers.

With the third one, I made the first two entries negative numbers, and then changed the criteria to say that the range for the data bars was -20 to 20. Since my largest positive value is 10, that cell's bar only covers a fourth of the cell width, half of the positive side. With my negative numbers, the data bar is red by default and, again, doesn't go to the end because the smallest number is -12 but I told Excel the range should go to -20.

Color Scales

Another way to visually see differences across your data is to use color scales. I like to use this one for my monthly revenue, ad cost, and profit numbers. It lets me quickly scan multiple years of monthly values for each, and see if things are going up or down based upon the darkness of each cell.

Month	Revenue
January	$1,868.00
February	$2,101.00
March	$2,562.00
April	$5,968.00
May	$6,164.00
June	$2,085.00
July	$1,550.00
August	$3,901.00
September	$4,530.00
October	$3,046.00

This is another one where you're basically just choosing your color scheme in the secondary dropdown men.

There are a variety of choices that involve green, red, and yellow as well as a couple that involve red, white, and blue instead. I prefer to use a custom color range, because to me red is bad and green is good, so applying a color scheme that uses red and green implies that you've "failed" for the red values and "succeeded" for the green values. But maybe none of them are good. Or maybe all of them are good. So I tend to use different shades of teal or orange or something like that. Like this:

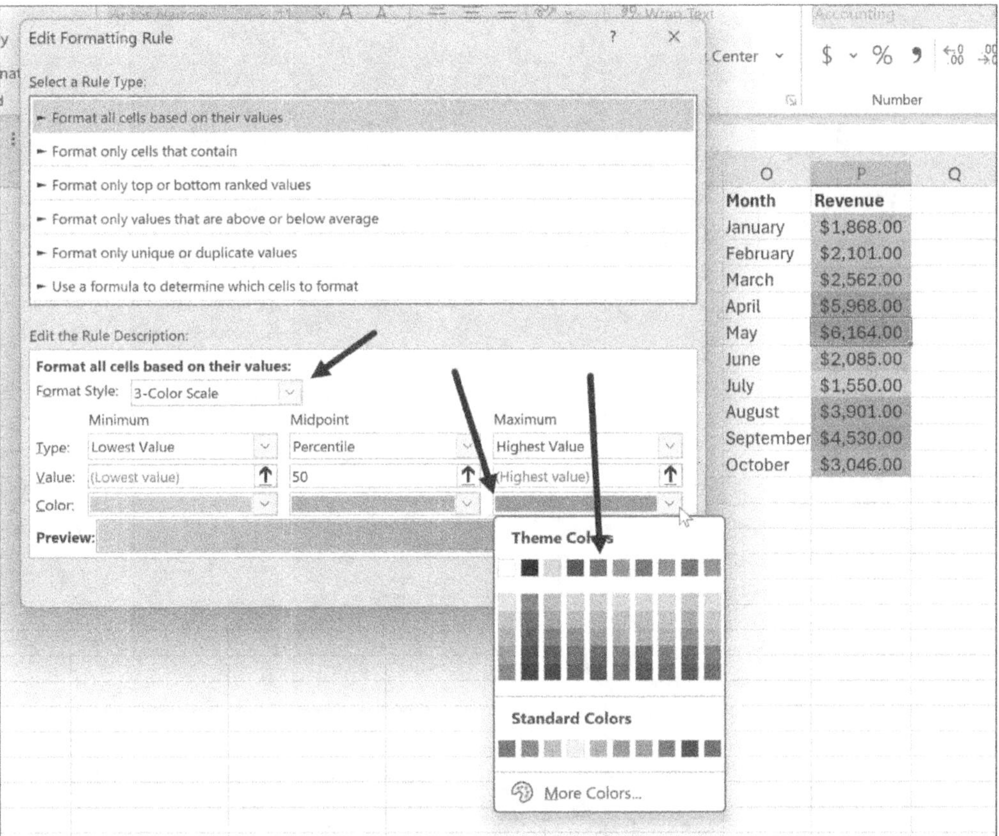

Here I edited the Format Style to use three colors. I then chose the first three colors in that fifth column of the theme colors dropdown menu to create my custom gradient. This blue color is neutral to me in terms of "bad" or "good", but at the same time the difference between the lighter fill color and darker fill color still tells me which months performed the best comparatively.

The default on this one is for Excel to use a percentile to bucket values around the minimum and maximum values in the range, but you can change that. It's possible to set specific numbers instead.

Icon Sets

The final way to visually represent your values is to use icon sets. Icon sets are basically images instead of colors. (Although many of the images also have colors as part of their composition.)

The secondary dropdown menu on this one allows you to choose the images you want to use.

Here I've chosen the "3 Traffic Lights" option that puts a green circle next to the highest values, a yellow one next to those in the middle, and a red one for the lowest values:

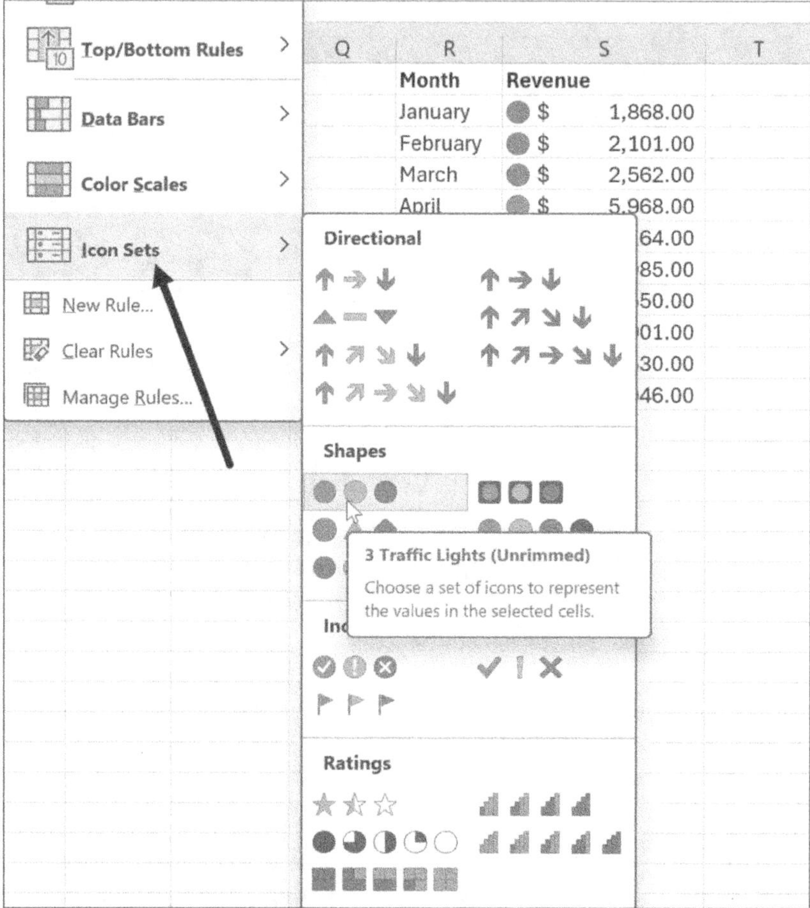

This is another one where if you're going to use it you probably want to customize the ranges used. The default is for Excel to take the values in the range, assign "good" to the top 33%, "okay" to the next 33%, and "bad" to the bottom 33%.

You can also set this one to just show the icons and not the values.

And you can also choose a different icon for each of the three buckets, but I wouldn't recommend it. They're grouped together for a reason.

Manage Conditional Formatting Rules

If you want to edit an existing rule, go to the Conditional Formatting dropdown menu, and choose Manage Rules. That will bring up the Conditional Formatting Rules Manager dialogue box:

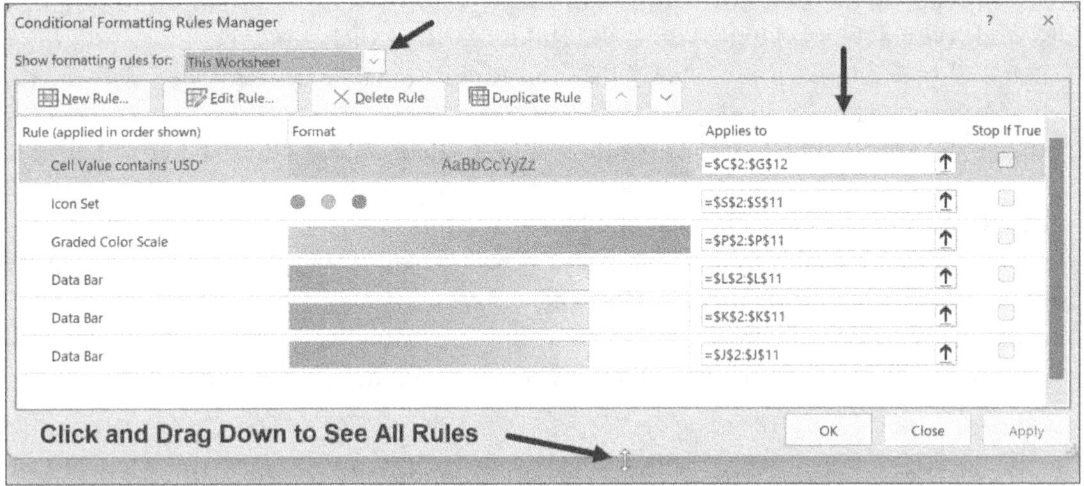

At the very top, you can see the dropdown menu for which rules to display. The default is "Current Selection," but you can change that to your current worksheet, any other worksheet in your workbook, or any pivot table in your workbook.

Above, I chose This Worksheet. I also clicked and dragged from the bottom of the dialogue box to make it big enough to show all of the conditional formatting rules I have applied to this worksheet.

Below that dropdown is a row with four main options: New Rule, Edit Rule, Delete Rule, and Duplicate Rule. There is also an up arrow and a down arrow.

And below that is the list of all conditional formatting rules that apply for your selection.

The first column for each rule shows the type of rule (Icon Set, Graded Color Scale, Data Bar, etc).

The next column shows the formatting each rule is using.

The third column shows which cells each rule applies to.

The fourth column has a checkbox for "Stop if True". The checkbox is for situations where you have more than one conditional formatting rule applied to the same cell range. Excel will work through the rules from top to bottom but stop if that box is checked, and the rule was triggered by the contents in the cell.

Edit Rule

To edit a rule that you've already created, click on its row in the rules manager, and then click on Edit Rule at the top of that dialogue box.

That will bring up the Edit Formatting Rule dialogue box. Make the changes you want, click on OK, and you will be brought back to the Rules Manager dialogue box.

If that's all you wanted to do, click OK, the Rules Manager dialogue box will close, and your rule changes will be applied.

If you're not done, you can click Apply to apply that change immediately, or wait until you're done all of your changes and click OK to apply all of them at once.

Above, with the highlight cells rules, if I had wanted to format based on whether the values were greater than or equal to $1200 (instead of greater than $1199), I would have applied one of the default options, and then come here and edited that rule.

As you can see below, the dropdown in the Edit Formatting Rule dialogue box for highlight cell rules, contains greater than or equal to, less than or equal to, and not equal to:

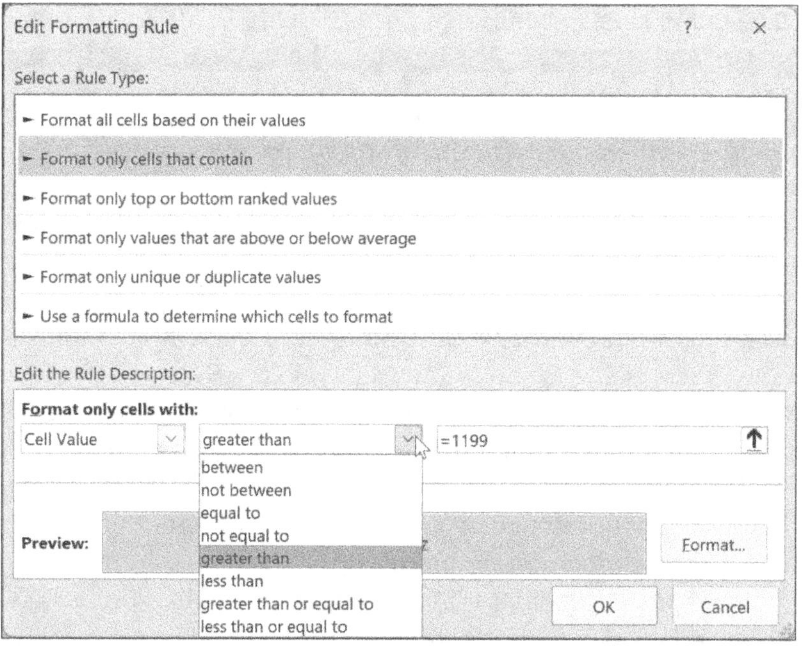

As you can see on the next page, the Edit Formatting Rule dialogue box for the "text that contains" rule will allow you to also format cells not containing, beginning with, or ending with your specified text:

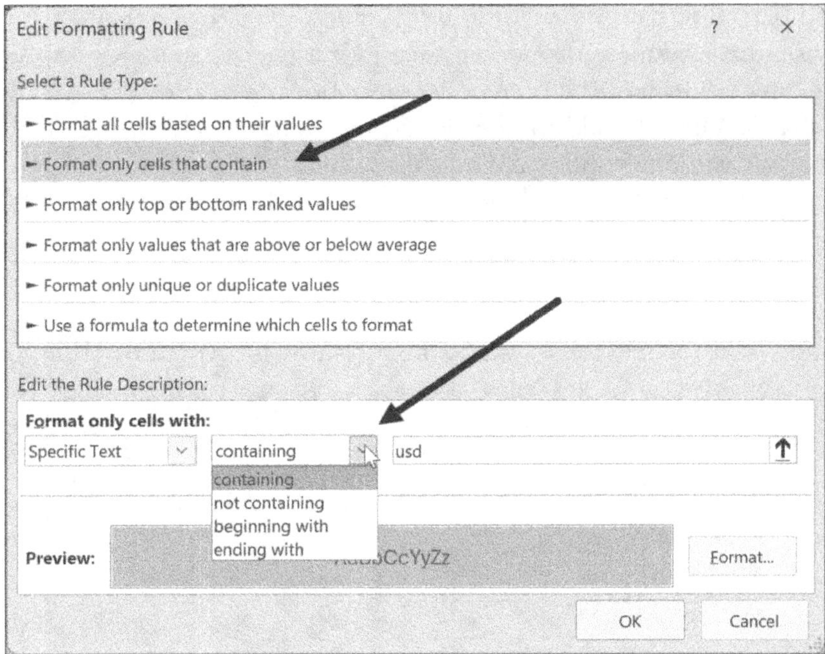

For the top/bottom rules, the Edit Formatting Rule dialogue box also lets you use standard deviations to flag your results:

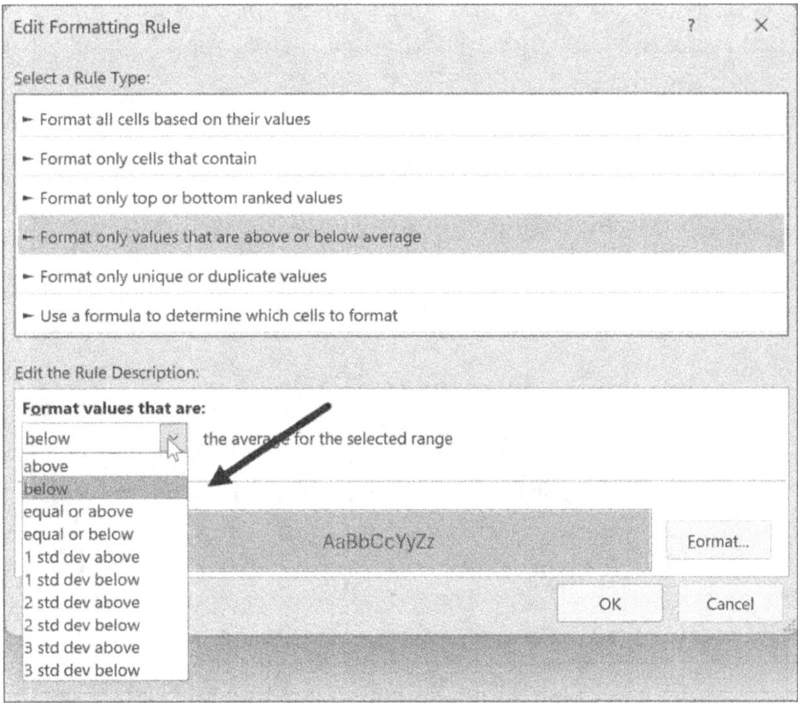

You can also reach the Edit Formatting Rule dialogue box by choosing More Rules at the bottom of any of the secondary dropdown menus, but if you use that option, you may have to change your category to find the correct list of options.

(Also note that you could build these rules from scratch by choosing New Rule from the main conditional formatting dropdown menu at the start, and then choosing the rule type you want, and going from there. I just find it easier to let Excel do most of the work first.)

Clear Rules

To remove conditional formatting, in the main conditional formatting dropdown menu you can hold your mouse over Clear Rules, and then choose to clear rules from the entire worksheet or the selected range of cells.

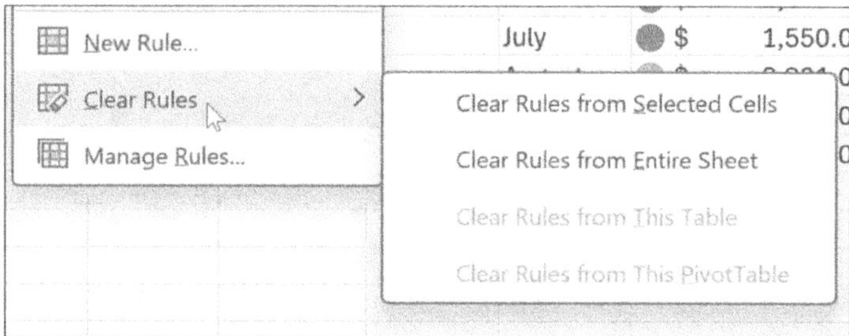

Your other option is to use the Rules Manager dialogue box. If you have a lot of cells that contain conditional formatting, but other conditional formatting you don't want to lose in that worksheet, that's probably the best option.

Delete Rule

To delete a rule, bring up the Conditional Formatting Rules Manager dialogue box by clicking on Manage Rules in the main conditional formatting dropdown menu. Click on the row for the rule you want to delete, and then click on Delete Rule at the top.

Duplicate Rule

To duplicate a rule, bring up the Conditional Formatting Rules Manager dialogue box, click on the row for the rule you want to duplicate, and then click on Duplicate Rule at the top.

Excel will put an exact duplicate of that rule at the top of your rules list. Use Edit Rule to make changes to it. (Or choose Cancel at the bottom to close the dialogue box without saving your changes.)

Multiple Rules On One Cell Range

It is possible to apply multiple conditional formatting rules to the same range of cells. For example, here I've applied red formatting to cells that are under $1,000 and kept the green formatting for cells over $1,199:

	A	B	C	D	E	F	G	H	I
1			Hours Worked						
2			20	25	30	35	40	45	50
3		$15	$300	$375	$450	$525	$600	$675	$750
4	Pay Rate	$20	$400	$500	$600	$700	$800	$900	$1,000
5		$25	$500	$625	$750	$875	$1,000	$1,125	$1,250
6		$30	$600	$750	$900	$1,050	$1,200	$1,350	$1,500
7		$35	$700	$875	$1,050	$1,225	$1,400	$1,575	$1,750
8		$40	$800	$1,000	$1,200	$1,400	$1,600	$1,800	$2,000
9		$45	$900	$1,125	$1,350	$1,575	$1,800	$2,025	$2,250
10		$50	$1,000	$1,250	$1,500	$1,750	$2,000	$2,250	$2,500

If the formatting you apply has no conflict, that's all you have to do. Just select that same range of cells twice and choose your formatting you want for each set of criteria.

But if you have rules that are applied to one cell range where there's a potential for conflict between the rules, then that's where you need to use the up and down arrows in the rules manager and/or the checkbox for Stop if True to make sure that when there's a conflict the correct rule takes precedence.

Conditional Formatting on Pivot Tables

It is possible to apply conditional formatting on a pivot table. To get started, it works the same way. Go to the pivot table, select the cells that you want to apply your formatting to, and apply your conditional formatting. (Be careful not to select subtotal and grand total fields, though.)

By default, Excel is going to set the range of cells covered by your pivot table conditional formatting to just the cells you selected. But for a pivot table, because they are dynamic, you very likely will want that to be set to a different option.

To do that, bring up the Conditional Formatting Rules Manager dialogue box by clicking on Manage Rules in the main conditional formatting dropdown menu.

Select the rule from the list, and choose Edit Rule.

That will give you a set of three options to choose from:

The first is the selected cells. The second is for all cells showing values for that field. The third is for the specific interaction between that field and any others you used to build the values in the table.

In this case that third option is for Sum of Converted Currency for Marketplace and Author Name. That's the one I want. That way if I add a new author or a new marketplace and refresh my pivot table, the conditional formatting will incorporate those changes.

* * *

Okay, so that was conditional formatting. It's a nice, easy way to flag your values in a data table to visually highlight what that data is telling you. But sometimes you don't want to have to show people the gory details of your data. In those cases, charts are a great way to visually summarize a lot of data. Let's cover those next.

Charts - Types

Okay, our next big topic is charts, which are yet another great way to visualize data. Sometimes taking a thousand rows of numbers and turning them into a pretty picture is truly the best way to understand what you're dealing with.

The way you build or format a chart is generally consistent across the various types of chart, but different charts are better used for different purposes, so I want to walk through chart types first, and then we'll get into how to actually insert charts and format them in the next chapter.

Let's start with a high-level summary for this chapter and then walk through examples.

Column charts, bar charts, and line charts are good choices for when you want to compare values using two different categories. For example, sales by store by month. The value is sales, the first category is store, the second category is month. I usually use these for time-series data where one of the categories is month, year, etc., but you don't have to. I could as easily use one of these chart types for sales by store for different formats (print, ebook, audio).

Pie, doughnut, and area charts are a good choice for when you're doing a "part of the whole" analysis. For example, total sales by store for a year. In that case, you want a visual that shows what part of the whole year's sales each store represented.

Scatter charts or histograms are a good way to visualize random data and look for patterns.

Okay, let's look at some actual charts now to help visualize what I just said. For most of this chapter the data table we'll be working with is this one that shows sales for four stores across six months and also includes totals for each store and for each month:

	A	B	C	D	E	F
1		Amazon	Kobo	Nook	Google	Total
2	January	$ 1,747	$ 353	$ 470	$ 65	$ 2,635
3	February	$ 1,616	$ 767	$ 445	$ 106	$ 2,934
4	March	$ 5,099	$ 420	$ 314	$ 1,132	$ 6,965
5	April	$ 4,596	$ 692	$ 140	$ 1,928	$ 7,356
6	May	$ 2,165	$ 809	$ 407	$ 1,090	$ 4,471
7	June	$ 2,502	$ 261	$ 244	$ 1,113	$ 4,120
8	Total	$ 17,725	$ 3,302	$ 2,020	$ 5,434	$ 28,481

(It's fake data so don't read anything into it or get hung up on if there's a weird number.)

First up:

Column and Bar Charts

Column and bar charts are essentially the exact same thing, it's just a question of whether the bars are vertical (column) or horizontal (bar). Excel includes both 2-D and 3-D versions of these charts.

In general, 3-D feels a bit gimmicky to me—like something that would be used in a bad consulting presentation. You do you, but if you're going to use 3-D, do it for a reason. (I do have an example of one possible use below and I have been known to be wrong before so there may be other uses out there.)

There are three main types of column and bar charts: clustered, stacked, and 100% stacked.

Clustered Charts

Here we have both a clustered column and a clustered bar chart that show the amount earned in each store for each month:

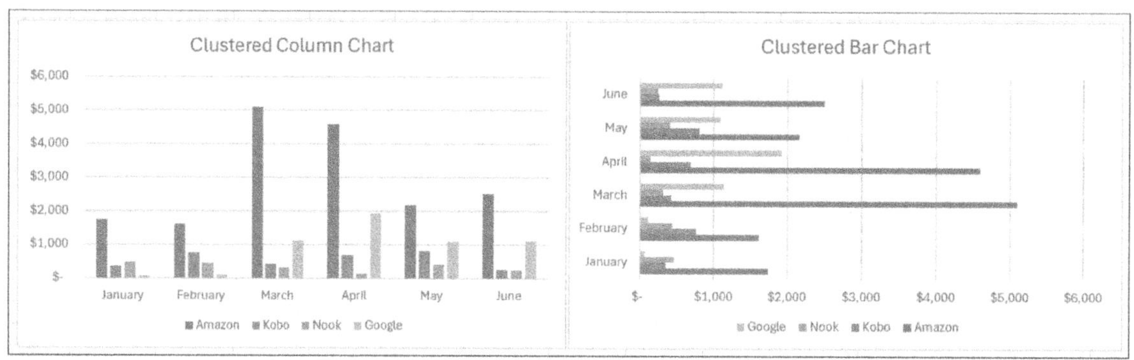

You can see that Excel created a separate column or bar for each store for each time period. The color of the column or bar stays the same for each store for each month, but the "height" of the column or bar varies month-to-month based on the sales for that particular store in that particular month.

Amazon, for example, is the darkest color. You can easily see that within each month Amazon had the highest sales compared to the other stores, but that it went up and down across the time period. You can also see that Google (the lightest colored column/bar) had a good month in April compared to its sales in other months.

Clustered columns are great for situations like this where you want to see the relative performance of a limited number of one category across a limited number of a second category. However, they can quickly get out of hand. Above, I have four stores and six months. That's easy enough to read. But imagine how busy this would get if I had ten stores across twenty-four months. It'd be a nightmare.

Also, note that it's pretty hard to see the *overall* change in sales month to month. You can see the obvious ones, like the increase from February to March, but what about March to April. Did total sales go up or down? It's not easy to see in this chart type. If that was something you needed to visualize, this chart would not be the best choice.

Stacked Charts

The next column and bar chart choice you have is a stacked chart:

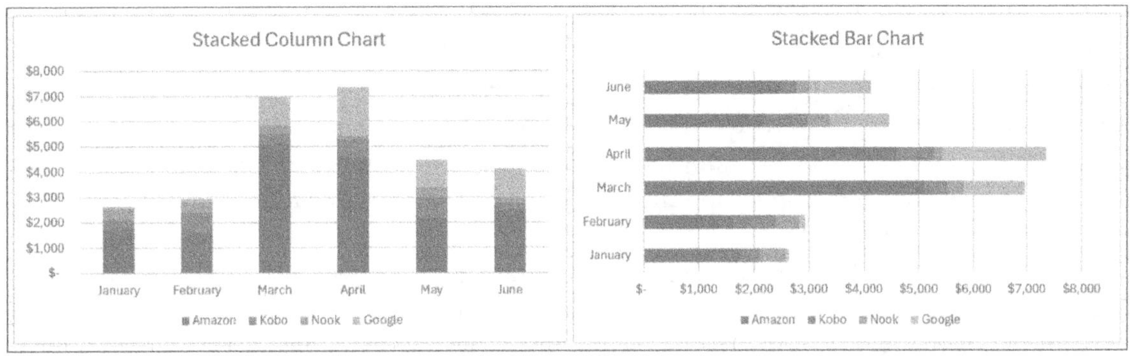

Stacked charts take the columns or bars used in clustered charts, and stack them on top of each other for each secondary category.

You can see here that instead of four separate columns or bars each month, there is one, and that each colored section in that one column or bar for the month represents the sales for a specific store for that month.

It's still possible to see relative performance between stores within a given month. But it can be harder to see how a specific store, like Google, did over time. Amazon is on the bottom so you can still see those changes month-to-month, but try matching up the sections for Kobo and comparing them to one another. Much harder to do.

The advantage to this chart type, though, is that you can easily see total performance across the time period much easier. Here we can immediately see that more was earned in April compared to March.

100% Stacked Charts

The next type of column or bar chart is the 100% stacked chart:

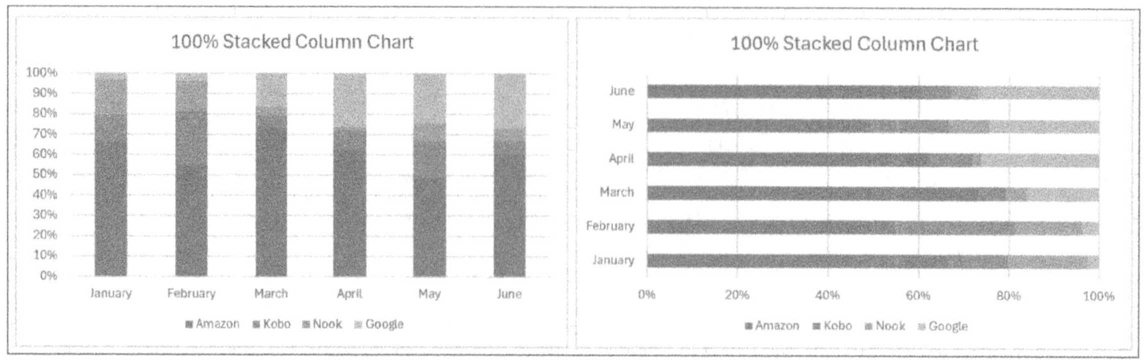

The column or bar "height" on this one is always going to be the same, because it always has to add up to 100%. In this case, the portion of the bar or column assigned to each store represents the *percent of the whole* for that store for that month. I mentioned before with pivot tables, that sometimes I'm not as concerned with total dollar value as I am with share of what was earned. Is one of my stores slipping so that even though my revenue is going up overall, that one store is in decline?

This chart type lets you see that better. Like the decline there March to April to May for Amazon. Why did Amazon's share of overall sales decline during those three months? Is this a good thing (I started selling better elsewhere) or a bad thing (my biggest source of revenue is in decline)?

I rarely use this chart type, though, because it can really hide key information. The problem with this chart type is that in one period you could have values of 1, 2, and 5, and in the next have 1000, 2000, and 5000, and they'd look exactly the same in the chart. If you're trying to pay your rent based on the amount you earn, the difference between making $8 in a month and $8,000 in a month is very important.

Same with disease analysis. Sure, it matters that Variant X is coming to dominate, but if Month 1 has 10,000 cases and Month 2 has 100, I think the 100 versus 10,000 is far more important than that the 100 comes 50% from Variant X instead of Variant Y.

3-D Column Chart

There is one type of column chart that is not mirrored as a bar chart, the 3-D Column Chart.

This one actually does provide information beyond what the standard 2-D charts provide, so I want to show it to you real quick.

The 3-D Column Chart is kind of like if you very carefully deconstructed the stacked column chart and put each piece that had been stacked one-by-one in a row behind the first piece. This lets you compare values for each store over time (left to right) as well as among stores for each month (front to back, back to front).

Here are two examples using the same data as above:

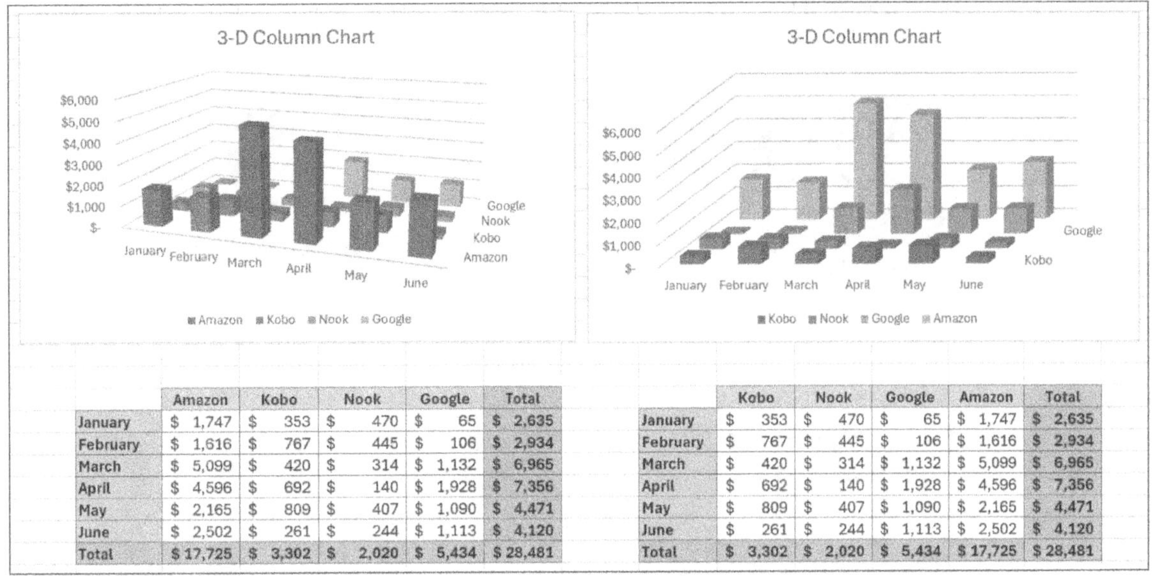

	Amazon	Kobo	Nook	Google	Total
January	$ 1,747	$ 353	$ 470	$ 65	$ 2,635
February	$ 1,616	$ 767	$ 445	$ 106	$ 2,934
March	$ 5,099	$ 420	$ 314	$ 1,132	$ 6,965
April	$ 4,596	$ 692	$ 140	$ 1,928	$ 7,356
May	$ 2,165	$ 809	$ 407	$ 1,090	$ 4,471
June	$ 2,502	$ 261	$ 244	$ 1,113	$ 4,120
Total	$ 17,725	$ 3,302	$ 2,020	$ 5,434	$ 28,481

	Kobo	Nook	Google	Amazon	Total
January	$ 353	$ 470	$ 65	$ 1,747	$ 2,635
February	$ 767	$ 445	$ 106	$ 1,616	$ 2,934
March	$ 420	$ 314	$ 1,132	$ 5,099	$ 6,965
April	$ 692	$ 140	$ 1,928	$ 4,596	$ 7,356
May	$ 809	$ 407	$ 1,090	$ 2,165	$ 4,471
June	$ 261	$ 244	$ 1,113	$ 2,502	$ 4,120
Total	$ 3,302	$ 2,020	$ 5,434	$ 17,725	$ 28,481

The reason I wanted to call this one out here is also because the order of your columns impacts the appearance.

In the left-hand 3-D chart, the tallest column is in front. This isn't because that is Excel's default. It's because Amazon was the first store listed in my data table, which I've added below the chart so you can see it.

In the right-hand 3-D chart, I moved Amazon's values to the last column. That put the largest values for each month in the back row and, I personally think, made the chart easier to read. Note, though, that it also changed the color assigned to Amazon and the other stores. That's because colors are just assigned down the line from first to last and Amazon is now last. (You can customize colors. We'll discuss that in the next chapter.)

Pie and Doughnut Charts

A doughnut chart is just a pie chart with the middle missing. I'd say pie charts are more of a traditional look while doughnut charts are more of a modern look, but it's the exact same information.

On the next page are examples using our data from above, that show share of total sales by store for the entire time period.

In both charts you can easily see that Amazon has the biggest share, and that Google is second. But note that these are part-of-the-whole-type charts, so you don't see actual values. You don't know if this is a chart of $8 in sales or $8,000 in sales.

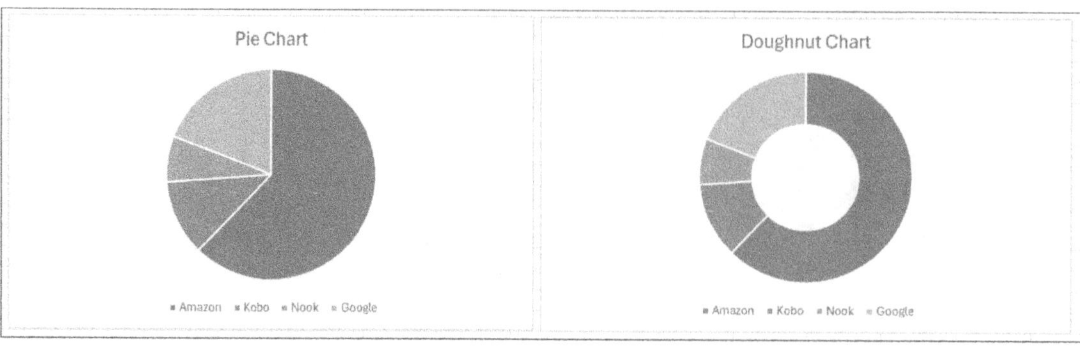

There are three other types of pie chart in Excel. One is a 3-D version, which I consider gimmicky. The others are a pie of pie chart and a bar of pie chart. I'll cover them so you understand them, but use them with caution.

Breakout Pie Charts

Pie of pie charts and bar of pie charts do the exact same thing, they break out a part of your data from your main pie chart into a separate chart. Here we have share of total sales by month in a standard pie chart, a pie of pie chart, and a bar of pie chart:

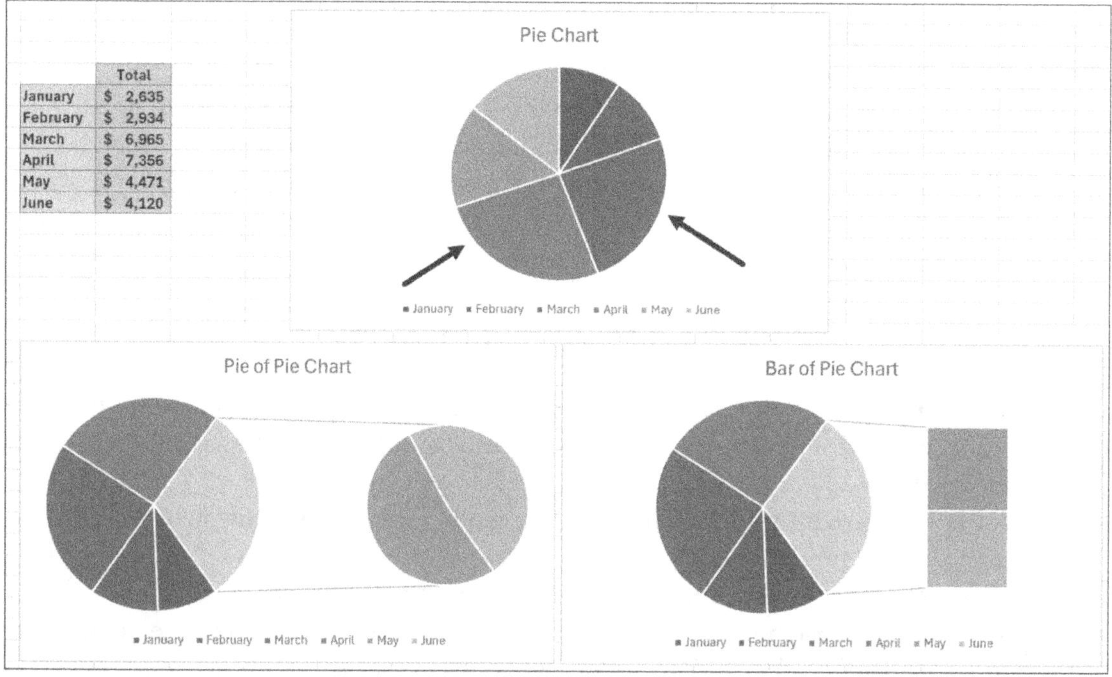

If you look at the standard pie chart, it's pretty easy to see that the two biggest months are March and April, the two bottom slices in the pie.

(In Excel you can hold your mouse over a chart element, like a pie slice, to see its label and value if you're not sure which color in the legend (guide) matches to that particular element. There are also formatting options to have Excel display labels and values on the chart itself that we'll cover in the formatting chapter.)

Okay. Now look at the pie of pie and bar of pie charts below that pie chart and try to figure out what you're seeing. It's the same information as in the basic pie chart.

If you just focused on the main pie chart in either one of those, you'd think that March and April, now on the left-hand side of the chart, are pretty much equal to that slice on the right-hand side, maybe even a little smaller. It would no longer be obvious that March and April were the best months because that third pie slice is just as big.

What is actually happening here is that the third pie slice there on the right side is a combination of two different months, May and June. And then that second chart on the right side, whether it be a pie chart or a bar chart, is just those two months charted against one another. (In other charts this could be many fields, but in this case Excel just chose those two.)

I do not find it intuitive to interpret these charts correctly. My natural inclination is to compare the size of the different slices to one another, which makes me think that May and June are the same size as March and April even though they're not.

The bar of pie chart is a little easier to understand, in my opinion, because it breaks that slice of the main pie chart into a bar chart, but I still think it's confusing because that secondary chart gives too much visual space to smaller values than it should.

I'm sure there are uses for these, just ask yourself before you use either one whether it helps explain your data or whether it causes confusion. If you're in a field where they get used often, most people will probably understand what you're doing, but if your chart has the chance to reach a wider audience, maybe find some other way to call out those smaller results, like a data table.

Also, these are good chart types to include labels with to help users understand what they're seeing. I have an example in the next chapter under Display Pie Chart Percent to show how I'd handle a pie of pie chart.

Line Charts

Line charts are great for seeing trends, but there are only two line charts I would recommend you use in Excel, Line and Line with Markers. The other line chart types Excel offers are stacked line charts like we looked at with column and bar charts, but they aren't intuitive. I'd avoid them and use area charts or bar or column charts instead. They're way too easy to misread.

Here is a Line chart showing total sales for each month:

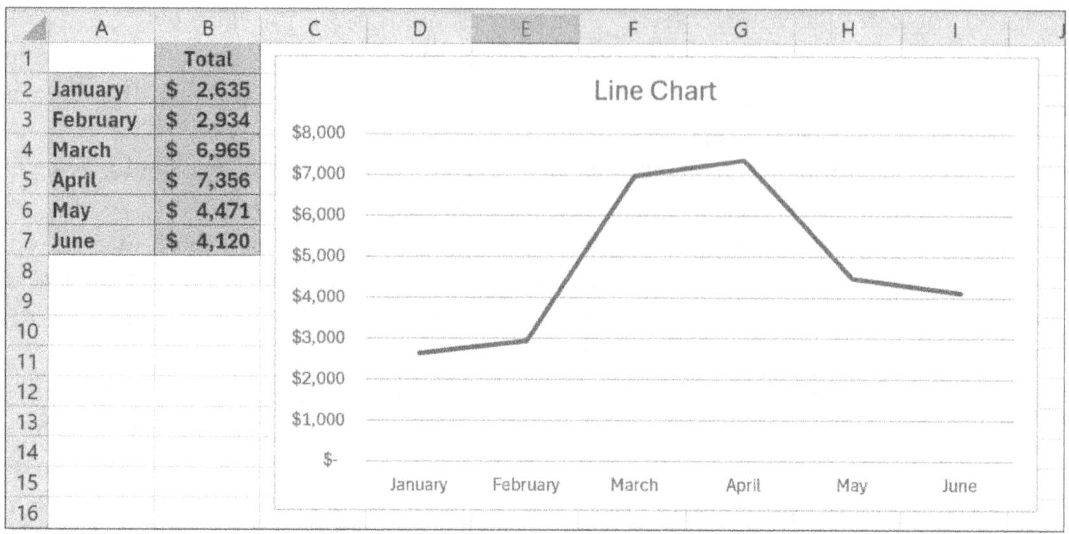

You can easily see how total sales were up in March and April, and how they stayed up a bit in May and June.

Here is a Line with Markers chart of sales for each store for each month:

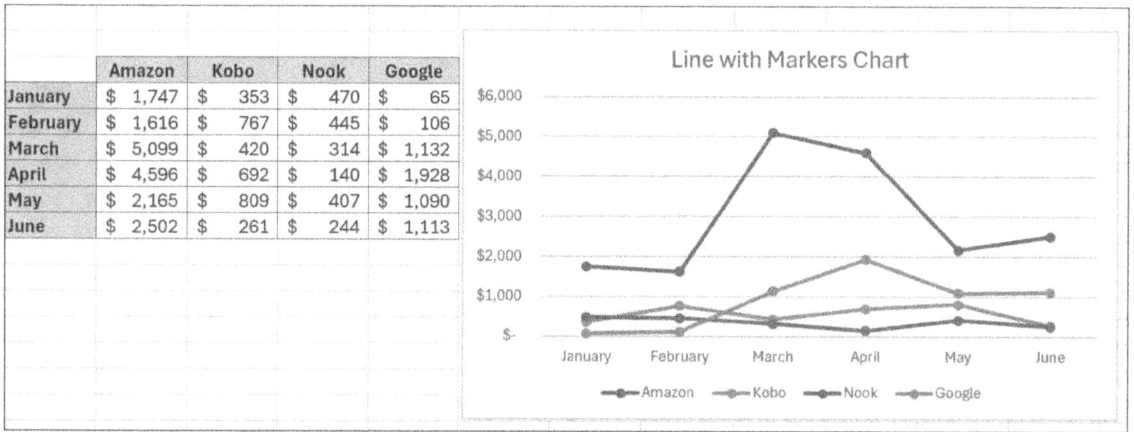

To include lines for each store, all I had to do was include the columns of data for the individual stores, Excel did the rest. The first column is the x-axis, the rest are charted against that.

Area Charts

We have all seen a lot of area charts over the last few years. Or maybe it's just me. A lot of the "share of variant" charts use an area chart to show which variants are gaining traction or fading away. Where the stacked line charts fail miserably, an area chart works. It basically creates a colored layer for each category where the width of the layer for a given period is determined by the value or percent of total for that period.

Here is a Stacked Area Chart and a 100% Stacked Area Chart for sales by store by month:

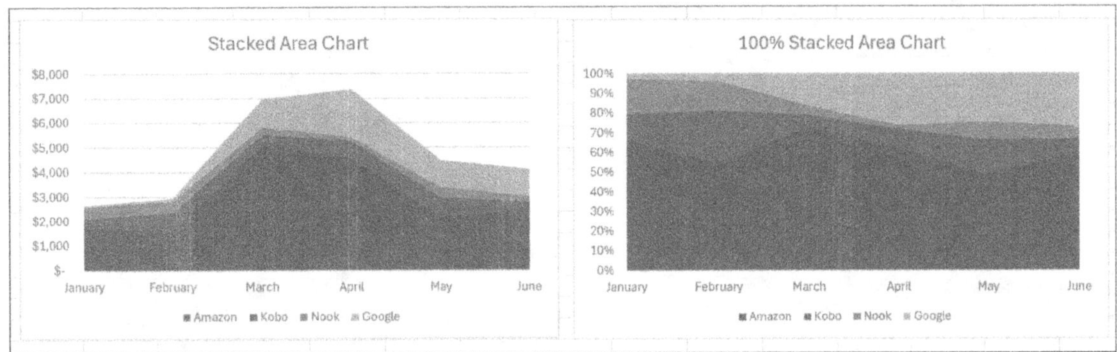

By filling in the space below each line, it becomes clear that the different pieces are stacked on top of one another to make a whole.

I think this chart type better shows the change for a specific store from period to period than a stacked column or bar chart, because even when a specific store is a small part of the whole, you can still see whether that layer gets bigger or smaller over time.

Of course, be careful once again with the 100% stacked chart since it doesn't show changes in overall total value. $8 and $8,000 can look the exact same.

Also, I'm thinking on this one that it's only good for time series data. I don't think I'd use it for sales by store by format, for example, because those don't really represent a continuum like time does. I looked online and found a few that broke that (like one that had car colors instead of months), but I think they were less successful than if they'd used a column or bar chart for that data instead.

Okay, next.

Scatter Plots

A scatter plot puts a dot on the chart for the intersection of two values. You can choose to just plot those dots (Scatter) or to plot those dots and connect them with a smooth line or a straight line (Scatter with Smooth Lines, Scatter with Straight Lines). If you connect dots with a line, you can also choose to include a marker for each data point (Scatter with Smooth Lines and Markers, Scatter with Straight Lines and Markers).

A scatter plot can be a good way to see clusters in data points or relationships between different data points. For this one we need new data points because a scatter chart is more likely to be used for random measurements of two variables than for the sales data we've been using.

On the next page is a basic scatter plot of nine data points:

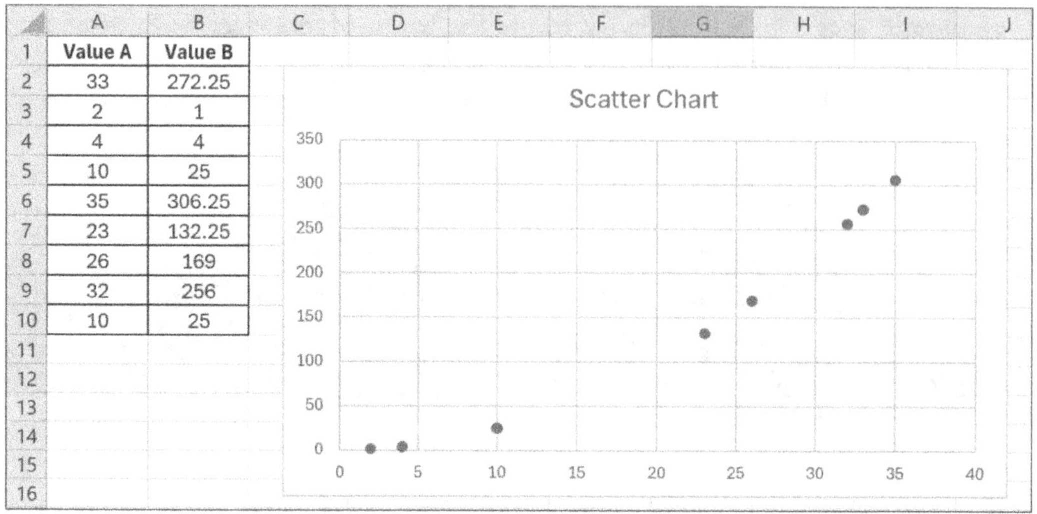

If I were to just look at the data in Columns A and B, I wouldn't be able to see that there's a relationship there. Maybe I could see that larger values of A also mean larger relative values of B, but that's about it. However, when I plot those values in a scatter chart, like I did above, suddenly we can see that there's a pattern there. Given the curve of that line, we also know it's likely exponential.

To confirm that, I really want to draw a line between those points. Problem is, if I do it with my data as it is now, it looks horrible:

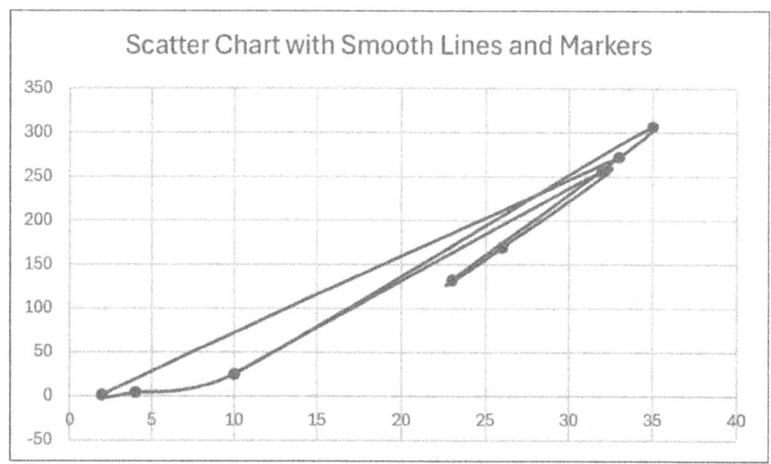

That's because Excel draws the connecting points between each line in order from first to last. It's basically assuming that there is a time component to the data you gave it, and that the order in which the data points were collected also matters.

If the order of the observations is not important, then sort your data before you create a scatter plot.

Here I sorted by the values in the first column and plotted again with a smooth line and it works:

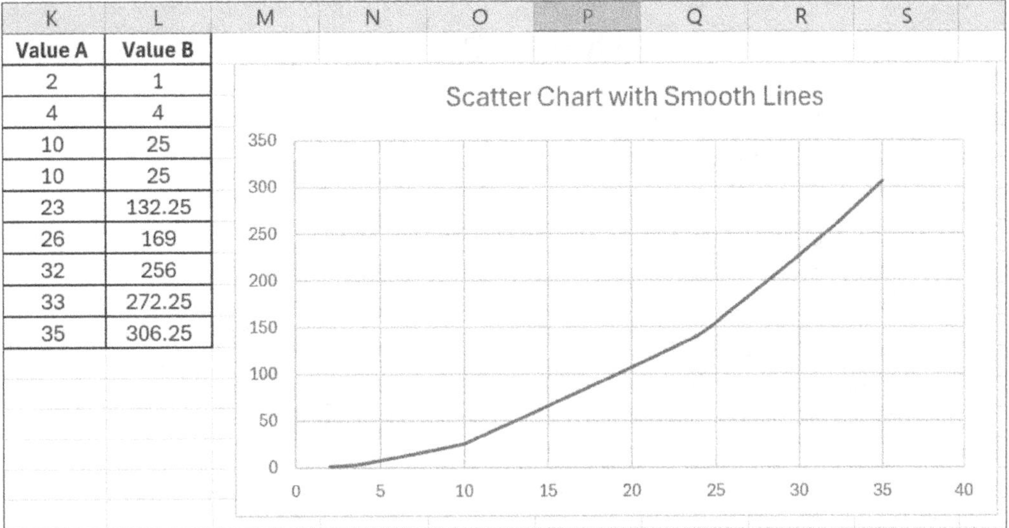

I can now clearly see a relationship between Value A and Value B.

With enough data points, the difference between smooth and straight lines becomes less important, but when you have fewer data points a straight line can more clearly show the lack of observations between two points.

It is also possible to have a scatter plot with more than two values plotted against the same base value. The first column of your data will be used to set the x-axis values, the remaining columns of data will then be plotted against the values in that first column.

Like this:

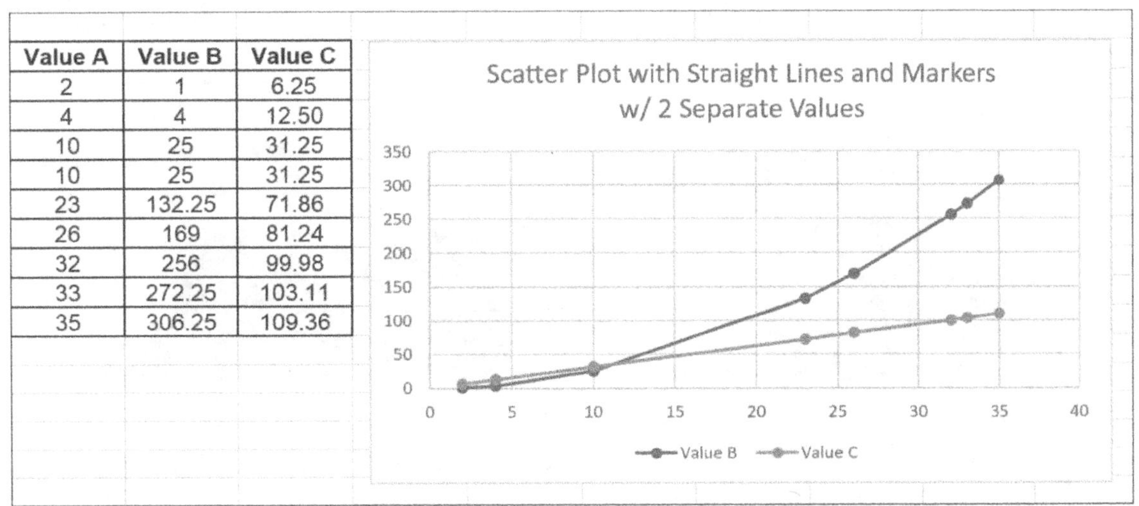

(You can do this without a line connecting the various points, but that might be a little hard to read because you'll just have a bunch of different colored dots on your plot.)

Bubble Plots

A bubble plot is like a scatter plot except you can have an additional value that is represented by the size of the bubble that plots each point.

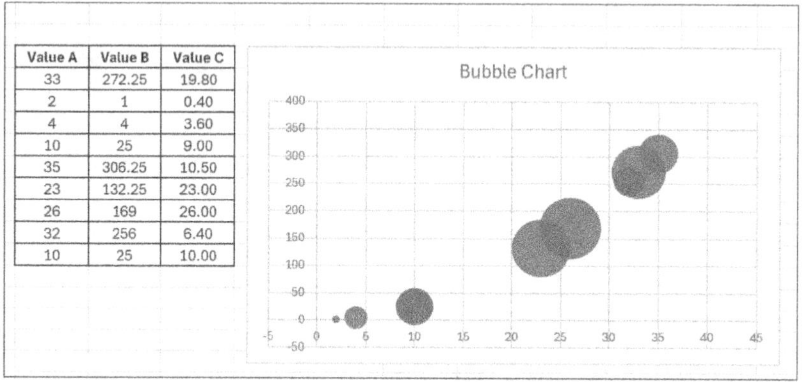

Histogram

Histograms take a set of values and place them into equally-sized buckets that cover the range of your data from smallest to largest. They're useful for seeing if there's a pattern to the distribution in your data. The more observations you have, the more clear any distribution will become.

Below we have two histograms, one with only 29 observations, the other with 100.

Both are using a data set that generates random whole numbers between the values of 5 and 60.

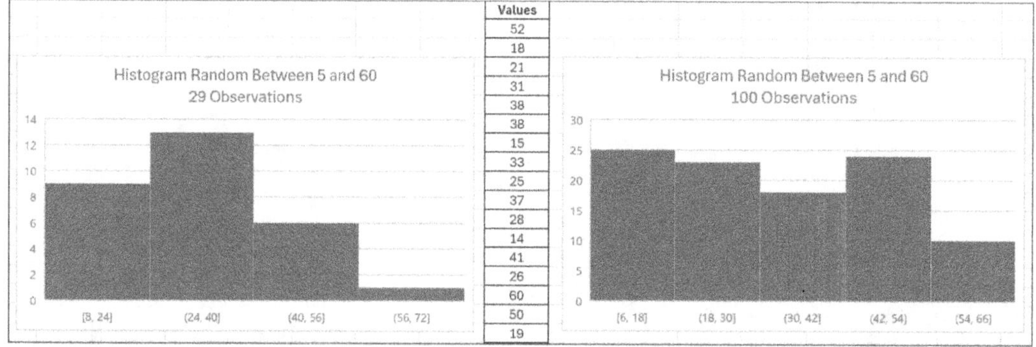

You can see that as the number of observations goes up, the buckets that Excel assigns get closer to the true range of the values. Also, the buckets start to even out in terms of the count of how many values fall into each bucket. With enough observations, we'd be able to see that the values are randomly distributed across that range.

With normally distributed data, the more observations you had the more the histogram would start to look like a standard bell curve.

It is possible to customize the range and number of buckets Excel uses for a histogram. We'll cover that in the next chapter.

Other Chart Types

Excel contains other types of charts such as a Treemap, a Sunburst, waterfall, surface, stock, radar, and box and whisker charts. You can also create maps that are filled in according to various values. I'm not going to delve into those here because I think most of the readers of this book won't need them. Just know that they exist if you do. (And remember that Excel actually has excellent help available on the Microsoft website as well as through the Help tab if you have the right settings enabled.)

Combo Charts

This is also just a quick mention. Excel lets you create combo charts so that you can combine two types of charts in one.

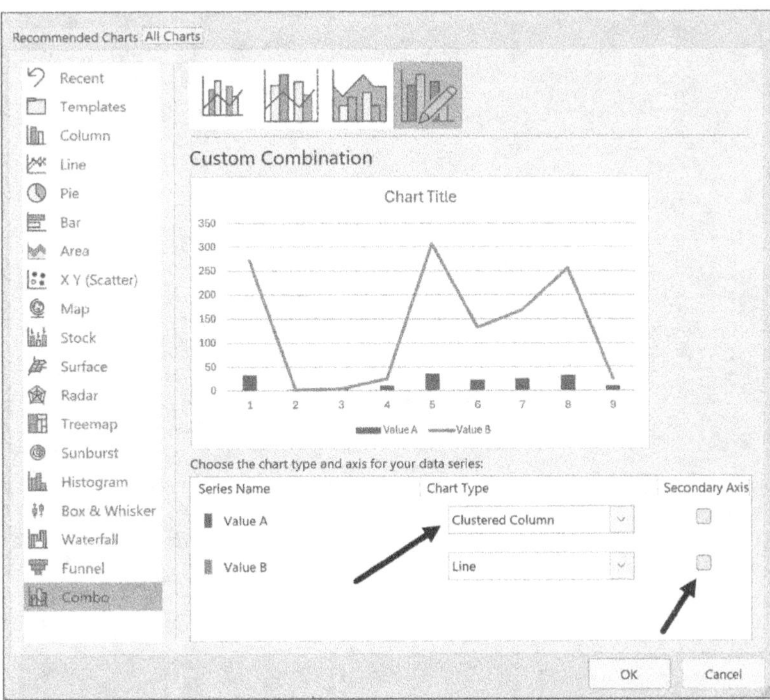

I was playing with this recently because I had downloaded a timeline template from the Office website and needed to understand how it worked.

What I figured out is that it was basically a line chart with values of zero paired with column charts that drew a bar for each point on the timeline. (Which meant that to get things lined up properly on the timeline I had to have my data points sorted by date, which was not obvious up front.)

It was a really interesting use of Excel. (That, me being me, I then expanded into using six different column charts so that I could color code different entries on the timeline.)

That's an advanced topic, though. Just know it exists if you want to try to go there at some point. And, if you do, use the secondary axis if your values are very different. (Like number of months and dollar value.)

Okay. Now that we've covered the different chart types, let's actually walk through how to create a chart and format it.

Charts – Insert and Format

Before you can create a chart, you need to format your data properly.

For column, bar, pie, and doughnut charts, you want to have labels across the first row and down the first column, and then your values in the cells in the table where those labels would intersect. Also, no subtotals or grand totals. If you do have grand totals, leave them out when you select your data.

As an example, this was the data table I worked with in the last chapter:

	A	B	C	D	E	F
1		Amazon	Kobo	Nook	Google	Total
2	January	$ 1,747	$ 353	$ 470	$ 65	$ 2,635
3	February	$ 1,616	$ 767	$ 445	$ 106	$ 2,934
4	March	$ 5,099	$ 420	$ 314	$ 1,132	$ 6,965
5	April	$ 4,596	$ 692	$ 140	$ 1,928	$ 7,356
6	May	$ 2,165	$ 809	$ 407	$ 1,090	$ 4,471
7	June	$ 2,502	$ 261	$ 244	$ 1,113	$ 4,120
8	Total	$ 17,725	$ 3,302	$ 2,020	$ 5,434	$ 28,481

For the bar and column charts, I selected Cells A1 to E7. For the pie and doughnut charts, I selected either Cells A2 to A7 and F2 to F7 (using the Ctrl key) or Cells B1 to E1 and Cells B8 to E8, depending on if I was looking at total sales by month or by store.

For the line graphs, scatter plots, bubble plots, and histogram, it was different. Those can work with one column of data. Put the label for the values in the first cell. If you want more than one line graph in a chart, or more than one set of data for a scatter plot, put the data in consecutive columns. The screenshots in the last chapter included examples.

Insert

Okay. Assuming you have a data table to work with, the first step for inserting a table is to select the cells that contain your data.

Next, go to the Charts section of the Insert tab, and find the dropdown menu for the chart type you want:

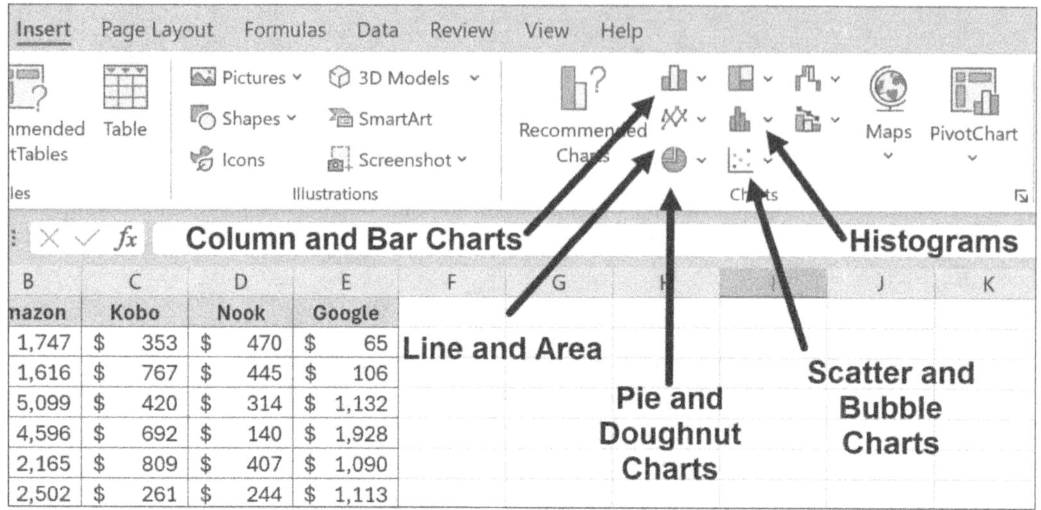

You can hold your mouse over each image on the menu tab as well as in the dropdown for each chart type, to see what kind of chart it is. This will also include a description of when it should be used. Here, for example, is the dropdown for column and bar charts where I am holding my cursor over the 2-D stacked column chart:

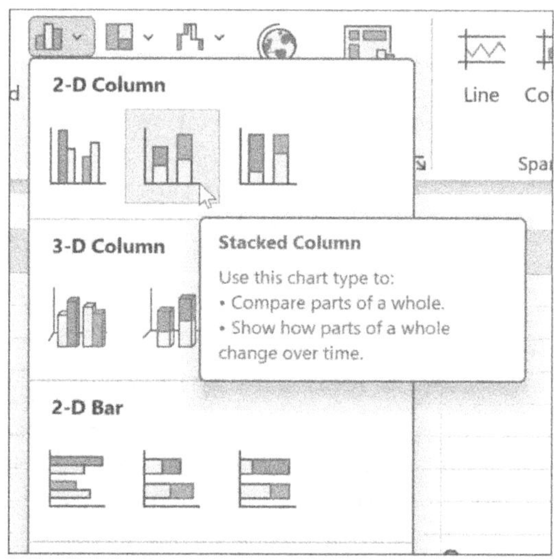

It says that the Stacked Column chart type is best to compare parts of a whole or to show how parts of a whole change over time.

If you have data selected when you hold your mouse over a chart type in the dropdown menu, the chart will appear in the background, allowing you to see what your data will look like. Click to actually insert it.

Another option, if you're not sure what type of chart to use, is to click on the Recommended Charts option in the Charts section of the Insert tab.

That will open the Insert Chart dialogue box to the Recommended Charts tab:

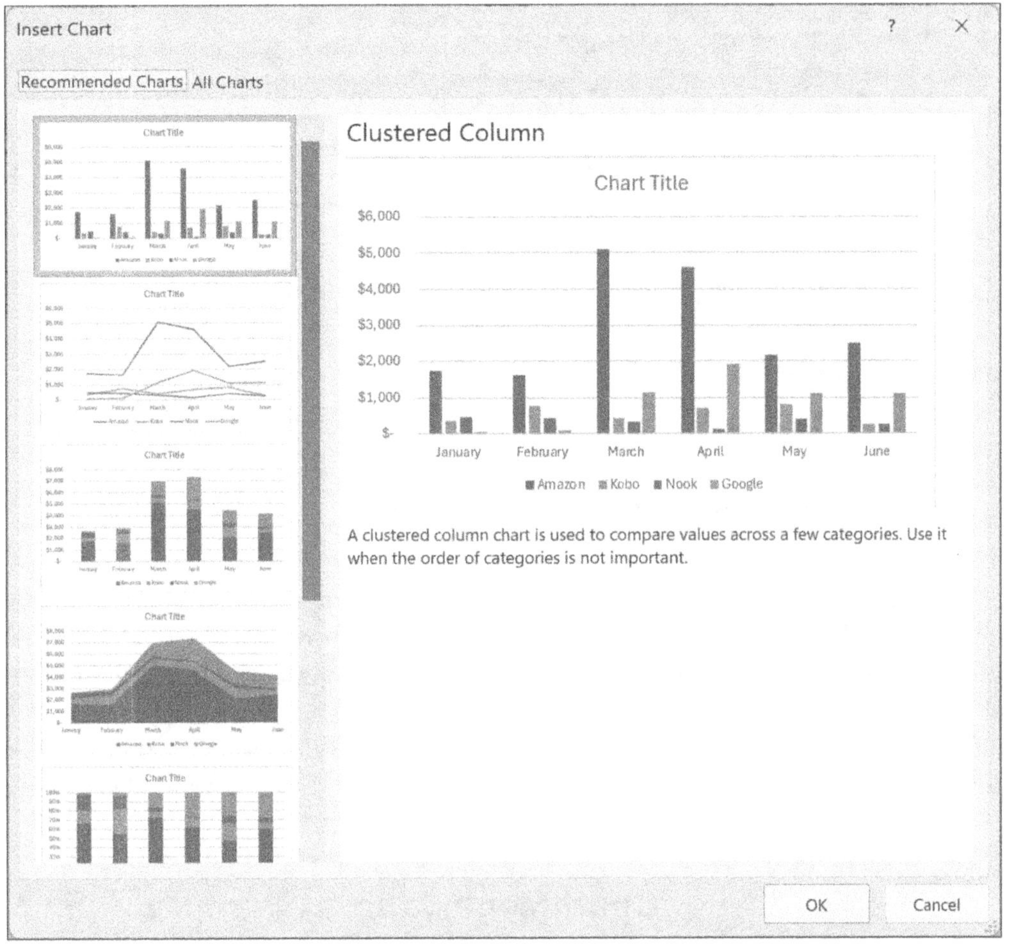

Click on the chart thumbnails on the left-hand side to see a larger sample of what your data would like like in that type of chart.

You should also see a description below the sample of what that chart type is meant to do.

Click OK to select the currently-displayed sample chart or Cancel to close without inserting a chart.

In that dialogue box, you can also click over to the All Charts tab at the top. That will show a listing of all the available chart types.

Click on a high-level chart type on the left, and then click on the icon for a specific chart type along the top, to see samples of what your data will look like using that specific chart type.

Here I've selected Bar on the left-hand side and Clustered Bar at the top:

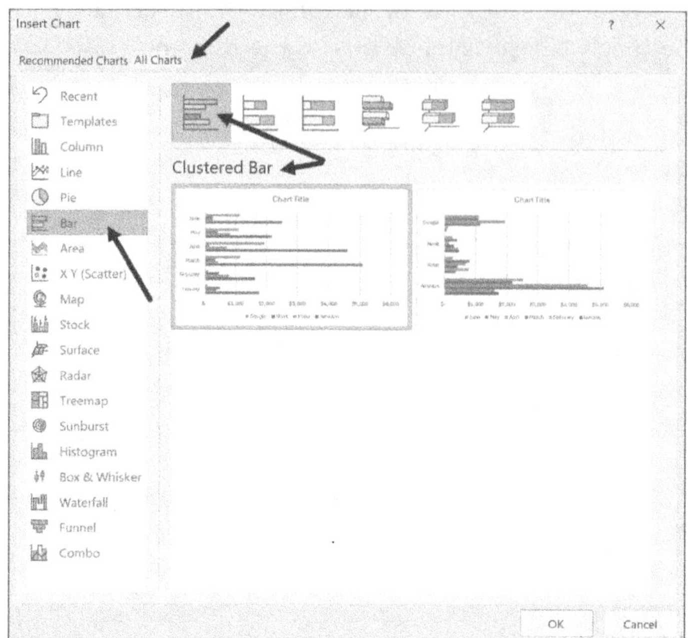

If you look at the sample charts in the All Charts section of the dialogue box, when there are two sample charts, like above, the left-hand image is usually how the chart will look with your data table formatted as is. The right-hand image is how the chart will look if you switch your row and column data.

In the image above, for example, the left-hand chart is sales by store by month and the right-hand chart is sales by month by store. (As we'll discuss soon, you can always switch row and column data after you insert a chart, too.)

Chart Menu Tabs

When you insert a chart into Excel and are clicked onto that chart, there will be two additional menu tabs available, Chart Design and Format.

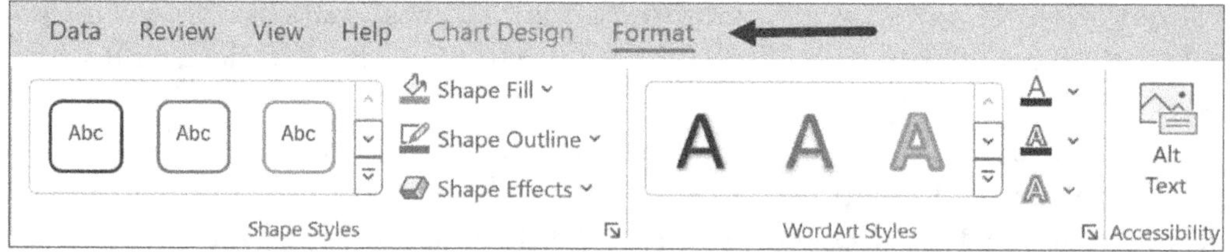

Chart Design is where you can choose the various chart elements for your chart, change your chart colors (like I've been doing throughout to make this print better in black and white), choose various suggested chart styles or layouts, switch your column and row data, change what data is being used in your chart, and change your chart type.

The Format tab is where you can manually change the formatting of your chart, such as the size or colors of different elements.

Chart Task Pane

It won't automatically be visible when you insert a chart, but there is also a chart task pane that will allow you to apply various formatting to the elements in your chart. We'll cover some of what you can do there, and how to open it, towards the end of this chapter.

* * *

Okay. Let's start talking about how to edit an existing chart. First up, all the ways you can fix an error if you didn't quite get it right when you inserted your chart.

Switch Row/Column

Here is a chart I just inserted in Excel:

	Amazon	Kobo	Nook	Google
January	$ 1,747	$ 353	$ 470	$ 65
February	$ 1,616	$ 767	$ 445	$ 106
March	$ 5,099	$ 420	$ 314	$ 1,132
April	$ 4,596	$ 692	$ 140	$ 1,928
May	$ 2,165	$ 809	$ 407	$ 1,090
June	$ 2,502	$ 261	$ 244	$ 1,113

It shows sales by store for each month. But what if I had actually wanted sales by month for each store?

The easiest way to make that change is to go to the Data section of the Chart Design tab, and click on Switch Row/Column. Immediately, I get this:

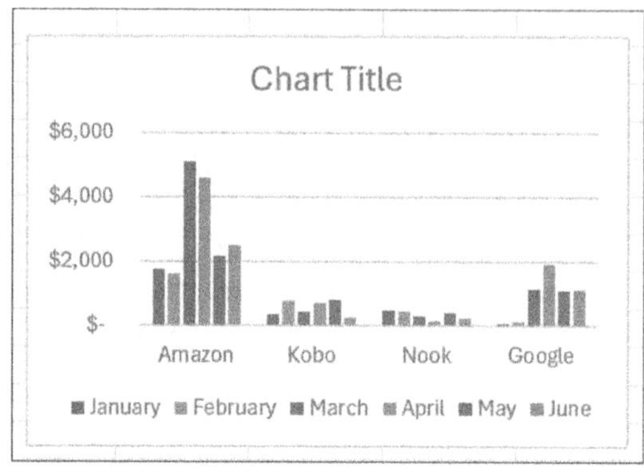

See how the axis is now the store names and the columns are now the months?

Change Data

What if you realize that you included fields in your chart that you didn't want to (like totals or subtotals), or you add more data after the fact and want to incorporate it?

For example, here I've added one more "store", Other.

	Amazon	Kobo	Nook	Google	Other
January	$ 1,747	$ 353	$ 470	$ 65	$ 50
February	$ 1,616	$ 767	$ 445	$ 106	$ 34
March	$ 5,099	$ 420	$ 314	$ 1,132	$ 123
April	$ 4,596	$ 692	$ 140	$ 1,928	$ 65
May	$ 2,165	$ 809	$ 407	$ 1,090	$ 228
June	$ 2,502	$ 261	$ 244	$ 1,113	$ 185

When you click on a chart, Excel will select the cells in your data table that are being used to create that chart.

Above, for example, Cells B1 through E1 are providing one of the categories, A2 through

A7 are providing the other, and B2 through E7 are providing the values. But note that none of the cells in Column F are currently selected.

One way to change the cells being used, is to left-click and drag from the bottom of the cell range that's already selected. In this case that would be the bottom right corner of Cell E7. (You may be able to see the angled, double-ended arrow there, but maybe not because it's a little small.)

When you left-click and drag to expand the selected cells, Excel should expand to capture both the header row and the cells with the values in them, but if it doesn't, then just do the same for the cell(s) with the header row value(s).

Another way to change your data, is to go to the Select Data option in the Data section of the Chart Design tab. Click on that to bring up the Select Data Source dialogue box:

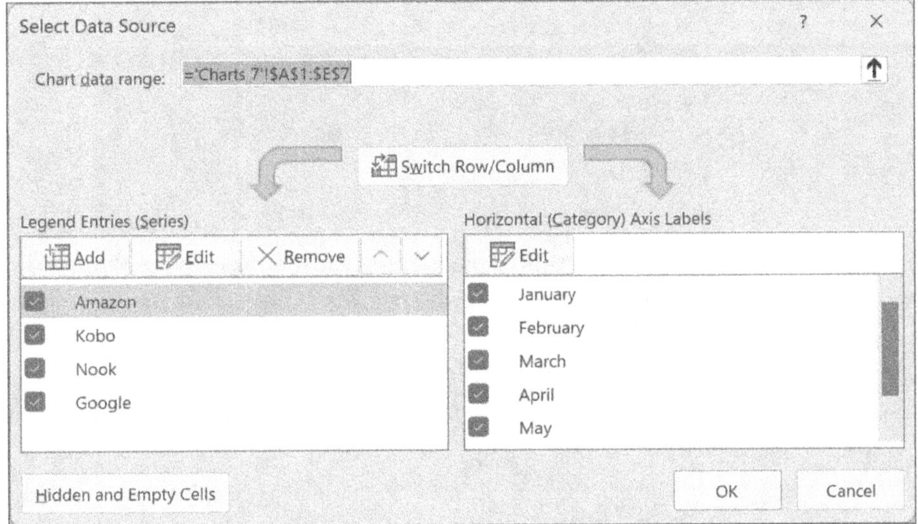

You can do a lot here, including switch your rows and columns, but if you're here to change your data, click into the Chart Data Range field at the top.

The Chart Data Range field does not work well if you click into it and try to use arrows. So one option is to click right next to the E, delete it, and replace it with an F.

The other is to select all of the text there now, delete it, and then go and select the correct cell range from your worksheet.

* * *

This dialogue box is also a great way to remove certain values from a chart after the fact.

For example, sometimes Amazon is so far out of range of the other stores for me, that having it in a chart obscures the detail for my other stores. When that happens, I open this dialogue box, and uncheck Amazon in the Legend Entries section on the left-hand side.

That removes the Amazon values from the chart.

*　*　*

This is also a place to go to fix the Legend Entries field names.

I generally recommend that you edit them in the data table itself, but sometimes that's not possible. If you need to edit them here, click on the value you want to change in the lower section of the Select Data Source dialogue box, and then click on the Edit option for that section.

This will bring up the Edit Series dialogue box:

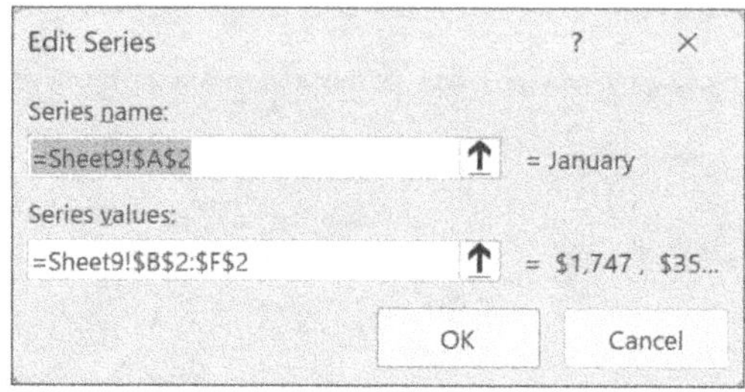

By default, the name fields will be cell references. You can see a sample value to the right.

For Legend Entries, click into the white box for Series Name, and type the label you want to use instead, and then click OK.

If you need to edit the Horizontal Axis Labels, that is a little different because it is a cell range, not a single cell. Instead of typing in one value, use curly brackets around your text, with commas to separate each entry.

{Entry 1, Entry 2, Entry 3}

For both, you can also replace the original cell reference or cell range reference with a different cell reference.

Use Cancel to close either of those dialogue boxes without making changes.

Change Chart Type

You can easily change an existing chart to a different chart type by clicking on the chart, and then using the Change Chart Type option in the Type section of the Chart Design tab.

Clicking on that will bring up a dialogue box that looks just like the Insert Chart dialogue box. From there, just find the chart type you want, click on it, and click OK.

*　*　*

Now that you have the chart set up the way you want, it's time to learn how to pretty it up.

Change Chart Title

If you've been trying things yourself as you read this book, you may have noticed that when a chart is inserted into Excel it has a default title of Chart Title. Not something you'll want to keep most of the time.

To change that title, click on it. You should see a box appear around the text. Select the text in that box by either left-clicking and dragging or using Ctrl + A, and then type the title you want.

You can format text in that box the same way as any other text in Excel using the Font section of the Home tab. That generally does everything I need for a chart title.

But if you want to get fancier, you can also use the WordArt Styles section of the Format tab to apply outlines to your text as well as special effects like shadow, reflection, and glow.

Another option for that is to right-click on your title box, and choose Format Chart Title from the dropdown menu. This will open a task pane on the right-hand side for Format Chart Title. Click around in the Title Options and Text Options to explore the choices available there.

Change Chart Colors (Easy Way)

To change your chart colors, an easy option is to click on the chart, and then go to the Chart Design tab. In the Chart Styles section, there is a dropdown menu for Change Colors.

Click on that to see almost 20 different pre-formatted color palettes:

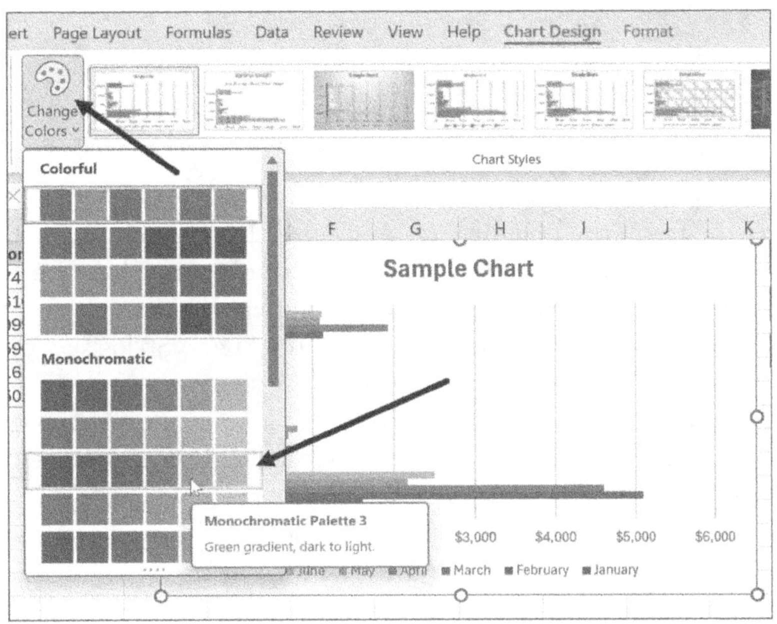

Hold your mouse over each one to see what it will look like. Click to apply.

This is especially useful if you're going to print in black and white. The monochromatic palettes ensure that different chart elements will be easily distinguishable from one another without relying on color difference to make that happen.

Change Chart Colors (Hard Way)

The hard way to change your chart colors is to do so one element at a time using the chart Format tab.

The first step is to click on an element in your chart. Here I've clicked on the blue column that represents April:

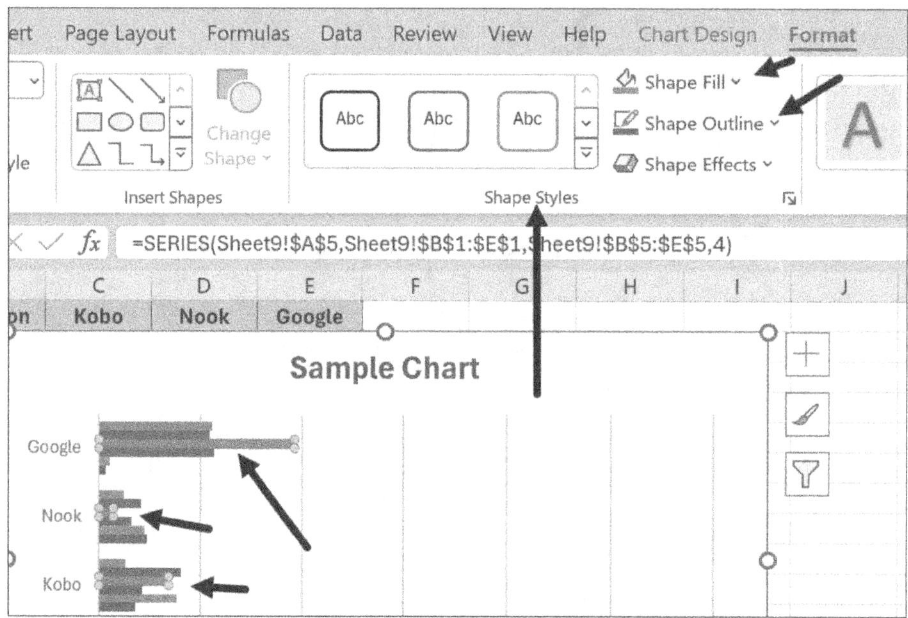

When I clicked on the first April column, Excel selected that column for each store. You may be able to see the dots on each corner for each of those columns. That means all of my April entries will change at the same time. If that doesn't happen, try again.

Once all of a specific element are selected, go to the Shape Styles section of the Format tab.

On the left-hand side are various pre-formatted styles. Click on the downward-pointing arrow with a line behind it to see the full list of options. Hold your mouse over each one to see what it will look like if applied

Here, for example, I have my mouse over a white shape with a colored outline in the first row, and you can see it applied in the chart in the background:

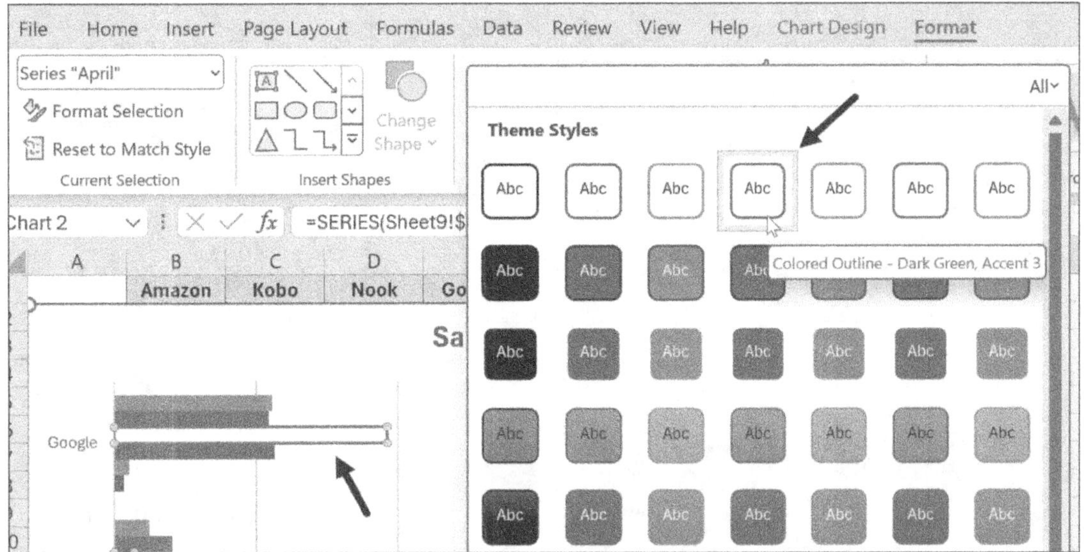

If you don't want to use one of those options, to the right of that are Shape Fill and Shape Outline dropdown options which will let you choose any color you want. (See the image on the last page.)

The More [Fill/Outline] Colors option in those dropdowns will bring up a Color dialogue box where you can choose other colors or input the values for a custom color.

For columns, bars, or pie slices, use the Shape Fill dropdown to choose a main color, and the Shape Outline if you want a different color around the edge.

For lines, use Shape Outline.

Shape Fill also has secondary menus for picture, gradient, and texture, but I would exercise caution in using them. You don't want your formatting to obscure your data.

Outline has secondary menus for line width (weight) and style (dashes).

Hold your mouse over each option to see what it will look like before you click to apply it.

It is possible to combine different fills and outlines for columns, bars, or pie slices like in the pre-formatted example above.

If you customize your colors, just pay attention so that you are keeping the colors distinct for each element. Pay attention to contrast between colors. It is possible to use two different colors that are so similar they might as well be the same, and that pretty much defeats the purpose of having distinct colors for distinct elements.

Change Chart Size

I often need to resize a chart in Excel. One option, if you know the size you want, is to go to the Format tab and enter values for height and width in the Size section:

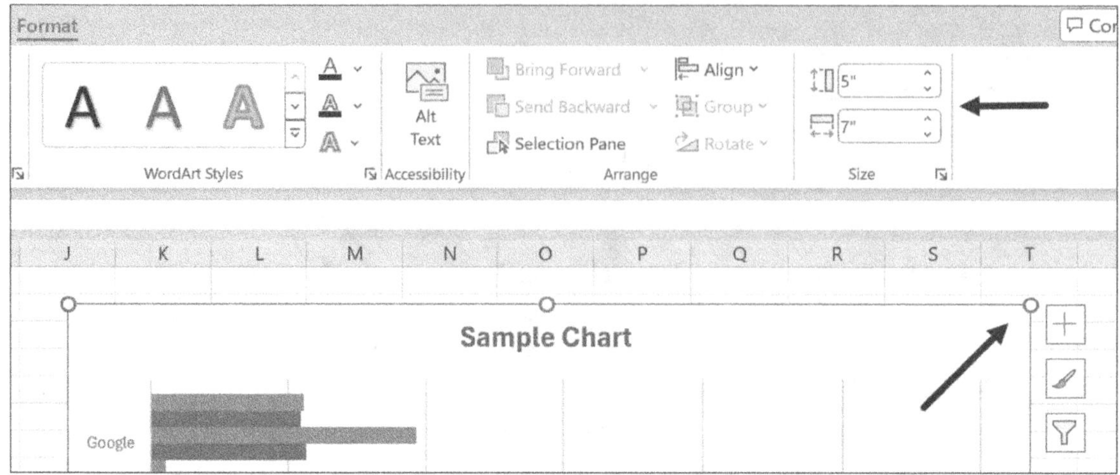

The other option, and the one I use most often, is to click on the chart, and then left-click and drag from one of the white circles around the perimeter. There should be one at each corner as well as one in the middle of each side.

You can see the one in the top right corner of the chart in the image above.

With either option, the size of the various elements in the chart should also adjust.

Chart Styles

Excel provides various pre-formatted styles for each chart type in the Chart Styles section of the Chart Design tab. They contain different colors, layouts, and effects, and will vary depending on the type of chart you chose, as well as any elements you've already added to your chart.

Here, for example, are some options for a column chart:

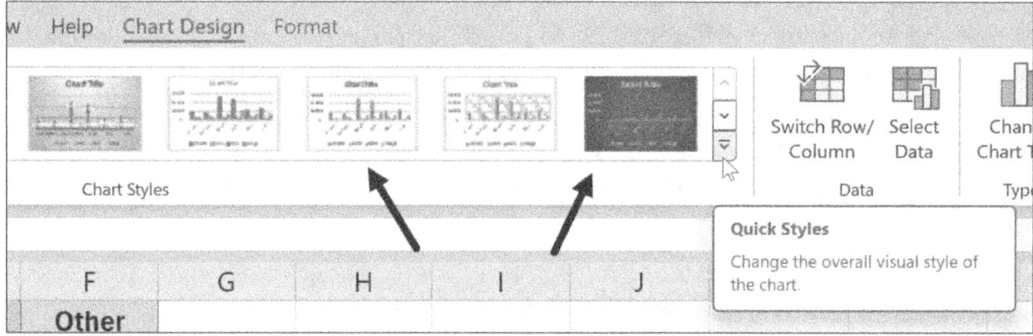

Click on the downpointing arrow with a line behind it in the bottom right corner to see the full set of choices available.

Hold your mouse over each one to see it applied to your chart. Click to keep it.

Personally, I don't think I've ever used any of these, but you should at least look at them once, because they might get you close to an appearance you like.

Quick Layout

Another pre-formatted option can be found in the Quick Layout dropdown menu:

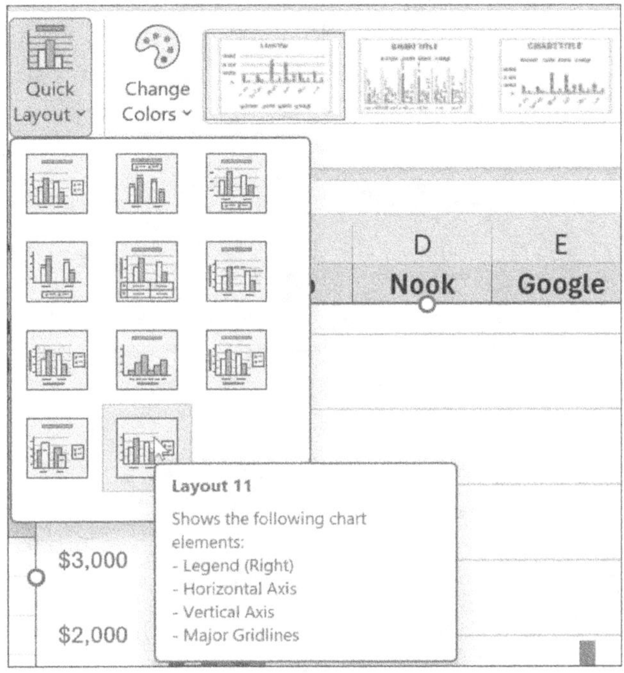

Quick layouts include different chart elements. For example, in the image above I have my cursor over Layout 11. Per Excel that layout would put the legend (that describes my values and their assigned colors) on the right, include a horizontal axis and a vertical axis, and add in major gridlines (which are lines that run across from the side to better help you determine the value that corresponds to a particular column).

Note from the thumbnail image that it would also remove my chart title.

Hold your mouse over each one to see what it will look like applied, click if you want to keep it.

Keep in mind that sometimes a layout will look horrible until you resize your chart to better display all of the elements. (Both here and if you customize your chart yourself.)

Like with chart styles, the quick layouts available will depend on your chart type.

It is possible to apply both a quick layout and a chart style to the same table, since quick layouts are primarily about what chart elements to include, and chart styles are more about the appearance of those elements.

But they do sometimes conflict. Where they conflict, whichever one you selected last will generally be the winner.

If you want to use these, you're just going to have to play around to see what you get.

Add or Modify Chart Element

At the far-left side of the Chart Design tab in the Chart Layouts section is the Add Chart Element dropdown. This is where I go when I want to customize my chart.

Click on the dropdown arrow to see the list of elements you can add or remove. If an element isn't available for a specific type of chart, it will be grayed out like Lines and Up/Down Bars are here:

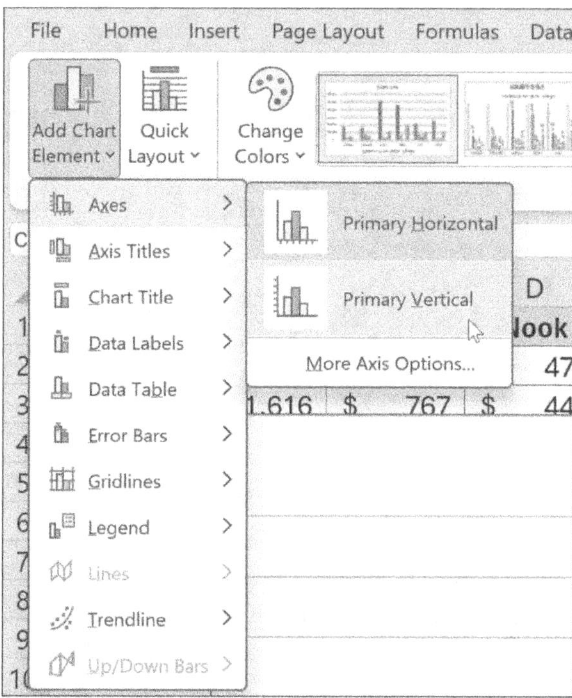

Each element has a secondary dropdown menu, like the one above for Axes, where you can see what choices are available.

Hold your cursor over each option in the secondary dropdown to see what would happen to your chart if you click on it. If the element is already there, clicking on that option will remove it. If it isn't there, then clicking will add or change it to that location.

Keep in mind for text elements that they can sometimes also be manually moved around or resized after you add them.

Now let's walk through each of those choices:

Axes

Your horizontal and vertical axes are what show the values. For a standard chart, horizontal is along the bottom, vertical is along the left side.

If you ever do a combo chart, it's possible to have a secondary vertical axis on the right side and a secondary horizontal axis along the top. The listed options will expand to also let you turn on or off those secondary axes.

Axis Titles

This option lets you add a text box to describe each axis.

Chart Title

This option lets you decide whether to have a chart title and, if you do, whether to put it above the contents of the chart or centered within the chart itself. I personally prefer to have it above, so all the charts in this book have the title in the Above Chart position.

Data Labels

The data labels option lets you decide whether to add the actual values to your chart. For me, I generally only like to do this on pie charts, because I use a data table with most of my bar or column charts that lists the values below the table. It can also get really busy, which makes the chart harder to read.

There are a number of choices about where to place your data labels if you choose to do so. The positions are not fixed.

Here are two options applied to a pie chart, inside end and outside end:

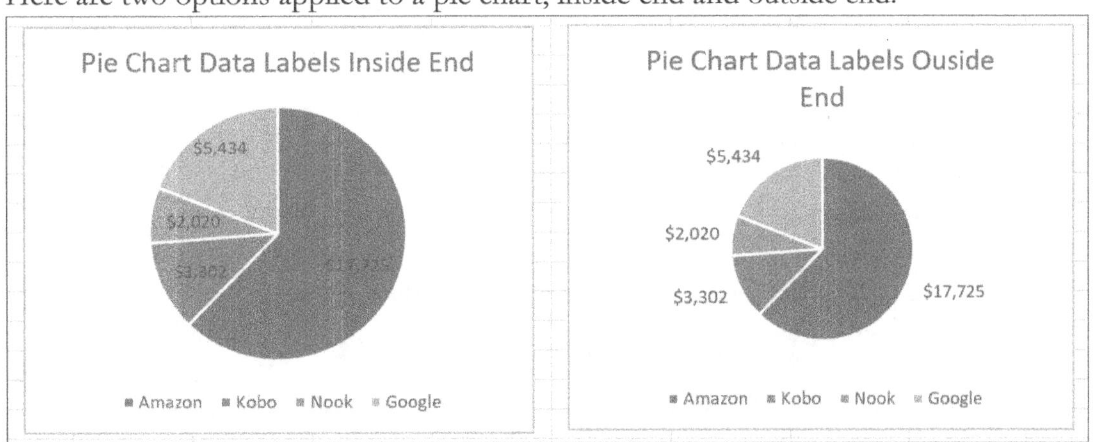

I prefer to have labels on the outside end. (Also, I'll show you how to do this later in the task pane, I tend to prefer to show the % value instead of the dollar value. You can show either one or both.)

You can also click and drag each text box to move them around.

Data Table

The data table option shows the data that created the chart in a table below it. Like here where you can see the dollar values for each store in each month below the columns that represent those values:

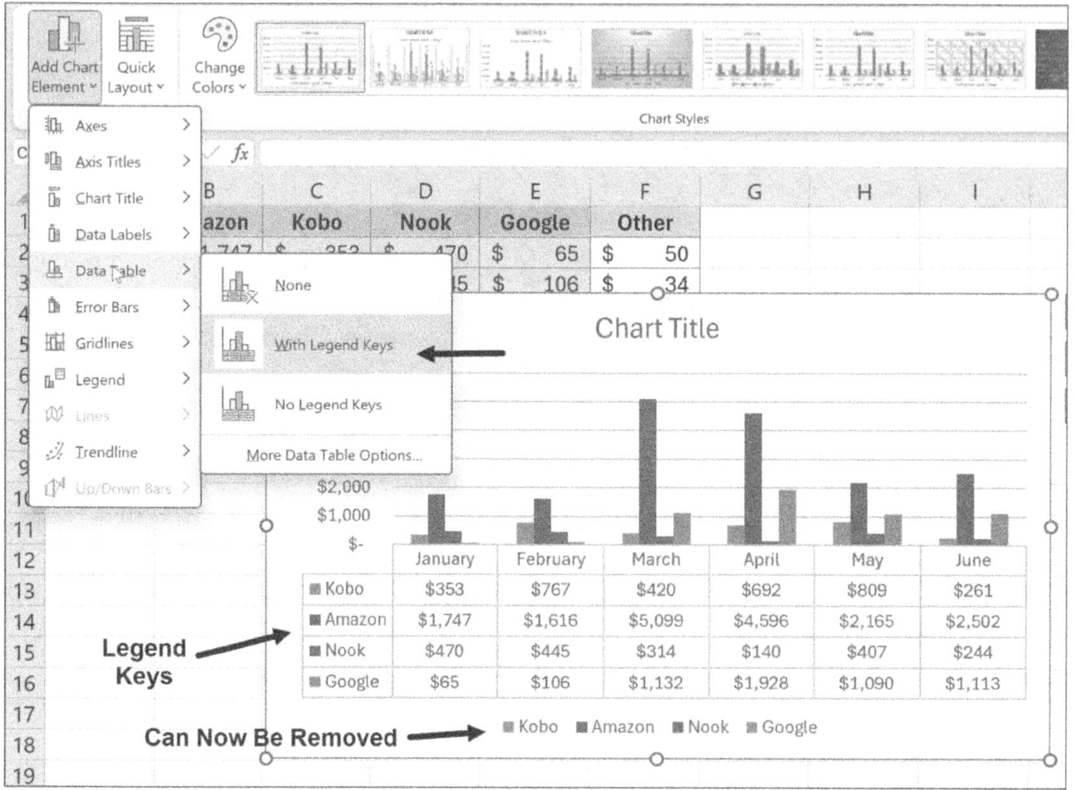

	January	February	March	April	May	June
Kobo	$353	$767	$420	$692	$809	$261
Amazon	$1,747	$1,616	$5,099	$4,596	$2,165	$2,502
Nook	$470	$445	$314	$140	$407	$244
Google	$65	$106	$1,132	$1,928	$1,090	$1,113

I often use this because I like to have the visual of the chart, but then I also like to see the actual numbers.

You can see that you have a choice to include legend keys or to leave them out. Above I included them. They show the color next to the store name in the data table. The nice thing about doing that is it lets you remove the legend as a separate element.

Error Bars

This option lets you add error bars to the results in your chart. The dropdown contains choices for standard error, percentage, and standard deviation and will apply to all of your category values. For example, with store in the column charts we looked at, you'd have one error bar for each store.

Choosing the More Error Bar Options will let you specify which category values to apply an error bar to. It will also open a Format Error Bars task pane with a custom and a fixed value option. The task pane allows you to control whether the bars go plus, minus, or both, and whether they have a cap at the end.

Gridlines

Gridlines can make it easier to read the data in a chart by providing lines in the background that a reader can follow to the axes to see the associated value.

You can add horizontal or vertical gridlines, and choose to include major lines and/or minor lines. Major lines have wider spacing between each line.

Legend

This option lets you choose where to place the legend (the guide that tells people what color corresponds to what label).

It can be on the top, bottom, left side, or right side. You can also manually position it if you need to as long as you add one.

It is also possible to remove the legend entirely, like I do when I use a data table with legend keys.

Lines

The lines option is available with line and area charts, and allows you to add drop lines and/or high-low lines.

Drop lines draw a vertical line from the top data point down to the horizontal axis.

High-low lines draw a vertical line from the top data point to the bottom data point for each entry.

Trendline

A trendline allows you to add a line onto your chart that either shows a linear or exponential trend based on the values in the chart, shows a linear forecast extrapolated from your values, or shows the moving average of your values.

When you click on this one, it will make you choose one of the values from your legend to create the line from.

The line it inserts will be a dotted line the same color as the category value you chose.

On the next page, for example, I've added trendlines for Amazon and Google:

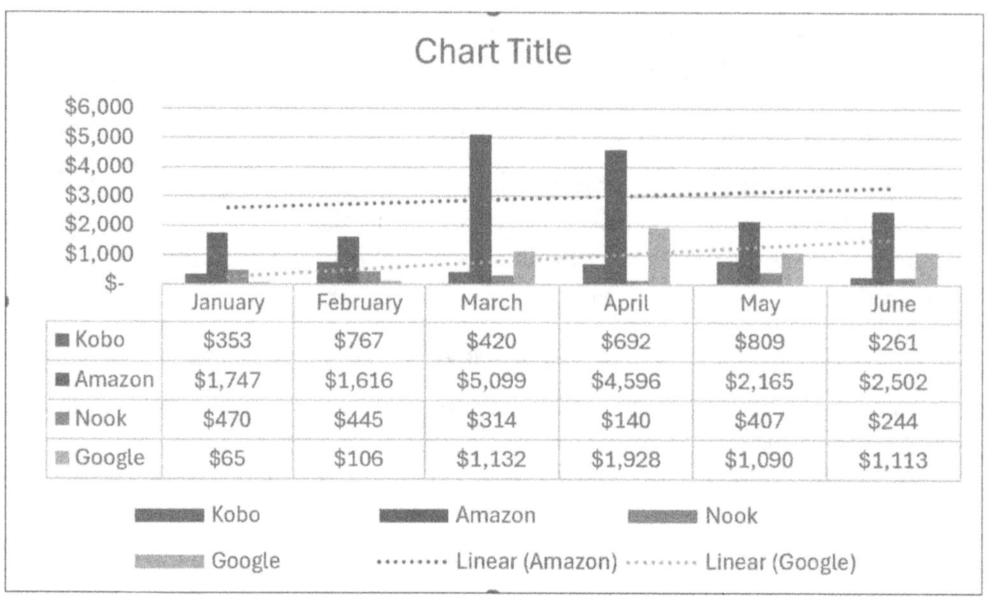

	January	February	March	April	May	June
■ Kobo	$353	$767	$420	$692	$809	$261
■ Amazon	$1,747	$1,616	$5,099	$4,596	$2,165	$2,502
■ Nook	$470	$445	$314	$140	$407	$244
■ Google	$65	$106	$1,132	$1,928	$1,090	$1,113

Make sure the type of trendline you choose makes sense for your data. Excel will apply whatever you tell it to, but sometimes the data doesn't justify that. A linear trendline, for example, is not a good choice to use with exponential data.

Up/Down Bars

Up/Down Bars are available for line charts. They draw a bar between two lines on the chart to show a visible change in the distance between the two from entry to entry.

* * *

Format Chart Area Task Pane

As I mentioned above, there is also a task pane option for formatting your chart.

You can open the task pane by double-clicking on your chart. Another option is to right-click on the chart and choose Format Chart Area from the dropdown menu.

You can also choose the More Options choice from any of the secondary dropdown menus for the chart elements.

Using the secondary dropdown menus is probably the best way to get you to the specific task pane you want to work with. You can always navigate there once the task pane is open, by using the dropdowns and icons at the top, but sometimes it's hard to know exactly where to go.

Here, for example, is the task pane that opens when I use the Data Labels secondary dropdown menu for a pie chart to choose More Data Label Options:

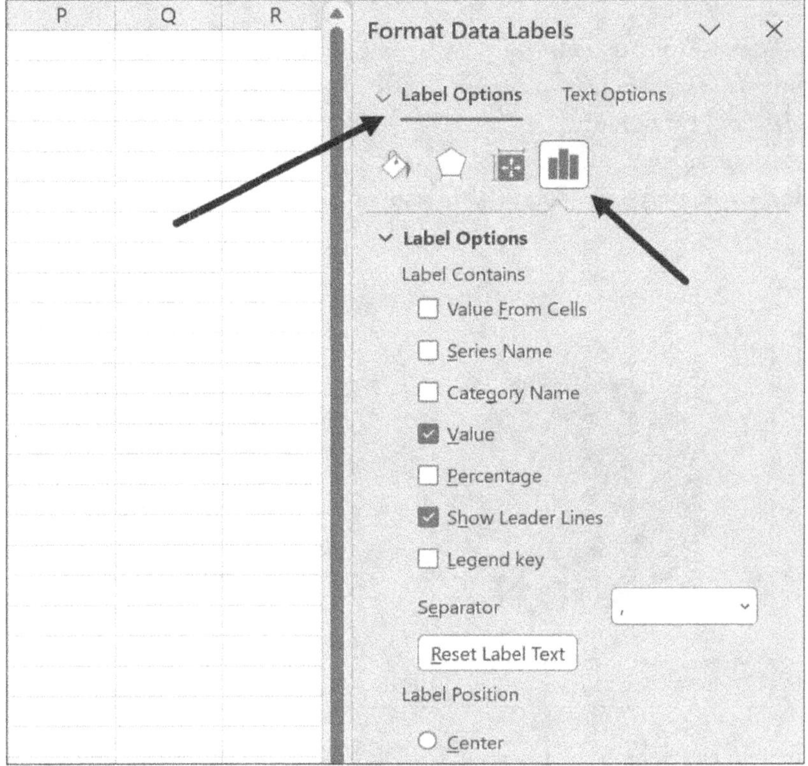

That brought me straight to where I can choose to show data labels as a percent. I could have also added data labels to the pie chart, opened the task pane, changed the top option to Series 1 Data Labels, and then clicked on the fourth icon for Label Options:

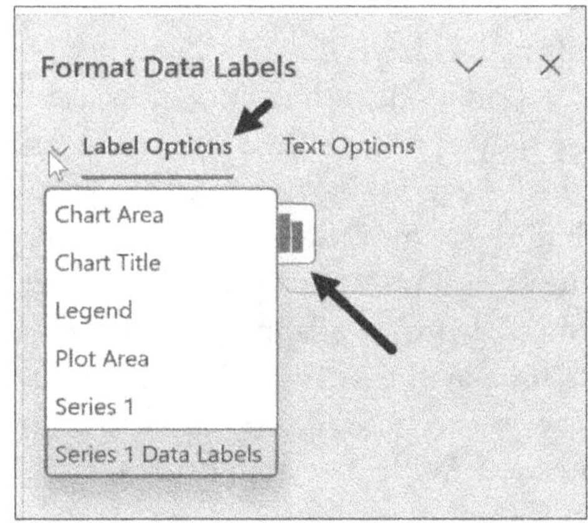

:

(You have to have already added data labels to use that dropdown in the task pane, though.)

Display Pie Chart Percent

The More Data Label Options task pane window (seen above) has a Label Contains section under Label Options. That section has checkboxes for Value, Percentage, and more. For a pie chart, Value is checked by default.

To include percent as well, just check the box for Percentage.

To only include the percent, like in this example, uncheck Value and check the box for Percentage.

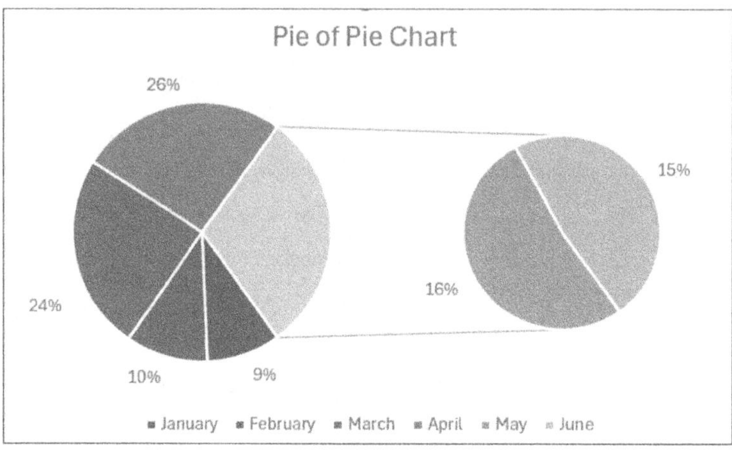

In the above chart I also deleted a box that showed 31% for the pie slice in the main pie chart that is broken out in the secondary chart. (You can do that by just clicking on a text box in the chart and using Delete.)

Leader Lines and Category Name

Two other choices there are Show Leader Lines and Category Name.

Leader lines should be turned on by default even if they aren't initially visible.

I like to have them, because they connect a data label to its element, so even if you have to move data labels around to make everything fit, you can still see what label goes to what element. (Just left-click and drag the text box for a data label to reposition it.)

On the next page, for example, is a pie chart with a lot of values where I had to move the data labels around to keep them from overlapping, and you can see the leader lines that connect each value back to its slice of the pie.

Note the other thing I chose to do here. I turned on Category Name for the data labels, too, so that a legend wasn't needed. With that many slices, trying to distinguish by color just doesn't work well.

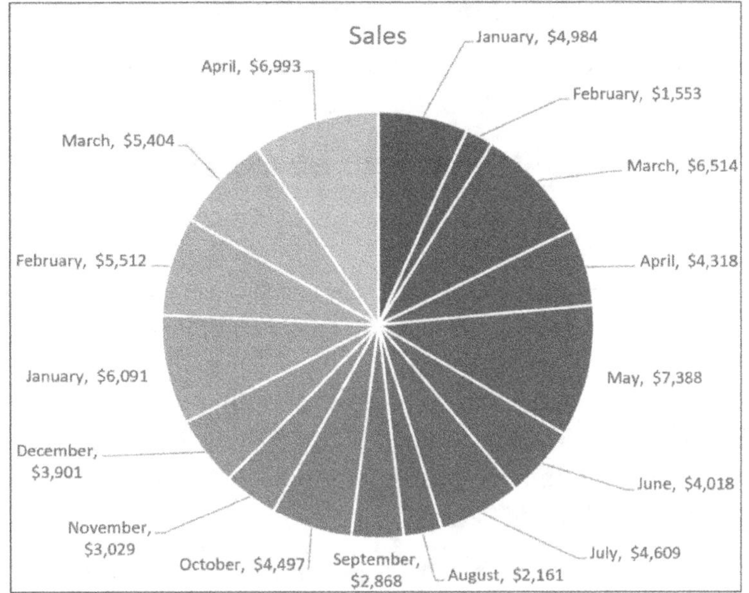

Explode Your Pie Chart

I sometimes like to "explode" a pie chart so that the various slices have space between them. That can be found by clicking on Series Options in the task pane dropdown, and then the third icon listed, which is also Series Options.

(If you can't find one of these settings, try clicking onto that element in your chart and then going to the task pane.)

The higher the percentage you input in the pie explosion box or choose using the slider, the more white space there will be between the various slices of the pie:

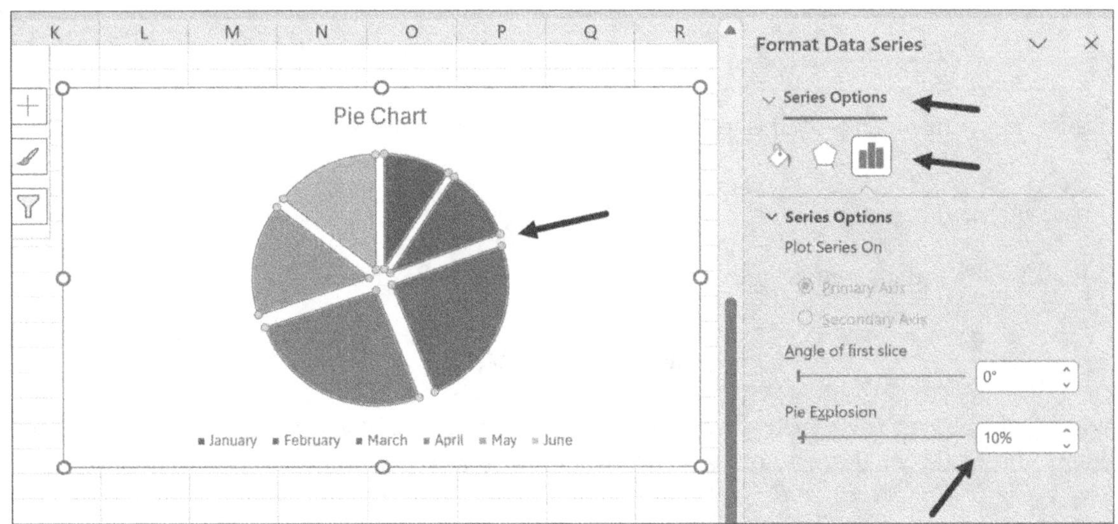

Rotate Your Pie Chart

You can also rotate your pie chart to control which slice is where. To do that, play with the Angle of First Slice setting also located in the Series Options section of the task pane.

Customize Your Histogram

The chart task pane is also the only way I know to customize the size of each histogram bin and the range of values used.

For this one you want Horizontal Axis, Axis Options.

The default is Automatic, but you can specify either the bin width or the number of bins instead.

You can also set the minimum and maximum values using the overflow and underflow bin fields. For example, here I have a range of 10 to 50 with five total bins. Anything under 10 gets dumped into the first bin, anything over 50 gets dumped into the last one. The three in between cover equal ranges of 13.33 each:

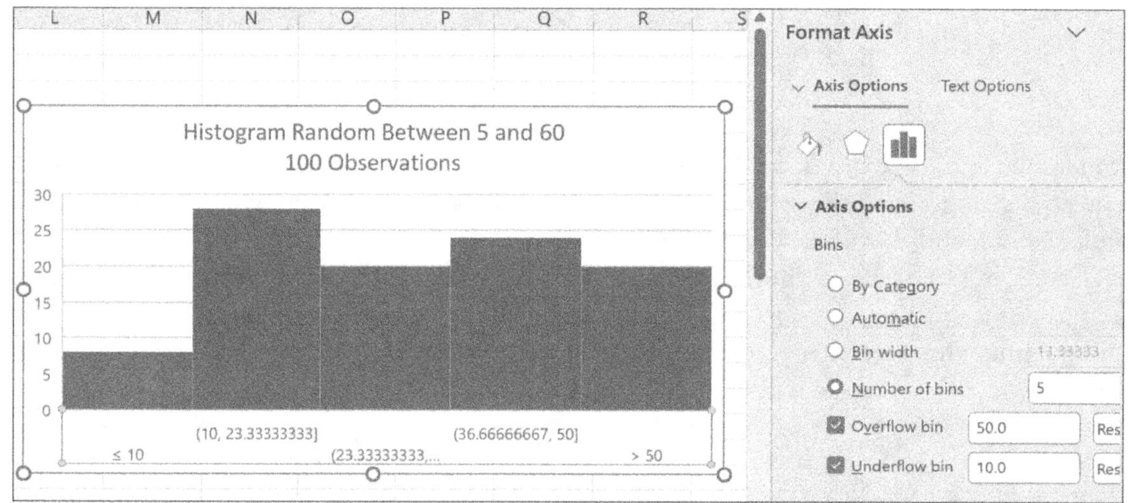

For this one, your chart will update when you click away from the task pane.

* * *

Finally, a few quick points on moving elements or charts around.

Move a Chart

If you need to move the whole chart, left-click and drag. Just be sure not to click on a specific element within the chart or you'll end up moving the element instead. (Remember, Ctrl + Z to Undo.)

You can also select a chart and use Ctrl + X to cut or Ctrl + C to copy, and then go to another worksheet, Word document, or PowerPoint presentation, and use Ctrl + V to paste. (Or your preferred method to copy/cut and paste, I just like the control shortcuts.)

Move or Resize a Chart Element

As I've mentioned a few times already, it is possible to move a chart element around, too. I often move data labels, for example. Just click on that element and drag.

But be aware that sometimes it may not work. I was just struggling to move the chart title on a histogram. I was able to do so just fine on other chart types, but for some reason histograms weren't cooperating with me.

When you click on a chart element that can be edited, there will be white circles at each corner and in the middle of each side that you can left-click and drag to resize. When you resize an element, all of the contents of that element—like the text within a legend—should also resize.

If you don't see white circles, but only blue ones at the corners, you should be able to move that element when your cursor has arrows pointing in four directions by left-clicking and dragging, but you won't be able to resize it.

In general, I don't find I need to manually move or resize elements in charts often. It's more that I accidentally do so sometimes when trying to move the whole chart around. Just remember that Ctrl + Z will undo any mistake you make with a chart.

Pivot Charts

Now that we've finished our discussion of charts, let's circle back to pivot tables, because it is possible to create a chart from data in a pivot table.

The first step is to build the pivot table that has the information you want to use in your chart.

Next, click on your pivot table, and either go to the Tools section of the PivotTable Analyze tab, or to the Charts section of the Insert tab. Both have a PivotChart option.

Click on the PivotChart icon to bring up an Insert Chart dialogue box:

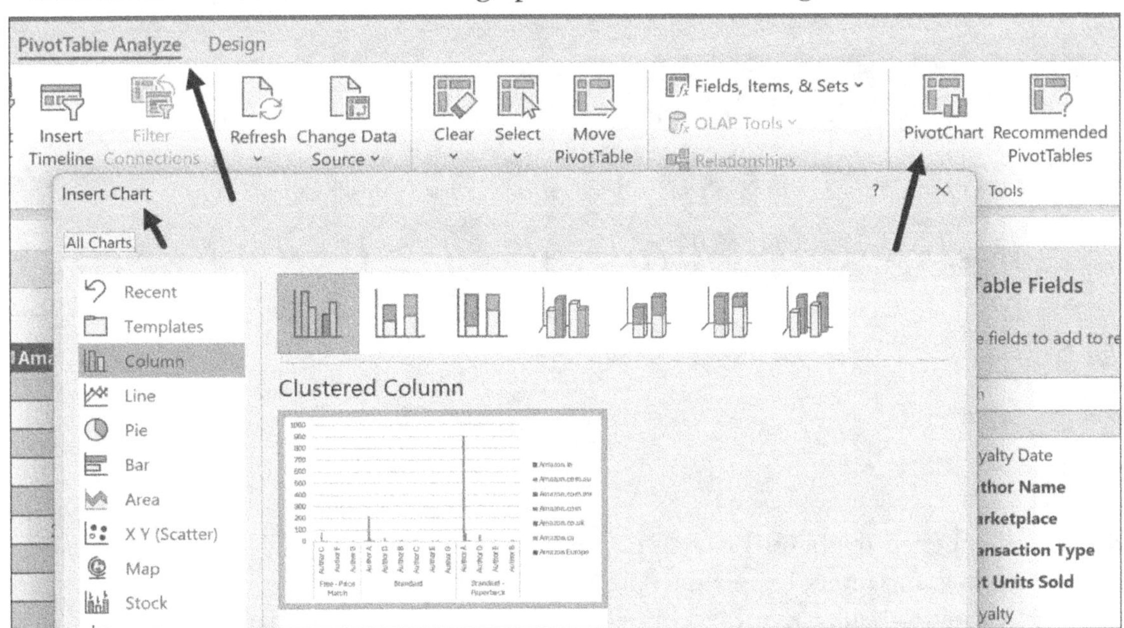

The preview for each chart type will show what your chart will look like given the data in the pivot table. Click on the chart type you want, and then click OK.

The pivot chart that Excel creates will be more dynamic than a standard chart:

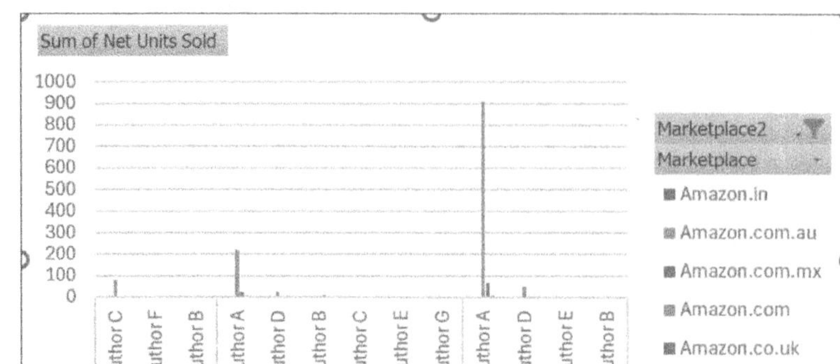

Each of the gray fields that you see in the chart above is a field from the pivot table. The ones that are being used to build the axes—in this case, transaction type, author name, and marketplace (with two levels because I have a group for Amazon Europe)—can be filtered right there in the chart.

Here, for example, I used the Marketplace dropdown and chose to only display results for Amazon Europe:

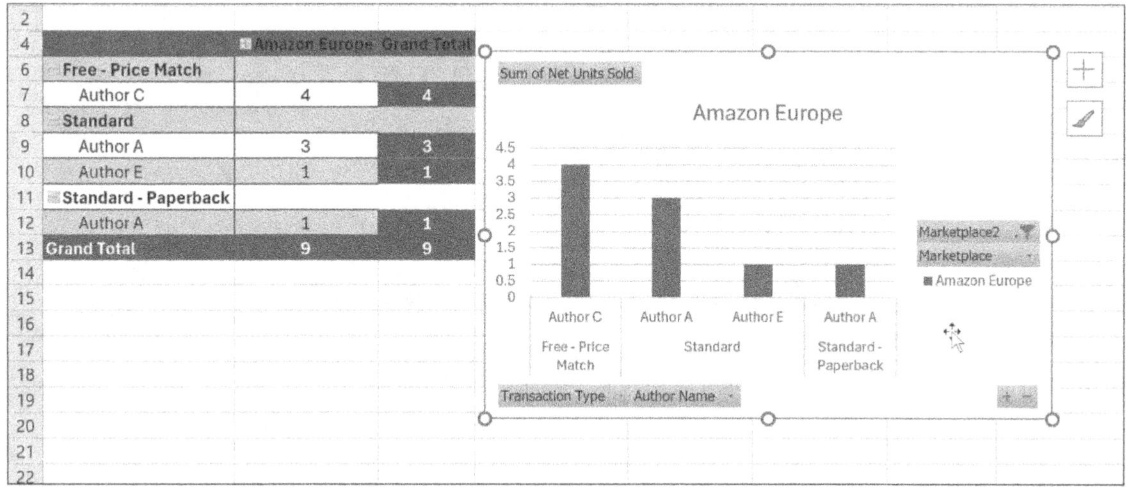

Note what happened to the pivot table in the background when I did that. It automatically updated based on the filters I applied to the chart.

It is important to realize that this connection exists. Because any changes you make to the pivot table will change your pivot chart, and any changes you make to the pivot chart will change your pivot table.

Also, I found that sometimes I needed to go to the pivot chart and update my filters there to see the full data in my pivot table.

If you ever create a pivot chart and you want to "lock it in" so that it can't be impacted by changes you make to the pivot table, you can copy the chart and then paste it special as a picture.

That will lock it in as is. You won't be able to edit it ever.

In terms of formatting your pivot chart, it basically works the same as a normal chart in terms of using the Design and Format tabs or the task pane. Just keep in mind that something like "switch row/column" will also be reflected in your pivot table. It will flip your entries from Rows to Columns and Columns to Rows.

I have found pivot charts particularly useful for things like isolating one value at a time. For example, we've been working with data here that covers different authors or different stores. With a pivot chart, I can use the filter functionality in the chart to quickly show me a chart for each author or each store. Doing that with a standard chart would be much more time-consuming.

Okay. Almost done. Let's cover a few more quick topics and then wrap it up.

Odds and Ends

I always go back and forth on what else people need to know to work in Excel at an intermediate level. For some people, inserting equations or illustrations might be a required skill, but for most people it isn't. Same with inserting symbols. I've devoted chapters to each before in other versions of these books, because sometimes when I'm exploring a new-to-me topic for the first time I like to dive in. But over time that "new information" excitement wears off and I realize no one really cares but me.

So I'm going to do a few topics in this chapter in a fast, high-level way so you know they exist and can go explore them further if they interest you.

Insert Symbols

It is possible that if you're working in Excel, especially if you're using it for text-based analysis, that you will need to insert a symbol at some point. For example, in my day job I have to insert the section symbol that gets used for legal writing. I've also in the past needed the copyright symbol.

There are keyboard shortcuts for these things, so if you use one a lot it may be worth a quick internet search to find the appropriate shortcut to use, but if it's just an occasional thing you need to do, click on the spot in the cell where you need the symbol, and then go to the Symbols section of the Insert tab and click on Symbol.

That will bring up the Symbol dialogue box:

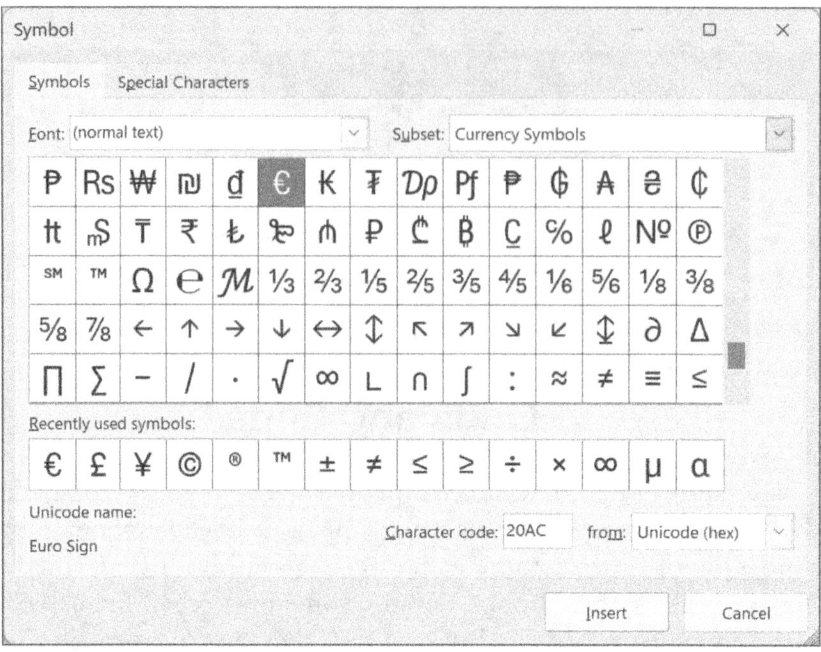

The symbols tab, which is the default, will show your recently used symbols at the bottom, or you can scroll through all of your fonts to find what you need. The dropdowns at the top let you choose a specific font or category of symbol to jump through the list faster. You can also click over to the Special Characters tab to find em dashes, en dashes, copyright, trademark, section, paragraph, etc.

Find the symbol you need, click on it, and then click on Insert.

The dialogue box will remain open. Close it by clicking on the X in the top right corner or Close in the bottom right.

Be careful with inserting symbols and then changing your font. For example, I just inserted a wheel symbol from Wingdings, but when I changed the font it became a right bracket. For common special characters, you're probably fine changing fonts, at least if you use robust ones—it will just change to that font's version of that character—but for more unique shapes or symbols, they can be specific to that particular font.

Once you insert a symbol, you can change the size and color just like any other text.

Insert Equations

In that same section (Symbols section of the Insert tab) is an option for Equation.

If you need to write math in Excel, this is the place to go. The dropdown there has common equations like the area of a circle, binomial theorem, Pythagorean theorem, etc. Click on one of those choices to insert a text box on top of your worksheet.

When you have an equation like this inserted onto your worksheet, and you are clicked onto it, there will be an Equation tab available that has a zillion components you can use to build an equation, as well as common structures you can insert, like fractions:

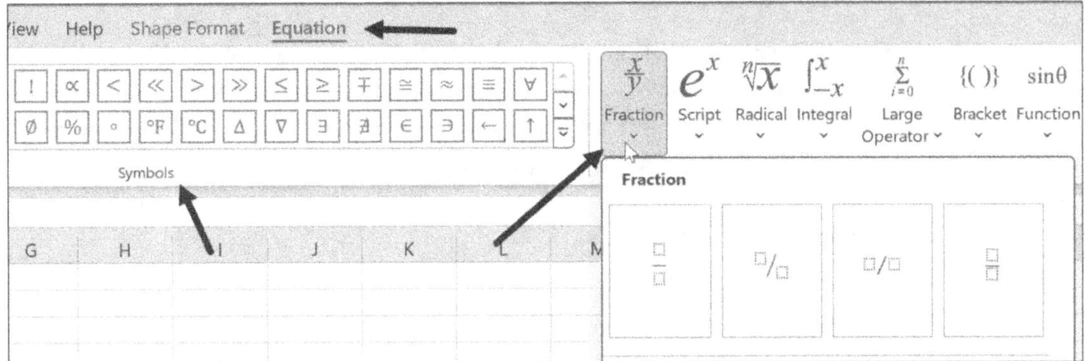

Click on an element to add it to your equation. If there are boxes, like with the fraction examples above, click on each box and then either type a value or click on another element to complete the box.

There is an option to "ink an equation" that lets you write the equation yourself with a stylus.

There are also three formats you can use for your equations depending on the notation style you prefer.

Insert Illustrations

You can also insert pictures, shapes, icons, 3D models, SmartArt, and screenshots in Excel. These options are found in the Illustrations section of the Insert tab. Most will insert on top of the worksheet, not in a particular cell.

You can change their size, color, etc. once inserted.

If you have more than one, you can control which one displays in the forefront or background when they overlap by using the Arrange section of the menu tab for that type of illustration.

Quick Access Toolbar

If you ever find yourself moving back and forth between two different tabs a lot, because you're using different tasks that are located in different tabs, it may be possible to add one or the other of them to the Quick Access Toolbar. This will make that task always available in the top left corner of your workspace.

To add another task to the Quick Access Toolbar, click on the downward-pointing arrow with a line at the end of your currently available tasks:

You can see that it says Customize Quick Access Toolbar in the image above when I hold my mouse over it. And that I currently have save, undo, redo, and format painter available.

When you click on that arrow, it will bring up a dropdown menu of popular options. Ones with a check next to them are displayed in the quick access toolbar, ones without a check are not. If you see the one you want, click on it to put a check next to it. If you don't see the option you want, click on More Commands.

That will open a dialogue box with all possible choices:

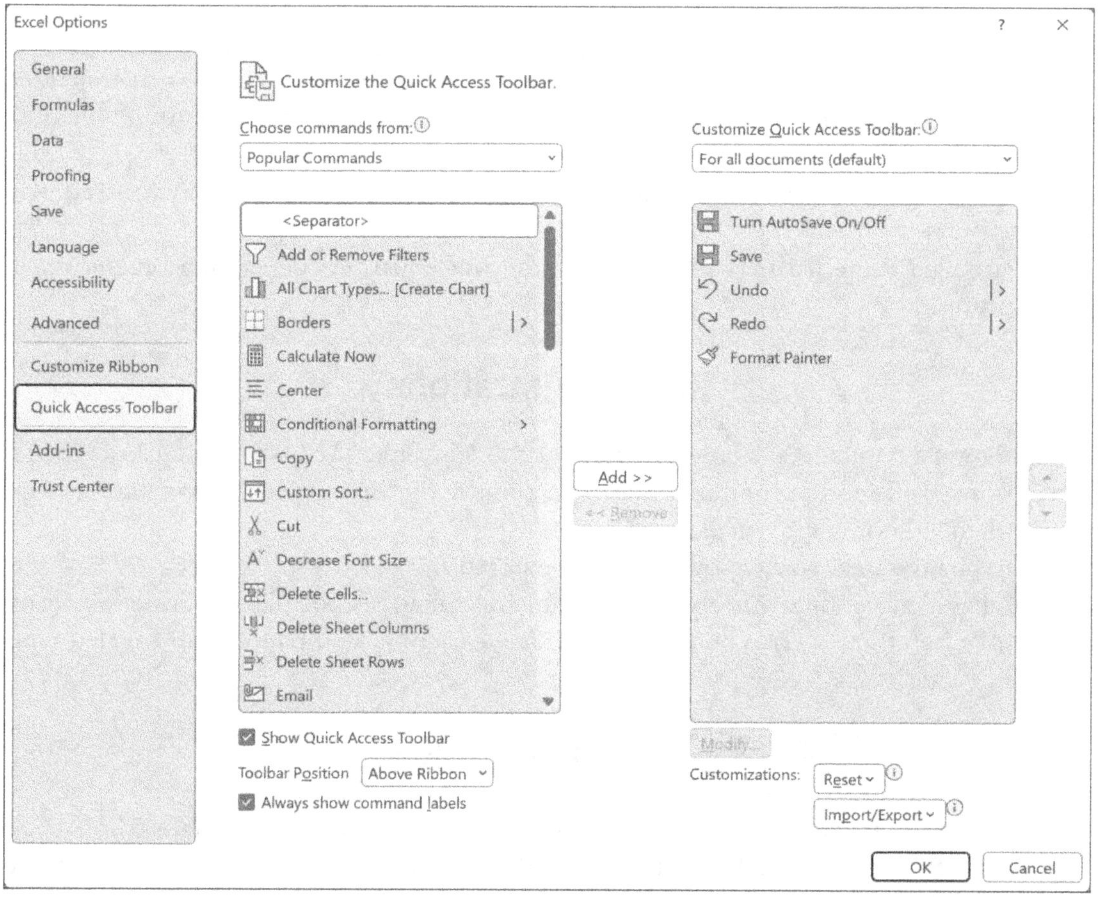

To add a task, find it on the left-hand side, click on it, and then click Add in the center. To remove a task, find it on the right-hand side, click on it, and then click on Remove in the center.

Excel Options

You may have noticed that the dialogue box above was called Excel Options, and that Quick Access Toolbar was just one of a number of options listed along the side.

That's because you can also open this dialogue box by going to the File tab and then clicking on Options in the bottom left corner. Excel Options lets you do a lot of different things to customize your Excel experience. I'd say it's worth exploring if there is anything Excel regularly does that annoys you or that you have to undo.

For example, I normally change the default save location. They love to save to OneDrive and I just want to save to my C drive.

I also tend to turn off certain error corrections, like turning (c) into the copyright symbol since I am more likely to be citing a rule. And I prefer to set my privacy settings to not access the internet or whatever it is they have going on with LinkedIn.

I would caution against getting too fancy with customizing your Excel options, though, because you still want to be able to use someone else's version of Excel when needed.

Zoom

It is possible to zoom in or out to increase or decrease the size of the cells in your worksheet and make their contents more or less visible.

If you ever need to do this, the easiest option is in the bottom right corner. There is a line there with a minus at one end, a plus sign at the other end, a percentage displayed for the current zoom level, and a perpendicular bar somewhere along the line

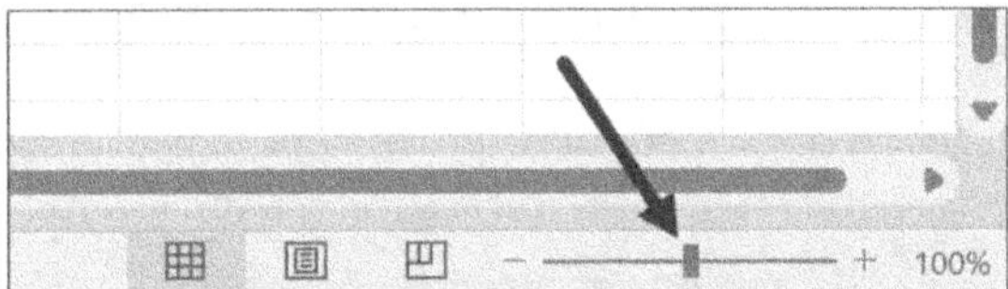

The perpendicular bar marks where you currently are. Click to the left of that bar to make things smaller, click to the right to make them bigger. You can also click and drag the bar.

Your other option is to go to the Zoom section of the View tab:

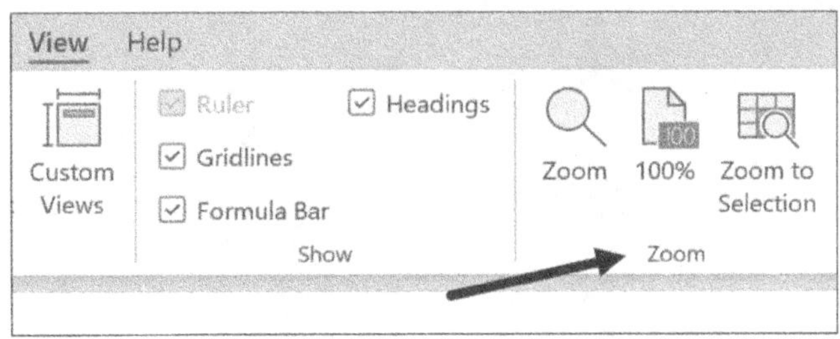

The 100% option there will take your view back to a 100% zoom level.

Clicking on the Zoom option will open a dialogue box with options for 200%, 100%, 75%, 50%, 25%, Fit Selection, or Custom.

Zoom to selection will zoom to show all of the selected cells. (Even if you select a lot of them, so be careful there.)

Note that zoom only affects the cells in your worksheet, not the menu up top, task panes, or dialogue boxes. You need to maximize Excel to take up your entire screen, use a bigger monitor, or change your Windows settings to get any of those to be larger.

Hide a Worksheet

If you ever need to hide a worksheet, right-click on its name and choose Hide from the dropdown menu.

Other worksheets will still be able to reference that one, but users won't be able to see it unless they unhide it. This can come in handy if you ever need to reference a list of values that don't need to be visible to users.

Unhide a Worksheet

To unhide a worksheet, right-click on a currently visible worksheet, and then choose Unhide from the dropdown menu. This will bring up an Unhide dialogue box that will list all hidden worksheets in that workbook. Click on the one(s) you want and then click on OK.

Navigate a Large Number of Worksheets

If you have a large number of worksheets in a workbook, right-click on the arrows at the left bottom end that you use to navigate between worksheets to bring up the Activate dialogue box:

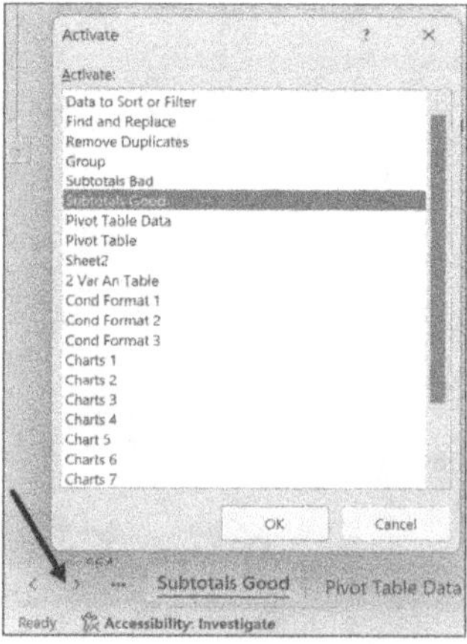

You can then click on the worksheet you want, and click OK to move to it.

Indent Text within a Cell

If you ever want to indent text or values within a cell, use the Increase Indent option that's located in the bottom row of the Alignment section of the Home tab. It has lines with a right-pointing arrow. You can indent more than once.

I've used this when I had a summary row above detailed rows of data and wanted to create a visual break between the two.

To remove an indent, use the Decrease Indent option which has the left-pointing arrow. If you indented more than once, you will need to decrease the indent more than once also.

The Format Cells dialogue box also has an Indent field in the Alignment tab that will let you specify the number of times to indent the text in the selected cell(s).

Notes in Excel

If you're using a worksheet that someone else created and you see a red mark in the top right corner of a cell, especially in a header row, it is possible that there are instructions or further explanation available for that field. Hold your cursor over that cell to see the comment:

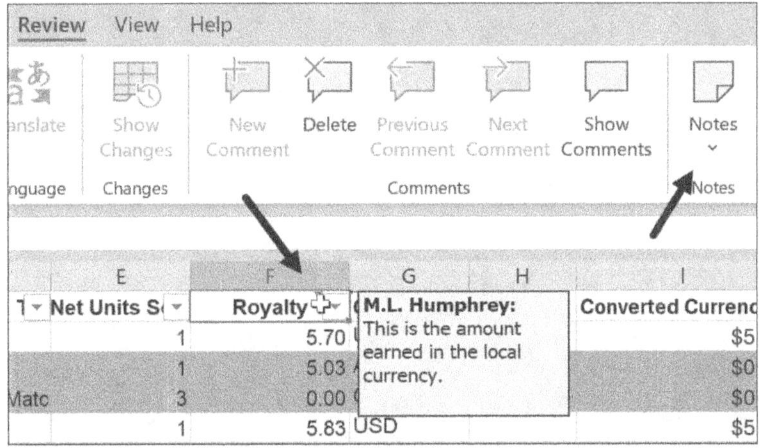

To add a note yourself, click on the cell, go to the Review tab, and use the dropdown under Notes in the Notes section. Select New Note and then type what you want in the note field that appears. You can also use the Notes dropdown to edit an existing note or move between the notes in a worksheet.

The show notes options available there will make notes visible by default.

Conclusion

Okay. That's all we're going to cover in this book. We're just over thirty thousand words which is pretty much the upper limit for one of these books. Past that point I think we cross the line from something a person can read cover to cover to a resource that only gets used for learning specific topics.

The next book in this series is going to dive in on the last big topic I want to cover with respect to Excel, which is how formulas and functions work. It covers about seventy total functions with fifty having their own chapter.

So what didn't I cover here that you may still need to know?

I didn't cover how to lock a workbook or cells from being edited. It's just not one I've had to use often. Same with the different workbook views or accessibility.

And there are definitely some very big more advanced topics out there like macros or PowerBi. There are plenty of books on those topics by people far better at using them than I am. Using them is like learning a computer programming language. Not for the faint of heart.

As a reminder, you can always go to the Help tab to search for how to do different things in Excel. There are also a zillion resources out there, and the Microsoft support website is great.

You can also reach out to me and I'll try to help, too, especially if something in here wasn't clear. Or if I got it wrong. I try to test everything I write in these books, but I am not perfect. Sometimes I test something and it works one way and that's how I describe it, and then later I happen to do it a little differently and it turns out there was a bit of nuance there that I'd missed the first time around.

This is the fourth series of these books I've written, so hopefully I've caught most of those issues by now, but I always find something the next time around.

And they do change Excel on a regular basis. Usually on the fringes, thankfully, but sometimes in more core areas. I think I mentioned that I've noticed that filtering is now a little wonky in Excel 365. The good news about working in Excel 2024 instead of Excel 365 is that it will remain stable for you as long as you use it. (Theoretically. I think sometimes they try to get in there and update things even on the stable versions.)

Anyway.

Good luck with it. You can do this. It's a lot to take in when you're just getting started, but remember that under all of this there is a certain logic. If you get stuck or confused, try to think about how something similar works in Excel, and then take that approach.

Also, remember that Ctrl + Z, Undo, is your friend. It will get you out of a lot of mistakes. And Esc is often a good way to just shut things down and back away.

Okay then. If you're ready to keep going, check out the next book in the series, *Excel 2024 Useful Functions*.

Excel 2024
Useful Functions

EXCEL 2024 ESSENTIALS - BOOK 3

M.L. HUMPHREY

CONTENTS

CONTENTS (CONT.)

Introduction

If you truly want to use Excel to its utmost, you have to learn how to use formulas and functions. Even if you're going to use it for text-based uses (which I do sometimes), there are functions that let you clean up text that are very useful to know, in addition to the many, many, many functions that perform actual mathematical calculations.

Now, this is the fourth time I've written a series of books on Microsoft Excel. And because I am wired weird, I like to actually write these books from scratch each time. I know what I've done before and sometimes reuse portions, but each time I sort of step back and say, "What should I cover in this book?" And even, "How many books should this series include?"

Functions is one of those areas where I've gone back and forth the most. The first time around, I started with just two books, *Excel for Beginners* and *Intermediate Excel*. I only covered a handful of functions in those books: SUM, IF, COUNTIFS, SUMIFS, CONCATENATE, and a special use of the TEXT function. I figured your average beginner really didn't need much more. And if they did, they could use Help to find it.

I wrote that entire series of books with the singular goal of teaching self-published authors how to use pivot tables, so I was trying to get to that point as fast as possible. Later, though, I ended up writing two more books in that series, *50 Useful Excel Functions* and *50 More Excel Functions*, that covered a hundred functions between them, with a chapter devoted to each one.

That was a lot, and it put me right at the edge of my comfort level to cover that many in detail, because I don't use that many day-to-day. But I wanted a good selection of functions across various uses for the variety of potential users who might read those books.

Some of the chapters were also very short. I included certain functions for completeness' sake. For example, I don't think I have ever used the PRODUCT function (which multiplies values), but I included it because I wanted to explain SUMPRODUCT (which sums the results of multiplied values across more than one range).

So the next time around I covered functions in only one book, which I think worked, too. But that book was bordering on being a little too much for someone to read cover-to-cover.

(And, yes, I really do hope that people will read this book that way, even though it's the length of a short novel.)

I did the same thing with the Excel 365 books.

Which leads us to now. There is so much that Excel can do, it can be overwhelming. I think I add value by cutting out the extraneous mess you don't need. I don't want to write a dictionary of Excel, others have done that, and probably more effectively. My thought is, "You have limited time, I have limited time, let's focus on what you might actually use some day."

But there still are times when it makes sense to cover a lesser-used function so you know it exists. Or to at least mention a different function so you'll recognize it if someone else uses it.

There are also a lot of good new Excel functions that even experienced users should learn to use like XLOOKUP, TEXTBEFORE, TEXTAFTER, TEXTJOIN, RANDARRAY, and IFS. But some of the core functions still do great work. The SUM or count functions are probably the functions you will use the most in Excel, no matter how sophisticated you get.

So as I wrote this book, I asked myself over and over, "Does this user need to know this right now?" Which led me to cover 50 functions in their own chapter and reference another 20, so 70 in total. I think that's a good solid base for you to start from.

If you must skip around, and I know some of you will, I've given you a chapter that lists the top functions I think you should learn, so at least cover those. You don't have to use them, but read those chapters to understand what's possible in Excel.

Also, be sure to read the non-function-specific chapters at the beginning and end of the book, because they apply no matter what functions you use.

Finally, I print these books in black and white to make them as affordable for readers as possible, but sometimes it is nice to see color images. The ebook versions of these books are in color and if you go to the About the Author section at the end of this book there is a discount code for buying the ebook off of my Payhip store.

Okay, then. First things first, we need to learn the basics of what formulas and functions are, where to find them, and how to use them.

Formulas Versus Functions

You can have a formula in Excel that does not include a function. But you cannot have a function in Excel without it being part of a formula.

Every formula in Excel is started with an equals sign (=), a minus sign (-), or a plus sign (+). That tells Excel, "This is a calculation or task that needs to be performed. It's not just text or a numeric value to store, I want you, Excel, to do something for me."

I personally start all of my formulas with the equals sign, but some people will come from a background where using the minus or plus sign works better for them. No matter which one you use, Excel will convert it to a formula that uses an equals sign.

Here is an example of the same calculation written three different ways:

What I Wrote	What Excel Changed It To	Visible Result
=4-2	=4-2	2
+4-2	=4-2	2
-2+4	=-2+4	2

The top row is how I would write it. This is basically saying, "Hey, Excel, take the number 4 and subtract the number 2":

$$=4-2$$

The second row starts the formula with a plus sign, but says the same thing:

$$+4-2$$

Excel changed that to:

$$=4-2$$

The third row starts the formula with a minus sign:

$$-2+4$$

Note I had to switch up the order of the numbers there to make it work. That's basically saying, "I have negative 2 here, can you add four to it?" Excel changed that to:

$$=-2+4$$

All three of the above formulas work to perform the same calculation. Personally, I find it easier to write =4-2, but you do you, whichever one works.

As you saw with the above examples, a formula can just include numbers and operator signs like minus (-) and plus (+) in one cell, which we'll cover in more detail in another chapter. But what makes Excel really powerful are two more things it can do: cell notation and functions.

Cell notation lets you shortcut the tedious task of typing in a bunch of numbers. While it is possible to write something like:

$$=1+2+3+4+5+6+7+8+9+10$$

or

$$=A1+A2+A3+A4+A5+A6+A7+A8+A9+A10$$

if those values are in cells in your worksheet, you can also just tell Excel to add a range of cells by using what I refer to as cell notation. A1:A10 refers to the values in Cells A1 through A10, for example. (We'll go into detail on that in a moment, too.)

Functions are basically a shorthand way to tell Excel what to do. For example, instead of the formula above where I put a plus sign between every single value I wanted to add, I can instead use the SUM function and cell notation:

$$=SUM(A1:A10)$$

tells Excel to go to the specified cells (A1 through A10), pull each value, and then add them all together.

SUM is one of the most basic functions in Excel, but there are far more complex functions that you can use. SUMIFS, for example, will take a range of values, compare them to your specified criteria, and only add the values where all of the criteria are met. I can tell Excel with one little function that I want it to add the dollar value of sales of blue widgets made to Colorado customers since July 1, 2024.

Giving Excel a function to use is like giving it an instruction sheet to follow. As long as you use the correct function, format your inputs correctly, and give the required inputs, Excel will do all the rest. That's the key, of course: Excel is only as good as the person using it. You give it bad commands or bad data, you will get bad results.

To summarize: A formula is essentially you telling Excel you need it to do something. You can have one formula per cell. A function is part of a formula. It's a shortcut way of telling Excel what you want it to do. A formula can include more than one function.

Cell Notation

As I noted in the last chapter, cell notation is crucial to working with formulas and functions in Excel. If you don't know cell notation, you will not get near the full value from Excel that you could.

First, the basics.

A cell is referenced (by default) using its column letter and its row number. The first cell in any worksheet is Cell A1. The last cell in a worksheet in Excel 2024 is XFD1048576.

You should be able to see the column and row for a given cell without much issue, but if you ever have doubts, look to the left of the formula bar above the active workspace. That will show the cell reference for the cell you're in.

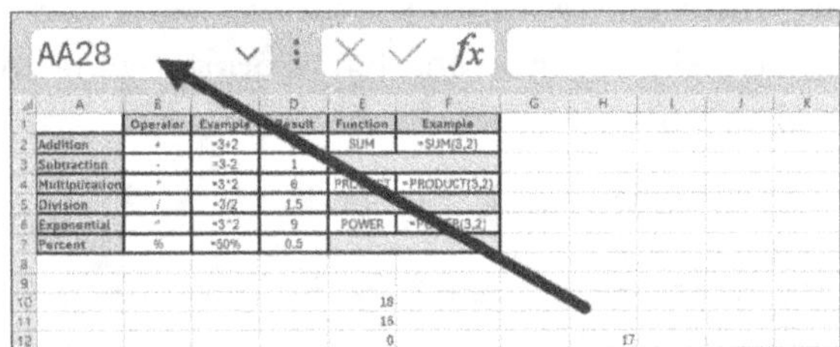

Here, for example, I am zoomed way out so that my column and row values are barely visible, but the formula bar stays the same size, and I can easily see that I'm in Cell AA28. (That only works, though, for a single cell. If you select a range of cells, that box will only show you the first selected cell in the range.)

To reference more than one cell, you have two options. You can use a comma (,) which you can think of as standing for *and*, or a colon (:) which you can think of as standing for *through*.

So if I write:

$$=SUM(A1,A2,A3)$$

that is saying to sum the values in Cells A1 *and* A2 *and* A3.

But I could also write that as:

$$=SUM(A1:A3)$$

which would be saying to sum the values in Cell A1 *through* Cell A3.

To reference an entire row or column, you just use the column letter or row number. So

$$=SUM(A:A)$$

will sum all values in Column A.

To sum across multiple columns or rows, start with the first letter or number, then use a colon, and end with the last letter or number in the range you want.

You can also combine commas and colons when referencing cells. So:

$$=SUM(6:8,11:12)$$

will sum the values in all cells in Rows 6 *through* 8 *and* in Rows 11 *through* 12.

If you want to reference cells in another worksheet or workbook, that is also possible.

For another worksheet in that workbook, write the name of the tab that has the data you want, followed by an exclamation point, and then the cell range. So:

$$=SUM(Operators!E10:E12)$$

is summing the values in Cells E10 through E12 in the worksheet named Operators in the current workbook.

To sum a worksheet in a different workbook, you can write the other workbook name in brackets, followed by the worksheet name in that workbook, followed by an exclamation point, followed by which cells to use:

$$=SUM([Book2]Sheet1!\$A\$1:\$E\$12)$$

If you're not sure how to reference a range of cells in a function, start it:

$$=SUM($$

and then when you reach the point in the function where you need the cell reference, select the cells you want by clicking and dragging. Excel will populate your function for you with the proper notation for those selected cells.

For cells I reference in other worksheets or other workbooks, I always do it that way because I can't be bothered to figure out how to write the worksheet or workbook reference portion properly.

You may still need to make edits, though.

I did that above for the last example, and Excel inserted $ signs for the cell range. Instead of writing A1:E12, it wrote \$A\$1:\$E\$12.

Using dollar signs has the effect of fixing that part of the cell reference. In this case, since it was on all parts of the cell range, that means that anywhere I copy that equation it will stay the same. Left as-is, the formula would continue to reference Cells A1 through E12 no matter where it was copied to. If I didn't want that, I'd have to remove them.

Those dollar signs have their uses. In the intermediate book, we were able to quickly build a two-variable analysis grid by fixing the row reference for the values across the top of the table and the column reference for the values down the side of the table.

So if you ever want to be able to copy a formula but keep one or more cell references in that formula fixed, use them.

This is probably a good time for a quick refresher on what happens to formulas when you copy them in Excel or cut them in Excel.

If you click on a cell that has a formula in it, *cut* that formula, and move it elsewhere, it will not change. Same with if you click on a cell, go to the formula bar, select the text from the formula bar, copy it, use Esc, go to another cell, and paste the text in.

If you *copy* a cell with a formula and paste it elsewhere, thought, the cell references in the formula will all update based on their new relative position.

This sounds horrible when you first hear about it, but that ability to copy a formula and have it adjust, is one of the most important things that Excel does for you.

Because let's say I have 100,000 rows of values in Column A and Column B, and for each row I want to add those values together. So I want =A1+B1 in Row 1, and then =A2+B2 in Row 2, and then =A3+B3 in Row 3, and so on for 100,000 rows.

I do not want to have to write 100,000 formulas to make that happen. And thanks to the beauty of how copied formulas work in Excel, I don't have to. All I have to do is write that first formula, =A1+B1, and then copy and paste it down 99,999 rows. Excel does all the rest for me.

But pay attention to this! Because copying and pasting formulas without fixing a cell reference is probably one of the most common mistakes I make.

For example, I will want to calculate the percentage share of each value in a table. That requires summing the total of all the values, and then dividing each individual value by the total. Here, for example, I have five values in Column A. The total of those values is 15:

	A	B	C	D	E
1	Value	Bad Formula	Bad Result	Good Formula	Good Result
2	1	=A2/SUM(A2:A6)	7%	=A2/SUM($A$2:$A$6)	7%
3	2	=A3/SUM(A3:A7)	14%	=A3/SUM($A$2:$A$6)	14%
4	3	=A4/SUM(A4:A8)	25%	=A4/SUM($A$2:$A$6)	25%
5	4	=A5/SUM(A5:A9)	44%	=A5/SUM($A$2:$A$6)	44%
6	5	=A6/SUM(A6:A10)	100%	=A6/SUM($A$2:$A$6)	100%
7					
8			190%		190%
9					

In both Cells C2 and E2 I have correctly calculated the share of the value in Cell A2. You can see the formulas I used in Columns B and D:

$$=A2/SUM(A2:A6)$$

and

$$=A2/SUM(\$A\$2:\$A\$6)$$

Both give me 1 divided by 15, which is 7%.

Where the issue comes in is if I then copy that formula down to the rest of the cells in each column. For the formula used in Cell C2 (which you can see written out in Cell B2), when I copy it down, the formula adjusts *all* of the cell references.

By the time we reach Row 6, the formula in Cell C6 (shown in Cell B6) is:

$$=A6/SUM(A6:A10)$$

That is wrong. We are no longer dividing by the total of all five values. We know it's wrong because the value in Cell C6 is 100%, and the total of all values in Column C, shown in Cell C8, is 190%.

For the formula used in Cell E2 on the other hand, which you can see written out in Cell D2, when I copy it down, the formula only adjusts the top value because those dollar signs in the formula keep the other cell references fixed.

$$=A6/SUM(\$A\$2:\$A\$6)$$

Perfect. That's what we wanted.

It continued to reference the sum of the correct cell range, A2 through A6, that we wanted to divide by, while also updating the value that needed to be divided for each line.

(And for the extra credit students, if I'd just used A\$2:A\$6 that would've worked, too, since I'm staying in the same column, but I prefer to lock in the whole cell reference because that's actually what I'm trying to do.)

This is why you have to, have to, have to, gut check your results when working with formulas.

Or find another way to verify a result. Here in Cells C8 and E8 I've totaled my percentages, because I know that I need a total of 100% if I'm calculating a share of the whole. They don't total to 100% in Column C, so I know I made a mistake there.

Always ask yourself, "Does this result make sense?"

Excel is not smarter than you. Excel is as smart as you. It is you using a tool that is more sophisticated than a calculator, but at the end of the day, it's still you using a tool.

Okay. Now let's discuss functions more.

Excel Function Basics

First, know that I will write all functions I refer to in this book with all caps, but you don't have to type them into Excel that way. So I'm going to write:

$$=SUM(A1:A10)$$

but you could type in

$$=sum(a1:a10)$$

and it would work just fine.

When you use a function, it needs to be followed by opening and closing parens.

Most functions will have required inputs that need to go between those parens—for example, SUM needs you to tell it what numbers to add together—but there are functions out there that do not require an input. For example TODAY() returns today's date.

You can use a function at any point in a formula.

$$=10\text{-}SUM(A1:A10)$$

is a perfectly valid formula that tells Excel to subtract the values in Cells A1 through A10 from 10.

Note that you don't put an equals sign before a function if it's not at the start of the formula. You just list it like you would any number in that formula.

You can also have more than one function in a single formula:

$$=SUM(A1:A10)+SUM(B1:B5)$$

is a perfectly valid formula that adds the values in Cells A1 through A10 and in Cells B1 through B5.

You can also "nest" functions. You do this when you put one function around another. For example:

$$=ROUND(SUM(A1{:}A10),2)$$

would sum the values in Cells A1 through A10, and then round the result to two decimal places.

If you nest functions, pay special attention to your opening and closing parens.

Sometimes it helps to think of a nested function as two parts:

$$=ROUND(x,2)$$

$$SUM(A1{:}A10)$$

where the x in the first function represents the second function. When you break two nested functions out this way, they should each stand on their own. ROUND would require a number there for x, but it is fully functional otherwise, with all required inputs and parens. SUM needs to be part of a formula, but it too is fully functional with all required inputs and parens.

Excel Function Notation

For every function, Excel provides a text description of what the function does:

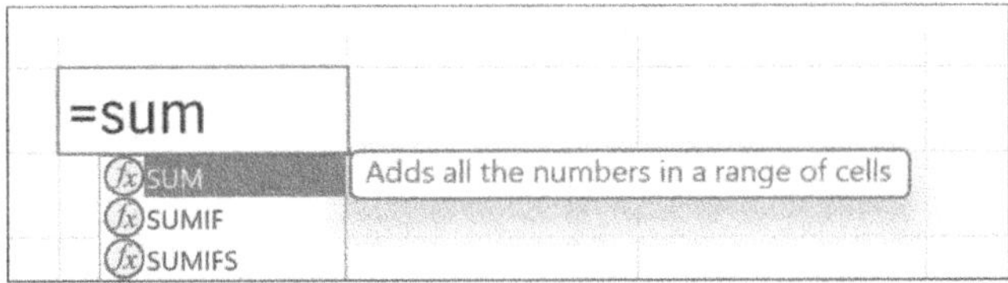

as well as a list of the inputs for that function:

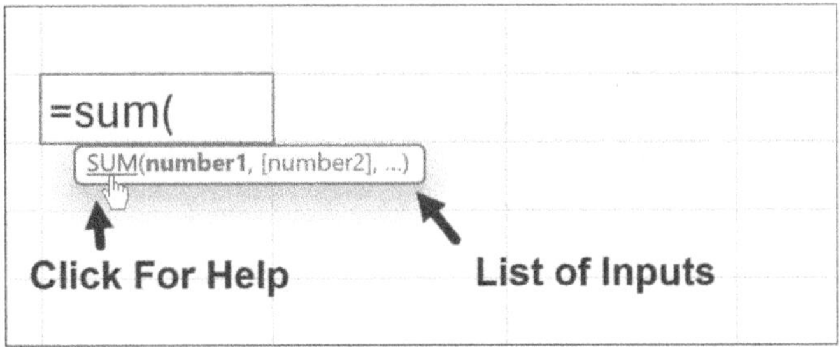

You can see above that the list of inputs for the SUM function are (number1, [number2], …)

Any input that's in plain text, like number1, is required. Any input in brackets, like number2, is optional. The dot, dot, dot at the end of a list means you can add more of the same inputs if needed.

So for SUM, that basically says, "The SUM function requires at least one number, but can take more than one. Separate each number you provide with a comma."

In this case, a "number" is very loosely defined, since it can be an actual number, a cell reference, a range of cells, or a named range.

$$=SUM(A1:B25)$$

is a perfectly legitimate use of SUM that only has one "number" input.

Other functions in Excel will have other types of inputs like TRUE/FALSE or lists where the value you provide specifies how that function works. (We will talk about them in detail under each specific function.)

When a function has multiple inputs that require different types of information, like XLOOKUP, you have to provide the inputs in the correct order with each input separated by a comma.

(It is possible to provide a list of values for an input into a function using curly brackets or a nested function. We'll cover a couple examples later, so don't worry about understanding how to do that right now.)

As you work through creating a function, the portion that is bolded in the description at any given time is the input you are currently being asked to give to Excel.

Where To Find Functions & How to Use Them

I am going to spend the majority of this book walking you through some of the most useful functions I know in Excel. But chances are you are either going to forget a function name or you're going to need a different function. So before we dive in, I want to discuss where you can go to see *all* the available functions, and to search for one you want.

Excel has an entire tab devoted to Formulas. Click there on the Formulas tab, and you'll see a Function Library section with various categories (Recently Used, Financial, Logical, Text, Date & Time, Lookup & Reference, Math & Trig, and More).

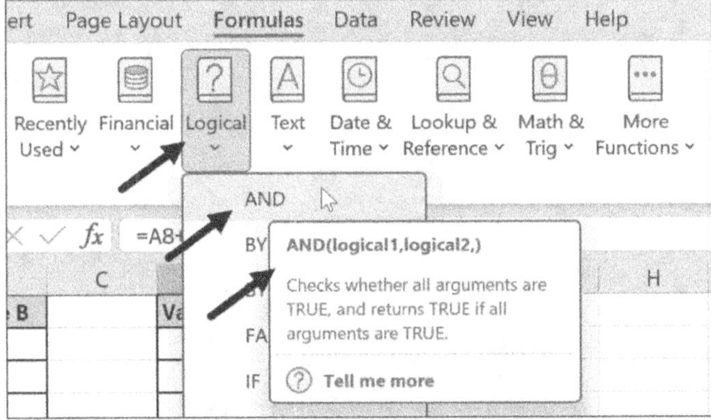

Each of those categories has a dropdown menu that alphabetically lists functions, like the one above for Logical. Hold your cursor over a function name to see a definition of what that function covers, like I have here for AND.

Personally, I don't think this is the ideal place to find a function you don't already know about, but it can be an interesting way to explore within a given category, like Text.

If you have a specific task in mind, it is better to bring up the Insert Function dialogue box. You can do this with Shift + F3, or, if like me you will never remember that, go to the Formulas tab and click on the Insert Function option on the far left:

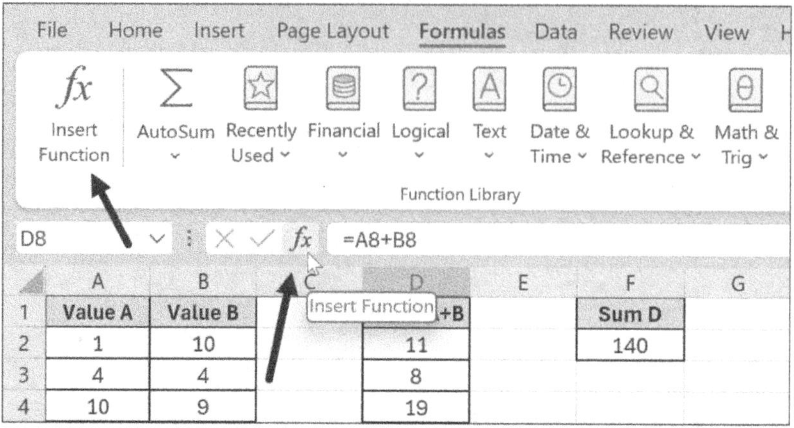

Another option is to click on the little function symbol in the formula bar that you can see above. However you do it, all three options will open the Insert Function dialogue box:

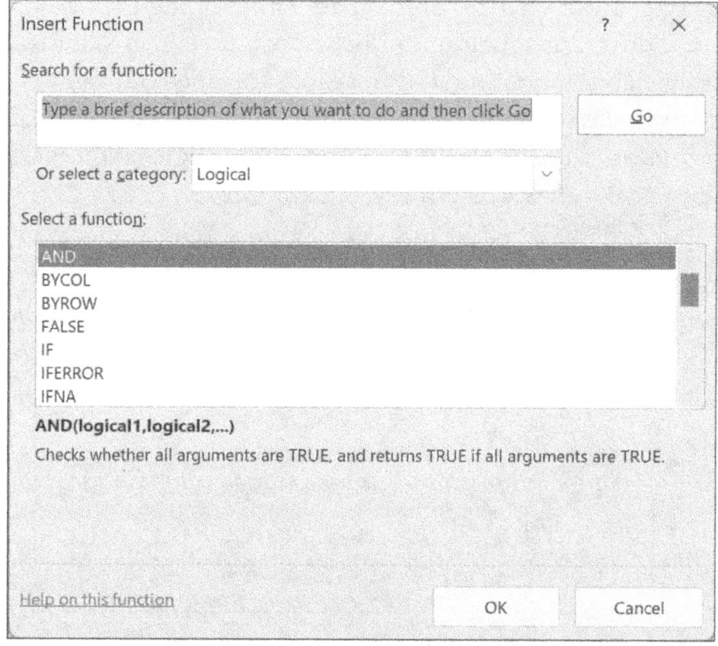

The Select a Category dropdown lets you choose a category and then see all functions for that specific category in the white box in the middle. But that's pretty much what you could do in the Formulas tab.

I prefer to search. Use the white Search For a Function field in the top section of the dialogue box to type a few keywords that describe what you're trying to do.

Click on Go and Excel will show you a list of possible functions in the Select A Function field in the middle of the dialogue box.

Click on each function in that list to see the function description and required inputs. Here I've searched for functions that let you "join text", andExcel gave me three options, CONCAT, CONCATENATE, and TEXTJOIN:

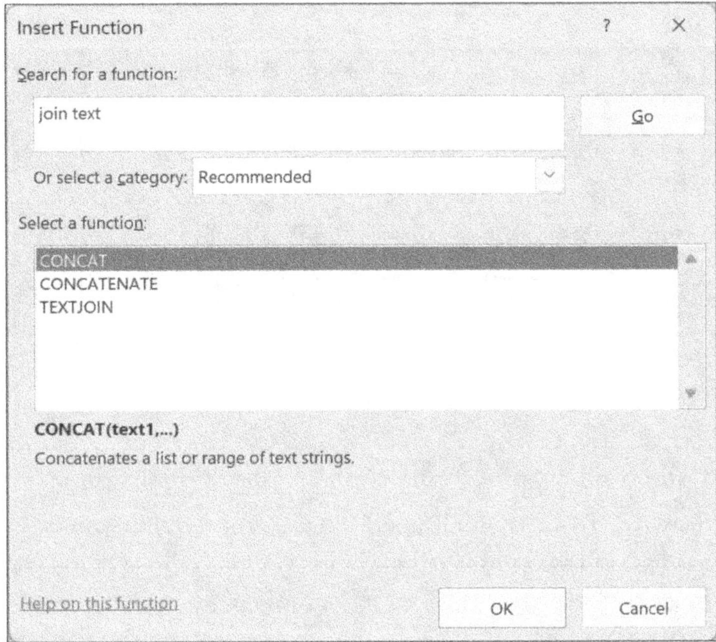

For each of the functions we're going to cover in detail in this book, I will give you that text description and list of inputs.

A few more things to point out here.

The Help On This Function link in the bottom left corner will bring up a web page that has help text specific to the selected function from the Microsoft website. (But only if you have your settings set to allow that.)

If you click OK, Excel is going to try to insert the selected function into the cell you were clicked into before you brought up the dialogue box.

It is also going to try to help you fill out the function with a Function Arguments dialogue box that will have fields for all of the required or optional inputs for that function.

On the next page is the one for TEXTJOIN, for example:

You can use this dialogue box if you find it helpful. It will show the result of the choices you've made in the bottom left corner where it says Formula Result =, which can be useful for a function you haven't used before.

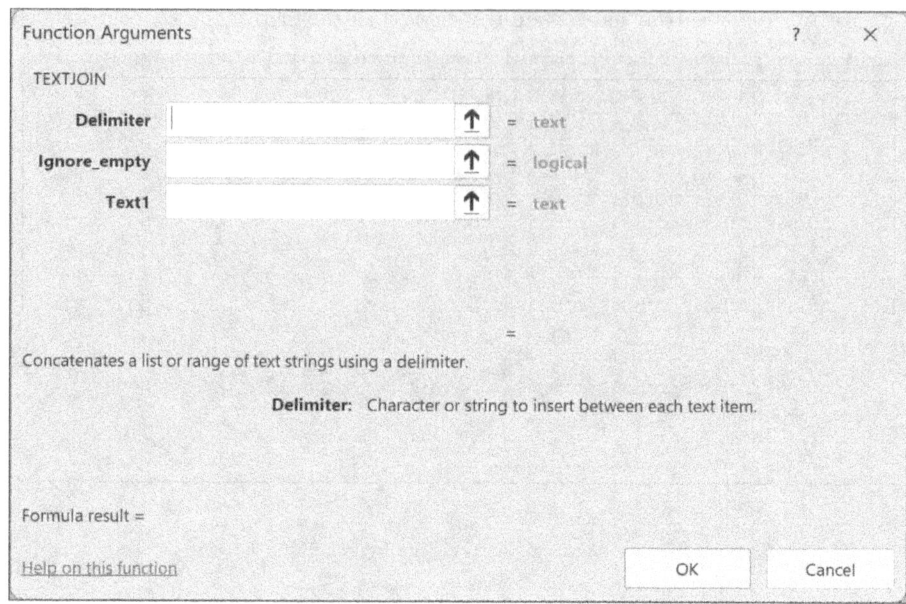

I personally prefer to work from the cell itself once I know what function I need, so let me walk you through how to do that now.

To start, go to the cell where you want your formula, and start entering it. When you reach the portion of your formula that requires a function, as you type the function name Excel will come up with a list that matches what you've typed so far:

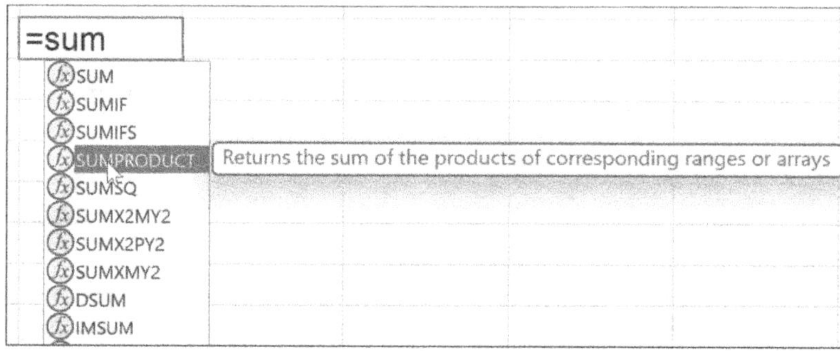

You can click on any entry in that list to see what the function does without changing what you've already typed in the cell.

To use a function from that list, double-click on the function name. Excel will add it along with the opening paren.

I usually just type in the function name myself, so have to add that starting paren when I do so.

Once you have the function name and opening paren, the text below your cell will show the function name and its required inputs:

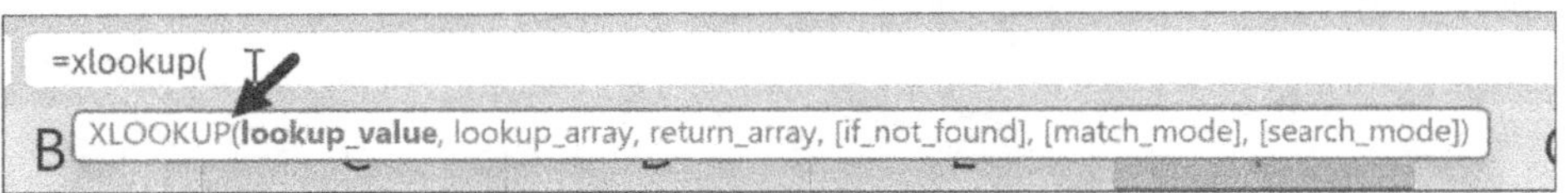

You can click on that function name to open the Help specific to that function.

A task pane should appear on the right-hand side of your workspace that is specific to that function.

(Note that this will only work if your options are set to allow help to open, otherwise you'll get an error message. Also, I can't promise that all Excel functions have their own dedicated help page, but the main ones do.)

If you click into the formula bar, you'll see the same text that you can link to help with and also the same list of inputs.

Either in the cell itself or in the formula bar, you then just walk through the function and provide each input as required. If this isn't a nested function, then close out the function with a closing paren when you reach the end.

* * *

One final tip for finding a function or figuring out how to use it: do a web search.

I often will wonder "Is this possible?" or "How would you do this?" Internet searches are the best way to find that answer. Micosoft's help is great for "how to" but less useful for "can you" type of inquiries.

Don't think you have to struggle alone, because chances are whatever you want to do has been done at some point by hundreds of others, some of whom asked how to do it and were told how in an online forum.

Now, keep in mind that web searches are probably becoming much less reliable these days thanks to AI and other crap, but there's still a lot of older help out there. (I'd say focus on results prior to about 2023 whenever possible.)

And if you're dealing with a newer function, the Microsoft support forums should still be a source of solid, reliable information on "can you" type of questions.

Okay, one more basic formula topic, and then we'll start working our way through actual functions.

Operators and Calculation Order

Before we dive into functions, I want to cover operators that you can use in formulas, and how Excel goes through and performs more complex calculations.

Here is a table of the most common mathematical calculations:

	Operator	Example	Result	Function	Example
Addition	+	=3+2	5	SUM	=SUM(3,2)
Subtraction	-	=3-2	1		
Multiplication	*	=3*2	6	PRODUCT	=PRODUCT(3,2)
Division	/	=3/2	1.5		
Exponential	^	=3^2	9	POWER	=POWER(3,2)
Percent	%	=50%	0.5		

The first column lists the type of calculation. The second column lists the "operator" you need to use to perform that calculation. (Operator is just a fancy way of saying the character you use.) The third column shows a formula that performs that calculation type. The fourth displays the result of the formula.

And then the last two columns show functions that can also be used for that type of calculation, and an example of them applied to the same numbers.

So, for example, for addition you use the plus sign (+) or the SUM function.

$$=3+2$$

returns the same result as

$$=SUM(3,2)$$

For subtraction you use the minus sign (-), for multiplication it's the asterisk (*) or PRODUCT function, and for division it's the forward slash (/).

To put one number to the power of another ,use the caret (^) or POWER function. To tell Excel to treat a number as a percentage, use the percent symbol (%).

You can also use greater than (>) or less than (<) operators when working with functions.

$$* * *$$

Within any given formula, Excel will perform calculations and complete functions in a set order. You can go to Help and look for "calculation operators and precedence" to see a full discussion of how this works, but here are the basics:

For the most part, Excel follows standard calculation rules and works from left to right.

Excel will start with all reference operators first. It will find anything that uses a colon or comma to reference a range of cells, and retrieve those values.

Next, it will apply any negatives that are in the formula.

Then percentages.

Then exponentials.

Then multiplication and division.

Then addition and subtraction.

Then any strings of text that need to be joined using the ampersand (&).

And finally, it will perform any equal to, greater than, or less than comparisons.

If you want a specific part of a formula calculated first before it is incorporated with the rest of the values in the formula, put parens around that part. So:

$$=2+3*5$$

will give a result of 17 because Excel multiplies 3 times 5 first and then goes back and adds 2. But

$$=(2+3)*5$$

will give a result of 25 because Excel does the part in parens, 2 + 3, first, and then multiplies that by 5.

As you can see, one misplaced paren and your results could be completely wrong. So always, always, always pay attention to what order things will happen in.

In the Formulas tab, there is an Evaluate Formula option in the Formula Auditing section. Use that to walk through a formula step-by-step, and see which calculations are being performed first.

We'll discuss that and other troubleshooting options at the end of this book. For now I want to dive in and start working with different functions.

Top Functions to Learn

Before we start with specific functions, here are the five that I think you should learn no matter what:

1. SUM

   I've already used this one more than once in examples in the introductory section. Pretty much anyone who is going to work with numbers in Excel will at some point want to add a range of numbers together. This function is how you do that.

2. TEXTJOIN

   This one also does what it says. It joins strings of text together. You can also tell Excel what character(s) to use to separate each text string.

3. IFS

   IFS lets you write formulas that return different results based on the data. Think of it as IF x, THEN y, ELSE z, but capable of much more complexity than that.

4. TRIM

   TRIM removes extra spaces from text strings and is good for cleaning up messy data.

5. XLOOKUP

   XLOOKUP will look for a value or the closest to that value in one columns, and then return that result or a value in another column.

These may not be the functions that you personally will use the most, but if you learn all five they will give you an understanding of how Excel functions work, and the variety of uses for them.

Now on to individual functions.

I've grouped them by type. We'll start with some Math & Trig and Statistical functions, then move on to Text functions, and then Date & Time functions. Finally, I'll round it out with a smattering of Logical, Lookup & Reference, and Information functions.

The SUM Function

Notation: SUM(number1,[number2], …)

Excel Definition: Adds all the numbers in a range of cells.

The SUM function is probably the most-used function in Excel. There are ways to see the sum of values in cells without using it (like selecting the cells and looking in the bottom right corner of the workspace), and the AutoSum option can sometimes substitute for actually writing the formula yourself, but if there is one function you learn in Excel, this is the one.

SUM technically only requires one input.

$$=SUM(3)$$

will give you a result. But the reason for that is that you can sum millions of records with just one input. For example,

$$=SUM(D:F)$$

will sum all of the values in Columns D, E, and F.

As you can see in my first example above, it is possible to list the values directly in the function. For example:

$$=SUM(2,3,4)$$

will add 2, 3, and 4 and give a result of 9. But the real power of Excel comes with cell references, like I used above to refer to all of the values in three columns.

If you have multiple non-adjacent cell references that you want to sum, just separate them with commas. Like so:

$$=SUM(1:1,3:3,7:7)$$

which would sum all of the values in Rows 1, 3, and 7.

You can also use the SUM function to get around the fact that there is no function for subtracting a large number of values. The reason Excel doesn't have a function for subtraction is because with subtraction the order matters. Three minus two is different from two minus three. But if you have a starting value and everything else is being subtracted from that value, then you can use the SUM function to create a very simple formula. Like this:

$$=H16\text{-}SUM(A{:}A)$$

Here I am taking the value in Cell H16 and subtracting from it the values in the cells in Column A. The reason this works is because

$$=H16\text{-}A1\text{-}A2\text{-}A3$$

is equivalent mathematically to

$$=H16\text{-}(A1+A2+A3)$$

As I mentioned previously, you can sometimes use the AutoSum function to build your SUM function for you. Just be sure to check that it captures the right cell range. If there are gaps in your data it's liable to stop at the first gap it finds, so instead of summing A2:A100 it tries to sum A52:A100.

The COUNT Function

Notation: COUNT(value1, [value2],…)

Excel Definition: Counts the number of cells in a range that contain numbers.

The COUNT function allows you to count how many cells within a selected range contain numbers. Excel sometimes refers to this as the Numerical Count option.

The "value1" input into the function is generally going to be a cell range. Note that since Excel stores dates as numbers, the COUNT function will count cells that contain dates as well.

Let's look at an example:

	A	B
1	Visible Value	Type of Value
2	12	Number
3	2-Jan	Date (1/2)
4	0.5	Number (1/2)
5	Ten	Text (Ten)
6	"1"	Text ("1")
7	1	Text ('1)
8		
9		COUNT
10	3	=COUNT(A2:A7)
11		
12		COUNTA
13	6	=COUNTA(A2:A7)
14		

In Cells A2 through A7 I have various values. A2 has the number 12, A3 had 1/2 which Excel turned into the date 2-Jan, A4 has '1/2 so it remained a number and shows as .5, A5 has the word Ten, A6 has the number 1 but in double quotes, and A7 has the number 1 but it was preceded by a single quote so is treated as text by Excel. You can see those value types in Column B.

In Cell A10, I used the formula

$$=COUNT(A2:A7)$$

The result is 3. Excel counted the two numbers in Cells A2 and A4 as well as the date in Cell A3. It did not count the text of a number nor did it count numbers preceded or surrounded by single or double quotes.

Let's look at another example:

	E	F
1	Visible Value	Type of Value
2	9	Formula (+ sign)
3	45305.50	Formula (SUM)
4	12452930.5	Formula (TEXTJOIN)
5		Blank
6	1 day	Text (1 day)
7		Formula (IFERROR blank)
8		
9		COUNT
10	2	=COUNT(E2:E7)
11		
12		COUNTA
13	5	=COUNTA(E2:E7)
14		

Here I've used a variety of formulas as well as included a blank cell and one that looks blank but is using a formula.

Cell E2 shows a value of 9 that was generated by using the plus sign to add two numbers together.

Cell E3 shows a value that was created by using the SUM function on three cells that had numbers in them.

Cell E4 looks like a number but it was created with the TEXTJOIN function so is in fact text.

Cell E5 is simply blank.

Cell E6 contains text that says 1 day.

Cell E7 looks like it's blank, but it was created using an IFERROR function that returns a result of "".

The COUNT function for Cells E2 through E7 returns a value of 2, for the values in Cells E2 and E3. Note that they are counted as numbers even though the actual contents in those cells are formulas that generated those numbers.

The COUNTA Function

Notation: COUNTA(value1, [value2],…)

Excel Definition: Counts the number of cells in a range that are not empty.

Where COUNT is limited to numbers (including dates), the COUNTA function will count any cells in a range that "are not empty".

The result of the COUNTA function is what is displayed as the Count value in the bottom right corner when you select a range of cells in Excel.

Let's look at those two examples from the COUNT function again.

In the first example where every cell had something in it, the COUNTA function returns a value of six, because none of the cells are empty. Even though some are numbers, one is a date, and some are text, it counts them all.

	A	B
1	Visible Value	Type of Value
2	12	Number
3	2-Jan	Date (1/2)
4	0.5	Number (1/2)
5	Ten	Text (Ten)
6	"1"	Text ("1")
7	1	Text ('1)
8		
9		COUNT
10	3	=COUNT(A2:A7)
11		
12		COUNTA
13	6	=COUNTA(A2:A7)
14		

In the second example (on the opposite page) it returns a value of five. That's because of the two apparently blank cells, E5 and E7. Only one of them is truly blank, E5. Cell E7 looks blank but there is a formula in that cell that's currently displaying a blank result, so it gets counted.

It is important to understand this distinction, because there will be times where you want to write a formula that returns a blank value, but the COUNTA function is going to pick up those "blanks" as if there was something in that cell.

COUNT won't, though, because the result isn't a number or date.

This is also important to understand for situations where you use the COUNTA function to calculate something like an average, where you need to accurately count which cells have values in them.

Let's look at one final example with COUNTA:

	H	I	J
1	**Visible Value**	**Type of Value**	
2	0.00	Sum Blank Cells using +	
3	0.00	Paste Special-Values H2	
4		Paste Special-Values E7 ("" result)	
5		Paste Special-Values E5 (blank)	
6	0	Sum Range using SUM	
7	0	Paste Special-Values H6	
8			
9		**COUNT**	
10	4	=COUNT(H2:H7)	
11			
12		**COUNTA**	
13	5	=COUNTA(H2:H7)	
14			

Again we have a range of six cells.

Cells H2 and H6 have formulas that sum values in blank cells. Since the formulas used + or SUM which apply to numbers, they are both treated as numbers and captured by COUNT and COUNTA.

In Cells H3 and H7, I took the numbers in Cells H2 and H6 and pasted them back in as just their values. Those also were captured by COUNT and COUNTA.

So far, so good.

The tricky one is Cell H4, which is a copy and paste special – values version of a blank result (""). COUNTA counts that cell. It considers it to be "not empty". But if I look in the formula bar (see image above) I will see nothing there. Nothing to delete..

Note that for Cell H5, which was a paste special – values version of a truly blank cell, COUNTA ignored it just fine.

It's only the values that come from a null value that are problematic. To really clear a cell like that, you can either select the cell, and then use Clear Contents from the Editing section of the Home tab, or click on the cell and use Delete or Backspace.

The AVERAGE Function

Notation: AVERAGE(number1, [number2],…)

Excel Definition: Returns the average (arithmetic mean) of its arguments, which can be numbers or names, arrays, or references that contain numbers.

Essentially the AVERAGE function combines the SUM and COUNT functions.

The way you calculate an average is you take a series of numbers, add them together, and then divide by the number of values you combined. So

$$=AVERAGE(A2:A7)$$

will return the same result as

$$=SUM(A2:A7)/COUNT(A2:A7)$$

Here is our data from before that we used for COUNT: but with AVERAGE applied:

	A	B	C	D	E
1	Visible Value	Type of Value		Column A Actual Number Value	
2	12	Number		12.00	
3	2-Jan	Date (1/2)		45293.00	
4	0.5	Number (1/2)		0.50	
5	Ten	Text (Ten)			
6	"1"	Text ("1")			
7	1	Text ('1)			
8				SUM(A2:A7)	45305.50
9					
10		AVERAGE		COUNT(A2:A7)	3
11	15101.8333	=AVERAGE(A2:A7)		D8/D10	15101.83333
12					
13		AVERAGEA		COUNTA(A2:A7)	6
14	7550.91667	=AVERAGEA(A2:A7)		D8/D13	7550.916667
15					

In Cells A2 through A7, we have the same values as before. We have three cells that have "numbers" in them and three that don't. (I put numbers in quotes since one of those numbers is in fact a date.)

Recall that COUNT returned a value of 3.

In Column D I have put the actual numbers that Excel is using for each one. That date, which displays as 2-Jan in Column A, is actually January 2, 2024 behind the scenes, which is stored by Excel as the number 45293.

(I'm on a PC. For PCs, Excel treats every date as a number counting from a start date of January 1, 1900 which has the value of 1.)

Which means to take an average over that range, Excel is going to add 45,293 to 12 and 0.5, to get a total of 45,305.50. For AVERAGE it will then divide that by 3, the COUNT result, giving the result of 15,101.833 shown in Cell A11.

* * *

Now, here's where things get a little tricky. Remember that bottom corner where you can just select a range of cells and see calculations without using a formula? The average value that Excel shows there is the one for AVERAGE, but the count value is for COUNTA.

They do not match up.

Which is fine, really, because chances are that the type of average you will normally want is one that looks at numbers only, while the type of count you want is for every cell that has a value.

So there's a reason they did it that way. Just keep it in mind, so you know which one you're getting if you use that option.

This also brings up another issue.

What if you really wanted the average across all six cells, not only the ones that currently have numbers in them?

To use AVERAGE, you'd need to put a number in every cell, even if that number was zero.

* * *

One final note: You may at times get a #DIV/0! Error message when you use AVERAGE on a range of cells. That happens when there are no numeric values in the range, so the COUNT is zero.

If that's because you haven't put in values yet, no problem, don't worry about it. If there are what you think are numbers there, no there aren't. Check your formatting.

The **AVERAGEA** Function

Notation: AVERAGEA(value1, [value2],…)

Excel Definition: Returns the average (arithmetic mean) of its arguments, evaluating text and FALSE in arguments as 0; TRUE evaluates as 1. Arguments can be numbers, names, arrays, or references.

AVERAGEA is *not* the same as taking SUM and dividing it by COUNTA. That is because AVERAGEA will assign a value of 1 to TRUE values, whereas SUM does not.

Here is an example:

	G	H	I	J	K
1				Cells G3:G8	
2	**Visible Value**	**Type of Value**		SUM	14
3	12	Number			
4	2	Number		COUNT	2
5	TRUE	Text (TRUE)		AVERAGE	7
6	FALSE	Text (FALSE)		=14/2	7
7	TRUE	Formula TRUE			
8	FALSE	Formula FALSE		COUNTA	6
9				AVERAGEA	2.666666667
10				=14/6	2.333333333
11				=16/6	2.666666667
12					

In Column G, there are two numbers and four TRUE or FALSE values. You can see in Cell K2 that SUM adds those values up to 14. But if we take the COUNTA value in Cell K8 and divide it by 14, the result is 2.33. The AVERAGE function, though, returns a value of 2.667.

That is because each TRUE value in a cell is counted as 1 by AVERAGEA, so it is using 16 as the summed value.

So you have to keep that distinction in mind when using AVERAGEA if there are TRUE or FALSE values in your data.

Now let's walk through an example that puts this to good use. Say that I want to know what percent of the class scored 90% or above on a test. I have 25 test results in Column O:

	O	P	Q	R	S	T	U
1	**Score**	**90% or Above**			**AVERAGEA**		
2	85%	FALSE	=IF(O2>=0.9,TRUE(),FALSE())		48%	=AVERAGEA(P2:P26)	
3	92%	TRUE					
4	96%	TRUE			12	=COUNTIF(P2:P26,TRUE)	
5	100%	TRUE			0.48	=R4/25	
6	77%	FALSE					
7	93%	TRUE					
8	81%	FALSE					
9	95%	TRUE					
10	100%	TRUE					
11	90%	TRUE					
12	77%	FALSE					
13	97%	TRUE					
14	74%	FALSE					
15	94%	TRUE					
16	79%	FALSE					
17	75%	FALSE					
18	100%	TRUE					
19	86%	FALSE					
20	100%	TRUE					
21	83%	FALSE					
22	88%	FALSE					
23	93%	TRUE					
24	73%	FALSE					
25	73%	FALSE					
26	84%	FALSE					
27							

I use an IF function, like I did in Column P, to identify those results that are 90 or above, and copy it down:

$$=IF(O2>=0.9,TRUE(),FALSE())$$

After that it's simple enough to use AVERAGEA on that range. Since TRUE is worth 1 and FALSE is worth 0, the AVERAGEA result is also a calculation of the percent of results that are 90 or above.

(To confirm that it worked, I used another function we'll cover later, COUNTIF, to count the number of values in Column P that were TRUE, and then I manually divided that result by 25 and got the same result. There's always more than one way to do something.)

If I'd wanted to see what percentage *weren't* 90% or above, I could either write the IF function differently to assign TRUE to values under .9, or I could subtract my AVERAGEA result from 1:

$$=1-AVERAGEA(P2:P26)$$

The MIN Function

Notation: MIN(number1, [number2],…)

Excel Definition: Returns the smallest number in a set of values. Ignores logical values and text.

MIN, short for minimum, returns the smallest *numeric* value out of the list of values you give it.

Much like SUM, COUNT, and AVERAGE, the MIN function requires a "number" input, but what you're usually going to do is reference a range of cells.

Here are some examples:

	A	B	C	D	E	F	G	H
1	Visible Value	Type of Value		Visible Value	Type of Value		Visible Value	Type of Value
2	12	Number		2	Number		-5	Number
3	2-Jan	Date (1/2)		TRUE	Text (TRUE)		0.5	Number
4	0.5	Number (1/2)		FALSE	Text (FALSE)		TRUE	Text (TRUE)
5	Ten	Text (Ten)					FALSE	Text (FALSE)
6	"1"	Text ("1")						
7	1	Text ('1)						
8								
9		MIN			MIN			MIN
10	0.5	=MIN(A2:A7)		2	=MIN(D2:D4)		-5	=MIN(G2:G5)
11								
12		MINA			MINA			MINA
13	0	=MINA(A2:A7)		0	=MINA(D2:D4)		-5	=MINA(G2:G5)
14								

In Column A, we have a range of values that includes three numeric values, 12 in Cell A2, the date January 2, 2024 in Cell A3 (which is also the number 45293), and the value 0.5 in Cell A4, as well as three text versions of numbers in Cells A5, A6, and A7.

The MIN function only looks at the numbers, so it returns a value of 0.5 for the minimum. You can see that in Cell A10.

The formula I used is in Cell B10:

$$=MIN(A2:A7)$$

In Column D, we have the number 2 in Cell D2, a TRUE value in Cell D3, and a FALSE value in Cell D4. Since MIN only looks at *numbers*, it returns a value of 2, which you can see in Cell D10 with the formula shown in Cell E10.

Column G has a negative value, -5, in Cell G2, a positive value, 0.5, in Cell G3, and then TRUE and FALSE in Cells G4 and G5.

This time MIN returns a value of -5, because that's the lowest numeric value in the range. You can see that in Cell G10 and the formula in Cell H10.

If MIN is referencing a range of only blank cells, it will return a value of zero, but if it is referencing a range of cells where some are blank and some have numbers, it will ignore the blank cells, and return the smallest numeric value in the range.

You can also set Excel to display the MIN result for a selected range of cells in the bottom right corner of your worksheet. The Min option is not available by default, though, so to do that, right-click where it says Count, Sum, and Average in the bottom corner, and then click on Minimum in the dropdown menu so that it's checked, like I have here:

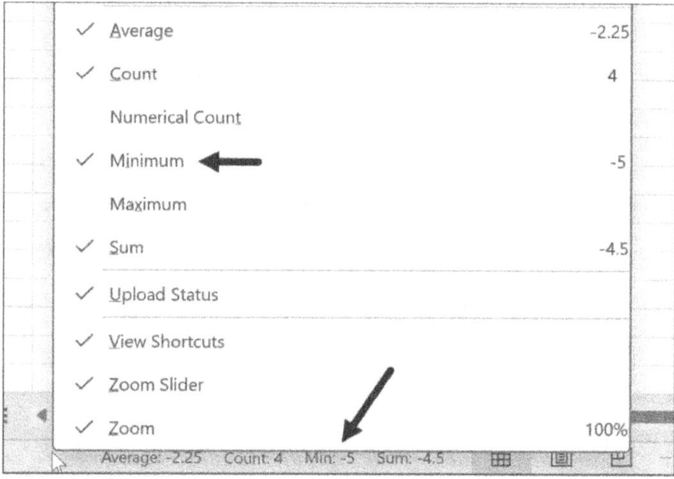

A Min value will only display in that section if at least one of the cells you select has a number in it.

The MINA Function

Notation: MINA(value1, [value2],…)

Excel Definition: Returns the smallest value in a set of values. Does not ignore logical values and text.

The difference between MIN and MINA, is that MINA will include text values and logical values like TRUE or FALSE. Any text, formula with a blank result, or FALSE value in a cell, will be treated as a value of zero for the MINA function, while TRUE will be given the value of 1.

In the examples in the MIN chapter, there were also results displayed for MINA. It returned a different result for the values in Column A and Column D. Let's walk through why.

In Column A, the text values in Cells A5, A6, and A7 are assigned a value of zero by MINA, which makes that the smallest value.

In Column D, MINA assigns FALSE a value of 0 and TRUE a value of 1. That makes FALSE the smallest value in the range, and also returns a result of zero.

For Column G, both MIN and MINA return the same result, -5. That's because even though MINA assigns values to FALSE and TRUE, a negative number is less than either assigned value.

Just like with MIN, MINA will return a value of zero if it is referencing a range of blank cells. Unlike MIN, MINA will ignore blank cells if there is *any value* in the referenced range. So one cell in the range with a value of TRUE in it, will result in a minimum of 1 even if the rest of the cells in the range are blank.

Also, be careful with MINA, because if you have a formula in your cell range that returns a blank result, that will count as a value. So you could only see TRUE results in your cell range, but because the formula in that range returned a blank value, the MINA result would be zero. (You probably won't see this often, don't worry.)

Finally, neither MIN nor MINA can work if there is an error in the cell range. They'll return the error message instead of a value.

The MAX Function

Notation: MAX(number1, [number2],…)

Excel Definition: Returns the largest value in a set of values. Ignores logical values and text.

The MAX function is the mirror of the MIN function, but instead of returning the smallest value in the range, it returns the largest.

Like MIN, MAX only looks at "numeric" values, which I put in quotes because dates are considered numbers by Excel, and chances are the number1 input that you provide the function will be a cell range not actual numbers.

Here are three examples of it applied to the same values we used for MIN and MINA:

	A	B	C	D	E	F	G	H
1	Visible Value	Type of Value		Visible Value	Type of Value		Visible Value	Type of Value
2	12	Number		0.5	Number		-5	Number
3	2-Jan	Date (1/2)		TRUE	Text (TRUE)		0.5	Number
4	0.5	Number (1/2)		FALSE	Text (FALSE)		TRUE	Text (TRUE)
5	Ten	Text (Ten)					FALSE	Text (FALSE)
6	"1"	Text ("1")						
7	1	Text ('1)						
8								
9		MAX			MAX			MAX
10	45293	=MAX(A2:A7)		0.5	=MAX(D2:D4)		0.5	=MAX(G2:G5)
11								
12		MAXA			MAXA			MAXA
13	45293	=MAXA(A2:A7)		1	=MAXA(D2:D4)		1	=MAXA(G2:G5)
14								

You can see the formula used for Column A's values in Cell B10:

=MAX(A2:A7)

Because Column A has that date value, the numeric equivalent, 45,293, is the largest value in that range.

In Column D there is only one numeric value, 0.5, so that is the value that MAX returns.

In Column G there are two numeric values, 0.5 and -5, and MAX returns the value 0.5 because it is the larger of the two numbers.

Just like MIN, MAX will return a value of zero for blank cell ranges or cell ranges that don't have any numbers in them. And if there is an error message in the range, it will return the error message.

You can also set Excel to show the Max value of a selected range of cells in the bottom right corner of the worksheet.

The MAXA Function

Notation: MAXA(value1, [value2],...)

Excel Definition: Returns the largest value in a set of values. Does not ignore logical values and text.

The MAXA function is the counterpart to MINA. It treats text and TRUE or FALSE values the same way, assigning a value of zero to text or FALSE values, and a value of one to TRUE values.

In the last chapter, you can see that I also applied MAXA to those values.

In Column A, MAXA returns the value of 45,293 because even assigning a value to the text entries there doesn't change that the date value is the largest value in that range.

In Column D, MAXA returns a different result from MAX. That's because TRUE is assigned a value of 1, which makes it the largest value in the range.

Same for Column G. MAXA returns a different result because TRUE, when assigned a value of 1, is the largest value in the range.

As with MAX, MAXA will return an error message if there's an error in the referenced range. It will also return a value of zero for a range of blank cells, but will ignore blank cells if there is any value in any cell in the referenced range of cells.

MAXA also has the issue MINA does, where it will treat a cell with a formula that returns a blank result as a zero, which means it can return a result you don't expect to see if you're dealing with negative numbers in your other cells. You might see − 5, -3, -2, and expect the MAXA result to be -2, but if there's a formula there with a blank result, you'll get a value of 0 as your maximum. Just something to keep in mind if things aren't working the way you think they "should".

The SMALL Function

Notation: SMALL(array, k)

Excel Definition: Returns the k-th smallest value in a data set. For example, the fifth smallest number.

What the SMALL function does is it looks at a range of values, puts them in order from smallest to largest, and then pulls for you the k-th smallest value.

I honestly don't use the SMALL function that much, but it is a handy one to know if you happen to need what it provides. Its counterpart, which is discussed in the next chapter, is the LARGE function.

This is the first function we've covered that *requires* more than one input. It's a pretty basic one, so nice for demonstrating a few things.

Look at the cell notation above, SMALL(array,k). That means the SMALL function requires that you provide two separate inputs, the range of cells (i.e. array) that contain your values, and then a number that represents the position you want to pull from. For example, entering 1 for your k-value will give you the smallest number in the range.

Both inputs are required for this function to work. SMALL will give you a "too few arguments entered" error if you fail to provide a value for k. It will give you a #NUM! error if you put a comma but leave the k-value blank.

Now let's look at a few examples of SMALL applied to a range of values.

On the next page, in Column A I have fifteen randomly-generated numbers that are not sorted. It makes it a little challenging to find the smallest number, doesn't it? It would be even more challenging to find the third or seventh smallest. Imagine if this were 1,000 entries instead of 15.

Yikes!

But that's what SMALL is for.

	A	B	C	D	E	F
1	**Values**					
2	670		**k-value**	**SMALL**	**k-smallest Result**	
3	353		1	=SMALL(A:A,C3)	113	
4	722		3	=SMALL(A:A,C4)	196	
5	196		7	=SMALL(A:A,C5)	528	
6	572		15	=SMALL(A:A,C6)	998	
7	528					
8	693		**k-value**	**LARGE**	**k-largest Result**	
9	198		1	=LARGE(A:A,C9)	998	
10	998		3	=LARGE(A:A,C10)	722	
11	113		7	=LARGE(A:A,C11)	662	
12	697		15	=LARGE(A:A,C12)	113	
13	456					
14	150					
15	958					
16	662					
17						

In Cells C3 through C6, I have four k-values: 1, 3, 7, and 15. That will give me the smallest number, the third smallest, the seventh smallest, and, since I have fifteen values, my largest.

I wrote a formula in Cell D3 that uses a column reference for my array and a cell reference for the k-value. This says, look at all the values in Column A and take the k-th smallest value where k is in Cell C3:

$$=SMALL(A:A,C3)$$

Writing it that way lets me copy the formula to Cells D4 through D6 without having to rewrite it. Excel automatically adjusts the k-value cell reference for me.

Note, too, that by using a cell reference in my formula, and showing the k-values in that table, I am also making my inputs visible, which is a data best practice. Anyone can quickly see from that table that the values in Column E are meant to return the first, third, seventh, and fifteenth smallest values.

One little bonus trick before we move on. Since we already learned COUNT, you can combine SMALL and COUNT together to return the largest value in the range for you using:

$$=SMALL(A:A,COUNT(A:A))$$

That sets the k value to whatever the COUNT of numeric values in Column A is, and will continue to work no matter the number of numeric values in Column A. It's a little twisty because you have to use the SMALL function to get the largest value, but it works..

The LARGE Function

Notation: LARGE(array, k)

Excel Definition: Returns the k-th largest value in a data set. For example, the fifth largest number.

As I mentioned in the last chapter, the SMALL function and the LARGE function are counterparts of one another. In the screenshot on the opposite page you can see formulas that use the LARGE function in Cells D9 through D12.

I once more used cell references to make my life easy, so the first formula there is:

=LARGE(A:A,C9)

But to get the largest value in Column A, you could also use:

=LARGE(A:A,1)

To get the smallest value in Column A when you don't know how many numbers you're dealing with, you could use

=LARGE(A:A,COUNT(A:A))

Or, since we know there are 15 values, you could use:

=LARGE(A:A,15)

The ROUND Function

Notation: ROUND(number, num_digits)

Excel Definition: Rounds a number to a specified number of digits.

The ROUND function does what you think it would, it rounds numbers.

Note that the ROUND function is another one that requires two inputs. The first input is the number that you want to round. That can be, and usually will be, a cell reference.

The second input is the number of digits you want to round to. This should be a whole number.

If it isn't a whole number, Excel will just ignore any decimal places, so using 2.73 for num_digits will be treated as 2.

A num_digits value of 0 will return a number with no decimal places. A positive num_digits value will return a number with that number of decimal places. A negative num_digits value will return a number rounded to the nearest tens, hundreds, thousands, etc.

For example, 12,345 can be rounded to 12,000 using:

$$=ROUND(12345,-3)$$

Note that the num_digits here is -3.

It is possible to format a number using a format like Currency or Accounting to make it look like you've rounded it to two decimal places, but when you use a number formatted that way in a formula, Excel will still use the original number. ROUND, on the other hand, transforms a number to truly only have the specified number of digits.

Okay. So, how does Excel round numbers?

It looks at the digit *one past* where you want to round to. If that digit is 0 through 4, it leaves the number you want to round to alone, and drops everything past that point. If the number is 5 through 9, it increases the number you want to round to by one, and also drops everything past that point.

If you're rounding to the left of the decimal place, it puts in zeroes to replace the numbers that were dropped..

Let's look at some examples:

	A	B	C
	Value	**Digits to Round**	**ROUND**
1			
2	123.123	2	123.12
3	123.123	0	123
4	123.123	-2	100
6	567.567	2	567.57
7	567.567	0	568
8	567.567	-2	600
9			
10	**Formula In Row 2:**		=ROUND(A2,B2)
11			

Here is a table with numbers in Column A. Rows 2 through 4 use the number 123.123 (so things should always round down) and Rows 6 through 8 use the number 567.567 (so things should always round up).

Because I'm lazy, I put the various num_digits values I wanted to work with in Column B. That let me write a formula in Cell C2 that I could then just copy to the other cells in Column C.

That formula was:

$$=ROUND(A2,B2)$$

Which is saying, "Take the value in Cell A2 (which is 123.123) and round it by the number of digits in Cell B2 (which is 2)."

In Column C you can see what the ROUND function does with each combination of the value in Column A and the num_digits in Column B.

For 2 digits, so Rows 2 and 6, 123.123 becomes 123.12 and 567.567 becomes 567.57. Both times, Excel went to the digit one past the second digit after the decimal, and then either rounded down (for a 3) or rounded up (for a 7).

For 0 digits, so Rows 3 and 7, 123.123 becomes 123 and 567.567 becomes 568. Again, Excel went to the first digit after the specified location, and then either rounded down (for a 1) or rounded up (for a 5).

For -2 digits, so Rows 4 and 8, 123.123 becomes 100 and 567.567 becomes 600. This one is a little harder for me to wrap my head around, but once more, Excel goes to the digit to the right of where we specified, so the 2 for 123.123 and the 6 for 567.567, and then rounds up or down accordingly.

If you want to force Excel's hand, there are two other functions, ROUNDUP and ROUNDDOWN, which will force Excel to always round up or always round down. Here you can see how those would work on these same numbers:

	A	B	C	D	E
1	Value	Digits to Round	ROUND	ROUNDUP	ROUNDDOWN
2	123.123	2	123.12	123.13	123.12
3	123.123	0	123	124	123
4	123.123	-2	100	200	100
6	567.567	2	567.57	567.57	567.56
7	567.567	0	568	568	567
8	567.567	-2	600	600	500
9					
10	Formula In Row 2:		=ROUND(A2,B2)	=ROUNDUP(A2,B2)	=ROUNDDOWN(A2,B2)
11					

Column D shows what happens when you use ROUNDUP. Column E shows what happens when you use ROUNDDOWN.

I used to do this for budgeting and it worked well. I would round all of my expenses up to the nearest five or ten dollars, and round all of my income down. It meant I always had a little extra I hadn't planned on. But in most situations, you'll want to use ROUND because it balances out over a lot of values, and keeps you close to the actual result.

Okay. Now on to a really simple one, absolute value.

The ABS Function

Notation: ABS(number)

Excel Definition: Returns the absolute value of a number, a number without its sign.

As the definition says, ABS gives you the absolute value of a number. Interestingly enough, it works on numbers that are stored as text even though a function like SUM won't.

It only takes one input, the number (or cell reference for the number, more like).

For example:

$$=ABS(A1)$$

would take whatever value is in Cell A1, and turn it into a positive number.

When I use ABS, I usually paste special-values after I'm done. Since ABS is a function, if you delete the cell that was being referenced by it, you will get a #REF! error. The only way to remove the original values but keep your absolute value result is to convert that result from formulas to values.

You may be wondering when you would use this. One example I have, is when I'm looking at financials and I have positive values of money coming in and negative values going out. To easily see the largest transactions, whether in or out, I will create a column with ABS applied to the sum of my Money In and Money Out columns.

$$=ABS(A1+B1)$$

I can then sort or filter on that column to get the largest transactions. If I didn't do that, the largest money out would be at the opposite end of the list from the largest money in if the data is sorted. And if I used a filter, I'd need to use a custom filter to show the largest negative and positive values at the same time. Using ABS is easier.

The **RANDBETWEEN** Function

Notation: RANDBETWEEN(bottom, top)

Excel Definition: Returns a random number between the numbers you specify.

In writing this book, I have used RANDBETWEEN more times than I can count. Because what it does is lets you quickly and easily generate a series of whole numbers that fall within the range you specify. So that range of numbers for MIN and MAX? Generated by RANDBETWEEN. And the numbers used for SMALL and LARGE? Same.

RANDBETWEEN takes two inputs, the lowest possible number in the range, and the highest possible number in the range.

For example, if I want random numbers between 65 and 100, I would use:

$$=RANDBETWEEN(65,100)$$

and then copy that formula down however many rows I need.

Now, in that case, I wanted percentage values. So I had to write it as:

$$=RANDBETWEEN(65,100)/100$$

because RANDBETWEEN only generates whole number values.

RANDBETWEEN can also generate negative numbers.

For example,

$$=RANDBETWEEN(-100,100)$$

will generate random whole numbers between negative one hundred and positive one hundred.

It is possible that a value will repeat if you have a limited range of numbers. Each cell is its own formula. So each cell is randomly pulling a value from the range you gave it, independent of the other cells using that formula.

There is another function, RAND, that is similar to RANDBETWEEN, but what it returns is a random decimal value greater than 0 and less than 1 that is evenly distributed.

I never use it because I think I get the same result with something like:

$$=RANDBETWEEN(0,1000000)/1000000$$

If you do use RAND, it does not require any inputs. You just write it and then follow it with empty parens. For another example of a function that works like that, see the TODAY function, because I can't actually write the RAND function here. If I do, Word will turn it into a block of random text.

One final warning. The numbers you generate with RAND or RANDBETWEEN are *not static*. Every time you hit F9, use another formula, add text to a cell and hit Enter, etc., all of your randomly-generated values will generate again, and *you can't get the old numbers back.*

Undo does not work.

So if you are generating a list of random numbers that you want to do something with, turn them into fixed values before you do anything else.

I usually use paste special-values, but if you need to lock your result down immediately, type your formula in like normal, and then use F9 instead of Enter when you're done, and before you leave that cell.

That will use your formula to perform the calculation and also immediately convert the cell contents to the result. Use Enter, Tab, or click away to then leave the cell. (If you use Esc it will revert to the formula.)

To apply the F9 trick to an existing cell with a formula, click into the formula bar, use F2 after clicking on that cell or double-click on the cell, and then use F9.

Now let's discuss a new-to-me function, RANDARRAY, which is going to be our first array function.

The RANDARRAY Function

Notation: RANDARRAY([rows],[columns],[min],[max],[integer])

Excel Definition: Returns an array of random numbers.

One of the reasons I like writing these books is because it forces me to think through the various tools I use when working in Excel, and dig for better answers.

For example, just now when I was writing the RANDBETWEEN chapter, I thought, "I wonder if Excel has a function for generating a *range* of random numbers instead of doing it just one cell at a time like I do with RANDBETWEEN."

The answer was yes, RANDARRAY.

First off, let me tell you what an array function is. It's a function that can return results in more than one cell at a time. We haven't dealt with one of these yet. They're fairly new to Excel. I think it's only been the last three or four versions of Excel that have had them. The way they work has also changed over time. This is a book for Excel 2024, so I'm not going to get into how they used to work, but keep that in mind if you ever have to use an older version of Excel. You may have RANDARRAY available, but need to go to the Help function to see how to use it.

Okay. So.

First thing to note with RANDARRAY: Every single input to the function is listed in brackets, which means they are all optional. You can just write

$$=RANDARRAY()$$

and you will get a result. It will be the same result as if you'd used RAND: One cell with a decimal value between 0 and 1.

But RANDARRAY can do so much more than that.

The first input to the function is rows. The default value is 1. You can leave this input blank if you want one row of results. Or you can put a positive whole number which will tell Excel how many rows you want to populate with random values.

The second input is columns. It works the same as rows. Default is 1. If you only want one column of values, leave it blank. Otherwise put a positive whole number for the number of columns you want.

If you try to use a 0 for rows or columns, you will get a #CALC! error. If you try to use a negative value you will get a VALUE! error. So you either have to leave the inputs blank, or you have to put a positive whole number. (You can technically put a decimal, like 2.5, but Excel is just going to take the whole number portion and ignore the rest.)

The next two inputs to RANDARRY are min and max. This is the number range you want Excel to use when generating your random numbers. Leave those values blank and you'll get results between 0 and 1.

The final input, integer, is a TRUE/FALSE input. The default is FALSE, or 0, which will return decimal results. Put TRUE here (or the value 1) to get only integer results.

To use the default value for any input, just skip putting a value, and use a comma to indicate you're providing the next input. Here, for example, I have a RANDARRAY formula that will create a 2 by 2 grid of 0 and 1 values:

$$=RANDARRAY(2,2,,,1)$$

I used 2 for rows, 2 for columns, but then left min and max blank so that meant my range was going to be between 0 and 1. But then I put 1, TRUE, for my last input, which limited the result to whole numbers. That means in each of the four cells where Excel returns a value, the value will either be 1 or 0.

Here is another example:

$$=RANDARRAY(,4,1,10,TRUE)$$

This tells Excel to generate whole number values between 1 and 10 in four cells in a single row. Here is the result when the formula is in Cell A1:

A1		f_x	=RANDARRAY(,4,1,10,TRUE)		
	A	B	C	D	E	F
1	8	7	7	8		
2						
3						
4						

A few more things to note about working with an array formula.

The formula goes in the first cell of the range where you want your values. So above, even though it gave me values in Cells A1 through D1, the formula I entered was entered into Cell A1.

When you're clicked away from cells that contain the results of an array formula, they look perfectly normal. It's only when you click onto them that you can see that the values were generated as part of an array function.

As you can see in the screenshot above, Excel puts a border around all of the cells that were populated using the array formula when you click on any cell in that range.

To edit an array formula, go to the top left cell of the range. The formula will show in the formula bar for any of the cells in the range, but will be grayed out for all but that top left cell.

Another thing to know about array functions is that they need enough room to work. You can't use an array function that takes up five rows by five columns if you already have text or values in that space. You'll get a #SPILL! error if there isn't enough room.

Every time you see #SPILL! that means that you are using an array function, and that the function doesn't have enough room to display its results. Either clear the contents of the cells that are blocking the formula, or move the formula to a cell where it has enough room. With RANDARRAY, you could also edit the formula to take up less space.

One more example before we move on. Here I nested RANDARRAY with decimal places within a ROUND function to generate a five-by-five table of currency values between 1 and 100:

$$=ROUND(RANDARRAY(5,5,1,100,FALSE),2)$$

This is what the result looks like:

C3	f_x	=ROUND(RANDARRAY(5,5,1,100,FALSE),2)

	A	B	C	D	E	F	G
1	71.25	37.72	5.06	53.69	75.44		
2	75.8	80.69	31.34	5.4	86.56		
3	31.01	10.45	23.9	3.63	87.18		
4	52.2	78.34	1.28	56.33	18.71		
5	35.71	24.09	63.54	68	79.79		

Note that even though I am clicked into Cell C3, the formula you see is the one that was entered into Cell A1. Also, that the cells that are the result of the formula all have a border around the perimeter. And that the formula in the formula bar is grayed out because Cell C3 contains results from the formula, but not the formula itself.

One final note. RANDARRAY is a random-number-generating function, so be sure to lock down your values before you use your random numbers for any sort of calculation or demonstration that requires the numbers to stay fixed.

As I said before, I generally use paste special-values, but F9 did lock in the values for me here just in a unique way. It listed the values that were generated within a set of curly brackets in the first cell of the range. So =RANDARRAY(2,2,1,10,1) became ={9,4;2,8} and displayed the values 9, 4, 2, and 8 in a 2 by 2 range of cells.

The SUMIFS Function

Notation: SUMIFS(sum_range, criteria_range1, criteria1, …)

Excel Definition: Adds the cells specified by a given set of conditions or criteria.

This is one of my favorite functions. I use it all the time. What SUMIFS does is lets you apply SUM to a range of values if certain criteria are met. There is an older function, SUMIF, that let you do this for one single criteria, but if you master SUMIFS, you won't need it.

Okay, so let's look at the required inputs.

The first input is the range of cells where the values you want to add up are located.

The second input is the first range of cells that contain information you want to evaluate. It can be the same range of cells as the ones you want to sum. Later, for example, I have a formula for determining the total value of purchases over $100.

The third input is your criteria you want to apply to that range of cells.

For this function that … at the end is important to understand. Because if you keep going, you need to actually add two additional inputs at a time. The next input you'd put there is the *second* range of cells that you want to evaluate. But you'd also then need to provide a fifth input, which is the criteria to use on that second range of cells.

This is what that would look like written out in notation format:

SUMIFS(sum_range, criteria_range1, criteria1, criteria_range2, criteria2,…)

The maximum number of criteria you can have is 127, although why you would ever want to do that, I do not know. That would be way too prone to error in my opinion.

Speaking of errors. If your cell ranges are not the same size for each range input (sum_range and each criteria_range), you will get a #VALUE! error. Excel needs to know what to match up.

I've only ever used SUMIFS (or any of the similar functions that we'll discuss next) with a table of data where my input ranges were in columns. But I did just try it with rows, and that worked, too. You can also use something like a 2x3 cell range, but all of your range inputs would then need to be 2x3 as well. The ranges always have to match up.

Your criteria can look at numeric values, dates, or text. You can also combine different types of criteria in the same function.

For example, I can have Excel sum transactions that occurred in 2024 (a date criteria), were over $100 (a number criteria), and involved customers in Alaska (a text criteria).

Let's now talk about how to write each of those properly.

For a number, you can either just write the number (22) or use quote marks around the number ("22").

For a greater than (>), less than (<), greater than or equal to (>=), or less than or equal to (<=) criteria, you need to put the whole expression in quotes. So greater than or equal to 22, would be ">=22" in that part of the function.

To evaluate dates, you also need to put them in quotes. So "7/23/2020" or "7/23/20" both work. If all else fails, convert the date you want to a number (44035 in this case), and write it that way, but you shouldn't have to do that.

It is possible to combine dates with the greater than and less than symbols as well. For example using ">5/1/2020" would look for any entry in the range after May 1, 2020.

You can also use cell references if the value you want is in a cell. (This is very useful for something like counting the number of sales per state. Create a list of all state abbreviations, write a formula that references the first entry in that list, use fixed cell references for your table or reference the entire column, and then just copy that formula down for all the states.)

To use greater than, less than, etc. with a cell reference, you have to write it as ">"& and then the cell reference. So

$$">"\&G25$$

would be how you write greater than the value in Cell G25.

To evaluate text, put it in quotes. So, "Alaska" would look for entries in that cell range for Alaska.

With text you can also use wildcards. An asterisk (*) represents any number of characters or spaces. So if I write

$$"*e*"$$

as my criteria, that would look for any entry that contains the letter e.

If I instead looked for

$$"e*"$$

that would look for any entry that *starts* with the letter e. And if I used

$$"*e"$$

that would look for any entry that *ends* with the letter e.

The other available wildcard is the question mark (?), which represents one single character, including a single space.

So if I looked for

"??e"

that would return any three-letter entry that ends in e.

But keep in mind that each question mark is a character/space so "??e" would not capture the entry "be" since it is only two letters.

Also. If you ever want to use text that includes an actual asterisk or a question mark in your criteria, precede the asterisk or question mark with a tilde (~).

Okay. Time to look at some examples. Here is our data:

	A	B	C	D	E
1	Date	Customer Name	Product	Units	Total Cost
2	2/6/2020	Lee	Widget	14	$ 31.50
3	2/25/2020	Morales	Whatchamacallit	3	$ 33.75
4	4/1/2020	Jones	Widget	8	$ 18.00
5	4/7/2020	Jones	Whatchamacallit	11	$ 123.75
6	4/25/2020	Phong	Whatsit	11	$ 14.85
7	4/28/2020	Gutierrez	Widget	9	$ 20.25
8	5/2/2020	Holsen	Whatchamacallit	24	$ 270.00
9	5/4/2020	Morales	Whatsit	15	$ 20.25
10	5/6/2020	Gutierrez	Whatsit	1	$ 1.35
11	5/26/2020	Lee	Whatchamacallit	3	$ 33.75
12	6/10/2020	Smith	Whatchamacallit	4	$ 9.00
13	6/12/2020	Smith	Whatsit	2	$ 2.70
14	7/11/2020	Holsen	Widget	6	$ 13.50
15	7/18/2020	Phong	Whatchamacallit	9	$ 101.25
16	7/23/2020	Fromer	Whatsit	11	$ 14.85
17					

We have date of transaction, customer last name, product, units bought, and total cost.

I want to answer the following questions using this data:

1. How much did customer Lee spend?

2. How much did customer Lee spend on or after May 1, 2020?

3. What was the total value of purchases over $100?

4. How many What-type products did customer Smith purchase?

Take a moment and think about how you'd do that. And then look here at how I did it:

Question	Formula	Result
How much did customer Lee spend?	=SUMIFS(E2:E16,B2:B16,"Lee")	$ 65.25
How much did customer Lee spend on or after May 1, 2020?	=SUMIFS(E2:E16,B2:B16,"Lee",A2:A16,">=5/1/2020")	$ 33.75
What was the total value of purchases over $100?	=SUMIFS(E2:E16,E2:E16,">100")	$ 495.00
How many What-type products did customer Smith purchase?	=SUMIFS(D2:D16,C2:C16,"What*",B2:B16,"Smith")	6

The first question was "How much did customer Lee spend?" Which means we want to sum the cost column, and we have one criteria to apply, that the customer last name be Lee.

Here that is:

$$=SUMIFS(E2:E16,B2:B16,"Lee")$$

Note here that our criteria was text, so Lee is in quotes.

The next question takes that first example and limits it with a second criteria to purchases made on or after May 1, 2020. Adding that to our formula we get:

$$=SUMIFS(E2:E16,B2:B16,"Lee",A2:A16,">=5/1/2020")$$

Note that the >= and the date itself are all in quotes together.

Now let's look at the third question, "What was the total value of purchases over $100?" With this one, the criteria range and the sum range are the same:

$$=SUMIFS(E2:E16,E2:E16,">100")$$

It also uses a greater than symbol with a number, so both have to be included in quotes. Another option would be:

$$=SUMIFS(E2:E16,E2:E16,">"\&100)$$

where we join the greater than symbol to the number using an ampersand.

The fourth question is "How many what-type products did customer Smith purchase?"

To solve this one, we have to think about our product types. We have Whatsits, Widgets, and Whatchamacallits. Two of those are "what-type" products, Whatsits and Whatchamacallits.

The simplest solution is to use the wildcard asterisk character to get our answer:

$$=SUMIFS(D2:D16,C2:C16,"What*",B2:B16,"Smith")$$

By using "What*" I captured both products. (Note that Excel is not case-sensitive with text criteria so it views what and What as the same.)

Another option would be:

$$=SUM(SUMIFS(D2:D16,C2:C16,\{"Whatsit","Whatchamacallit"\},B2:B16,"Smith"))$$

Note that I used curly brackets to create a list for that particular input. And that because the list didn't use the plural of each product name, I had to be careful to use "Whatsit" instead of "Whatsits" and "Whatchamacallit" instead of "Whatchamacallits".

Also, it required SUM around the SUMIFS function, because otherwise it returns separate results in separate cells for Whatsit and Whatchamacallit.

Finally, note that this last example used a different sum range (Column D), because we were adding up units this time rather than amount made.

One final thought, I always like to test things like this on on a small range of my data where I can also manually compute the answer. That lets me confirm that the result my formula returns is what I'd expect.

One mistake I often make when initially writing a formula or filter or anything else involving numbers, is that I will write it as "greater than" or "less than" when what I really want is "greater than or equal to" or "less than or equal to". So I always try to test my edge cases. For example, with the $100 or more question, I'd use fake data that included values of 99.99, 100, and 100.01 to see if the result matched my expectations.

The other things I check for if I get an error message or my formula isn't working as expected, is that my quotes, commas, and cell ranges are where and what they should be.

The COUNTIFS Function

Notation: COUNTIFS(criteria_range1, criteria1, …)

Excel Definition: Counts the number of cells specified by a given set of conditions or criteria.

Where SUMIFS sums values based on the criteria you give it, COUNTIFS counts them. Despite the name, the type of count function used here is COUNTA, which, if you recall, counts more than just numbers. (This is good, actually, I just mention it lest there be confusion.)

Note that since COUNTIFS is just counting results, it doesn't require that first input that SUMIFS does. It jumps right into the criteria ranges.

Also, just like SUMIFS has SUMIF, there is a COUNTIF function that can be used for one criteria. You can actually turn a COUNTIF function into a COUNTIFS function just by adding an S to the function name. (You can't do this with SUMIF and SUMIFS because the inputs are in a different order.)

In terms of building a COUNTIFS function, most of what you need to know was already discussed in the SUMIFS chapter. They handle criteria in the exact same way. So let's just dive in and walk through some questions we can answer with COUNTIFS.

Using the same data from the SUMIFS chapter, how would you answer the following questions:

1. How many transactions were there for customer Phong?

2. How many purchases did customer Phong make of Whatchamacallits?

3. How many purchases of more than ten units were made in April 2020?

4. How many purchases of Widgets and Whatsits were made?

Let's start with the first one: "How many transactions were there for customer Phong?" You just need Column B for this one, right?

If you did this manually, you would look down Column B, and every time it says "Phong", you would count that entry. Written as a formula it looks like this:

$$=COUNTIFS(B:B,"Phong")$$

The next question, "How many purchases of Whatchamacallits did customer Phong make?" takes that initial count but refines it to only transactions in Whatchamacallits.

That requires two pieces of information, customer name and product. As a formula it looks like this:

$$=COUNTIFS(B:B,"Phong",C:C,"Whatchamacallit")$$

(Note here that I'm using the entire columns for my cell ranges. I have nothing below my data table, so I can get away with that.)

The next question is a bit trickier: "How many purchases of more than ten units were made in April 2020?"

The first part is easy enough, it's just using the Units column and looking for any value greater than ten. But stop and think about what it means to be in April 2020. Clearly you need to use the Date column, but how would you write that?

Here's what I ended up doing:

$$=COUNTIFS(D:D,">10",A:A,">=4/1/2020",A:A,"<5/1/20")$$

I used two criteria on the same column. The date needed to be on or after April 1, 2020, that's the first criteria I used, and also before May 1, 2020, that's the second criteria I used.

Was is the most elegant and streamlined solution? Maybe not. But on something simple like this, "if it works, it works" is a good approach to take. When you're dealing with 15 rows of data you can be a bit clunky.

Okay. Final one: How many purchases of Widgets and Whatsits were made?

We can't use the wildcard symbol like we did in the last chapter, so we need to come up with another approach. This is the one I came up with:

$$=COUNTIFS(C:C,"Widget")+COUNTIFS(C:C,"Whatsit")$$

And it worked.

But as you may recall from the SUMIFS chapter, I could have also used:

$$=SUM(COUNTIFS(C:C,\{"Widget","Whatsit"\}))$$

Let's explore what happens when I don't surround that with SUM.

On the next page is a screenshot of a table I created with my product names in Column H. In Cell I2, I put the following formula:

$$=COUNTIFS(C:C,H2:H4)$$

I2   fx =COUNTIFS(C:C,H2:H4) ← Formula

Product	Count of Sales
Whatsit	5
Widget	4
Whatchamacallit	6

Array Result

That returns an array result. Excel filled Cells I2 through I4 with the count for each product type itself.

I didn't have to copy a formula to get this result, Excel just did it.

Pretty interesting, huh?

The **AVERAGEIFS** Function

Notation: AVERAGEIFS(average_range, criteria_range1, criteria1, …)

Excel Definition: Finds average (arithmetic mean) for the cells specified by a given set of conditions or criteria.

AVERAGEIFS works much like SUMIFS, except it is looking for the average of the values that meet the specified criteria.

This uses the AVERAGE function, not the AVERAGEA function, so the values you want to average have to be numbers or dates. If you try to apply it to a range of values that are all TRUE/FALSE or text values, it will return a #DIV/0! error.

If the range has numbers in it as well as TRUE/FALSE and/or text values, it will only average the number results. (Which means be careful that the range of values you use are all actually numbers since it won't look at any numbers stored as text.)

(Also, you can use it with dates, which are technically numbers. It will give you a date that's within the range of the dates that meet your criteria, I'm just not quite sure how you'd interpret the result.)

There is an AVERAGEIF function, but if you master AVERAGEIFS you won't need to use it.

Since at this point I think you have the general gist of how each of these functions work, let's just look at a few examples.

First, using the data table we used for SUMIFS and COUNTIFS, how would you calculate the average amount customers spent per transaction when they bought Whatsits?

This requires looking at Total Cost based on only one criteria, product. The formula is:

=AVERAGEIFS(E2:E16,C2:C16,"Whatsit")

What if we wanted that same calculation, but for all three product types? Just like with COUNTIFS, it turns out we can do this with an array:

I2			f_x	=AVERAGEIFS(E:E,C:C,H2:H4)	
	H			**I**	**J**
1	**Product**			**Average Spent**	
2	Whatsit			$ 10.80	
3	Widget			$ 20.81	
4	Whatchamacallit			$ 95.25	
5					

In this case I put

$$=AVERAGEIFS(E:E,C:C,H2:H4)$$

into Cell I2, and it populated the values for Cells I2 through I4.

Finally, how would you write a formula to calculate the average amount customers spent per transaction on Whatsits in June? I wrote it like this:

$$=AVERAGEIFS(E2:E16,C2:C16,"Whatsit",A2:A16,">=6/1/2020",A2:A16,"<7/1/20")$$

The MINIFS Function

Notation: MINIFS(min_range, criteria_range1, criteria1, …)

Excel Definition: Returns the minimum value among cells specified by a given set of conditions or criteria.

MINIFS gives you the minimum value within a range of cells that meet your chosen criteria. There is not a corresponding MINIF function.

MINIFS uses the same type of criteria that we discussed in detail in the SUMIFS chapter, and it will also return an array of values for you like we showed in the SUMIFS, COUNTIFS, and AVERAGEIFS chapters.

Here is an example of results using both MINIFS and MAXIFS to get minimum and maximum spend per transaction for each customer:

Customer	Min Spent in One Transaction	Max Spent in One Transaction
Fromer	$ 14.85	$ 14.85
Gutierrez	$ 1.35	$ 20.25
Holsen	$ 13.50	$ 270.00
Jones	$ 18.00	$ 123.75
Lee	$ 31.50	$ 33.75
Morales	$ 20.25	$ 33.75
Phong	$ 14.85	$ 101.25
Smith	$ 2.70	$ 9.00

This was built with just two formulas:

=MINIFS(E:E,B:B,H2:H9)

in Cell I2 (the second cell in the second column). And in Cell J2:

=MAXIFS(E:E,B:B,H2:H9)

One new little thing to point out for this chapter: If you get results like I did here using an array (the H2:H9 part of each of those formulas), you can't then sort that table of data by the results.

When I first did this one, I had the customer names in random order based on what Remove Duplicates gave me. After I added my MINIFS formula using an array, I tried to sort it alphabetically. It wouldn't let me.

There are two ways to fix that. One is to paste special-values for that table now that the results are there, and then sort.

The other option, which is what I did, was to move the two cells that have the formulas in them to somewhere else for a moment, sort the customer names in the table, and then bring those two formulas back.

Your other option, of course, is to not use an array in the formula. Just write the formulas in Cells I2 and J2 with a reference to H2 only, and then copy the formulas down.

You can still filter a table using an array result without issues. It seems to just be the Sort option that's affected.

The MAXIFS Function

Notation: MAXIFS(max_range, criteria_range1, criteria1, …)

Excel Definition: Returns the maximum value among cells specified by a given set of conditions or criteria.

MAXIFS is our final [Function]IFS function, and it takes the maximum from a range of specified cells based on your criteria. By now you hopefully know how that works. If not, go read the SUMIFS chapter and just think "maximum" instead of "sum" everywhere.

Like MINIFS, it does not have a corresponding single criteria function. (This is because by the time they created the MINIFS and MAXIFS functions they had not gotten around to creating a MINIF or MAXIF function yet, so one was never needed.)

In the MINIFS chapter, you can see an example of MAXIFS applied to the data table we've been working with, and looking at transaction amount for each customer.

In this chapter I wanted to bring it all together with a new example that uses COUNTIFS, AVERAGEIFS, MINIFS, and MAXIFS.

On the next page we have a table of test scores for eighteen students in Professor Jones's class. I want to know if there's any difference between how males and females perform:

I'm using arrays here. That means the formula for MAXIFS in Cell I2 is

$$=MAXIFS(\$A\$2:\$A\$19,\$B\$2:\$B\$19,\$E\$2:\$E\$3)$$

Note that I used $ signs to fix the references to the data table and to the two values I wanted to evaluate. I did that so I could copy the formula in Cell F2 to Cells G2, H2, and I2, and only have to adjust the function name. (I am very lazy, sometimes to the point of creating more work for myself.)

What did that tell us?

We have 8 men and 10 women in the class. The average class score for men is 79 and for women is 94. The range for men is 70 to 94. The range for women is 89 to 100.

	A	B	C	D	E	F	G	H	I
1	Score	Gender	Professor			COUNT	AVERAGE	MIN	MAX
2	100	Female	Jones		Male	8	79.125	70	94
3	89	Male	Jones		Female	10	94.2	89	100
4	98	Female	Jones						
5	89	Male	Jones						
6	70	Male	Jones						
7	70	Male	Jones						
8	71	Male	Jones						
9	90	Female	Jones						
10	80	Male	Jones						
11	70	Male	Jones						
12	89	Female	Jones						
13	89	Female	Jones						
14	91	Female	Jones						
15	97	Female	Jones						
16	94	Male	Jones						
17	95	Female	Jones						
18	100	Female	Jones						
19	93	Female	Jones						
20									

It looks like we have a difference there. Just be careful coming to a conclusion as to why. We don't know if that's the teacher's bias, or maybe this class meets at eight in the morning, and there are four male students who are good friends in the class who really like to party on Thursday nights, and end up missing Friday's quizzes.

The MEDIAN Function

Notation: MEDIAN(number1, [number2],…)

Excel Definition: Returns the median, or the number in the middle of the set of given numbers.

Alright, shifting gears a bit, let's talk about the MEDIAN function, which returns the middle number in a range of values. Once more, the notation for the function shows number1, number2, etc., but really the input that you're going to provide will almost always be a cell range. Like:

$$=MEDIAN(A:A)$$

$$=MEDIAN(A1:A26)$$

$$=MEDIAN(A2:A26)$$

All of those would return the middle value in a range of numbers in Cells A2 through A26, because MEDIAN ignores any blank cells or cells with text in them. It just looks at numbers. (But do be careful if there are dates in your cell range, because those are numbers to Excel.)

So, simple enough.

One thing to watch out for with MEDIAN, though, is when you have an even number of results. Because it will *average* the two results closest to the middle.

If you have a binary data set, like the one in the image on the next page, that can give a very misleading result.

In this data set, you either win or lose. You either get 100 or you get 0. But the median result (and the average), would tell you that the middle is around 50. It's not. No one ever gets 50. If this was betting money, that's fine. You're going to land around $50 over time. But what if you can't afford to land on zero? It would be important to know that you will half the time.

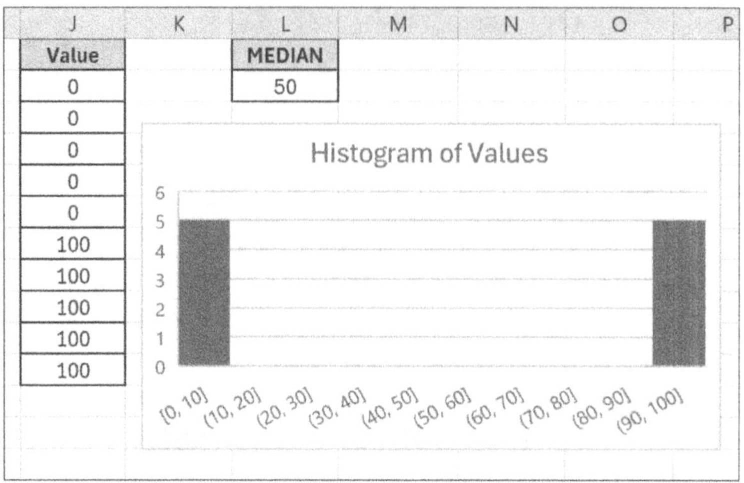

Add one more result on either end, and MEDIAN would return a value of 0 or 100. Which is more honest in a sense? But really MEDIAN is just not the best choice to use for that kind of data.

Graphing your data in some way, like I have here with the histogram, can help you make a better choice about which function to use, if any.

Before we move on, I want to show you an example where MEDIAN is a better choice to use than AVERAGE, and that's in a data set that has "skew" to it, so the "typical" result is not going to be close to the average.

Here we have twenty-five results in Column A that show annual author income:

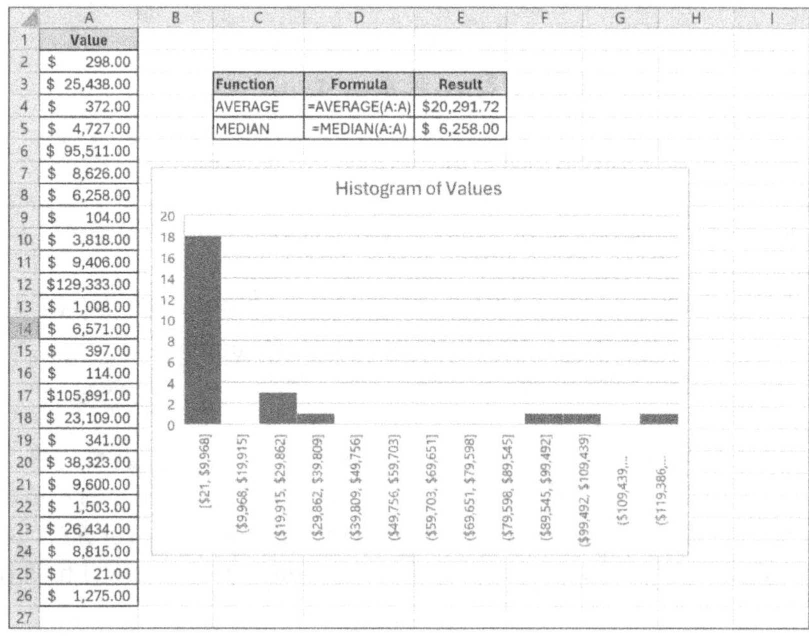

This is made-up data, but it's based on practical experience, too. Most authors don't make much, while some do very, very well. There's also the occasional author who does okay, but not great.

Look at the histogram in the image above. See how most of the values fall in that first bucket? Eighteen out of twenty-five, or 72%, are less than $10,000.

But note, too, that the upper end of this range has someone over $120,000. In this case, $129,333. (In real life, there'd be some over a million.)

In Cell E4 we have the average of the values, $20,291.72. The problem is that because the data has such skew, most authors will never earn that much.

In Cell E5 we have the median of the values, $6,258. That's much more realistic. It's a third of the average, but if you lined up the twenty-five authors and asked the one in the middle what they earned, that's where they'd be. If you were making career decisions off of this data? Much better to have the median than the average.

Now, remember, this is made-up information. Do not actually go out and make life decisions based on it. But if you ever see one of those "the average college grad earns $X" figures, that's a good time to remember that often the highest-earning members of a group skew the average in an unrealistic way. Include just one billionaire in a set of numbers like this, and it looks like everyone is doing well when really only one person is.

Okay. Next up is another way to look at this sort of data, mode.

The MODE.MULT Function

Notation: MODE.MULT(number1, [number2],…)

Excel Definition: Returns a vertical array of the most frequently occurring, or repetitive, values in an array or range of data.

This is another one of those functions where the notation lists numbers, but realistically the input you're going to provide is just a single cell range.

What MODE.MULT does is it returns the most common value(s) in your data set. Here:

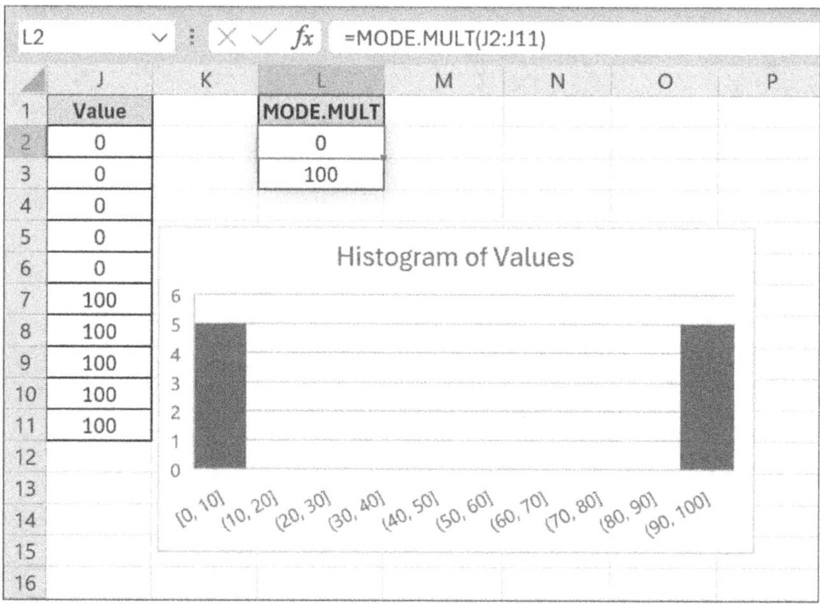

Because 0 and 100 both occur five times, they are both returned when I use MODE.MULT on that range of values. The formula I used is:

$$=MODE.MULT(J2:J11)$$

Very easy.

This is an array function. It will return all of the values that are most-frequently occurring. If there is only one, it will only return one.

Note that it also only works on numbers (including dates, which will return in their numeric form).

If it doesn't have enough room to return all of the values, you'll get a #SPILL! error.

If there are no duplicate values in a range, it will return an #N/A result.

Simple enough.

Two final points to make here.

One, there are two other functions, MODE and MODE.SNGL that are like MODE. MULT but flawed, because they only return one value. So in our example above, where two values occur at equal frequency, they would only return one of them, giving an incomplete result.

Two, MODE.MULT treats each unique value separately. So if you had 98, 99, 100, 1, and 1 in a range, it would return 1 as your most frequent result. Even though 98, 99, and 100 are close to one another, they are each unique values to MODE.MULT. It doesn't group results. So it is often not the best choice if your data isn't in clear distinct buckets like 1 through 5 for customer ratings.

Fortunately, there is another function that you can use to look at how often results fall into various ranges, FREQUENCY. Let's talk about that one now.

The FREQUENCY Function

Notation: FREQUENCY(data_array,bins_array)

Excel Definition: Calculates how often values occur within a range of values and then returns a vertical array of numbers having one more element than Bins_array.

The FREQUENCY function is an array function like MODE.MULT, but what it does is lets you count values that fall within a range, not just the most commonly occurring values.

There are two inputs into the FREQUENCY function, your values (the data array) and then the set of values you want to use to create separate buckets to put those numbers into (the bins array).

If you want a count for every single value in your range, then your bins_array input should be the list of unique values (in Column L in the image below):

	J	K	L	M	N	O
	Value		**Unique Values**	**Frequency**		
2	0		0	5		
3	0		100	5		
4	0			0		
5	0					
6	0					
7	100					
8	100					
9	100					
10	100					
11	100					
12						

Formula bar: M2 =FREQUENCY(J2:J11,L2:L3)

To create that list, copy your values (the same as your data_array input), paste them elsewhere, then apply Remove Duplicates from the Data Tools section of the Data tab to that list. Excel will take the full list of values and reduce it down to one entry for each unique value. You can then use that list as your bins_array.

Once you have your list , put your FREQUENCY formula in the cell next to the first value in the list, like I've done above in Cell M2.

You can see the formula I used:

$$=FREQUENCY(J2:J11,L2:L3)$$

Because my list of values, in this case 0 and 100, is all of the unique values in my data, I end up with a table of each unique value and how often it occurs in my data range.

Note that there is also an "overflow" value in Cell M4 of zero. You need to leave room for that, or else you'll get a #SPILL! error.

Also, I just tested this and it will work even if your list is not in numeric order as long as your list has all of the values in the table.

Now let's look at how to get a count across a *range* of values instead.

It turns out what we did above was not really "count everything equal to 0 or 100". What it actually was, was "count everything up to zero, and then count everything up to 100, and then count everything over 100". It just worked the way it did, because we'd captured all the unique values in the table with the set of bins we used.

But what if you want results that are close to each other to be in the same group, like here:

	A	B	C	D	E	F	G
1	Value		Lower Limit	Upper Limit	Frequency	Percent	
2	$ 298.00		$0	$500	7	28%	
3	$ 25,438.00		$501	$2,500	3	12%	
4	$ 372.00		$2,501	$10,000	8	32%	
5	$ 4,727.00		$10,001	$50,000	4	16%	
6	$ 95,511.00		$50,001	$75,000	0	0%	
7	$ 8,626.00		$75,001	$100,000	1	4%	
8	$ 6,258.00		$100,001	$125,000	1	4%	
9	$ 104.00		$125,001		1	4%	
10	$ 3,818.00						
11	$ 9,406.00						
12	$129,333.00						
13	$ 1,008.00						
14	$ 6,571.00						
15	$ 397.00						
16	$ 114.00						
17	$105,891.00						
18	$ 23,109.00						
19	$ 341.00						
20	$ 38,323.00						
21	$ 9,600.00						
22	$ 1,503.00						
23	$ 26,434.00						
24	$ 8,815.00						
25	$ 21.00						
26	$ 1,275.00						
27							

In the table above, I shaded all of the author incomes up to $500 red using conditional formatting. I want those values considered in one group. The way to do that is to use bins_ array values that set the upper limit for each bucket.

I did that in Column D. But to make things easier to read, I also put values in Column C that are just there for my or a viewer's information.

Column C is not used by the FREQUENCY function, but putting those values there shows anyone looking at the counts in Column E that we're dealing with a range of values, not one specific value.

For example, the count in E2 is for any author income equal to or less than $500, not just income equal to $500. Without Column C that wouldn't be obvious.

I shaded Column C in gray to visually separate it from the actual input and output of the FREQUENCY function.

Okay.

What is actually driving the FREQUENCY function are the values in Column D. I manually chose those values. They could be anything.

You can see that I did not choose equal intervals. My first one is a $500 range, but the fourth one is a $40,000 range.

I felt like it was important to call out values under $500, but I didn't want a 250-plus row table of results to get to the highest income. So I traded exact comparability between different "buckets" for an easily read table of data.

Whatever values you choose is what Excel will use. It is completely up to you.

The formula here is:

$$=FREQUENCY(A2:A26,D2:D8)$$

Just like with our last example, the results in Column E go one row past the values I gave to Excel. That's because the last bucket is basically a count of anything over the last value you give. In this case, we have one result, $129,333, that gets counted.

Now, counts are all well and good, but I work better with percentages, so I added a calculation in Column F that converts my counts into a percent of the whole calculation. (And shaded it gray since it's not part of the input or the output of the FREQUENCY function.)

With that I can see that 28% of the results are $500 or less and that 32% are between $2,500.01 and $10,000.

If all I wanted was the percentage, I could've combined two functions in Column E to get:

$$=FREQUENCY(A2:A26,D2:D8)/COUNT(A:A)$$

A final note. While FREQUENCY ignores blank cells and text, it does work with dates. Here I have an example looking at how many dates fell in each year range:

	O	P	Q	R	S	T
1	**Value**		**Beginning**	**Ending Date**	**Frequency**	
2	1/1/2021			12/31/2019	0	
3	1/2/2020		1/1/2020	12/31/2020	6	
4	3/1/2020		1/1/2021	12/31/2021	3	
5	3/1/2020		1/1/2022	12/31/2022	1	
6	1/1/2020		1/1/2023		0	
7	9/2/2021					
8	3/1/2021					
9	4/1/2020					
10	4/1/2020					
11	3/1/2022					
12						

Formula bar: S2 =FREQUENCY(O2:O11,R2:R5)

Cool, huh?

* * *

Alright, I don't know about you, but I've had enough of math for now. Let's move on to a completely different use of Excel functions and look at functions you can use on text.

The TRIM Function

Notation: TRIM(text)

Excel Definition: Removes all spaces from a text string except for single spaces between words.

The TRIM function is a good one to know when you need to clean up text entries. Sometimes people will combine text and it will have extra spaces between words, or you'll get data where someone (even yourself) typed an extra space at the end or at the beginning of the entry. TRIM is the way to clean that all up.

It says the input is text, but usually I just reference the cell that contains that text instead.

$$=TRIM(A1)$$

Remember to lock in the result when you're done. I use paste special-values for that. Until you do so, the contents of the new cell are still a formula that references the original cell. If you delete that original cell, you will get a #REF! error in the cell that has your formula.

You can also nest a function within the TRIM function. For example, back in the day I would have used CONCATENATE to join strings of text together into one entry, such as first name, middle name, last name. Problem is, if there's no middle initial, that would generate an extra space in the result. Wrapping TRIM around the function fixed that issue:

$$=TRIM(CONCATENATE(B2," ",C2," ",A2," ",D2))$$

TRIM will also work on numbers that it perceives as text such as 123 456 789.

The TEXTJOIN Function

Notation: TEXTJOIN(delimiter, ignore_empty, text1, …)

Excel Definition: Concatenates a list or range of text strings using a delimiter.

TEXTJOIN is a newer function, but it's one I've come to love. (For some reason I can love Excel functions and pets much more easily than humans. Go figure.)

Anyway. What it does is it takes text inputs and joins them into a single entry. You can tell it how to separate those entries with what you provide as the delimiter(s).

You can also tell it how to deal with empty fields so that you don't run into the issue I mentioned with CONCATENATE where you get an extra space and need to use TRIM to clean it up.

Here is our data table and result:

	A	B	C	D	E	F
1	**First Name**	**Middle Initial**	**Last Name**	**Suffix**	**Full Name**	**Formula**
2	John		Lee	Jr.	John Lee Jr.	=TEXTJOIN(" ",TRUE,A2:D2)
3	Sarah	J.	Morales		Sarah J. Morales	=TEXTJOIN(" ",TRUE,A3:D3)
4	Lee	K.	Jones	Esq.	Lee K. Jones Esq.	=TEXTJOIN(" ",TRUE,A4:D4)
5	Ann		Phong		Ann Phong	=TEXTJOIN(" ",TRUE,A5:D5)
6	Jose	A.	Gutierrez		Jose A. Gutierrez	=TEXTJOIN(" ",TRUE,A6:D6)
7	Dean		Holsen		Dean Holsen	=TEXTJOIN(" ",TRUE,A7:D7)
8	Francisco	R.	Morales		Francisco R. Morales	=TEXTJOIN(" ",TRUE,A8:D8)
9	Marney	B.	Smith		Marney B. Smith	=TEXTJOIN(" ",TRUE,A9:D9)
10	Kelly		Fromer		Kelly Fromer	=TEXTJOIN(" ",TRUE,A10:D10)
11						

Columns A through D have the text we want to join together.

Column E is the result of using this TEXTJOIN formula in Row 2 and copying it down:

=TEXTJOIN(" ",TRUE,A2:D2)

Column F shows the formula for each row.

Now let's break that down.

The first input is the delimiter. This is just a fancy way of saying "what is between the entries". The delimiter I used is a single space. I had to put it into quotes since I typed it directly into the function.

The second input is a TRUE/FALSE input where you tell Excel whether to ignore empty cells or not. Since I don't want those weird extra spaces when a middle name or suffix is missing, I put TRUE. If I had said FALSE, there wouldn't be any text to put there, but Excel would include the delimiter, and I'd end up with two spaces next to each other or an extra one at the end.

Finally, the third input is for text. Excel lets you list each text reference individually, separated by a comma. But it also let me use a cell range since my inputs were in the order I wanted: A2:D2.

This would also work, it just takes a little more effort to create:

$$=TEXTJOIN(" ",TRUE,A2,B2,C2,D2)$$

If the resulting text string is too long (32,767 characters) Excel will return a #VALUE! error.

TEXTJOIN is very easy to use compared to CONCATENATE or CONCAT, which is how I would've done this before. With those functions, you have to list the delimiter as a separate entry each time, so you have A2," ",B2," ", etc. all the way down the line.

Based on that difference, you might think CONCATENATE (I never used CONCAT but it was the shortened name they came out with at some point) is the way to go if you want to use different delimiters, because you can manually add each one as you create your text string.

But it turns out that TEXTJOIN also lets you have multiple delimiters.

You have two options.

First, you can include them in the function itself by using curly brackets around your list of delimiters, putting each one in quotes, and separating them with a comma. Here, for example, I have space, space, and then a comma with a space:

$$=TEXTJOIN(\{" "," ",", "\},TRUE,A16:D16)$$

It's a little hard to read after the fact, but pretty easy to create.

Second, you can put your delimiters into cells, like I did on the next page in Cells G20 to G22. Cells G20 and G21 have spaces, Cell G22 has a comma and a space.

If you do that, you can then reference that cell range as your first input. For example, the formula I used in Cell G16 was:

$$=TEXTJOIN(\$G\$20:\$G\$22,TRUE,A16:D16)$$

Note that I put $ signs on the cell references for the first input. That lets me copy the formula to other cells while still referencing the range of cells with my delimiters in them.

	A	B	C	D	G	H
15	**First Name**	**Middle Initial**	**Last Name**	**Suffix**	**Full Name**	**Formula**
16	John		Lee	Jr.	John Lee Jr.	=TEXTJOIN($G$20:$G$22,TRUE,A16:D16)
17	Lee	K.	Jones	Esq.	Lee K. Jones, Esq.	=TEXTJOIN($G$20:$G$22,TRUE,A17:D17)
18						
19					**Delimiters**	**Description**
20						Space
21						Space
22					,	Comma, Space
23						

Now. We have a problem. Look at the values in Cells G16 and G17. G17 is great and perfect and wonderful. Lee K. Jones, Esq. is exactly what we wanted. But John Lee Jr. is not. Why?

Because it turns out that if you give Excel more than one delimiter to use, it will go to that list of delimiters only when it needs one. So what happened here for John Lee Jr. is that it needed a delimiter between John and Lee, so grabbed that first space. Then I told it to skip the middle initial if it was empty, so it did. When it needed another delimiter to put between Lee and Jr., it grabbed the next delimiter in the list, which was the second one, a space.

You might think that the way to solve this is to change that TRUE to a FALSE and surround the whole thing with TRIM. But no. That doesn't work. You end up with a comma at the end of all of the entries that don't have a suffix. (How do I know? I tried it. It's always good to experiment in Excel and see what you get.)

As of now, I think the best way to solve this would be an IFS function (which we discuss later in the book) where you'd use a conditional statement that said "(a) if there's no suffix, then use a space and skip blanks, (b) but if there is a suffix, then don't skip anything and use this list of delimiters but trim out extra spaces".

=IFS(ISBLANK(D3),TEXTJOIN(" ",TRUE,A3:D3),TRUE,TRIM(TEXTJOIN($G$20:
$G$22,FALSE,A3:D3)))

It looks ugly, and uses ISBLANK, which is another function we haven't covered that just asks if a cell is blank or not, but I think it works.

Break that down and we have these two TEXTJOIN functions:

TEXTJOIN(" ",TRUE,A3:D3)

TRIM(TEXTJOIN($G$20:$G$22,FALSE,A3:D3))

Since we used TRUE in the first one, we don't need TRIM. But since we used FALSE for the second one, any time there is a missing middle initial we'd have a double space without TRIM, so we need it.

(That was fun for me, but probably not for you. Just let it sit there for now as one of those things Excel can do if you are willing to explore and experiment to find a solution.)

Okay.

One more thing to know about delimiters. If you use a list of different delimiters, and Excel needs more than the list you gave it, Excel will circle back to the start of your list. So be sure you've thought through the different iterations of your results and how those will work with the delimiters you've provided if you're going to provide more than one delimiter.

The LEFT Function

Notation: LEFT(text, [num_chars])

Excel Definition: Returns the specified number of characters from the start of a text string.

The LEFT function is one of three functions you can use to extract part of a text entry. It does exactly what it says it will do. It takes x number of characters from the left of an entry.

Even though it lists the first input as text, I almost always use a cell reference for that first input to indicate where my text is located.

I recently used this on a database of case numbers where some entries were just a number 1234 stored as text, but others were 1234N or 1234Jones. Easy enough for me to extract the number portion from a range of values in Column A with:

$$=LEFT(A2,4)$$

and copy it down all the rows of data.

Of course, that doesn't always work so nicely. Here you can see an example where it didn't work in Row 6:

	A	B	C
1	**Case Number**	**LEFT Result**	**Formula**
2	1234	1234	=LEFT(A2,4)
3	1234N	1234	=LEFT(A3,4)
4	1234Jones	1234	=LEFT(A4,4)
5	123	123	=LEFT(A5,4)
6	123N	123N	=LEFT(A6,4)
7			

That's because the first four characters in Cell A6 were a three-digit case number followed by an N. It worked okay with Row 5, though, that had just three characters, all the number portion of a case number.

So you have to still pay attention to your data and check your results when you use this.

This was a very clean example for using LEFT. Sometimes I have to get fancier and combine it with other functions, like LEN, if the number of characters needed varies.

Another thing to note, the number of characters input is optional. If you leave it out, you'll get the left-most character in the cell.

There is a counterpart to LEFT, LEFTB, that is designed to work with languages like Chinese, Japanese, and Korean where you specify the number of bytes instead of the number of characters.

The RIGHT Function

Notation: RIGHT(text, [num_chars])

Excel Definition: Returns the specified number of characters from the end of a text string.

The RIGHT function works just like the LEFT function, except it pulls the designated characters from the right end of the referenced text.

So, for example, one of the reports I receive sometimes at work is a report that includes entries like 125 USD, 272 AUD, 456 CAD, etc. I use the RIGHT function to extract the currency (USD, AUD, and CAD) from those cells.

=RIGHT(A2,3)

(I can then use LEN and LEFT to pull the numbers as well.)

If you omit the number of characters input, you'll get just the right-most character.

The counterpart to RIGHT for entries in languages like Chinese, Korean, and Japanese is RIGHTB.

The MID Function

Notation: MID(text, start_num, num_chars)

Excel Definition: Returns the characters from the middle of a text string, given a starting position and length.

The MID function completes our trio of functions for extracting text from a text string. It's basically for when the text you want isn't on the left or the right end of the text entry, but is somewhere in the middle. Note that it requires an additional input, start_num, because you have to tell it where to start in addition to the number of characters you want.

The inputs to this function are all required, none are optional. If you omit one, Excel will tell you that you didn't provide enough inputs.

Also, you have to provide a value of 1 or more for start_num. You can leave num_chars blank, but then your result will also be blank.

MID also has a counterpart, MIDB, for languages like Chinese, Japanese, and Korean.

Here is a use of MID on the text "$10 dollars" where I want the dollar value:

$$=MID("\$10\ dollars",2,2)$$

The first input is the text, which I provided within the function this time so put in quotes. (It could also be a cell reference like I used with LEFT and RIGHT.)

The second input tells Excel where to start in that text string. Just count characters (including spaces) to where the first character you want is. In this case, I wanted to skip that initial dollar sign and pull the 1, so I wanted to start on the second character.

The third input is how much of the remainder of the text string you want. Here I knew the number I wanted was two digits, so the value I gave Excel was 2.

You will find that for large sets of data that have some variability in them, MID works best when combined with LEN, which we'll discuss next. For example, if the next entry was $123 dollars and the one after that was $1234, this formula wouldn't work.

The LEN Function

Notation: LEN(text)

Excel Definition: Returns the number of characters in a text string.

I think of the LEN function as the length function, because that's basically what it's doing. It's telling you the length of a text string. It only has one input, the text you want Excel to use to count the number of characters. As with RIGHT, LEFT, and MID, that first input can be a cell reference. LEN also has a LENB counterpart.

Let's revisit that example from the MID chapter. It was easy enough for me to extract the number from $10 dollars using MID. But then that wasn't going to work for $123 dollars or $1234 dollars.

But let's look at those again:

$10 dollars

$123 dollars

$1234 dollars

They're pretty consistent, aren't they? They all start with a currency symbol ($), then there's the number that can vary in length, then there's a space, and then the word "dollars".

We could manually count the number of characters in " dollars" (8), or we could use

=LEN(" dollars")

to have Excel count for us.

But we still need one more piece of information to extract the number. We need the length of the entire text string. Fortunately, LEN can calculate that, too.

Perfect. Now let's look at some sample data and apply it:

	A	B	C	D
1	Value	Number Only	Easy Formula	Hard Formula
2	$10 dollars	10	=MID(A2,2,LEN(A2)-9)	=MID(A2,2,LEN(A2)-(LEN(" dollars")+1))
3	$123 dollars	123	=MID(A3,2,LEN(A3)-9)	=MID(A3,2,LEN(A3)-(LEN(" dollars")+1))
4	$1234 dollars	1234	=MID(A4,2,LEN(A4)-9)	=MID(A4,2,LEN(A4)-(LEN(" dollars")+1))
5				

Column A has the value we want to extract from, Column B has the result, and Columns C and D have different formulas for how to do this.

Column C has the more manual version, which for Row 2 is:

$$=MID(A2,2,LEN(A2)-9)$$

Let's break that down. It says, "Look in Cell A2, go to the second character, and pull x characters where x is equal to the length of the entire entry minus 9." Why 9? Because we need to remove the dollar sign, the space, and the word dollars to get to the length of the actual number we're trying to extract.

Column D has a version where I have Excel do the math on how many characters to exclude:

$$=MID(A2,2,LEN(A2)-(LEN("\ dollars")+1))$$

Instead of my putting in the value 9, I have:

$$(LEN("\ dollars")+1)$$

Okay. So hopefully you can now see how to use RIGHT, LEFT, MID, and LEN to extract part of a text entry. Now let's cover two new functions that may make this even easier, TEXTBEFORE and TEXTAFTER.

The **TEXTBEFORE** Function

Notation: TEXTBEFORE(text, delimiter, [instance_num], [match_mode], [match_end], [if_not_found])

Excel Definition: Returns text that's before delimiting characters.

They make this look really complicated, don't they? But really it's just a big fancy function to say "I want the text that falls before this other text."

Note that the only required inputs are the text and the delimiter. All the rest is optional.

So let's go back to Cell A2 with its entry of "$10 dollars" from the last chapter.

If I want to extract the dollar sign and number, so drop the part that says " dollars", I can just write:

=TEXTBEFORE(A2," dollars")

For me personally, it's easier to understand what I'm telling it to do to use " dollars", but that doesn't mean I can't simplify it down later. I could actually use:

=TEXTBEFORE(A2," ")

That tells Excel to pull everything before the first space. Since there is only one space in the entry, it's that simple.

Okay. So that is TEXTBEFORE at its most basic. Your first input is the text or cell reference where the text is. Your second input is where in that text to draw the line.

But you can get fancier.

The third input is instance_num. Sometimes you'll have a text string and want to remove the text before a certain point, but maybe the delimiter you want to use for that is one that appears earlier in that text string, too.

Here is an example:

	A	B	C
8	Value	Isolate Name	Formula
9	John Lee Investigator	John Lee	=TEXTBEFORE(A9," ",2)
10	Lee Jones Lawyer	Lee Jones	=TEXTBEFORE(A10," ",2)
11	Kelly Fromer Teacher	Kelly Fromer	=TEXTBEFORE(A11," ",2)
12			

I have three listings where the information is first name, space, last name, space, profession. To isolate just the name in Cell A9, I can use:

$$=TEXTBEFORE(A9," ",2)$$

That's saying, "Look at the text in Cell A9, find the second space, and bring back everything before that point".

If the text entries had been something like "Kelly Fromer, Teacher" then we'd need to use a comma and a space as our delimiter:

$$=TEXTBEFORE(A13,", ")$$

Of course, as you may remember when we were using TEXTJOIN, data isn't always that neat and tidy. You may have variation in the number of spaces in different cells.

It turns out, your instance number can also be a negative number.

If you do that, Excel will start at the end instead of the beginning of your text. So with entries like, "Joseph L. Jones, Jr., Teacher" and "Daphne Clark, Astronaut" I'd use:

$$=TEXTBEFORE(A21,",",-1)$$

That looks for a comma delimiter, but it does it from the end, so I don't end up dropping the suffix from someone's name. (I don't need to include the space after the comma in the delimiter, because we're pulling everything to the left of the comma. I could use it, but it's not needed.)

The match_mode input lets you say whether Excel should be case-sensitive when it looks for the delimiter.

This was another one that I had a hard time thinking up an example for, but with my Google book links, I'll often add &gl= and then the two letter country abbreviation at the end to link to Google stores in different countries. So let's say I was trying to extract a website address that didn't have that on the end. TEXTBEFORE is one way I could do that.

Here we go:

	A	B	C
13	Website*	Case-Sensitive	Formula
14	www.Abs&Glutes.com&gl=AU	www.Abs&Glutes.com	=TEXTBEFORE(A14,"&gl",,0)
15		Not Case-Sensitive	Formula
16		www.Abs	=TEXTBEFORE(A14,"&gl",,1)
17			
18	*Completely made up - do not blame me if it's real and weird.		
19			

This (made up) website address, Abs&Glutes.com, includes &Gl in the name. If I don't tell Excel to treat my delimiter, &gl, as case-sensitive, Excel won't pull the full website address for me.

The formula I need is:

$$=\text{TEXTBEFORE}(A14,\text{"\&gl"},,0)$$

where that 0 in the last position tells Excel to treat &gl separate from &Gl.

Another thing to note about the formula I used here is that I didn't need the instance_num input, so I just left it blank. If you're not comfortable doing that, you could also use:

$$=\text{TEXTBEFORE}(A14,\text{"\&gl"},1,0)$$

The next optional input is match_end, which according to Excel "treats the end of text as a delimiter". I went to the help text to understand what this meant, but it was not in fact helpful.

I think I know what this is for, though. If you use a delimiter that isn't contained in the text in that cell—so a comma when the cell has no commas—Excel is going to by default generate a #N/A error as your result. But if you put 1 for this input, Excel will instead return the full text in the cell.

If you want something else returned instead of the full text or #N/A, that's where the final input, if_not_found, can be used. It only gets used if the input before it for match_end is 0 or blank, *and* there is no match to the delimiter.

You can use a number for this input. Excel will return that number as text. If you want to put actual text, be sure to surround the text with quote marks.

Here is an example with text:

$$=\text{TEXTBEFORE}(A23,\text{","},,0,0,\text{"Nothing There"})$$

I suspect you'll only use the last two optional inputs when you're getting some sort of error in your results that needs to be overcome by suppressing the #N/A error, which can interfere in certain calculations.

The other time you may see a #N/A error for this function is if the instance_num you use is greater than the number of times the delimiter occurs in the text.

You may also see a #VALUE! error if the instance_num you use is a larger number than the length of the text in the cell. So, for example, 4 in a cell that only has the word "ten".

You will also see that if you list zero for the instance_num.

Okay, that was kind of fun to explore, let's now look at its counterpart, TEXTAFTER.

The TEXTAFTER Function

Notation: TEXTAFTER(text, delimiter, [instance_num], [match_mode], [match_end], [if_not_found])

Excel Definition: Returns the text that's after delimiting characters.

TEXTAFTER is the counterpart to TEXTBEFORE. They actually have the exact same inputs, it's just which side of the delimiter you return.

Let's revisit two of our examples from the TEXTBEFORE chapter:

	A	B	C
8	Value	Isolate Profession	Formula
9	John Lee Investigator	Investigator	=TEXTAFTER(A9," ",2)
10	Lee Jones Lawyer	Lawyer	=TEXTAFTER(A10," ",2)
11	Kelly Fromer Teacher	Teacher	=TEXTAFTER(A11," ",2)
12			
13	Value	Isolate Profession	Formula
14	Joseph L. Jones, Jr., Teacher	Teacher	=TEXTAFTER(A14,", ",-1)
15	Daphne Clark, Astronaut	Astronaut	=TEXTAFTER(A15,", ",-1)
16			

In Rows 9 through 11 I had first name, last name, profession, all separated by a single space. To get the profession from those cells, all I had to do was change my TEXTBEFORE formula that extracted the names to TEXTAFTER:

$$=TEXTAFTER(A9," ",2)$$

This formula looks in Cell A9, finds the second space, and brings back everything after that.

In Rows 14 and 15 we have profession separated out with a comma and a space, but there's also a name with a comma and a space before the suffix.

Fortunately, I can use a delimiter that is a comma and space combined, and then a -1 for instance_num to pull profession:

$$=\text{TEXTAFTER(A14,"", "",-1)}$$

Just like with TEXTBEFORE, the match_mode input is used to determine if the delimiter should be case-sensitive. Match_end is used to return the entire cell contents instead of an #N/A result when there's no match to the delimiter, and if_not_found is used to return a custom result instead of #N/A or the entire cell contents.

One final example for you.

In the MID chapter, we wanted to extract just the number from entries like $123 dollars and $1234 dollars. You can also do that using a combination of TEXTBEFORE and TEXTAFTER. Specifically:

$$=\text{TEXTBEFORE(TEXTAFTER(A2,"\$"),"" "")}$$

That says, "take text after the dollar sign and then, from that result, take the text from before the first space".

It might be easier to understand written as:

$$=\text{TEXTBEFORE(TEXTAFTER(A2,"\$")," dollars")}$$

But that limits it to entries that use dollars, whereas the first example would work with a variety of currencies.

Also, for the bored overachievers, it turns out you can give Excel a list of delimiters to use with these ones, too.

Here I have a variety of currency entries, and I want to remove the currency symbol from before all of them. I can do that with a TEXTAFTER formula:

	A	B	C
17	**Value**	**Remove Currency Symbol**	**Formula**
18	$10 dollars	10 dollars	=TEXTAFTER(A18,{"$","£","€"})
19	£123 pounds	123 pounds	=TEXTAFTER(A19,{"$","£","€"})
20	€1234 euros	1234 euros	=TEXTAFTER(A20,{"$","£","€"})
21	€1234 euros, $10 dollars, £123 pounds	1234 euros, $10 dollars, £123 pounds	=TEXTAFTER(A21,{"$","£","€"})
22	$10 dollars, £123 pounds, €1234 euros	10 dollars, £123 pounds, €1234 euros	=TEXTAFTER(A22,{"$","£","€"})

Look at Rows 18 to 20. What I did here is used curly brackets around the different delimiters I wanted Excel to use.

$$=\text{TEXTAFTER(A18,\{"\$","£","€"\})}$$

It looked for each delimiter and then when it found one of them, extracted the text past that point. Pretty cool, huh?

But now look at Rows 21 and 22 where it didn't work so well. Note that it stopped as soon as there was a match to any delimiter, so you can't extract all of the currency symbols this way.

Based on the results in those rows, I think Excel starts at the first character and goes through its list looking for each delimiter you give it. If there's a hit on a delimiter, it will give you all the text after that point. If not, it goes to the next *character* in the text, and does the same thing. Not very helpful for a scenario like in Rows 21 and 22, but very nice for Rows 18 and 20, especially if you referenced a cell range for your delimiters. Like this:

$$=TEXTAFTER(A28,\$D\$28:\$D\$30)$$

where the delimiter values are in Cells D28 to D30 instead of listed directly in the function.

If I had a really long list of data entries I was working with, that included a variety of currency symbols, I'd probably use LEFT to extract them from all my entries, and then Remove Duplicates to create a unique list of the currency symbols in my data, that I could then reference with my TEXTAFTER formula.

(Of course, then we have to pause and ask why we're doing that, because if you are going to add those numbers together, that would be a very bad idea. You'd still need them to be separated by currency type because you can't just add USD, BRL, JPY, etc. values to one another without converting everything to one currency. Right? Right.)

Okay, enough nerding out on that. On to the next. Three more text-related functions to cover, and then we'll get to some date functions. Are you excited? No? Fair enough.

The LOWER Function

Notation: LOWER(text)

Excel Definition: Converts all letters in a text string to lowercase.

You are less likely to need this function in Excel than the equivalent option in Word, but it (and its related functions that we'll cover in a moment) is still useful to know.

What LOWER does is it takes a text string and puts all of the text in lower case. While you could enter the text directly into the function itself by using quotes

$$=LOWER("ALRIGHT")$$

you are more likely to use a cell reference with this function.

So why use it? It can help sometimes to convert different entries like "ALRIGHT", "Alright" and "alright" to the same case.

Whether lower case is the best choice is another question, but standardizing capitalization is probably where I would use this the most.

Keep in mind that this is still a function, so until you paste special-values or otherwise lock in the result(s) as text, it is still a formula that is referencing the initial cell. If you delete that initial cell, your formula result will turn into a #REF! error.

The UPPER Function

Notation: UPPER(text)

Excel Definition: Converts a text string to all uppercase letters.

The UPPER function is like the LOWER function except it puts everything in upper case letters.

It works the same way. You can enter text directly into the function using quote marks around the text, or reference a cell that contains your text.

And the same caution as with LOWER. This is a formula. Lock it in before moving on so that you don't end up with an error message if you delete the source cell(s). There is an example using UPPER in the next chapter.

The PROPER Function

Notation: PROPER(text)

Excel Definition: Converts a text string to proper case; the first letter in each word to uppercase, and all other letters to lowercase.

The PROPER function is the final in this trio of functions. What it does is capitalizes every single word.

This is not the same as title case, which has a set of rules about which words to capitalize. For example, in title case you generally don't capitalize "to" or "and" in a title. Proper just goes through and capitalizes each and every first letter of a word. (Excel does not have a title case option.)

Same caveats. You can reference text directly using quotes, but are more likely to reference a cell that contains your text, and you should lock down the result after you're done.

All three of these are good functions to wrap around another function. So, for example, you may use TEXTJOIN to bring together the text in three different cells. Wrapping that text in LOWER, UPPER, or PROPER would then create standardized capitalization for your finalized entries.

For example, on the next page is a screenshot of different ways I used UPPER and PROPER to create a standardized address entry.

In Row 2 there are values for the street (123 man St in Cell F2), city (El paso in Cell G2), and state (Tx in Cell H2), but they're not capitalized properly.

In Row 5 I used TEXTJOIN to create an address entry. Within that, I used PROPER to capitalize the street and city names, and UPPER to capitalize the state abbreviation:

```
=TEXTJOIN(", ",TRUE,PROPER(F2),PROPER(G2),UPPER(H2))
```

The result was:

123 Main St, El Paso, TX

	E	F	G	H
1		**Text 1**	**Text 2**	**Text 3**
2		123 main St	El paso	Tx
3				
4	**Formula**	=TEXTJOIN(", ",TRUE,PROPER(F2),PROPER(G2),UPPER(H2))		
5	**Result**	123 Main St, El Paso, TX		
6				
7	**Formula**	=TEXTJOIN(", ",TRUE,UPPER(F2:H2))		
8	**Result**	123 MAIN ST, EL PASO, TX		
9				
10	**Formula**	=UPPER(TEXTJOIN(", ",TRUE,F2:H2))		
11	**Result**	123 MAIN ST, EL PASO, TX		
12				

Much better. I took a different approach in Row 8, and put everything into upper case within the TEXTJOIN function:

=TEXTJOIN(", ",TRUE,UPPER(F2:H2))

That gave me:

123 MAIN ST, EL PASO, TX

In Row 11, I created the same result by wrapping UPPER around the TEXTJOIN function instead using:

=UPPER(TEXTJOIN(", ",TRUE,F2:H2))

Since it's only one function being applied to all of the text entries, UPPER can go on the outside of TEXTJOIN just as easily as on the inside.

Okay, enough of text, on to dates.

Excel and Dates

Before we explore various functions related to dates in Excel, it's important to review how Excel handles dates. What I'm going to discuss here applies to PCs. If you have a Mac, the start date is different.

Behind the scenes, each date is stored as a number. If you type the number 1 into a cell in Excel, and then convert that to a date, you will see that Excel views the number 1 and the date 1/1/1900 as equivalent. Each date from that point forward moves forward by one whole number.

If you are ever dealing with specific times in Excel, it treats hours, minutes, and seconds as fractions of a number. So the value 3.25 is also the date and time January 3, 1900 at 6:00 AM. You have twenty-four hours in a day, and 6:00 AM is one-fourth of the way through a day. The number 3 is two days past the start date of January 1, 1900.

This is nice, because it's lets you easily do math with dates. You can quickly calculate the number of days between two dates using subtraction, because to Excel that's just like subtracting 42321 from 42444.

But you have to be careful with dates in Excel, too.

First, Excel can't handle dates before January 1, 1900. It doesn't convert those to numbers, they are seen as text and not seen as dates. I personally have worked with at least one data set (that included founding dates for companies that dated back to the 1800s) where this became a problem. I ended up with a data set where Excel could not work with some of the values.

The other thing you need to know about dates in Excel is that if you give Excel just part of a date, it will guess the rest of the date. So if I put in Jan-2025, Excel is going to turn that into January 25 of the current year and give it a numeric value. January-2025 becomes January 1, 2025. If you put 3/4 and tab to another cell, Excel will convert that to a month and day of the current year; for me, March 4, 2025.

You won't automatically see this in what displays in the cell, though.

If you go back and click on that cell, you can see the full date in the formula bar.

Excel will always create a full date. Always.

This becomes especially important if you, like me, are a little lazy, and only put the last two years for your dates.

Excel has a rule for how it assigns each two-digit year to a century. As I write this it is the mid- 2020s, and Excel is going to look at an entry like 1/1/35 and turn it into 1935 even though I am more likely to mean 2035.

According to the Excel website help, as of right now, a two-digit year ending in 00 through 29 is interpreted as the years 2000 through 2029, but a two-digit year ending in 30 through 99 is interpreted as the years 1930 through 1999.

We are about three years from that being a big issue with new data inputs.

You can manually change the setting in your systems to modify which years end up in which centuries, but I think the better bet is to really try hard to always use a four-digit year, because if it's computer-dependent, it's way too easy to forget that a different computer doesn't work the way yours does.

To learn more about this, look for a help topic on how two-digit years are interpreted.

In the past I've thought this was a big issue for older data, too, but I've finally realized it's not.

Because Excel converts every date to a number when you enter it, that century assignment by Excel locks in at the time you enter your date.

Which means whatever conversion issue exists only exists at that point in time. Enter the date correctly and you're fine.

So this is something you should pay close attention to when you or other users enter your data. If you know you have a system where all dates need to be in the future, maybe set up a rule to restrict what can be entered into those cells. Or apply conditional formatting to flag entries that are in the past.

One final comment on dates. If you're ever subtracting dates and getting weird results, it may be worth checking to see if the dates you're using include time of day information.

Usually when I'm dealing with dates, I want them to be whole numbers. I want today, but not today at two in the afternoon.

To fix dates that include time information, TRUNC will cut off a number to make it a whole number. Which means using something like:

$$=TRUNC(G21,0)-TRUNC(G22,0)$$

where your dates are in Cells G21 and G22, will ensure that you don't get a wonky answer based on time of day information that changes the result. (Say, 11:45 PM on Monday subtracted from 2:00 AM on Tuesday giving a zero answer instead of 1.)

Okay. Now let's discuss some actual date-related functions.

The TODAY Function

Notation: TODAY()

Excel Definition: Returns the current date formatted as a date.

The TODAY function does exactly what it says, it returns the current date. Behind the scenes the value is a whole number. So it's today's date at midnight.

Note that there is no required input into the TODAY function, so you just use opening and closing parens with nothing between them when you use it, whether it gets used standalone or as part of a larger formula.

It's a great one to know about in case you ever have calculations where you want to know the number of days from now. So, maybe you want to know which bills are over 30 days past due. You can use the date of the invoice and TODAY to make that calculation. Here is what that formula looks like where the date of the invoice is in Cell A2:

$$=TODAY()-A2$$

I would probably pair this with an IF or IFS function to suppress any results for customers who still have time to pay before being overdue. Like this:

$$=IF(TODAY()-A2<30,"",TODAY()-A2)$$

What that formula basically says is that if taking today's date and subtracting the date in cell A2 gives you a value less than 30, then just return a blank result, otherwise do the calculation. (We're going to cover IF and IFS soon, so flag this as something to come back to then.)

If you don't lock in your result, each time you open that file, TODAY will pull the current date. Depending on what you're using it for, you may not want that, so be sure to lock the result down immediately if needed.

(This happens often in Word. People will use the equivalent of the TODAY function to create a memo template, and then use the template but fail to lock in the date field when they use it. Six months later they go to open that important memo showing that they did X on Y date and the memo shows the current day's date instead. Yikes. Not something you want to have happen.)

If the time of day is also important, then you need to use a different function, NOW. Let's discuss that one next.

The NOW Function

Notation: NOW()

Excel Definition: Returns the current date and time formatted as a date and time.

NOW is very much like TODAY except it will also return the time of day down to the second.

Behind the scenes, instead of getting a whole number, you will get a number that includes a decimal portion representing the current hour, minute, and second.

You can't see on the surface that it goes to the second, but if you use

$$=SECOND(A2)$$

where A2 is the cell that contains your NOW result, you can then use F9 to refresh the result and see it change. (Or you can just trust me on this.)

Like TODAY, NOW has no inputs, just include the opening and closing parens so that Excel can recognize it as a function and not a named value.

To write it standalone:

$$=NOW()$$

To use it in a formula:

$$=NOW()-A2$$

or

$$=A2-NOW()$$

Don't forget, that if you need to lock your result down immediately, you can either use paste special-values or type your formula in like normal but then use F9 to convert it from a formula to a calculation. If you use F9 it will return the numerical equivalent of the date, so you'll need to reformat the result.

The YEAR Function

Notation: YEAR(serial_number)

Excel Definition: Returns the year of a date, an integer in the range 1900-9999.

The YEAR function lets you extract the year portion of a date. (In the function notation date is referred to as a serial number.)

So if I have 1/15/2024 as my date in Cell A2, then:

$$=YEAR(A2)$$

will return a result of 2024.

The MONTH Function

Notation: MONTH(serial_number)

Excel Definition: Returns the month, a number from 1 (January) to 12 (December).

The MONTH function works just like the YEAR function except the value it returns is a number between 1 and 12 that represents which month that date falls in.

Again, Excel stores dates behind the scenes as numbers, so it doesn't matter to Excel whether you write dates like an American with 7/1/24 meaning July 1, 2024 or like a European where that is January 7, 2024.

Theoretically, your version of Excel is set to your geographic location so it stored that date properly for you when you entered it.

But if you are having weird calculation issues around dates, then maybe that's something worth checking by using the MONTH function. Point it at that 7/1/24 entry and see what it returns for you.

So, for a date in Cell A1 you'd use:

=MONTH(A1)

The DAY Function

Notation: DAY(serial_number)

Excel Definition: Returns the day of the month, a number from 1 to 31.

The DAY function is like the MONTH function except it will return the number for the day portion of a date. July 1, 2024 will give a result of 1.

$$=DAY(A1)$$

where A1 contains your date. Or

$$=DAY("1/12/25")$$

$$=DAY(45669)$$

if you want to use the date in the formula.

Again, since Excel stores dates as numbers, the order in which someone might write a date when they enter it shouldn't impact the result as long as they provide the date in the correct format for their location.

As you can probably guess at this point, there are also functions for HOUR, MINUTE, and SECOND. They work the exact same way. If you have a whole number, like I did above, they will return a result of zero, so they really only provide useful information when you have time of day included in a date.

The TEXT Function

Notation: TEXT(value, format_text)

Excel Definition: Converts a value to text in a specific number format.

There is one aspect of the TEXT function that I love and the rest of it I think you should never try to learn. In the past I've covered both to be thorough, but I'm not going to do that this time. You can look it up if you want.

Okay. So what TEXT does that I love, is it can take a date and return the name for the month or the day of the week. Here are examples using March 7, 2024:

	Date	Formula	Result
1	Date	Formula	Result
2	3/7/2024	=TEXT(A2,"d")	7
3	3/7/2024	=TEXT(A3,"dd")	07
4	3/7/2024	=TEXT(A4,"ddd")	Thu
5	3/7/2024	=TEXT(A5,"dddd")	Thursday
6	3/7/2024	=TEXT(A6,"m")	3
7	3/7/2024	=TEXT(A7,"mm")	03
8	3/7/2024	=TEXT(A8,"mmm")	Mar
9	3/7/2024	=TEXT(A9,"mmmm")	March
10	3/7/2024	=TEXT(A10,"y")	24
11	3/7/2024	=TEXT(A11,"yyy")	2024
12			

Column A has the date. Column B has the formula I used for each row. Column C has the result of that formula.

The first four rows have formulas for returning the day portion of the date.

=TEXT(A2,"d")

=TEXT(A3,"dd")

$$=\text{TEXT(A4,"ddd")}$$

$$=\text{TEXT(A5,"dddd")}$$

A single d in quotes will return the one-digit day value, 7, two will return a two-digit result, 07, three will return the short name of the day of the week, Thu, and four returns the long name of the day of the week, Thursday.

The next four rows do the same for month using "m", "mm", "mmm", or "mmmm". And you get similar results. A one-digit month, a two-digit month, the abbreviated month name, the full month name.

The final two rows use "y" or "yyy" to return a two-digit year or a four-digit year. (You could also use "yy" or "yyyy" to return a two-digit and four-digit year, respectively.)

If you put the text for the second input into a cell, you can just reference the cell, no need for quotes:

$$=\text{TEXT(A2,E1)}$$

Converting dates to their name has come in handy for me more than once. The original reason I figured out you could do this was because I needed to know days of the week for a large table of dates, and figured there had to be some way to do it, which, fortunately, there is.

* * *

Okay. On to the next section.

We only have eight functions left, but two of them are two of the most useful ones you'll learn, IFS and XLOOKUP, but also some of the harder ones to use when you're just getting started. (Unless your mind naturally works that way, of course. We are all wired differently.)

The IF Function

Notation: IF(logical_test, [value_if_true], [value_if_false])

Excel Definition: Checks whether a condition is met, and returns one value if TRUE, and another value if FALSE.

The IF function will always be one of my first loves even though the IFS function is a much better choice for most uses these days. It still has its uses though, so I want to cover it here first before we move on to IFS.

At its heart, the IF function lets you give two possible answers. Think of writing an IF function as saying, if this is true, then return that result, but if it isn't true, then return another result.

That seems pretty basic, right? Okay, so you can return two different results, who cares? Oh my sweet summer child, there is so much power in being able to react in real-time to different outcomes.

(Especially when you have more than two possible outcomes, but that's what IFS is for.)

I mean, think about real life. If someone is nice to you, you want to be nice to them. But if they hit you, you probably want the choice to react differently, don't you? You don't want to only be able to be nice no matter what.

(Clearly I am writing this chapter at the end of a long week. Let's get it back on track with some examples. But first let's look at the inputs.)

The first input to the IF function is described as "logical_test". This is the question you are asking. Is the value in Cell A2 greater than 5? Does it contain this word? Is the result of that formula TRUE?

The second input, value_if_true, is what to do if the answer to that question is yes.

The third (and final) input, value_if_false, is what to do if the answer to that question is no.

Now, it looks like they're both optional, right? They're both in brackets. But actually, you must have one or the other. You will get an error message if you only have one input for the IF function.

So let's go back to that IF function I shared earlier for TODAY:

$$=IF(TODAY()-A2<0,"",TODAY()-A2)$$

What was the question I was asking? Let's look at what I listed for the first input:

$$TODAY()-A2<0$$

That's asking if today's date minus the date in Cell A2 is less than zero. If it is, what did I tell Excel to do?

$$""$$

That basically is returning a blank result. I could've also used

$$=IF(TODAY()-A2<0,,TODAY()-A2)$$

but that returns a result of 0 and I'd prefer it to look blank. I could've just as easily had it return text, and used something like:

$$"NOT DUE YET"$$

Or a value

$$5$$

Or the value in a cell:

$$A2$$

Any of those would work. You can see that text requires quotes, but the others just need to be listed between the commas.

Finally, what did I tell Excel to do if it *wasn't* true? That's the last input to the function:

$$TODAY()-A2$$

I told Excel to go ahead and display the result of the calculation.

This is a very common use of IF for me. I like to suppress messy error messages that are only there because there's no data yet. There are other functions like IFERROR that can also do that for you, that we'll cover soon, but they're so easy to do, I just build my own.

For example. If I use

$$=B1/C1$$

and there's no value in Cell C1, then I get a #DIV/0! error message. I will often do this instead:

$$=IF(C1="","",B1/C1)$$

That's just saying, if Cell C1 is blank, keep this cell blank, too. Otherwise, divide the value in B1 by the value in C1.

Okay.

So that was the basic approach with IF functions. Think of them as IF – THEN – ELSE statements. Those are your three inputs. If you can figure out how to describe your question as a calculation, that's your first input. And then you tell Excel what to do if that's true (THEN) and what to do if it isn't (ELSE).

If you're good with what we've talked about so far and don't want to go further, skip the rest of this chapter. But for the curious, let's keep going.

Before IFS existed, I did a lot more with the IF function using what I refer to as nested IF statements. This may be something you'll see in older Excel files, or that you yourself may need if you ever have to use an older version of Excel.

Think of a nested IF statement as saying, "If this is true then do A, but if it isn't true then is this other thing true? If it is, do B. Otherwise, is this third thing true? If so do C. Otherwise do D."

For our visual learners, this is what that looks like drawn out:

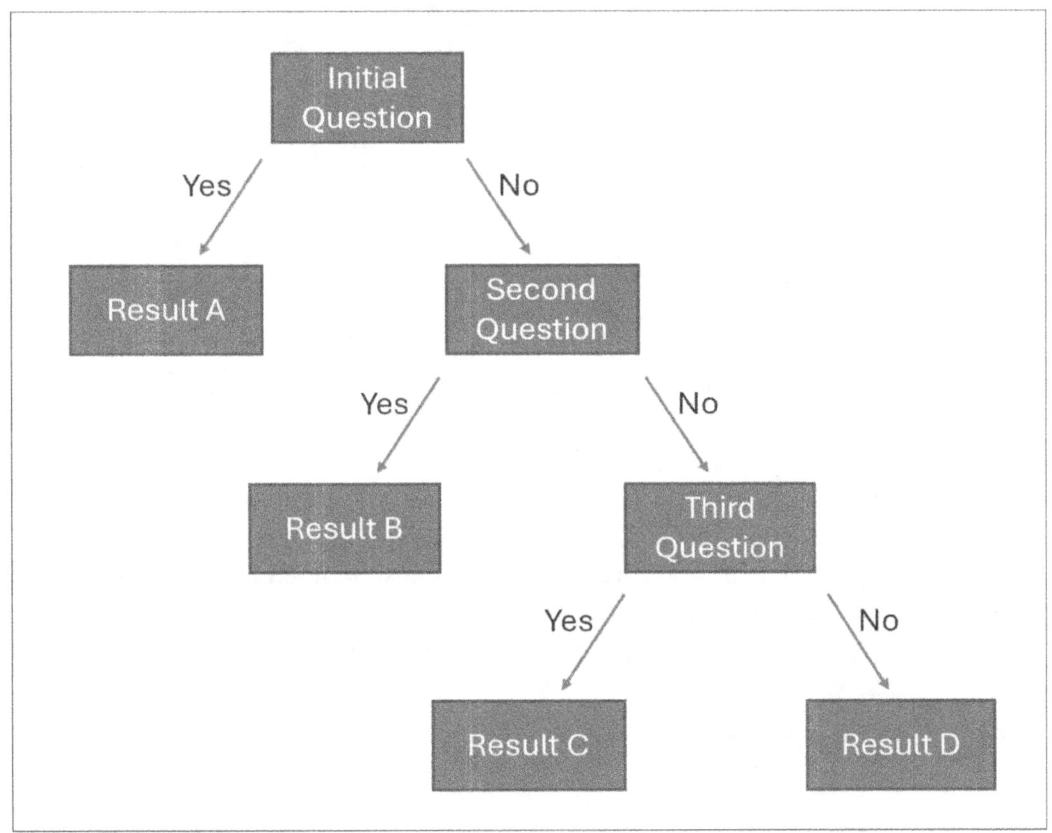

You can keep going as long as you want with that. I've gone nine or ten IF statements deep that way. The only real constraint is the challenge in writing one of these without making a mistake.

The classic example I've used in the past for this was a discount table. I think nowadays I'd use XLOOKUP instead, but the example still holds, so let's use it.

Here we go:

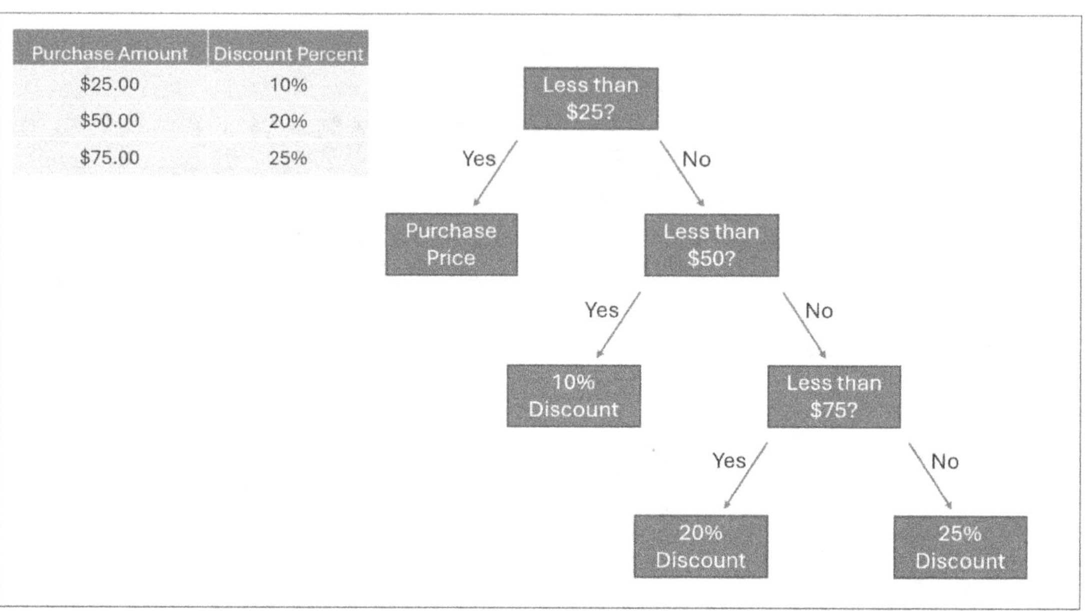

In the top left corner of this image, I have a discount table. If you spend $25, you get a 10% discount. Spend $50, get 20%. Spend $75, get 25%. I've also translated that into our IF-THEN-ELSE flowchart.

First question, is the amount less than $25? If so, you pay the purchase price. No discount.

Next question, is it less than $50? (Implied in the second question is that it is $25 or more already.) If so, then you get a 10% discount.

Final question, is it less than $75? (Implied here is that it is $50 or more.) If so, then you get a 20% discount. If not, then it must be $75 or more and you get a 25% discount.

On the next page is a table of values using that discount table where the price after discount is calculated using nested IF functions.

Our table is in Cells A1 through B4. Row 8 is the first calculation for a purchase price of $25:

=IF($A8<$A$2,$A8,IF($A8<$A$3,$A8*(1-$B$2),IF($A8<$A$4,$A8*(1-$B$3),$A8*(1-$B$4))))

	A	B	C	D	E
1	Purchase Amount	Discount Percent			
2	$25.00	10%			
3	$50.00	20%			
4	$75.00	25%			
5					
6					
7	Customer Purchases	Price after Discount		Formula	
8	$25.00	$22.50		=IF($A8<$A$2,$A8,IF($A8<$A$3,$A8*(1-$B$2),IF($A8<$A$4,$A8*(1-$B$3),$A8*(1-$B$4))))	
9	$50.00	$40.00		=IF($A9<$A$2,$A9,IF($A9<$A$3,$A9*(1-$B$2),IF($A9<$A$4,A9*(1-$B$3),$A9*(1-$B$4))))	
10	$75.00	$56.25		=IF($A10<$A$2,$A10,IF($A10<$A$3,$A10*(1-$B$2),IF($A10<$A$4,A10*(1-$B$3),$A10*(1-$B$4))))	
11	$15.00	$15.00		=IF($A11<$A$2,$A11,IF($A11<$A$3,$A11*(1-$B$2),IF($A11<$A$4,A11*(1-$B$3),$A11*(1-$B$4))))	
12	$60.00	$48.00		=IF($A12<$A$2,$A12,IF($A12<$A$3,$A12*(1-$B$2),IF($A12<$A$4,A12*(1-$B$3),$A12*(1-$B$4))))	
13	$80.00	$60.00		=IF($A13<$A$2,$A13,IF($A13<$A$3,$A13*(1-$B$2),IF($A13<$A$4,A13*(1-$B$3),$A13*(1-$B$4))))	
14	$40.00	$36.00		=IF($A14<$A$2,$A14,IF($A14<$A$3,$A14*(1-$B$2),IF($A14<$A$4,A14*(1-$B$3),$A14*(1-$B$4))))	
15					

(This is why IFS is so beautiful, because that looks pretty scary, doesn't it? I'm having flashbacks to learning how to use a slide rule in 9th grade. Like, why? But trust me that this can be useful to learn.)

Let's break this down step by step.

What is the first part of this formula?

$$=IF(\$A8<\$A\$2,$$

Okay. So we have an IF function. What question is this asking?

$$\$A8<\$A\$2$$

"Is the value in Cell A8 (our customer purchase price), less than the value in Cell A2 (our first discount cutoff)?"

Always be careful with your edge cases. Does $25 earn a discount? Or do you have to be over $25?

Here I was fine because $25 earns a discount so we want to ask if we're under that.

Okay. So we have the first question we're asking. Note the dollar signs for any reference to the discount table so we only have to write this once and can then just copy it down. (Honestly, I write it first and then go back and put in the dollar signs.)

What do we want Excel to do if the value in Cell A8 is less than the value in Cell A2?

The answer is whatever is after that comma and before the next one:

$$\$A8$$

If the purchase amount is less than our first discount level, then it says to return the purchase amount. Makes sense. So far so good.

Here's where it gets "fun". What do we want Excel to do if that isn't the case? The entire rest of the formula:

$$IF(\$A8<\$A\$3,\$A8*(1-\$B\$2),IF(\$A8<\$A\$4,\$A8*(1-\$B\$3),\$A8*(1-\$B\$4)))$$

Yikes! That's a lot.

But really it's just the rest of the flow chart. So what is the next step saying?

$$IF(\$A8<\$A\$3$$

Is the value in Cell A8 that we already know is \$25 or more, less than the value in Cell A3 (our second discount cutoff)?

If it is, then what?

$$\$A8*(1-\$B\$2)$$

Then take the customer purchase price in Cell A8, and multiply it by one minus the value in Cell B2, which is the corresponding discount rate if you get to \$25.

Note that's B2 not B3. Because if our customer purchase price is less than our second discount threshold, we want to give the customer the first-level discount.

And we do one minus that value, because we're taking off 10% for the customer. They still need to pay 90% of the original purchase price. (You could simplify your IF function by putting 90% into the table and doing the math in advance if you wanted, but I prefer to do it this way.)

Okay. What if our customer purchase price is *not* under that second discount cutoff? Then we have the remainder of the formula to work through:

$$IF(\$A8<\$A\$4,\$A8*(1-\$B\$3),\$A8*(1-\$B\$4))))$$

It still looks pretty ugly, but now we're down to a simple IF function with two extra parens at the end to close out the first two IF functions.

I like to write nested IF functions this way because they're easier to close out. You can also write a nested IF function that builds from the center outward instead, but then you have to put each closing paren in the midst of the formula, which is more error prone.

If your formula generates an error message, look for missing parens or commas first. That's usually going to be your problem. Also, one way to troubleshoot a complex nested IF function is to replace the messiness with a placeholder. That whole original formula becomes:

$$=IF(\$A8<\$A\$2,\$A8,ELSE)$$

You can then ask, does that make sense? If it does, then you can look at the ELSE part separately.

Okay, now on to IFS which is the newer, better way to write conditional formulas that have more than two outcomes.

The IFS Function

Notation: IFS(logical_test1, value_if_true1,…)

Excel Definition: Checks whether one or more conditions are met and returns a value corresponding to the first TRUE condition.

Technically, the IFS function can completely replace the IF function, but I still prefer to use IF for simple THIS-or-THAT comparisons. Where IFS really shines is when applied to multi-step IF-THEN-ELSE IF-THEN-ELSE type analysis.

The notation only shows you two inputs for IFS: what question you're asking (logical_test1) and the value if that's true (value_if_true1), but for me it really takes more inputs than that to do what I do with IF or IFS.

Let's go back to that first IF example we had where we wanted to keep a cell blank when there was no number to divide by.

Here it is:

$$=IF(C1="","",B1/C1)$$

Take a moment and try to think how you could convert that to an IFS function. According to the notation there, you only need two inputs:

$$=IFS(C1="","")$$

That is a working function. You will get a result. But there's no calculation. Could you get it to do a calculation with just two inputs?

Maybe one of these works:

$$=IFS(C1<>0,B1/C1)$$

$$=IFS(NOT(ISBLANK(C1)),B1/C1)$$

The first one is saying that if Cell C1 is not equal to zero, do your calculation. The second uses two functions we haven't covered yet. It basically says that if Cell C1 is not blank then do the calculation. Problem is, both of those return #N/A when Cell C1 doesn't have a value in it.

So really, not what I want. To use IFS in the way I want, I need to give Excel more.

When you add one more comma to one of these IFS functions, Excel's going to show you that you need to start adding additional inputs in pairs:

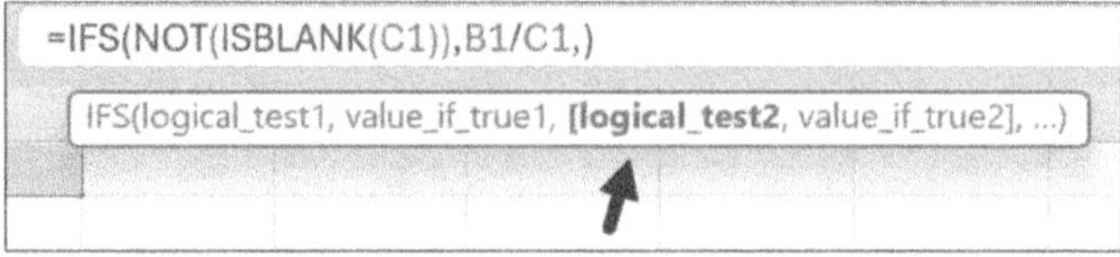

It puts logical_test2, value_if_true2 in the same set of brackets. Meaning if you add one, you have to add the other.

So how would you do that. Because all we really wanted was to do the calculation, right? We wanted to take this

$$=IFS(C1="","")$$

and add one more input for the calculation, but it wants two inputs.

(Do you hate me yet for not just explaining? Yeah, sorry. Trying to keep you awake.)

Here's the answer:

$$=IFS(C1="","",TRUE,B1/C1)$$

We add a new test that you can't fail. TRUE. TRUE is TRUE. And if that's the case, then do the calculation.

So we end up with a formula that basically says, "If Cell C1 is blank, then return a blank value, otherwise, if TRUE is TRUE, which it always is, divide the value in Cell B1 by the value in Cell C1."

I made you walk through this thought process in the hopes that it would stick better for you, because I do not find it intuitive. I always need to remember that my last input is not just, "do the thing", it's a final test that can't be failed, and *then* "do the thing".

You may be wondering why Excel does this. Can't they just default it somehow? And maybe they could've if they'd listed "final result" as the *second* input, but they didn't build it that way. It probably would've been a little counterintuitive. So you have to put TRUE (or some other test that can't be failed) as your final logical test to let Excel know you're done.

Just for kicks, I just tried setting the last test to 2=2, like so:

$$=IFS(C1="","",2=2,B1/C1)$$

and that worked, too.

Excel doesn't know how long your decision tree is, so that final logical test is how you stop.

If you don't give the IFS function a stopping point and none of your prior criteria are met, you'll get a #N/A error message.

Okay, you probably hate IFS right now. But let's go back to our complicated nested IF function and replace it with an IFS function. For those of you who skipped that section, don't worry, just notice how complex this is and that it uses three different IF functions nested together to get results:

$$=IF(\$A8<\$A\$2,\$A8,IF(\$A8<\$A\$3,\$A8*(1-\$B\$2),IF(\$A8<\$A\$4,\$A8*(1-\$B\$3),\$A8*(1-\$B\$4))))$$

Here is that discount table but now using IFS to calculate discounts:

	A	B	C	D	E
1	Purchase Amount	Discount Percent			
2	$25.00	10%			
3	$50.00	20%			
4	$75.00	25%			
5					
6					
7	Customer Purchases	Price after Discount			Formula
8	$25.00	$22.50			=IFS($A8<$A$2,$A8,$A8<$A$3,$A8*(1-$B$2),$A8<$A$4,$A8*(1-$B$3),TRUE,$A8*(1-$B$4))
9	$50.00	$40.00			=IFS($A9<$A$2,$A9,$A9<$A$3,$A9*(1-$B$2),$A9<$A$4,$A9*(1-$B$3),TRUE,$A9*(1-$B$4))
10	$75.00	$56.25			=IFS($A10<$A$2,$A10,$A10<$A$3,$A10*(1-$B$2),$A10<$A$4,$A10*(1-$B$3),TRUE,$A10*(1-$B$4))
11	$15.00	$15.00			=IFS($A11<$A$2,$A11,$A11<$A$3,$A11*(1-$B$2),$A11<$A$4,$A11*(1-$B$3),TRUE,$A11*(1-$B$4))
12	$60.00	$48.00			=IFS($A12<$A$2,$A12,$A12<$A$3,$A12*(1-$B$2),$A12<$A$4,$A12*(1-$B$3),TRUE,$A12*(1-$B$4))
13	$80.00	$60.00			=IFS($A13<$A$2,$A13,$A13<$A$3,$A13*(1-$B$2),$A13<$A$4,$A13*(1-$B$3),TRUE,$A13*(1-$B$4))
14	$40.00	$36.00			=IFS($A14<$A$2,$A14,$A14<$A$3,$A14*(1-$B$2),$A14<$A$4,$A14*(1-$B$3),TRUE,$A14*(1-$B$4))
15					

And here is the formula for Row 8. Still lengthy, but much easier to write. Let's walk through it.

$$=IFS(\$A8<\$A\$2,\$A8,\$A8<\$A\$3,\$A8*(1-\$B\$2),\$A8<\$A\$4,\$A8*(1-\$B\$3),TRUE,\$A8*(1-\$B\$4))$$

First, let's remove all the dollar signs, which only matter if you want to copy it:

$$=IFS(A8<A2,A8,A8<A3,A8*(1-B2),A8<A4,A8*(1-B3),TRUE,A8*(1-B4))$$

Step one of the formula asks a question:

$$IFS(A8<A2$$

Is the value in Cell A8 less than the value in Cell A2?
Step two tells you what to do if the answer is Yes:

$$A8$$

Return the full customer purchase price from Cell A8.
That's pretty much what the IF function version does, too.
Step three is where things get simpler. Instead of using another IF function, we can just ask another question:

$$A8<A3$$

Is the value in A8 less than the value in A3?
The task to perform if that's the case is:

$$A8*(1-B2)$$

Apply the discount percent in Cell B2 to the value in Cell A8.
Next up is another question and task if true:

$$A8<A4,A8*(1-B3)$$

Is the value in Cell A8 less than the value in Cell A4? Apply the discount in Cell B3 if so.

And then our final question and task if true, which it better be, because our question was the answer, TRUE:

$$TRUE,A8*(1-B4)$$

Apply the highest discount to all remaining purchases.

I know it still feels complex to walk through an example like this, but trust me when I tell you it's much easier to write it.

If you ever get stuck with IFS, it's probably going to be because you asked the wrong questions or told Excel to perform the wrong tasks (rather than a missing paren or comma which is often the issue with IF). So if you aren't getting the right result, draw it out and replace the questions with the cell references that ask the questions.

Like so:

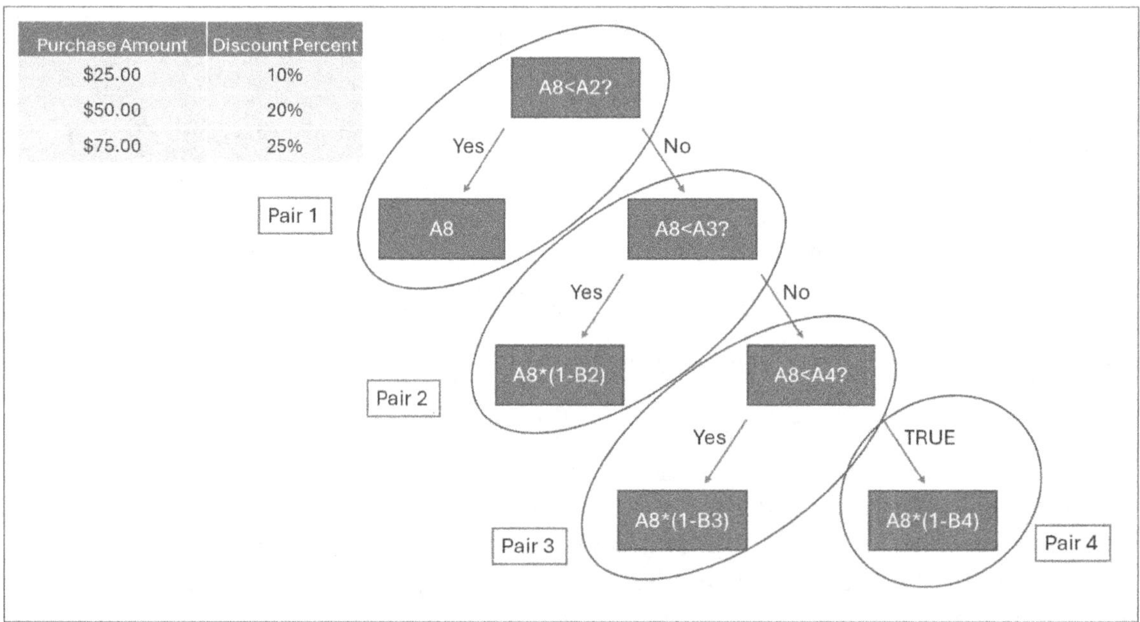

You can then check your IFS function against each paired set, circled in the diagram above.

Alright. That was a lot. If you're reading this book straight through, stand up, stretch, take a walk, take a nap, take a break.

(Honestly, sometimes getting a good night's sleep after you first learn something hard, is the best way to give your mind the time to process and absorb what you learned. Trust me. Sleep is better than all night cram sessions. Just, you know, at least read the material once before you go to sleep.)

The IFNA Function

Notation: IFNA(value, value_if_na)

Excel Definition: Returns the value you specify if the expression resolves to #N/A, otherwise returns the result of the expression.

The IFNA function basically lets you suppress a #N/A result so that it isn't visible. Going back to our divided by zero IFS example from the last chapter:

$$=IFS(C1<>0,B1/C1)$$

I could take that and surround it with IFNA to keep it from showing the #N/A error message when C1 is empty or equal to zero:

$$=IFNA(IFS(C1<>0,B1/C1),"")$$

If you leave the value_if_na blank it will return a value of zero:

$$=IFNA(IFS(C1<>0,B1/C1),)$$

You can also have it return text:

$$=IFNA(IFS(C1<>0,B1/C1),"Not applicable")$$

One more thing to keep in mind with IFNA is that the only error type it suppresses is the #N/A error. So if I had

$$=IFNA(B2/C2,"Not applicable")$$

and C2 was blank, I would still see the #DIV/0! error message. The reason to use it instead of IFERROR, which we'll cover next, is it doesn't hide important error messages you do need to see like #REF!

The IFERROR Function

Notation: IFERROR(value, value_if_error)

Excel Definition: Returns value_if_error if expression is an error and the value of the expression itself otherwise.

IFERROR works just like IFNA except it suppresses more error messages. It will suppress #N/A, #REF!, #VALUE!, #NUM!, #NAME?, #NULL!, and #DIV/0!

It also works with array functions just fine. (As does IFNA.) With an array function, if there are no errors, you'll still get all of your results, but if there are any errors in the range you'll get whatever you specified for value_if_error. You can see this by using:

$$=IFERROR((RANDARRAY(2,4)/0),"Issue")$$

That should generate a two by four grid of cells with the word "Issue" in them.

IFERROR does not suppress a #SPILL! error. You can see that by typing something in one of the fields that has the "Issue" result in that last example.

The AND Function

Notation: AND(logical1, [logical2],…)

Excel Definition: Checks whether all arguments are TRUE, and returns TRUE if all arguments are TRUE.

Technically, you just need one input for this function to work, the first logical statement, but I almost always have at least two.

I don't think I've ever used the AND function by itself. You could. You could have it evaluate all of your criteria are met, but usually I am asking a question like that because I want to do something with the answer. Which is why I usually combine this function with an IF or IFS function.

Let's walk through an example.

One of the places I publish my ebooks is on Amazon. For as long as I've been publishing with them, they've had different payouts for different price points. If you're under $2.99 (USD) they pay 35%. They also pay 35% if you're over $9.99. In between $2.99 and $9.99 they pay 70%. Which means that to earn 70% you need to both be greater than or equal to $2.99 AND less than or equal to $9.99.

So we have two questions that need to be TRUE to earn 70%.

The first one: Is my price greater than or equal to $2.99? If the value is in Cell A1, that would be written as:

$$A1>=2.99$$

You can put that into the AND function as a single input

$$=AND(A1>=2.99)$$

If the value in Cell A1 is greater than or equal to 2.99 we will get a TRUE result. If it's less than 2.99 we will get a FALSE result.

But that's not really an "and" sort of evaluation, even though we used the AND function for it.

So let's add our second question. Is the value in Cell A1 less than or equal to 9.99?

$$A1<=9.99$$

Add that to our AND function and we get:

$$=AND(A1>=2.99,A1<=9.99)$$

For this to return a value of TRUE, the number in Cell A1 has to be both greater than or equal to $2.99 AND less than or equal to 9.99.

Here I've taken a range of values, $3.99, $0.99, $10.99, $2.99, and $9.99. For all of them I've applied the AND formula from above that includes both criteria. For the ones that aren't our edge case I've also used AND formulas that look at just one of the two criteria at a time:

	A	B	C
1	**Value**	**AND Result**	**AND Formula**
2	$3.99	TRUE	=AND(A2>=2.99)
3	$3.99	TRUE	=AND(A3<=9.99)
4	$3.99	TRUE	=AND(A4>=2.99,A4<=9.99)
5	$0.99	FALSE	=AND(A5>=2.99)
6	$0.99	TRUE	=AND(A6<=9.99)
7	$0.99	FALSE	=AND(A7>=2.99,A7<=9.99)
8	$10.99	TRUE	=AND(A8>=2.99)
9	$10.99	FALSE	=AND(A9<=9.99)
10	$10.99	FALSE	=AND(A10>=2.99,A10<=9.99)
11	$2.99	TRUE	=AND(A11>=2.99,A11<=9.99)
12	$9.99	TRUE	=AND(A12>=2.99,A12<=9.99)
13			

Column A has the values to evaluate, Column B has the TRUE/FALSE result, and Column C shows the formula used in that row.

Rows 2 through 4 evaluate $3.99, and since $3.99 is both greater than $2.99 and less than $9.99, we get TRUE for all three formulas.

Rows 5 through 7 evaluate $0.99. In this case, the value is not over $2.99, so that returns a FALSE, which means our combined AND formula does as well.

Rows 8 through 10 evaluate $10.99. Since this value is over $9.99, that AND function returns a FALSE result, which means the combined formula does as well.

Make sense? Individual parts of an AND function can be TRUE, but if everything isn't TRUE, the AND function will return a result of FALSE.

Finally, in Rows 11 and 12 we have the two edge cases, $2.99 and $9.99, to make sure the combined AND statement returns the correct result.

Now let's combine AND with an IF function. This table takes various price points and calculates the payout at various price points:

	F	G	H
1	Value	IF(AND) Result	IF(AND) Formula
2	$0.99	$0.35	=IF(AND(F2>=2.99,F2<=9.99),F2*0.7,F2*0.35)
3	$2.99	$2.09	=IF(AND(F3>=2.99,F3<=9.99),F3*0.7,F3*0.35)
4	$3.99	$2.79	=IF(AND(F4>=2.99,F4<=9.99),F4*0.7,F4*0.35)
5	$9.99	$6.99	=IF(AND(F5>=2.99,F5<=9.99),F5*0.7,F5*0.35)
6	$10.99	$3.85	=IF(AND(F6>=2.99,F6<=9.99),F6*0.7,F6*0.35)
7			

Column F has the prices, Column G has the result, and Column H has the formula. For Row 2 the formula is:

$$=IF(AND(F2>=2.99,F2<=9.99),F2*0.7,F2*0.35)$$

This formula starts with IF, so we know that we have two possible outcomes. The first one is:

$$AND(F2>=2.99,F2<=9.99)$$

Is the value in Cell F2 both greater than or equal to $2.99 AND less than or equal to $9.99? If so, then:

$$F2*0.7$$

Multiply the price by 70% to get the payout.
If not, then:

$$F2*0.35$$

Multiply the price by 35%.

Now. For the overachievers, I actually used a slightly different formula than that, because I only wanted two decimal places in my results.

The formula I actually used was:

$$=ROUND(IF(AND(F2>=2.99,F2<=9.99),F2*0.7,F2*0.35),2)$$

That looks really complex until you replace the IF function with an X:

$$=ROUND(X,2)$$

So basically I just surrounded our IF function with a ROUND function because the actual results were numbers like 3.8465 and I wanted currency results instead.

The OR Function

Notation: OR(logical1, [logical2],…)

Excel Definition: Checks whether any of the arguments are TRUE, and returns TRUE or FALSE. Returns FALSE only if all arguments are FALSE.

The OR function works much like the AND function, except you will get a TRUE result if any of the inputs you provide the function are true.

Let's go back to our Amazon payout example. We could write a formula that uses the OR function instead, as long as we realize that Amazon pays 35% if a book is priced under $2.99 OR if it is priced over $9.99.

Here's our first table of prices we could charge, but with OR now:

	A	B	C
1	Value	OR Result	OR Formula
2	$3.99	FALSE	=OR(A2<2.99)
3	$3.99	FALSE	=OR(A3>9.99)
4	$3.99	FALSE	=OR(A4<2.99,A4>9.99)
5	$0.99	TRUE	=OR(A5<2.99)
6	$0.99	FALSE	=OR(A6>9.99)
7	$0.99	TRUE	=OR(A7<2.99,A7>9.99)
8	$10.99	FALSE	=OR(A8<2.99)
9	$10.99	TRUE	=OR(A9>9.99)
10	$10.99	TRUE	=OR(A10<2.99,A10>9.99)
11	$2.99	FALSE	=OR(A11<2.99,A11>9.99)
12	$9.99	FALSE	=OR(A12<2.99,A12>9.99)
13			

Rows 2 through 4 still use $3.99, but now all three of those are FALSE. This value is not less than $2.99, nor is it greater than $9.99, which means the combined result:

$$=OR(A4<2.99,A4>9.99)$$

is also FALSE.

Rows 5 through 7 still use 99 cents. Row 5 is TRUE because it is less than $2.99. Row 6 is FALSE because it is not greater than $9.99. The combined formula is also TRUE because only one of the two conditions needs to be met.

Okay. Now on to the IF function wrapped around an OR function:

	F	G	H
1	**Value**	**IF(OR) Result**	**IF(OR) Formula**
2	$0.99	$0.35	=IF(OR(F2<2.99,F2>9.99),F2*0.35,F2*0.7)
3	$2.99	$2.09	=IF(OR(F3<2.99,F3>9.99),F3*0.35,F3*0.7)
4	$3.99	$2.79	=IF(OR(F4<2.99,F4>9.99),F4*0.35,F4*0.7)
5	$9.99	$6.99	=IF(OR(F5<2.99,F5>9.99),F5*0.35,F5*0.7)
6	$10.99	$3.85	=IF(OR(F6<2.99,F6>9.99),F6*0.35,F6*0.7)
7			

Let's look at the formula for Row 2:

$$=IF(OR(F2<2.99,F2>9.99),F2*0.35,F2*0.7)$$

That is saying, if the price in Cell F2 is less than 2.99 OR greater than 9.99, then multiply it by 35%, otherwise multiply it by 70%.

So we had to swap where we did the multiplying by .35 and by .7, because the TRUE outcome here means the lower payout. But we get what we need this way just as easily as we did with AND.

So to recap: Use AND when there are multiple criteria that all have to be met. Use OR when any one of the criteria must be met but you don't have to meet them all.

Finally, I was using cell references for these examples to make it easy, but all of the criteria we covered in the SUMIFS chapter can be used here. You can use text, date, or number criteria.

The **ISBLANK** Function

Notation: ISBLANK(value)

Excel Definition: Checks whether a reference is to an empty cell, and returns TRUE or FALSE.

What ISBLANK does is looks at the cell or cell range you provide, and tells you whether the cell or cells in the range are blank.

Blank means no text or formula or "" result. It has to be truly blank.

It doesn't pick up formatting, so that's fine, but it will give a FALSE result if there is a formula in that cell, or if you had a null result returned that you copy pasted – special values.

If you run into Excel saying that a cell that looks blank is not blank, you can use Clear Contents in the Editing section of the Home tab to truly clear that cell of any content.

If you use a cell range, ISBLANK will return an array result equal to the size of the selected range, and will provide a distinct result for each cell in the range.

This is one of those functions that on its own you probably won't use often. Maybe to troubleshoot some data that isn't working the way it looks like it should. For example, maybe COUNTA is returning a count even though there's nothing to see.

It's more likely you'll use it to trigger an IFS or IF function like I did with the two examples earlier in this book. Here's the one I used with TEXTJOIN to help determine when to use different sets of delimiters:

=IFS(**ISBLANK**(D16),TEXTJOIN($G$21:$G$22,TRUE,A16:D16),**ISBLANK**(B16), TEXTJOIN($G$21:$G$22,TRUE,A16:D16),TRUE,TEXTJOIN($G$20:$G$22,TRUE,A16: D16))

And here's the one I used with IFS to say only do this calculation if Cell C1 is not blank.

=IFS(NOT(**ISBLANK**(C1)),B1/C1)

The NOT Function

Notation: NOT(logical)

Excel Definition: Changes FALSE to TRUE, or TRUE to FALSE

Before this week I would've told you that I have yet to find a good use for the NOT function. Because it's basically a function that takes a result, like TRUE, and replaces it with its opposite, FALSE. I can usually find a better way to do that. For example, the help on this one has a sales commission calculation that I could do much easier in other ways.

But earlier in this book, I actually reached for NOT to write a formula for you, so I figured I should include it.

Here's the formula again.

$$=IFS(\textbf{NOT}(ISBLANK(C1)),B1/C1)$$

What is this doing:

$$NOT(ISBLANK(C1))$$

By surrounding ISBLANK with NOT we're basically asking if there's something in that cell. That is a nice, legitimate use of NOT that I can get behind because as I write this I am not aware of the existence of a "not blank" counterpart to ISBLANK.

I do expect that when you get into writing macros in Excel—which are littles scripts to get Excel to perform complex tasks for you—that this one could come up more often. But for normal, everyday people like you and me, I'd say the uses are pretty limited.

But if you are ever thinking to yourself, "Gosh, I wish I could take this yes/no question I asked and turn it into its opposite," this is how you'd do that.

Okay. On to something more useful, XLOOKUP. And closing in on the end of this book. (Aren't you excited?)

The XLOOKUP Function

Notation: XLOOKUP(lookup_value, lookup_array, return_array, [if_not_found], [match_mode], [search_mode])

Excel Definition: Searches a range or an array for a match and returns the corresponding item from a second range or array. By default, an exact match is used.

I love this function so much I'm pretty sure I proposed marriage to whoever created it in one of my books. (Not seriously, of course. That would be the bad kind of weird and none of us want to be that.)

Anyway. XLOOKUP lets you take a value, the lookup_value, and then look in a range of cells, the lookup_array, to return a result from a designated range of cells that match up to the lookup array, the return_array.

Your lookup array and your return array can be the same, but they will often be different. For example, you'll look up customer number and want to return customer name.

The other inputs into the XLOOKUP function are optional. They let you tell Excel what to do if there is no match found, whether to match exactly or find the closest result (which is often helpful when you use the same lookup and return array), and how to search.

This is a newer function, so a lot of people aren't using it yet. You may instead stumble upon the VLOOKUP function, which I'll cover in the next chapter. But trust me when I tell you, that this is the function you want to use if at all possible.

Okay. So examples.

Let's start with an exact match example. Here is a table of customer transaction information:

	A	B	C	D	E
1	**Date**	**Customer**	**Product**	**Units**	**Total Cost**
2	2/6/2020	123456	Widget	14	$ 31.50
3	2/25/2020	78542	Whatchamacallit	3	$ 33.75
4	4/1/2020	698124	Widget	8	$ 18.00
5	4/7/2020	12793	Whatchamacallit	11	$ 123.75
6	4/25/2020	3267	Whatsit	11	$ 14.85
7	4/28/2020	4937	Widget	9	$ 20.25

Who is customer 78542? We can go manually look in our customer data table to see it's Shane Morales:

	G	H	I
1	**Customer Number**	**Customer Last Name**	**Customer First Name**
2	3267	Gutierrez	Luisa
3	4937	Holsen	Gary
4	12793	Phong	Bob
5	78542	Morales	Shane
6	123456	Lee	John
7	698124	Jones	Sheila

But what if we want to do this for a thousand transactions? That would be annoying. That's where XLOOKUP can come in handy. We can take the customer number in the first table, look it up in the second table, and then pull the first and last name of each customer. Let's build this for first name.

The first input is what we are looking up.

I want to look up the customer account number in Cell B2, so I start with:

$$=XLOOKUP(B2,$$

Next, where am I looking for this?

In my case, all of my information is in the same worksheet and the customer information table has account numbers in Column G, so I can write:

$$=XLOOKUP(B2,G:G,$$

If it were in a different worksheet, I'd just go to that worksheet and click on the column that had customer number in it and end up with something like

$$=XLOOKUP(B2,'Customer Data'!G:G,$$

The next input is what information we want to pull. First name results are in Column I for me, so that's what I'll use. I could stop there. Everything past that point is optional and I'm okay with the defaults. That would get me:

$$=XLOOKUP(B2,G:G,I:I)$$

But let's keep going.

The next input is what to put if there is no listing for what you're looking for. The default is to return #N/A. If you want it to return text, put the text in quotes. Like so:

$$=XLOOKUP(B3,G:G,I:I,"Unknown Customer Number")$$

This would return the text "Unknown Customer Number" if there wasn't an exact match between the number I'm looking up and the table I'm looking in.

The next optional input is match_mode. You have four options. If you use zero, 0, Excel looks for an exact match. This is the default option. Your other match choices are -1, which looks for an exact match but will go to the next smaller item in the list if there is no exact match, 1, which looks for an exact match but will go to the next higher item in the list if there isn't an exact match, and 2, which is a wildcard character match.

To use 2, the lookup value you use needs to contain a * or ? wildcard. If I looked for "*Jones", this would tell Excel to match to something like "A Jones".

(Also, just a note as I was playing with this, that Excel treated "Jones" and "Jones " the same for search purposes. It didn't treat that extra space as making the value different. It seems sometimes Excel does and sometimes it doesn't, so you kind of have to test it for search, filter, or functions.)

Okay, so in this instance we want an exact match. We could just put a comma and no number or we can put 0.

$$=XLOOKUP(B3,G:G,I:I,"Unknown Customer Number",0)$$

The final input is how to search the list. For an exact match it shouldn't matter what you use.

The two main choices are 1 to search first-to-last and -1 to search last-to-first. Excel does the heavy lifting behind the scenes for those two choices, and puts everything in order for you.

There are other options, but they both require that the lookup_array already be sorted. 2 will search your list assuming the data is sorted in ascending order, and -2 will search assuming the data is sorted in descending order. Do not use them if your data is not sorted properly, and you're trying to find the closest value. You will get an incorrect result.

One more really cool thing to share, and then we'll do a more complex example:

You can have Excel return more than one value at a time for you. For example, in my advertising spreadsheet I have Excel look up the title of my book in a list that then lets it return the author name, the series name, and the official identifier for that book. I used to use three separate formulas to do this, but with XLOOKUP I can do it with one.

Let's go back to our example above:

$$=XLOOKUP(B2,G:G,I:I)$$

If I wanted to return both last name and first name from our customer table at the same time, I would simply list the column range as my last input:

$$=XLOOKUP(B2,G:G,H:I)$$

That assumes, of course, that I want Column H returned before Column I. If I want Column I first and then Column H, I couldn't use this trick, I'd need separate formulas for each lookup array. (And I did try curly brackets on this one and they won't work. So your columns have to be in the same order or you have to write the formulas one lookup array at a time.)

Okay.

Now let's go through an example where we don't want an exact match by revisiting the discount table we used for the IFS function.

I had to make one edit, which was to add a row for no discount. Here we go:

	A	B	C	D	E
1	Purchase Amount	Discount Percent			
2	$0.00	0%			
3	$25.00	10%			
4	$50.00	20%			
5	$75.00	25%			
6					
7					
8	Customer Purchases	Price after Discount		Formula	
9	$25.00	$22.50		=$A9*(1-XLOOKUP($A9,$A$2:$A$5,$B$2:$B$5,,-1,1))	
10	$50.00	$40.00		=$A10*(1-XLOOKUP($A10,$A$2:$A$5,$B$2:$B$5,,-1,1))	
11	$75.00	$56.25		=$A11*(1-XLOOKUP($A11,$A$2:$A$5,$B$2:$B$5,,-1,1))	
12	$15.00	$15.00		=$A12*(1-XLOOKUP($A12,$A$2:$A$5,$B$2:$B$5,,-1,1))	
13	$60.00	$48.00		=$A13*(1-XLOOKUP($A13,$A$2:$A$5,$B$2:$B$5,,-1,1))	
14	$80.00	$60.00		=$A14*(1-XLOOKUP($A14,$A$2:$A$5,$B$2:$B$5,,-1,1))	
15	$40.00	$36.00		=$A15*(1-XLOOKUP($A15,$A$2:$A$5,$B$2:$B$5,,-1,1))	
16					

That's a lot to absorb. Let's look at the formula in Row 9:

$$=\$A9*(1-XLOOKUP(\$A9,\$A\$2:\$A\$5,\$B\$2:\$B\$5,,-1,1))$$

Those dollar signs are all there to fix cell references to make it easy to copy, so let's take them out for now:

$$=A9*(1-XLOOKUP(A9,A2:A5,B2:B5,,-1,1))$$

Real quick, I want to show you what happens when I replace the entire XLOOKUP function with X:

$$=A9*(1-X)$$

So what this is really doing is having XLOOKUP pull a discount percentage for us. Great. How is it doing that?

$$XLOOKUP(A9,A2:A5,B2:B5,,-1,1)$$

The first input, what to look up, is Cell A9. That's the customer's purchase price.

The next input is our lookup array, Cells A2 through A5. Those are the dollar values for the discount thresholds. Think about that one for a moment. We're not going to have exact matches to those values most of the time. So how would you use those cutoffs? (Hold that thought for now.)

The third input, is our return array, Cells B2 through B5. So we're pulling the discount percentages based on the discount thresholds.

With me so far?

The next input is blank. That's what we'd return if there was a failed lookup. I don't expect to have that, so I'm fine with a default #N/A error message. (Which did happen the first time I ran this. Because I'd forgotten to add that Row 2 that has 0 and 0% and it's needed for this to work.)

The fifth input is very important. I used -1.

That says, "Look for my purchase price. If you can't find an exact match to the purchase price, then drop back to the next lowest value."

So if I have $37.50, I want Excel to drop back to the discount percent for $25. We didn't reach the $50 discount level, we have to go back to the one we did reach.

I used 1 for the final input here, but I didn't need it. My data is sorted in ascending order, so the only option that wouldn't work is -2.

Excel went through for each of my values, looked for the customer's purchase price, compared it to the discount table, and gave the discount percent that the customer had reached. I needed that $0 level for it to have somewhere to drop back to when a customer hadn't reached the first discount threshold.

Great, so that worked.

But where I think XLOOKUP really shines, is with data that is messier. Let's look at an example.

In the table on the next page, Rows 1 through 9 are our data set, which contains information about different books, author, series, title, wordcount, hours to write, and genre.

The unique value that we can look up, Title, is in Column C. There can be duplicates in the other columns, such as author name or series name, but there is only one example of each Title in this table.

I want to look for author name (in Column A) and series (in Column B) for each title.

How would you do that?

You can see how I did it in Rows 12 through 14. The formula I used for Title H is in Row 12:

$$=XLOOKUP(A12,C2:C9,A2:B9,,0,1)$$

	A	B	C	D	E	F
1	Author Name	Related Series	Title	Wordcount	Hours to Write	Genre
2	Author A	Series A	Title A	26,527	26.5	Non-Fiction
3	Author A	Series C	Title C	7,893	6	Non-Fiction
4	Author A	Series C	Title E	4,997	4	Non-Fiction
5	Author A	Series C	Title F	7,976	4.25	Non-Fiction
6	Author A	Series C	Title G	57,900	23	Non-Fiction
7	Author A	Series A	Title H	8,284	5.75	Non-Fiction
8	Author B	Series B	Title B	46,204	54.25	Spec Fiction
9	Author B	Series B		6,079	4	Spec Fiction
10						
11	Value	Formula			Result	
12	Title H	=XLOOKUP($A12,$C$2:$C$9,$A$2:$B$9,,0,1)			Author A	Series A
13	Title E	=XLOOKUP($A13,$C$2:$C$9,$A$2:$B$9,,0,1)			Author A	Series C
14	Title B	=XLOOKUP($A14,$C$2:$C$9,$A$2:$B$9,,0,1)			Author B	Series B
15						

That says, look for the value in Cell A12, Title H, in Cells C2 through C9. When you find an exact match, pull the values in Columns A and B from the same row.

Because I wanted it to return results from both Columns A and B, the results show up in Cells E12 *and* F12. Cell E12 is where the actual formula that returns that result is. Since this is an array result, I would see a #SPILL! error in Cell E12 if there was already something in Cell F12.

One final cool thing that XLOOKUP can do (and that I always forget about), is return results between two points. If you combine it with SUM, it can return the sum of the result for a range of cells.

Here we go:

	A	B	C	D	E	F	G	H
1		Units Sold		Start	End	Formula	Result	
2	January	1,253		January	March	=XLOOKUP(D2,$A$2:$A$13,$A$2:$B$13):XLOOKUP(E2,$A$2:$A$13,$A$2:$B$13)	January	1253
3	February	1,417					February	1417
4	March	1,406					March	1406
5	April	929						
6	May	850		January	March	=SUM(XLOOKUP(D2,$A$2:$A$13,$A$2:$B$13):XLOOKUP(E2,$A$2:$A$13,$A$2:$B$13))	4076	
7	June	965						
8	July	736						
9	August	660						
10	September	710						
11	October	1,041						
12	November	942						
13	December	1,159						
14								

Columns A and B have total units sold for each month for a year. Column A has the month, Column B has the number of units sold.

In Rows 2 through 4 of Columns G and H, I have sales results for January, February, and March. These are there as the result of the XLOOKUP function you can see in Cell F2 that was used in Cell G2.

Let's look at it in closer detail:

=XLOOKUP(D2,$A$2:$A$13,$A$2:$B$13):XLOOKUP(E2,$A$2:$A$13,$A$2:$B$13)

That looks complicated, but split it at the colon and you get two XLOOKUP functions:

XLOOKUP(D2,$A$2:$A$13,$A$2:$B$13)

XLOOKUP(E2,$A$2:$A$13,$A$2:$B$13)

One is looking up the value in Cell D2, which is January. The other is looking up the value in Cell E2, which is March. That colon is basically saying "through".

So Excel pulls the results not just for January and March, but for any months between them. In this case, just February, and returns an array result in Cells G2 through H4.

In Cell G6, I took that formula and wrapped it inside a SUM function. You can see the formula I used in Cell F6:

=SUM(XLOOKUP(D2,$A$2:$A$13,$A$2:$B$13):XLOOKUP(E2,$A$2:$A$13,$A$2:$B$13))

Once more, it looks messy, but it's basically

=SUM(X)

Where X is the individual results from the XLOOKUP functions we just discussed, which returned the number of units sold for January *through* March.

Pretty cool, huh?

One more for you:

	A	B	C	D	E	F	G	H
1		Units Sold		Start	End	Formula	Result	
2	January	1,253		January	December	=XLOOKUP(D2,$A$2:$A$13,$A$2:$B$13):XLOOKUP(E2,$A$2:$A$13,$A$2:$B$13)	January	1253
3	February	1,417					February	1417
4	March	1,406					March	1406
5	April	929					April	929
6	May	850					May	850
7	June	965					June	965
8	July	736					July	736
9	August	660					August	660
10	September	710					September	710
11	October	1,041					October	1041
12	November	942					November	942
13	December	1,159					December	1159
14								
15				January	December	=SUM(XLOOKUP(D2,$A$2:$A$13,$A$2:$B$13):XLOOKUP(E2,$A$2:$A$13,$A$2:$B$13))	12068	
16								

All I did here was change the value in Cell E2 to December instead of March, and Excel pulled results for January *through* December.

Now, this worked because I have my months in the correct order. But if I move December to Cell A4, then Excel will stop at that point and not keep going. Using the colon basically says "pull the result for this first value and keep pulling results until you pull the result for the second value."

The VLOOKUP Function

Notation: VLOOKUP(lookup_value, table_array, col_index_num, [range_lookup])

Excel Definition: Looks for a value in the leftmost column of a table, and then returns a value in the same row from a column you specify. By default, the table must be sorted in an ascending order.

I'm covering VLOOKUP here because you may still run into it at times, and it is important to know how it works so you can deal with it if you do. But both VLOOKUP (vertical lookup) and HLOOKUP (horizontal lookup) have been effectively replaced by XLOOKUP (lookup in any direction).

The first thing to notice is the start of the definition: "Looks for a value in the leftmost column of a table." Technically you could define your table as starting in the third column to get it to work, but the problem for me with VLOOKUP is that it can only pull results that are located in the lookup column or to the right of it.

So that example I had earlier where we looked up Title in Column C, and then returned author and series from Columns A and B? You can't do that with VLOOKUP. You'd have to change the order of the columns in the source table to use it.

Also, look at the end of that definition: "By default, the table must be sorted in an ascending order." VLOOKUP requires you to sort your data or it won't work properly. That's not an issue with an exact match, but it is an issue with the approximate match choice.

Since I am normally someone using Column C to pull data from Column A, and also working with data that isn't sorted, I kind of hate VLOOKUP. Fortunately, now that XLOOKUP exists, I never have to deal with it.

But as I've said more than once at this point, a lot of people really like VLOOKUP, which means that if you're ever working in an environment where other people have built your files, or where people have been working in Excel for a long time, you may run into it. So best to understand it.

Let's go back to my Title example:

	A	B	C	D	E	F
1	Title	Author Name	Related Series	Wordcount	Hours to Write	Genre
2	Title H	Author A	Series A	8,284	5.75	Non-Fiction
3	Title F	Author A	Series C	7,976	4.25	Non-Fiction
4	Title A	Author A	Series A	26,527	26.5	Non-Fiction
5	Title C	Author A	Series C	7,893	6	Non-Fiction
6	Title E	Author A	Series C	4,997	4	Non-Fiction
7	Title G	Author A	Series C	57,900	23	Non-Fiction
8	Title B	Author B	Series B	46,204	54.25	Spec Fiction
9		Author B	Series B	6,079	4	Spec Fiction
10						
11	Value	Formula			Result	
12	Title H	=VLOOKUP($A12,$A$2:$F$9,{2,3},FALSE)			Author A	Series A
13	Title E	=VLOOKUP($A13,$A$2:$F$9,{2,3},FALSE)			Author A	Series C
14	Title B	=VLOOKUP($A14,$A$2:$F$9,{2,3},FALSE)			Author B	Series B
15						

First, note that I moved the Title column to Column A. I had to do that, because I wanted to pull author name, and I can't pull anything to the left of my lookup column.

I also mixed up the order just to show you that when you're looking for an exact match, it's okay to have your data not sorted.

Let's walk through this, because I was able to return two results, but I had to take a different approach to do it.

My results are once again in Rows 12 through 14. Columns E and F have the results with the merged cells that stretch across Columns B through D showing the formulas I used.

This is the formula used in Cell E12 to look up Title H, which is listed in Cell A12:

$$=VLOOKUP(\$A12,\$A\$2:\$F\$9,\{2,3\},FALSE)$$

The first input is the value we want to look for. That's in Cell A12, Title H.

The next input is the table we want to look in. The first column of this cell range HAS TO BE the column that contains the value you're looking for. Even if it's not the first column in your actual data table, it has to be the first column in the range you give Excel.

Here that wasn't a problem, because I moved Title to Column A. So the table I listed here stretches from Cell A2 to Cell F9. (I could've also started with Cell A1 and been fine.)

The third input is what column contains the information we want to return. This is always going to be a number. The way you figure out what number this should be is by counting from your lookup column to where the value you want to return is.

So if you want to return the value from that exact same column, you'd use 1. If you want to return a value from the next column over, use 2. Etc., etc.

Here I wanted to replicate what we did with XLOOKUP and return both Author and Series at the same time. At first I didn't think it was possible, but then I remembered that the old school way of telling Excel you have a series of values is to use squiggly brackets. So I used squiggly brackets around the numbers for both columns I wanted, separated by a comma.

$$\{2,3\}$$

And it worked! So you can do that. Yay. (But use XLOOKUP instead.)

Finally, the last input for VLOOKUP lets you say whether you want an exact match or an approximate match. Approximate match is the default choice.

If you're data is not sorted by that lookup column and you use approximate choice, you are going to get bad results, even if the value you're looking for is an exact match to a value in the table.

To have Excel look for an exact match, like I did here, you must put FALSE for the last entry. It's weird, but I don't make the rules.

Now let's look at that discount table example where we don't want an exact match and where the data table has to be sorted for it to work:

	A	B	C	D	E
1	**Purchase Amount**	**Discount Percent**			
2	$0.00	0%			
3	$25.00	10%			
4	$50.00	20%			
5	$75.00	25%			
6					
7					
8	**Customer Purchases**	**Price after Discount**		**Formula**	
9	$25.00	$22.50		=$A9*(1-VLOOKUP($A9,$A$1:$B$5,2))	
10	$50.00	$40.00		=$A10*(1-VLOOKUP($A10,$A$1:$B$5,2))	
11	$75.00	$56.25		=$A11*(1-VLOOKUP($A11,$A$1:$B$5,2))	
12	$15.00	$15.00		=$A12*(1-VLOOKUP($A12,$A$1:$B$5,2))	
13	$60.00	$48.00		=$A13*(1-VLOOKUP($A13,$A$1:$B$5,2))	
14	$80.00	$60.00		=$A14*(1-VLOOKUP($A14,$A$1:$B$5,2))	
15	$40.00	$36.00		=$A15*(1-VLOOKUP($A15,$A$1:$B$5,2))	
16					

My VLOOKUP formulas are visible in Column E. Here is the one I used for Row 9 where the customer purchase amount is in Column A:

$$=A9*(1-VLOOKUP(A9,A1:B5,2))$$

Replace the VLOOKUP portion with X and you have:

$$=A9*(1-X)$$

So VLOOKUP here is just pulling the discount percentage for us.

The VLOOKUP portion says, "Look for the value in Cell A9 in the first column of the cells in the cell range from Cell A1 to Cell B5. Return a result from the second column. No exact match required, so if there isn't an exact match, when you hit a higher value than the value in Cell A9, drop back to the previous row."

Note that this only worked with VLOOKUP because the discount percentages were listed to the right of the purchase amount thresholds, so if you use VLOOKUP think through your column order before you build your data table.

$$* * *$$

Okay. That was our last function. But before we close out, I want to cover best practices, troubleshooting, and error messages.

Best Practices

There are some best practices for working with functions and data that will make your life easier. You don't have to do any of this, but it will shortcut some issues that you'll run into otherwise.

Remember: Garbage In Garbage Out

You have to remember that Excel isn't some really competent assistant who will raise concerns with you. It's a computer program that does X when you tell it to do X. If you tell Excel to do the equivalent of banging its head against a wall, it will do that. If you tell it to add all of the sales in CO when the data uses Colorado, it will tell you there are no sales.

That is not Excel's fault. That is yours for writing a bad formula and not looking at your data.

So look at your data before you use it. Does it seem complete? Does it seem accurate? Are there any quirks to the data, like multiple values for the same thing?

For example, I once worked with a data set that was old enough it started with paper-based forms. The older entries had about fifteen variations on how to write Colorado, whereas the newer data all used CO. I could've easily seen the more recent values, and assumed that it was all like that, and then failed to pull any older results.

So take time to explore your data before you try to use it.

Standardize Your Data

Try to standardize your data as much as possible.

In my current day job, I work with a lot of bank records. Which means I may have records that read John Smith, J. Smith, John and Sarah Smith, and J.L. Smith Industries that all represent money from the same person.

I could just take those entries as they come and miss the big picture of how much money came from or went to John Smith. But for my purposes, it's better to add a new column that standardizes all of those values as belonging to John L. Smith/J.L. Smith Industries so that when I sum or create a pivot table, I get those grouped together.

Don't Mess With Your Raw Data

Always work from a copy of your data. Never work with the raw data. Keep the data as it originally was in some location where you won't lose it and won't alter it.

Why? Because we're all human and we all make mistakes. Maybe I think that John Smith, J. Smith, John and Sarah Smith, and J.L. Smith Industries are all the same person. If I were working directly on my original source data, I might be tempted to replace all of those values with John L. Smith/J.L. Smith Industries. But what would I do if I later learned that J.L. Smith Industries is a company run by the father of John Smith? Or that J. Smith is John's sister Janet?

If you keep your raw data, you can always go back to it and start over again.

Track Changes You Make to Your Data

Ideally, you'd also record all the things you did to change the data. In programming languages, like R for example, the script you write should work from the raw data file to final analysis. But the reality is that you are highly unlikely to think to do that.

I sometimes get close to this with worksheet names. One worksheet tab name is Raw Data, the next is Dedupe, etc.

But I have certainly been caught out by manual changes I made to clean up data and then couldn't replicate three months later.

Keep Versions

If I'm working on a really complex analysis, I also like to keep workbooks of the different steps and versions that got me to the final result.

Sometimes I'll work on a project that has multiple problems to solve. When that happens, I will save a version of the workbook at each step I solve with a name that lets me keep track of the various versions and know which one is the current one.

My general naming convention is to start each file name with YYYYMMDD so that my files will sort in the correct order no matter when I last saved edits to them.

So I might have 20241117 Sales Analysis for 2023 Sales. And then 20241120 Sales Analysis for 2023 Sales when I take the next step three days later.

If I ever have two versions of a file for the same date, I will add v1 or v2 to the name. If you add it after the name, the name of the file up to that point needs to be the exact same for both files.

I will also sometimes (like with PDF'ed emails) use military time. So 20241117 1131 Sales Analysis for 2023 Sales would be the version of the file saved at 11:31 in the morning of November 17, 2024. And 20241117 2331 Sales Analysis for 2023 Sales would be the version saved at 11:31 that same night.

Lock Down Results

A lot of the analysis I do is one-off analysis. I'm not building a calculation that will be used repeatedly over time. I'm analyzing a table of data for this one purpose, and will never come back to it.

In those instances, what I will often do is use Paste Special – Values to lock in the results of my analysis. I usually have the calculations on one worksheet, and then just copy and paste special to a new worksheet where I finalize my counts, sums, etc. using that locked-in data. This is because I don't want to accidentally delete a column and lose values that were feeding a formula like I would when using TRIM, LEFT, RIGHT, MID, etc.

Just be careful that you do this at the end, not when the analysis is still in process. You don't want to remove your formulas, add data, and not have it incorporated.

Make Assumptions Visible

It can be tempting to put all of the inputs into a formula in a cell in your worksheet to keep things clean and tidy. Don't.

For example, if I want to calculate the profit I'd make on selling a house, I might put the real estate fee of 6% directly into the formula rather than in its own cell, because that's not a number I expect to change. But assumptions like that can be crucial to decision-making. And someone else looking at your calculation won't be able to tell you their opinion on the result if they don't know the assumptions you made to get to that number.

Another example:

For book sales, I get paid in about six different currencies each month. I have formulas that take values for each currency and change it to U.S. dollars for me. To work, each of those formulas uses an exchange rate that was current as of the time I created the formula. But it's important to know what exchange rate that is, because as economies strengthen or weaken, the number to convert from one currency to another can shift, sometimes drastically.

For example, over the last five years, there have been times when 1 pound sterling was equal to 1.09 U.S. dollars and times when it was equivalent to 1.41 dollars. If you have 1000 pounds sterling, that's over a $300 difference. Bury that number in a formula and it's unlikely anyone will see it and choose to revisit. Put it in a field where it's seen every single time that worksheet is open, hund someone is more likely to notice and update the value.

Test Your Formulas

It's always a good idea to either test your formula on a smaller population of data where you can manually verify the result, or to find an alternative way to validate it.

For example, I was recently counting results that met certain criteria. I knew that the total across all of those counts needed to equal the total rows of data. So I was able to say, "I have 121 rows of data, do my numbers for these counts also total to 121?" If they didn't, then I was missing something somewhere.

Also be sure to test edge cases. I am notorious for needing to rewrite a formula for the edge case. Is that formula looking at values of 25 or more, or values over 25? Which did you want? Which did you get?

Always try to run a formula using any thresholds or breaks like that, to confirm that it's going in the right direction.

For really complex formulas where there are lots of different calculations feeding into the ultimate result, I will often build each part of the calculation separately first to confirm it works, and then combine them all to get the final result. I then manually combine each component and compare that to my formula result.

Look For Simpler Answers

Check to see if Excel already has a calculation for what you want to do.

For example, my default when calculating total cost for a series of purchases is to write a formula that multiplies units times cost per unit for each purchase, and then sum the results. But the SUMPRODUCT function can do that, too.

There has been more than one occasion where I was saved a lot of manual effort by using a function. So before you start some sort of lengthy, manual calculation or clean-up process, take a moment and see if there's a way to use functions to save yourself time. (Chances are there is. Even if it's something like combining NOT and ISBLANK together to find cells that aren't blank.)

Consider Compatibility Issues

This is a book on Excel 2024. I have assumed throughout that you have Excel 2024, and that anyone you're going to work with also has it or Excel 365, so will be able to use anything you create. But one of the areas where Microsoft has been making great strides in recent years, is in adding exciting new Excel functions. (Yes, I really did just use the word exciting with respect to Excel functions.)

This is great. Unless you have to share your workbook with someone with an older version of Excel.

Many years ago, I needed to build a complex calculation for a client using Excel. I found the *perfect* function for what I needed to do, SUMIFS. I spent hours building that workbook to incorporate all the different data feeds, and set up these conditional sum calculations with multiple inputs for their monthly reporting. It was a thing of beauty. I was so proud of what I'd done.

And then I gave it to the client.

Who happened to be using an older version of Excel that didn't have SUMIFS.

They couldn't use the workbook I'd created for them. I had to go back and recreate what SUMIFS does using multiple SUMIF functions. I could've saved myself a lot of time and energy if I'd realized before I started that SUMIFS was (at the time) a new function that not everyone had.

So new functions (or functionality) are great, and you should absolutely use them for your own work when they make sense, but be careful when you're trying to create something for a wider audience.

This is also a time to mention that some users (those with pre 2007 Excel, which are hopefully rare at this point) also have to use a different file format (.xls) than the current default (.xlsx). So you may at times have to save a file down to .xls format and test it out before you can give it to that other person. There will be a number of functions that don't work and you'll also run into issues with filtering, pivot charts, pivot tables, etc.

So, save yourself heartache, and think about your intended audience before you start. Just because you can do something doesn't mean you should.

Tips For Troubleshooting Formulas

I've touched on this at times throughout this book, but I wanted to include a specific chapter on how to troubleshoot formulas.

General Tips

The most common error I make with formulas is putting my parens in the wrong spot or forgetting one. We saw how easy that can be with the nested IF function examples. Sometimes Excel notices and will fix this for you. Sometimes you have to find it yourself. One way to see if you've made a mistake is to click into the formula bar and arrow through your formula. Excel will bold both the opening and closing parens as you reach each opening paren.

Another error I commonly make is copying a formula that requires a fixed cell reference without putting in my dollar signs first. I then have to go back to the first formula, add my dollar signs to lock in the cell reference, and then copy and paste again.

I also sometimes forget the quote marks around text or, if I'm copying and pasting from elsewhere, accidentally use curly quotes. Formulas in Excel only work with straight quotes. I've tried throughout this book to change curly quotes to straight quotes for you, but I may have missed a few. And most folks who write something out for you elsewhere won't even think to change it over.

Also check for missing a comma between inputs.

And then, of course, you have miscellaneous issues like referencing the wrong cell(s), putting inputs in the wrong order, or using the wrong function or input value, which for me are less common but could be a bigger issue for a new user.

How To See Formulas

By default, when you type a formula into a cell and then move away from that cell, Excel is going to display the result of the formula, not the formula itself. But for troubleshooting, you will need to see the formula.

The easiest way to do so is to click back onto the cell and look in the formula bar:

Here I have a formula in Cell D1 that adds the values in Cells A1 and A2.

You can also double-click on a cell to see the formula in the cell itself:

A nice perk to doing it that way, is that Excel will also color-code the cells that correspond to each cell reference in the formula. In this example, Cell A2 is colored blue as is the A2 portion of the formula, and Cell B2 and the reference to B2 in the formula are red.

That color-coding makes it very easy to see if the wrong cell is being referenced by a formula.

Another way to see the color-coding of a formula is to click into the formula bar after you've selected a cell.

Also, you can use F2 after selecting a cell.

Be careful, though, because with all of these options that show the color of the various components, if your cursor is somewhere that you could add a cell value, Excel will try to add any cell you click over to. I sometimes have issues with arrowing over as well. So use Esc, Enter, or tab to exit that cell.

To see the formulas in *multiple* cells at once, go to the Formula Auditing section of the Formulas tab and click on Show Formulas:

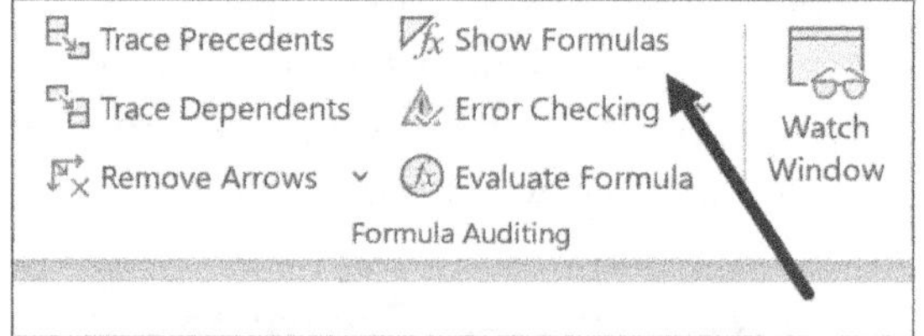

This is useful for troubleshooting tables like this one that is supposed to be adding the values in Columns A and D. It starts out fine, but in Row 8 you can see that the result is wrong:

	A	B	C	D
1	Value A	Value B		Value A+B
2	1	10		11
3	4	4		8
4	10	9		19
5	5	2		7
6	7	4		11
7	4	5		9
8	9	4		9
9	4	2		13
10	6	8		6
11	7	5		14
12	7	1		12
13	9	4		8
14	2	7		13

The wrong results continue through Row 14.

I could click into each of the cells that are wrong to see their individual formula, but that would be time consuming, and chances are the issue is the same for all of the wrong cells.

Show Formulas makes every single formula in the worksheet visible:

	A	B	C	D
1	Value A	Value B		Value A+B
2	1	10		=A2+B2
3	4	4		=A3+B3
4	10	9		=A4+B4
5	5	2		=A5+B5
6	7	4		=A6+B6
7	4	5		=A7+B7
8	9	4		=A7+B7
9	4	2		=A8+B8
10	6	8		=A9+B9
11	7	5		=A10+B10
12	7	1		=A11+B11
13	9	4		=A12+B12
14	2	7		=A13+B13

(When you click on this option, it may change the width of your columns, too, but they will go back to their original width when you turn it off, so don't worry about fixing them.)

I can now see that the formula in Row 8 is wrong because it's trying to add values from Row 7, and that this error carries down the rest of the column. Easy enough to copy the formula from D7 to those cells.

To turn it off, just click on Show Formulas again.

(Note that it works on a worksheet by worksheet basis. You either can see all formulas in a worksheet or none, and you have to turn it on or off for each worksheet separately. With the screenshots in this book because I needed to see a formula and a result of a formula at the same time, I used the single apostrophe at the beginning of cells twhere I wanted to keep the formula visible.)

How to See Connections Between Values

Another little trick that can sometimes come in handy for troubleshooting is seeing precedents, which is just a fancy way of saying that you can ask Excel what values are feeding into your formula.

This option is also in the Formula Auditing section of the Formulas tab. Click on a cell and then click on the Trace Precedents option. You'll get something like this:

	A	B	C	D	E
8	9	4		9	
9	4	2		13	
10	6	8		6	
11	7	5		14	

This shows that the cells that are feeding into the value in Cell D9, to create the total of 13, are coming from Cells A8 and B8. Not what we wanted.

Another option in the Formula Auditing section of the Formulas tab is to see Dependents. That shows you where a cell's values are being used.

You can have multiple precedents and dependents traced at a time, but it may be confusing to do so. You also have to set them up one-by-one.

(Personally, I just do this in my head, but I can see that it would be nice sometimes to visualize cell connections if you're working on a complex formula.)

To turn off tracing, go to the Remove Arrows option in the Formula Auditing section of the Formulas tab. Click Remove Arrows to remove all tracing or use the dropdown to turn off only precedents or only dependents.

Note that Ctrl + Z, Undo, does not work to remove tracing. If you apply a precedent or dependent, and want to remove it, you have to use Remove Arrows.

Flagged Formulas

In the examples above, I had multiple cells where the formula was wrong. Excel can't really help with that. But it can sometimes help when just one formula doesn't match the rest.

In the screenshot on the next page, the only cell with a "bad" formula is Cell D8. It's adding values from Row 7. But all the other formulas are doing the same thing, adding the cells from their own row.

In situations like this, Excel can be very good at recognizing when something doesn't match a pattern. You can see that it flagged that cell with a dark green mark in the corner. And note that this mark would be there even when formulas are not visible, I've just made them visible so you can see why Excel did that:

	C	D
1		**Value A+B**
7		=A7+B7
8		=A7+B7
9		=A9+B9
10		=A10+B10
11		=A11+B11

Click on the cell, and you'll see a yellow warning triangle. You can also hold your mouse there to see the cause of the issue:

	C	D	E	F
1		**Value A+B**		**Sum D**
7		9		
8	⚠ ▾	9		
9		0		
10		14		

That says, "The formula in this cell differs from the formulas in this area of the spreadsheet."

You can then click on the triangle, to again see why Excel flagged the cell, in this case "Inconsistent Formula":

	C	D	E	F
1		**Value A+B**		**Sum D**
7		9		
8	⚠ ▾	9		
9				
10				
11				
12				

That dropdown will also list a suggested way to fix the issue. In this case, "Copy Formula From Above."

You can also choose "Ignore Error" if it was a deliberate choice, and you don't want to see that mark in the corner. (I usually just ignore them.)

Formula Error Messages

In the past I've titled this chapter "when things go wrong", because they will at times. I've been using Excel for thirty years at this point, maybe more, and I still manage to mess it up sometimes. That's just life.

The key when you mess up is to not panic, and to figure out how to fix it. Knowing what error messages Excel generates and why, will help with that.

I'm giving an overview here. If you want more detail or examples, search help using the text in the name of the error and then the word "error". So search for "REF error" or "SPILL error". (Don't include the pound sign or exclamation point because you won't see a result if you do that for some of the errors discussed below.)

Okay. Without further ado:

#REF!

The #REF! error message is one of the easiest ones to fix if you catch it fast. It basically means that you have deleted or moved information that the formula was referencing.

I will often get this error message when I do something like use TRIM to remove extra spaces from a column of values, and then decide to delete the original column of data:

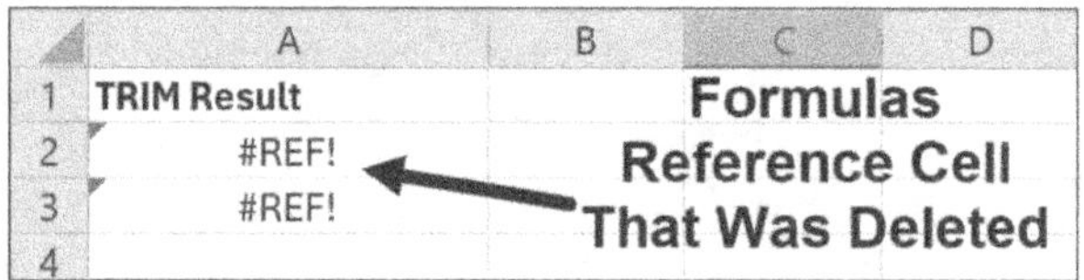

When you have a #REF! error and it isn't obvious what the issue is, it can help to look at the formula in that cell, to see which part of the formula is missing:

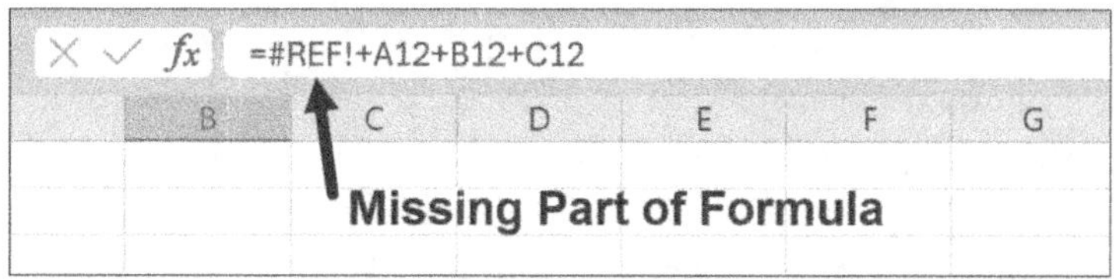

Be careful, though, because formulas are dynamic and adjust as you delete cells. This formula currently says

$$=\#REF!+A12+B12+C12$$

So we know we're missing a value that was added to the other three values. What is not obvious from this is that we deleted *Column A*.

The original formula was

$$=A12+B12+C12+D12$$

but when I deleted Column A everything shifted over a column, and the formula adjusted B12 to A12, C12 to B12, and D12 to C12. So you have to do a bit of mental gymnastics sometimes to actually figure out what is missing.

Also, note that I had a formula in that second example that referenced specific cells one-by-one. Had I used the SUM function for that cell range A12:D12 instead, Excel would've just adjusted the summed value and not generated an error message.

Always be careful when you delete data in a worksheet that has formulas to make sure you aren't inadvertently taking away crucial information.

(It is a good thing, generally, that Excel just adjusts the value for you when you use a cell range, but also something to be aware of.)

#VALUE!

Another type of error you are likely to see is the #VALUE! error. According to Excel, this error is "Excel's way of saying, 'There's something wrong with the way your formula is typed. Or, there's something wrong with the cells you are referencing.'"

Even they admit it can be a very vague type of error. In my experience, numbers or dates that aren't properly formatted as numbers or dates can be key drivers of this error message.

Here is an example where I managed to generate one:

The cell generating an error message has a formula that subtracts the date in the top cell

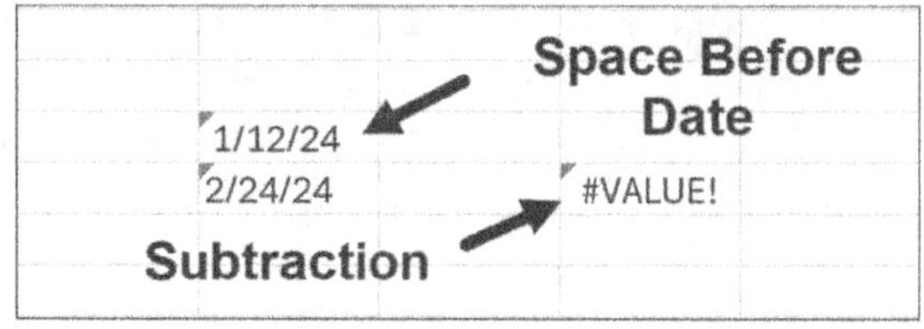

from the date in the bottom cell to calculate a number of days between the two dates, which is normally not a problem. But in this case it is treating one of those dates as text, so it can't perform a mathematical calculation on those two cells.

If you look at Excel's help on this, it's also possible that a regional setting that uses the minus sign for a list separator could be causing the issue.

Another cause of this can be hidden characters such as a single apostrophe (') or a space in a cell. Excel recommends filtering your data to find these, choosing the blank result from the filter list, and then clearing the contents in all of those not-really-blank cells.

#DIV/0!

The #DIV/0! error means that you have a formula that is dividing by zero. I often see this one when I create a table with a calculation that uses division, but where the table doesn't have values in it yet.

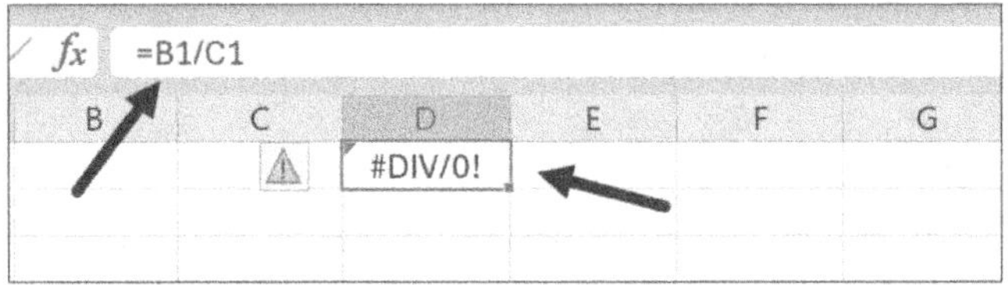

Above you can see that I have a formula dividing the value in Cell B1 by the value in Cell C1, but both are blank so it generates an error.

As we discussed previously, this is one I sometimes suppress using an IF or IFS function. You can also use IFERROR to suppress it.

#N/A

An #N/A means that Excel didn't find what it was looking for. For example, if you use XLOOKUP and don't tell Excel what to do when it doesn't find a match, you will get this as your result. Other functions where this can happen are VLOOKUP, HLOOKUP, MATCH, etc.

You may be expecting this. And with certain functions, like XLOOKUP, you can tell Excel to return a different result, like text that explains no match was found.

But other times, this can be a clue that your data is not formatted the way you want it to be.

If I have a value I'm looking for in another table, and I'm not getting matches even though I know I should, that may mean that my value and the values in the table are formatted as different types of data. For example, I may have a date formatted as a date in my current table, but my lookup table has dates formatted as text. In that instance, I won't see a match.

It can also indicate issues like an extra space at the end of one of the entries that you can't see.

If you run into this error message and don't want to see it, you can use the IFNA function to replace or suppress it.

#NUM!

According to Excel, you'll see this error when "a formula or function contains numeric values that aren't valid." (Note that I had to go to their website for that explanation because searching for it via the help in Excel gave me no result.)

The example they give in their help text is if you try to use $1,000 instead of 1000 in a formula. Problem is, they won't even let you do that anymore. It tells you there's an error in your formula and offers to fix it for you before it ever generates that error message.

The other place you may see this error is if the result is too big or too small for Excel to display. I just put

$$=123456789^{\wedge}123456789$$

in a cell, and it gave me that error message.

Most of us will never have this issue, but if you do, ask yourself whether the result you were looking for was supposed to be a really, really big number or a really, really small number. If it wasn't, you probably did something wrong, like leaving out a decimal or a plus sign between two numbers.

Excel's help also says you'll see this error with iterative functions like IRR or RATE when they can't find a solution.

#SPILL!

As we've seen, some of the newer functions in Excel return more than one result. To do so, they need enough room. You will see a #SPILL! error if Excel can't display the full results because there's already content in the cells where it would place the result.

You can either move the data in those cells elsewhere, or move the formula somewhere that gives it enough room to display all of the results.

You may also see this error if there is a merged cell within the range. It can't put results into merged cells.

If you're not sure where the formula wants to put results, click on the cell with the formula. You'll see a dashed border around the cells the formula needs to use.

You can also click on the yellow error triangle to ask Excel to show you the cells that are obstructing the formula by choosing Select Obstructing Cells from that error dropdown.

#NAME?

Usually I see this error because I start a function and hit Enter too soon. Typing =RANK and hitting enter will generate this error, for example. My solution is to go back and finish what I started, or delete it.

Excel says the top reason for this error is typos. So if you type in a formula that uses a function and get this error, make sure you typed the function name properly. It can also be because you failed to use quotes around text or to put a colon or comma in place.

(If this happens to you a lot, Excel recommends using the Insert Function dialogue box to build your functions.)

Circular Reference

If you ever get a circular reference error, it means that you are somehow referencing the current cell with the formula you're trying to put there.

I most commonly make this mistake when I try to put a total at the bottom of a column of values, but reference the entire column in my formula. SUM(A:A) doesn't work if the formula is in Cell A20.

But it can be an indirect issue, too, where you reference a cell that references a cell that references your current one.

As soon as you write the problematic formula and hit enter, Excel will show you a dialogue box telling you there's a problem:

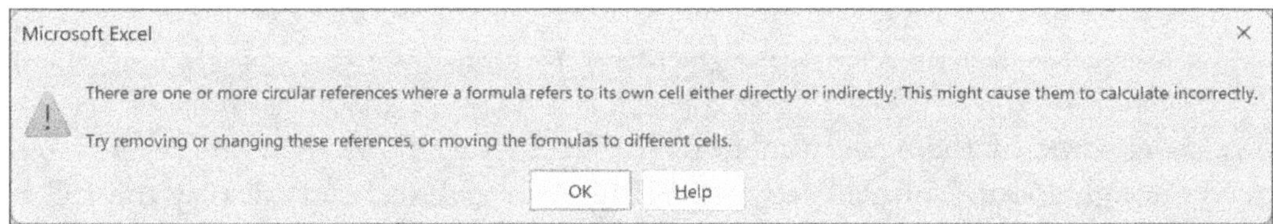

If you say OK, Excel will let the formula stand with a zero value. (Excel does this because sometimes people want that. They want an iterative calculation. But most people don't.)

I usually say OK and then go fix it myself immediately rather than try to have Excel help me, because I usually know exactly what I did as soon as Excel points it out to me.

If you're not sure what's causing the problem, the bottom left corner of your workspace will tell you one of the cells that is causing the issue:

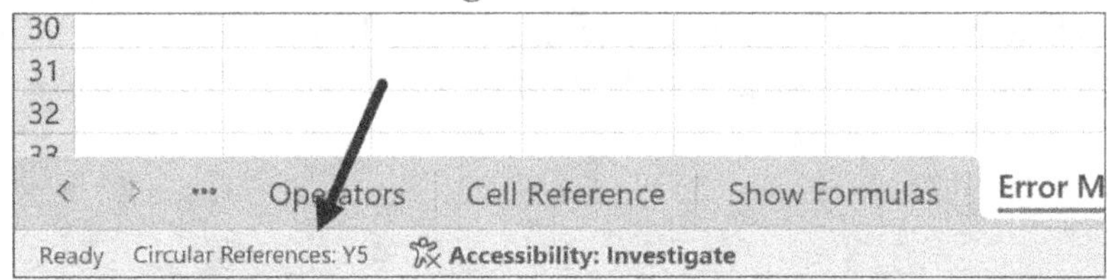

If it's still not obvious what the issue is, this is where tracing dependents and precedents helps. If you leave a circular reference in a workbook, Excel will tell you about it every time you open that workbook.

Too Few Arguments

Another error I sometimes see is when I don't provide enough arguments for a function.

For example, the ROUND function requires the number you want to round as well as the number of digits to use. I will sometimes just reference the cell, close out the function, and hit enter. When I do that, I get this:

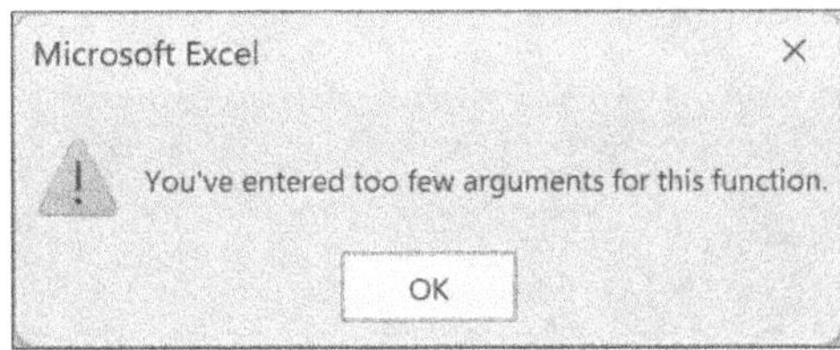

You'll only see this if you leave out a mandatory input.

Sometimes I see this error and wonder why because everything is in there, but then I realize I'm missing a comma or a closing paren somewhere in a complex formula.

The easiest way to see that, if it isn't obvious to you when you glance back at the formula, is to walk through each input. As you click on the cell ranges or values you provided for that function, you'll see the text describing that input bolded in the function description below. Like here where I'm clicked on U:U and Excel tells me that should be my lookup_array.

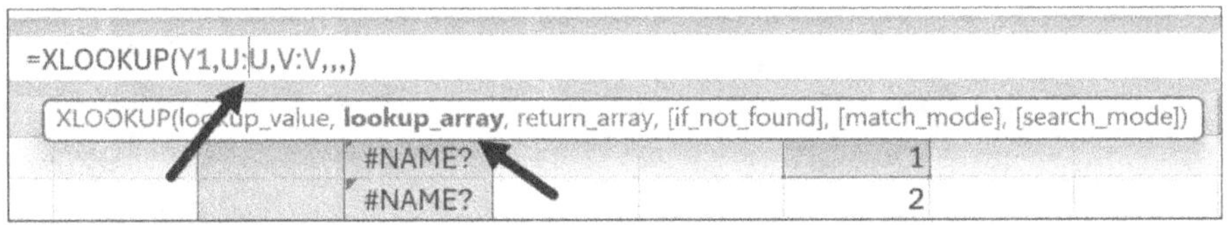

Too Many Arguments

It is also possible to get an error message for too many arguments. This is also usually caused by a paren or comma being in the wrong place or missing, so just walk back through the function and make sure everything is the way it should be.

General Wonkiness

Sometimes I will write a formula and the answer just doesn't seem right. I'm not getting an error message, but what Excel is telling me just isn't what I would expect to see. If I walk through the formula and don't see any obvious errors, that's when I will take each component and separate them out and make sure the separate components work as expected. I'll also make sure my data is formatted and/or sorted correctly.

If all else fails, I start over. And if I still can't get it? I read the Help, do a web search to see if anyone else has had that issue, or I find another way to get the same result.

Sometimes it also helps to just step away for a bit and let your mind sort it out in the background while you do something else.

Conclusion

Okay, that's it. That was an introduction to formulas and functions that is just shy of the length of a full-length novel. If you stuck with me to the end, good on you. I personally think what you learned here will be incredibly useful to you in navigating Microsoft Excel and unlocking its power.

Right now, I never want to see another Excel function again, but there are a lot more of them, even aside from the ones I casually mentioned here or there. So feel free to explore and see what else is out there.

You could also go look at one of my older titles *50 More Excel Functions* which covers some functions we didn't cover here. Or not.

At the end of the day, Excel is very logical. Once you start to understand some parts of it, the rest will fall into place. Expect there to be rules and commonalities. When you're learning something new, you can often look to what you already know to help with that.

Good luck with it. Reach out if you have any questions on what we covered here. Don't take it personally if something doesn't work the way you want it to the first time around, just step back, and walk through it from start to finish. Stay calm, figure out where you went wrong, and fix it.

You've got this.

Index

About the Author

M.L. Humphrey is a former stockbroker with a degree in Economics from Stanford and an MBA from Wharton who has spent close to twenty-five years as a regulator and consultant in the financial services industry.

You can reach M.L. at mlhumphreywriter@gmail.com or at mlhumphrey.com.

If you want to buy this book as an ebook, use code EXCEL2024 at https://payhip.com/mlhumphrey to get a fifty percent discount.

Common Control Shortcuts

Task	Ctrl + ...
Bold Text	B
Close File	W
Copy	C
Cut	X
Filter	Shift + L
Go to end of range	[Arrow]
Italicize Text	I
New File	N
Open Find dialogue box	F
Open Replace dialogue box	H
Paste	V
Print Screen (Go To)	P
Redo	Y
Save	S
Select All	A
Select cells in that direction	Shift + [Arrow]
Underline Text	U
Undo	Z